HAVEN OF THE MASSES

MAP
1
CHILE
PERU
TARAPACA
BOLIVIA
TROPIC OF CAPRICORN
ANTOFAGASTA
ATACAMA
ARGENTINA
COQUIMBO
ACONCAGUA
VALPARAISO
SANTIAGO
O'HIGGINS
COLCHAGUA
CURICO
MAULE
TALCA
LINARES
CONCEPCIÓN
ÑUBLE
ARACAU
BIO BIO
MALLECO
CAUTIN
VALDIVIA
OSORNO
LLANQUIHUE
CHILOE
AYSEN
MAGALLANES
PACIFIC OCEAN
ATLANTIC OCEAN
20º
25º
30º
35º
40º
45º
50º
55º
70º

World Studies of Churches in Mission

HAVEN OF THE MASSES

A Study of the Pentecostal Movement in Chile

by

CHRISTIAN LALIVE D'EPINAY

LONDON
LUTTERWORTH PRESS

First published 1969

Translated into English by Marjorie Sandle

7188 1599 8

Printed in Great Britain
by Billing & Sons Limited
Guildford and London

To my parents

CONTENTS

PAGE

PART FOUR

THEOLOGICAL AND ECUMENICAL ASPECTS

MAPS AND DIAGRAMS

ACKNOWLEDGEMENTS

This study forms part of a research project organized by the
WORLD COUNCIL OF CHURCHES.
It was carried out in Chile under the auspices of the
CONCILIO EVANGELICO DE CHILE,
in association with the
COMUNIDAD TEOLOGICA EVANGELICA DE CHILE.

Those who collaborated in the work in Chile were Pastor Udo HAUSER and Mr. Francisco VENDRELL, advocate. Research is never the work of one man alone. In particular anyone responsible for a study of Protestantism in Latin America should not forget to pay homage to the great forerunner, Emile G. Léonard.

I also wish to thank Professors R. Girod of the University of Geneva, John Housley of the Comunidad Teológica Evangélica de Chile, C. Munizaga of the Universidad de Chile, and Father R. Poblete, S.J., of the Universidad Católica de Chile, for their valuable advice, and express my gratitude to Pastors S. Araya, J. Beaty, Enrique Chavez and Victor Pavez, who initiated me into Chilean Protestantism.

Finally, this work would not have seen the light of day without the help of hundreds of people who are the players in the human and religious adventure I have tried to describe. It is my hope that this non-theological approach to a religious movement will be a contribution to the understanding of Pentecostalism and will sensitize the Chilean Pentecostalists to the problems of development which their country is experiencing.

C. L. E.

Santiago, March 1966
Geneva, December 1966

EDITORIAL FOREWORD

No other volume in this series demonstrates more successfully the value of allying theological with sociological competence. The former has enabled the author to understand the real issues of this study from an ecclesial point of view, the latter has given him the ability to set forth the sociological data so clearly that readers have the option of agreeing with his conclusions or of differing from them at certain points.

The subject-matter is fascinating, and of far greater importance than many may at first think. Pentecostalism is still a fast-growing, not a dwindling, movement. As the pressures of an increasingly organized secular and technological society are more and more felt by ordinary men and women who are sure only of their faith in God, what will happen? Members of traditional, 'mainstream' Churches, whose hold on Christian faith and sense of Christian purpose is manifestly weakening, cannot afford longer to ignore or slight those whose Christian vitality is still strong and whose missionary fervour remains. Here again one may readily perceive the Devil's typical strategy of dividing good things, so that instead of complementing and reinforcing one another, they become mutually antagonistic and thus perverted.

The crucial fact to be recognized, considered and acted upon, is that we are dealing with an unfinished story. This applies *inter alia* to the chapter on 'Ecumenism on Trial'. One or two of my colleagues would like to challenge both the accuracy of the history given, and the soundness of certain views expressed, but I am sure that here, as at all other points, what was written in good faith should in good faith be allowed to stand. When we are thinking of possibilities regarding future participation either in the Ecumenical Movement or in the development of Chilean society, we must leave room for further guidance from the Holy Spirit to these churches which so fervently believe in His power to lead them. It is on that note that the book concludes. It echoes, perhaps unwittingly, the contention for which Roland Allen lived and wrote all his life.

Those whose faith and practice have here been investigated and appraised may find it difficult not to feel that this study has been an attack upon them. But the author's whole tone, while manifesting an admirable as well as necessary objectivity, also betrays a fine Christian sympathy, in spite of the adverse judgments to which his research has led. The title of the book is a quotation from a Pentecostalist pastor's own description of the function of his Church. It is earnestly to be hoped that in the long run Pentecostalist leaders will realize the value to their movement of recognition of its present weaknesses.

This work, although done in conformity with the specifications of this total W.C.C. study project, has also been successfully presented by M. Lalive to the Faculty of Theology of the University of Geneva, as part of the requirements for its Licentiate's degree. At the time of undertaking the project, M. Lalive was already a Licentiate in Sociology of that University, and assistant to its chair of Sociology. Page xiii above gives the names of Pastor Hauser and Mr. Vendrell as two important collaborators in this work, and also records several other acknowledgements. Tribute must further be paid to the excellent services of Miss Marjorie Sandle, as translator from French to English; and to the Theological Education Fund for contributing more than half of the expenses of the undertaking. This volume has already been published in Spanish, under the title *El Refugio de la Masas.*

Geneva VICTOR E. W. HAYWARD
January 1969

INTRODUCTION

I. THE AIM OF THE STUDY

THIS STUDY is one of a series planned by the Research Department of the International Missionary Council (now the Department on Studies in Mission and Evangelism of the World Council of Churches). The series was originally entitled 'Studies in the Life and Growth of the Younger Churches', but this was later changed to 'Churches in the Missionary Situation: Studies in Growth and Response'.

Thirteen of these studies, done in four continents, have been completed or are nearing completion. Nine have been published already.[1]

In order to draw up an applicable framework for this piece of research, and thus to define in the most flexible way the object of our study, we started from the project's title. In speaking of 'churches in the missionary situation', and qualifying the expression by using the concepts of 'growth' and 'response', we are analysing not the religious movement itself, cut off from its social context, but the Church at grips with the environing society, linked necessarily to that society by the very fact of its claim to be missionary, to be delivering a message directed to the people of the country. A first formulation of the objective might have been given thus:

To comprehend the Protestant religious systems in the dialectic which unites them, at different levels, with Chilean society.

In a word, it was a question of studying the Protestant churches ***in*** Chilean society.

Discussion and reading in Geneva helped to define what was to be the focus of the work, by drawing our attention more particularly to one religious movement, *Pentecostalism.* In Chile this term describes (we shall later give better definitions) a popular form of Protestantism in which emotion prevails rather than reason, which is divided into a multiplicity of denominations and belongs to Troeltsch's 'sect' type. Its astonishing numerical growth and its financial and organizational independence make it particularly suitable for a study in depth. Naturally this study could not totally ignore the other Protestant denominations (Methodist, Presbyterian, Baptist, Anglican and Lutheran, to name only the most important), especially as Pentecostalism in Chile resulted from a schism with Methodism. We decided, however, not to deal with the so-called 'traditional' forms of Protestantism, except in so far as an understanding of the Pentecostalist phenomenon required it.

A study of the dialectic uniting Pentecostalism with society may be subdivided into three parts, each corresponding to a basic question:

1. What are the factors which at the beginning hindered and restricted, but later favoured, the planting of Protestantism and the expansion of Pentecostalism in Chile?

Here the question is one of analysing the introduction of Protestantism, the birth and growth of Pentecostalism, as a function of the history and sociology of Chile. This is the subject of the first part of our work, in which we establish the place of Protestantism in the general development of Chilean society.

2. What are the sources of inspiration of Pentecostalism in its social forms of expression? *To what extent* are its organization, conception of power, collective behaviour and activities, subject to the influence of socio-cultural models which are dominant in Chilean society? To what extent can one perceive other influences at work, whether opposed to those of the surrounding milieu or merging with them?

Though the first question is seen in a diachronic perspective, that of the second is synchronic: it is a matter of studying the Pentecostalist socio-cultural system in relation to some of the Chilean socio-cultural systems, as well as those of the missionary movements, such as Methodism, which had a direct influence on this sect. This is the objective of Part II.

3. Does the Pentecostalist movement in turn exert an influence on Chilean society? If one is ready to agree that Chile is a country aiming at achieving socio-economic development, the question may be put thus: does Pentecostalism bring with it, consciously or unconsciously, directly or indirectly, elements which make a positive contribution to the country's development?

First we ask how Chile produced a new religious movement. Then, by analysing different layers ('stages in depth', to use G. Gurvitch's terms) composing the Pentecostalist social phenomenon, we seek to show to what degree it is a body foreign to its environment, or how far it has become 'Chileanized'.[2] Finally we investigate the role it plays in the development process in Chile (Part III).

In Part IV we deal with certain phenomena which are peculiar to Pentecostalism, and also with the question of inter-church or ecumenical relations. Though this part does not exactly fit into the same pattern as the first three, the reader will see that the surrounding society remains the warp to which both religious practices and beliefs and also ecumenical problems are related as the weft.

2. CONDITIONS UNDER WHICH THE STUDY WAS CARRIED OUT[3]

The World Council of Churches engaged me to carry out a study on the given theme, but did not impose any scheme of research. As the person responsible for the field work, I was left completely free, both in working out the theoretical framework and the presuppositions of the project, as well as in its actual realization. The only restrictions weighing on the researcher were time and money, although even in these fields there was a certain margin for negotiation, since I had 22 months in which to do the work, whereas the original plan had been for 12 months only, and the budget was increased proportionately.

My time schedule had been drawn up as follows (leaving out of account the travelling time for the voyage out and home):

1. *Preparation:* 3 months (September 1964 to February 1965, half-time).

During this period, the following work was accomplished:

learning Spanish;
library work on Latin America in general and Chile in particular, on Pentecostalism and the history of religions in Latin America;
preparation of a research plan.

2. *Field Work:* 13 months (March 1965 to March 1966).

Two people who were connected with the field work devoted half their time for a whole year to collaboration in the project. They were Mr. Udo Hauser and Mr. Francisco Vendrell. Each of them undertook periods of participant-observation and carried out various tasks.

Mr. Udo Hauser, a Chilean whose ancestors came from Germany in the middle of the nineteenth century, belongs to a Pentecostal denomination. This qualification led him to take charge in particular of the enquiry among Pentecostalists, carried out by means of a questionnaire. Mr. Vendrell, a Methodist lawyer, for his part carried out various pieces of research in libraries and archives. His report on ecumenism provided the foundation for the chapter on this subject.

3. *Compiling and Writing the Report:* 4½ months (May to mid-September 1966).

An experienced research worker knows that the time given to actual research will be much less than he appears to have on paper. In working with men and observing the life of human societies, their liberty must be respected, and one must enjoy their full agreement and participation; that is, one must interest them in the work of research. The research has to be accompanied and sustained by much hard work on 'human relations', and it takes only a little thing to upset people's confidence in the research worker. Two episodes may illustrate the difficulties with which I met in my stay in Chile.

Well in advance the World Council had obtained the consent of the *Concilio Evangélico de Chile* (C.E.C.) to the project. However, from about June 1965 the letters sent by the World Council to the President of the C.E.C. remained unanswered, and in the end I left for Chile without knowing whether I should be welcomed by the organization which was supposed to be sponsoring the research and organizing certain practical details. When I reached Santiago, I met the President of the C.E.C., who was certainly surprised to see me and to hear my plans. Not until two months later, when friendly relations between us had been established, did we have an opportunity of discovering the mutual misunderstanding which had arisen from the fact that the address which the World Council had used for its letters proved to be that of the *former* President of the C.E.C., who, apparently, had not forwarded the mail. This explained for me the hesitations and misunderstandings which marked my path during the first two months of my stay in Chile.[4]

Once relations with the C.E.C. had been put on a normal footing, I was able to get the necessary introductions for visiting the leaders of the Pentecostal Churches, to explain my work to them and try to obtain the letters of introduction from them which would enable me to have free entry into their different congregations. Anyone who has special knowledge of the sects knows that they exclude observers, who can enter only if they obtain authority from the leaders. If he has this authority, then the observer finds the doors open and the most generous and touching hospitality will be shown him. But without it, he will be treated with the utmost suspicion.

At the very moment when a climate of confidence had been achieved between the denominations I wished to study and myself, an event took place which, it would not be an exaggeration to claim, caused the greatest injury to research in social science. I refer to the *Camelot Plan*.[5]

Briefly, a United States professor had proposed (at the end of 1964 and the beginning of 1965) to the Chilean universities that they should collaborate in carrying out a project of the *American University* of Washington, the object of which 'is to determine the possibility of establishing a general model of social systems which would make it possible to foresee, prevent and influence the politically significant aspects of social changes or mutations in the developing countries of the world'.[6]

The funds available appeared astronomical to the Chileans (1 to 1½ million dollars per annum for four years). Suspicions were aroused, and it came to light that both the theory of this project and its financial resources originated not in the universities of the U.S.A. but in the Defence Department. The enquiry of the Special Commission of the Chilean Chamber of Deputies came to the following conclusion:

> The Camelot Plan is part . . . of a vast international plan designed to defend the supposed interests and security of the United States . . . without being submitted to any norm other than that of its own convenience, without paying any respect to the inter-American juridical system, and without understanding that there may exist in Latin America popular movements which are alien to North American experience, and on which foreign countries should refrain from making pronouncements to the people of those countries where such movements develop, in conformity with the self-determination of nations.[7]

This affair,[8] which was given much space in the press (first by the left-wing, and later also by the right and centre), profoundly influenced public opinion, to such an extent that severe 'spy-fever' shook the people. Sociology became synonymous with espionage.[9] Neither I nor my collaborators thought that it would have repercussions on our work, until two leaders of denominations made it known, indirectly, that their Churches no longer wished to take part in the project.

It was then necessary again to visit, explain, plead, convince. To say that I was not an American, but a Swiss, and therefore the citizen of a country which did not have the necessary means to send 'marines' to South America; that I worked for the W.C.C., an organization whose participants included the churches of the U.S.S.R. as well as the U.S.A. and Chile, too, and did not have the reputation of being a nest of spies, etc. Little by little all returned to normal, although right up to the time of my departure each time I met a new acquaintance allusions to the Camelot Plan came up!

Every time a similar incident occurred, the corollary was a serious loss of time which might have been devoted to research; nevertheless this was an excellent initiation into Chilean reality and the psychology of the people. Such incidents were the occasion for weaving bonds of deep sympathy with several church leaders, getting to know them better and of understanding more deeply their way of going about things. *A posteriori* I am convinced that the conflict situations which I had to overcome made me susceptible of a deeper understanding of the churches than if, on arriving in Santiago, I had found everything perfectly in order for the organization of the research. In particular, the tensions in which, in self-defence, I found myself taking sides, taught me the strategy to be followed in the very involved game of interdenominational relations.

3. METHODS OF RESEARCH

In the main, three methods of research were used: an analysis of written documents, observation-participation, and lastly an enquiry conducted by means of a questionnaire, supplemented by different types of interviews.

(A) WRITTEN DOCUMENTS

These documents can be subdivided as follows:

(i). Documents produced by Chilean Pentecostalists themselves: denominational newspapers; psalters; handbooks, etc. Though difficult of access (of the three principal collections we were able to study only one completely), the newspapers were valuable for establishing the history of the denominations. Their analysis underlines the absence of any original contribution to theology by Chilean Pentecostalism, and even the absence of any systematic theology beyond the Confession of Faith.

(ii). Books and articles on Protestantism in Chile, generally from a confessional source (Catholic or Protestant). The work of Father Ignacio Vergara, *El Protestantismo en Chile,* should be especially mentioned; it is surprisingly objective in its approach to the subject. Father Vergara has accomplished a gigantic task, making an inventory of the Protestant and Pentecostal denominations in Chile and giving for each of them a historical sketch and a description of its present state. Though some errors were found in his work, this was inevitable since it was impossible for him to check all the information he received (especially on the number of members or points of historical derivation), and also since Protestantism in Chile is unstable, and each month sees denominations born, renamed, dividing or even disappearing. This book, which is a veritable dictionary and genealogical tree of Chilean Protestantism, made it unnecessary for us to undertake a similar enquiry and enabled us to turn immediately to problems of genesis and structure.

We should also mention the *Official Census Returns* and the statistical information therein.

(iii). Books and articles on the history, sociology, economy and politics of Chile.

(B) OBSERVATION-PARTICIPATION

Anyone who has made a special study of the sects knows that, in this type of society, there is no room for a neutral observer. The group would not understand it if one attended its activities without being existentially interested in its message and its faith. The visitor is compelled to participate, i.e. to sing, pray and preach, so that the so-called 'participatory observation' is not a matter of choice but of necessity.[10]

This method is not without its inconveniences. The observer (especially if he is a foreigner, as in this case) is an object of interest to the congregation. He cannot avoid being put in a seat of honour on the dais behind the pulpit. Since he is asked to preach, or at least to 'give a message', he takes part in the worship by speaking and his presence undoubtedly has an influence on the psycho-sociological progress of the ceremony. In fact this influence does not always operate in the same way: it may happen that the presence in the group of a foreign observer prevents any charismatic manifestations, but sometimes it stimulates them, as the congregation wishes to give the visitor an opportunity to observe the presence of the Spirit.

These inconvenient aspects may be corrected by making oneself well known to a certain number of congregations, who become so accustomed to the visitor's presence that he becomes part of the furniture. As I was living in Santiago, I was able after several months to move almost unnoticed in some congregations. During the periods of observation in the mining areas, or in the country districts, I decided to spend at least two weeks at a time in each place, and as I attended worship every day, at the end of a week the members had almost become accustomed to my presence.

Another problem is that of the subjective nature of the observations and interpretations made by the 'observer-participant'. In fact an enormous socio-cultural gap existed between me and the Chilean Pentecostal church members. Being Swiss, not Chilean, of French mother tongue, a member of the Reformed Church and university-educated, did not all this prevent me *a priori* from interpreting correctly what I observed?

Thus it was necessary to set up controls for myself of two sorts. The observations collected by my two Chilean collaborators provided the first. One of them was himself a Pentecostalist; he acted as a 'participant-observer'[11] and described the phenomena from the 'inside'. The other collaborator, a Methodist, stood midway between us. Thus, when we attended the same events, we were able to check our descriptions and to check the place we gave to the different actors, actions and objects.

The second control came from the very large number of discussions we had with pastors, groups of elders and of church members. We asked them, for example, immediately after a ceremony, to describe it for us and explain it.

One may question the limits of an observer's participation. For example, I was often asked if I took part in the charismatic phenomena and spoke in tongues myself. The question of the degree of participation arises from two other problems, one methodological and the other moral. Methodologically speaking, as Malcolm J. C. Calley[12] has very well put it, participation in the life of a congregation must not be pushed too far, otherwise one would link oneself too closely with that particular one and lose the opportunity of moving around from one church to another. In that case, personal participation (authentic or pretended) in ecstatic manifestations or glossolalia would be interpreted by the group as baptism of the Spirit, which would automatically make the subject of the experience an integral member of the congregation. Therefore the observer should confine himself to preaching, prayer and joining in collective responses. To my mind, there is also a moral problem. Can one pretend to participate, thus deceiving the congregation about oneself, to the point of feigning an ecstasy or speaking in tongues? The reply brings up a value judgment. In my own case, the congregations always knew for whom I was working, that I was a believer but not a Pentecostalist, and that I was making a study of their churches. Though I preached and sang together with them, I myself never underwent any charismatic experience, and, following the same line of thought, I always maintained a certain degree of detachment during collective prayer, when each person prays aloud with many gestures, for this custom lies just at the crossroads of reasoning and emotional participation. At those times I knelt with the rest, but neither spoke nor moved.

The reader may be interested to know that I emerged from this long period of observation convinced that the phenomena called 'charismatic' (dancing, speaking in tongues, prophesying, ecstasy, trembling, etc.) are very rarely simulated. Though I never had to make an effort to remain an 'observer', I am sure that, had I been a Chilean peasant or labourer, I would have been caught up by the power of this collective contagion, of which I have felt the 'impact'.[13]

Besides participating in community activities, I had the opportunity of joining in the family life of the Pentecostalists, generally with the pastors, but also with ordinary members. I was their guest for about fifty meals, which were unique opportunities for seeing the kind of life they lead, their rules of behaviour, and understanding the meaning of certain observances and beliefs, etc. Whenever I had a letter of introduction from the leader of a denomination, I was always and everywhere given a very warm welcome and treated as a brother who, because he was a foreigner, was forgiven for not being a Pentecostalist!

(c) INVESTIGATION AND INTERVIEWS

Besides observation-participation, which enables one to get a first-hand view of the whole group, we carried out interviews of different kinds: life histories of the pastors, life histories of church members and accounts of their conversion; conversations on specific questions with the leaders ('superintendents' and pastors), group discussions with members of local councils of Protestant churches, conversations with non-Protestants (group or individual)—priests, politicians, local government officials, school teachers, trade unionists, social and medical workers, employers; in short, all the types of people who by reason of their profession knew something about Pentecostalism or the Pentecostalists.

All these interviews were conducted according to the 'non-directed' method—the person interviewed was not given a questionnaire, but the investigator had a scheme to follow. As often as possible the conversation was recorded. If not, the investigator made notes, preferably during the interview or else immediately afterwards.

INVESTIGATION AMONG THE PASTORS, USING QUESTIONNAIRE

We also wished to obtain quantifiable information (i.e. to go on to make an enquiry by means of a questionnaire) about the pastors. Our plan was to use this method to study the following subjects: their conception of the pastor's role and function, their vision of society (the 'world'), and their attitude towards other Christian denominations.[14]

1. *Problems in Choosing a Sample*

(*a*) There were difficult problems to be overcome in choosing the sample. To begin with, just as there is neither law nor rule governing the use of the title, so there is no central organization able to provide a complete list of Pentecostalist pastors. Anyone can call himself a pastor. Because of the very large number of Pentecostalist denominations,[15] and their complete independence from one another, it was impossible to obtain a list of the pastors of all the principal denominations, or to compile one quickly. Since we had not enough time to work out a sample on a complete base, we decided to choose five Pentecostal denominations from which we could obtain lists of pastors and their addresses, and confine ourselves to these.

These denominations were:[16]

(i). The *Iglesia Metodista Pentecostal*, the mother church of Chilean Pentecostalism, by far the largest in the country today (along with the *Iglesia Evangélica Pentecostal*). It has about 90 pastors holding charges, and congregations all over the country. Its headquarters are in Santiago, but the present bishop, Pastor M. Mancilla, lives in the south at Temuco.

(ii). The *Iglesia Pentecostal de Chile*, which broke away from the above in 1946, has about 40 pastors. Geographically it extends from the Peruvian frontier to Puerto-Montt. The centre of this church is at Curico, where its superintendent and founder, Enrique Chavez, is the pastor.

(iii). The *Misión Iglesia Pentecostal* was founded in 1952 after a schism in the *Iglesia Evangélica Pentecostal*, and it has 22 pastors. Its headquarters are in Santiago, where its founder, Victor Pavez Ortiz, is leader of one of the congregations. Its geographical extent is more restricted.

(iv). The *Corporación Iglesia del Señor*, one of the many denominations whose titles include the words Iglesia del Señor, all of which broke away originally from the Methodist Church in the second decade of this century. Its spread is confined to the region between the Bio-Bio river and the town of Puerto-Montt.

(v). The *Iglesia de Dios*, which is an offshoot of the *Church of God* (Cleveland) and originated in the missionary activities of the latter from 1950 onwards. In our sample this is the only denomination which is not completely national.

(*b*) Once we had defined the population of Pentecostalists on whom we wished to carry out our questionnaire enquiry, a second problem arose, that of *interpreting the results*. Even though they were clear in themselves, in that marked tendencies were apparent, we did not know whether these tendencies were specifically related to the *Pentecostalist* pastors of Chile. In order to be able to emphasize the characteristics which were peculiar to Pentecostalism, it was necessary to compare them with control samples. We therefore decided to use the same questionnaire on a group of *Chilean* pastors of three 'traditional' Protestant denominations: Methodist, Presbyterian and Anglican.

Then, taking advantage of an invitation from the *Facultad Evangélica de Teología* in Buenos Aires, we were able to use the questionnaire on all the students there preparing for theological examinations.

(*c*) Thus we had three populations to deal with, the common denominators being that they all belonged to the Protestant family, and were all either carrying on a pastoral ministry or preparing to do so. There then remained a third difficulty to be overcome. We already knew that to send the questionnaire by post would be to doom our enquiry to failure: in Chile, especially in the cultural milieu of the Pentecostalists, no one answers letters.[17] An investigator had to visit each pastor in the sample. Because of the distances to be covered, the difficulty of access to certain regions, and also the limitation of time and money at our disposal, it was clear that we could not establish the sample simply by drawing lots.

To resolve this difficulty, we abandoned the probability method of sampling. We decided to *choose three provinces, and investigate all the pastors of the chosen denominations living in those provinces*.

The practical advantages of such a procedure are obvious. The chief disadvantage is also clear: since we did not choose our sample at random, we were not able to apply to the whole body of pastors the statistical results obtained from the sample. *Statistically speaking*, our results are valid for the pastors of the three provinces investigated, but on a strict view are confined to those provinces only. Nevertheless, we shall see later on whether arguments which are not statistical but

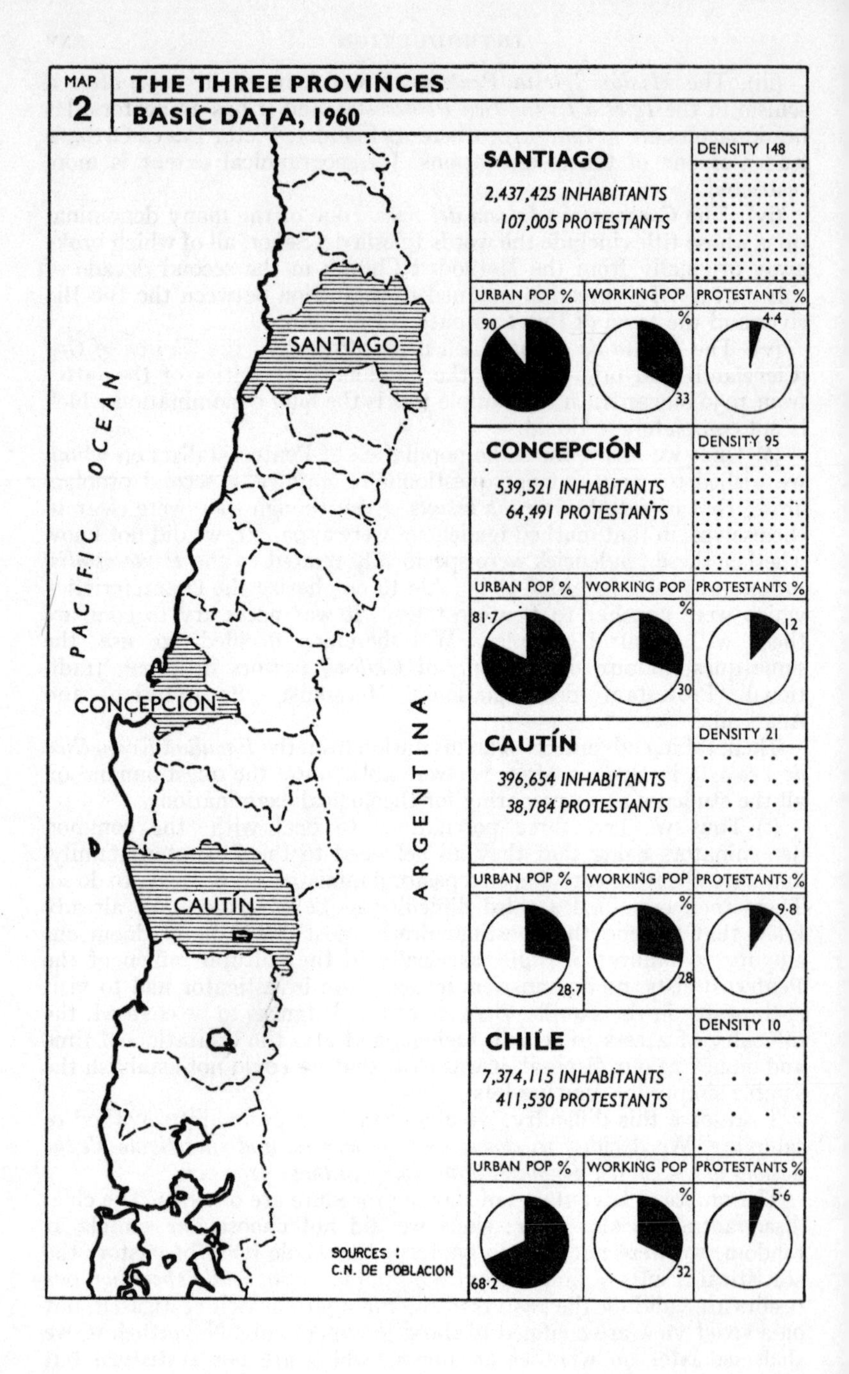
MAP
2
THE THREE PROVINCES
BASIC DATA, 1960
PACIFIC OCEAN
ARGENTINA
SANTIAGO
CONCEPCIÓN
CAUTÍN
SOURCES :
C.N. DE POBLACION
SANTIAGO
2,437,425 INHABITANTS
107,005 PROTESTANTS
DENSITY 148
URBAN POP %
WORKING POP %
PROTESTANTS %
90
33
4·4
CONCEPCIÓN
539,521 INHABITANTS
64,491 PROTESTANTS
DENSITY 95
URBAN POP %
WORKING POP %
PROTESTANTS %
81·7
30
12
CAUTÍN
396,654 INHABITANTS
38,784 PROTESTANTS
DENSITY 21
URBAN POP %
WORKING POP %
PROTESTANTS %
28·7
28
9·8
CHILE
7,374,115 INHABITANTS
411,530 PROTESTANTS
DENSITY 10
URBAN POP %
WORKING POP %
PROTESTANTS %
68·2
32
5·6

Table 1. Demographic characteristics of the provinces investigated (1960)*

PROVINCE	POPULATION	DENSITY PER SQ. KM	URBAN POP. %	% OF POP. WORKING	PROTESTANTS NO.	PROTESTANTS %
Santiago	2,437,425	148	90·0	33	107,005	4·4
Concepcion	539,521	95	81·7	30	64,491	12·0
Cautin	396,654	21	28·7	28	38,784	9·8
CHILE	7,374,115	10	68·2	32	411,530	5·6

* Table prepared on the basis of publications of the *Dirección de Estadísticas y Censos,* Santiago.

Table 2. Distribution of the working population (12 years old and over) of the three provinces, according to type of economic activity, 1960(%)*

ECONOMIC CATEGORY		SANTIAGO	CONCEPCION	CAUTIN	CHILE
0	Agriculture, hunting, fishing	8·4	16·7	55·7	27·8
1	Extractive industries	0·6	9·2	0·2	3·8
2–3	Manufacturing industries	26·8	24·0	9·9	17·9
4	Building industry	6·2	7·0	3·3	5·7
5 & 8	Service industries	31·0	22·9	15·7	23·6
6	Commerce, banking, insurance	14·0	9·1	6·5	10·1
7	Transport and communications	4·9	5·0	3·0	4·9
9 & 10	Unspecified occupations	8·1	6·1	5·7	6·2
TOTAL	%	100·0	100·0	100·0	100·0
	Actual	835,412	164,024	119,990	2,388,667

* Table prepared on the basis of Cuadro no. 24 (pp. 54–56) of *Población del País, Caraterísticas básicas de la Población,* Dirección de Estadísticas y Censos. The exact content of the categories corresponds with international classification methods as defined in the United Nations Paper Series M, N*4, Rev. 1.

purely qualitative could not after all enable certain general conclusions to be drawn.

2. *The Choice of Provinces*

Since we were limiting our investigation to three provinces, it was important to select them on the one hand for the density of Protestants, so as to meet a sufficient number of pastors there, and on the other for their socio-economic milieu. Each province being quite distinct from the others, by analysing the replies in each, one can find out whether the socio-economic milieu has an influence on the pastors' opinions. For that reason our choice fell on Santiago, an urban province, Cautin, a rural province, and Concepcion, a mixed province.

Santiago. These tables omit an important fact: 82·2 per cent. of the population lives in the metropolitan district of Gran Santiago. Thus this province is completely dominated by the life of the capital and its tentacles, the population of which is more than one quarter of the population of the whole country. One out of every two persons employed works in 'service industries' (categories 5–8): the tertiary sector is very dominant.

Cautin is quite the opposite: there, the manufacturing and construction industries play only a minor part and the provincial capital, with its 72,000 inhabitants, is chiefly an agricultural market and administrative centre. Agriculture employs more than half the working population, and services (5–8) one quarter.

Concepcion is between the two; a good third of the working population is occupied in services (5–8); just under a third is in manufacturing and building, and a little more than a quarter in agriculture and the extractive industries (in the coal mining area in the south of the province). Thus all the main branches of economic activity are present in Concepcion in nearly equal ratios. Another notable difference is that, while Santiago Province is just one unconfined city, and Cautin has only one town, Temuco, of more than 20,000 inhabitants, Concepcion has six towns of over 20,000 inhabitants.

3. *The Three Samples*

Having made these selections, the framework for the investigation was settled. The samples are defined as follows:

(i). The whole of the *theological students* of the F.E.T. in Buenos Aires (38 persons). This institution has the well-merited reputation of being the peak of Reformed thought in the southern half of Latin America. Created on the initiative of the Methodists, it seeks to be interdenominational and to serve all the Protestant churches of the *Cono Sur*[18] (Peru, Bolivia, Chile, Paraguay, Argentina and Uruguay), a large proportion of whose ministers it trains.

Whatever ecumenical overtures it may make, it goes without saying that the Faculty serves mainly the traditional Protestant denominations; it is rare for a Pentecostalist to come to study there, and the Methodist element predominates to the extent of constituting 72 per cent. of the student body. In the same way, the Argentinians outnumber the rest of the students (56 per cent.), and the Chileans alone form a minority group of any size (19 per cent.).

The students have all completed secondary education in their respective countries. They can obtain the B.D. in three years, and the licentiate (equivalent to M.A.) after two further years. The vast majority live in college, on the F.E.T. campus.

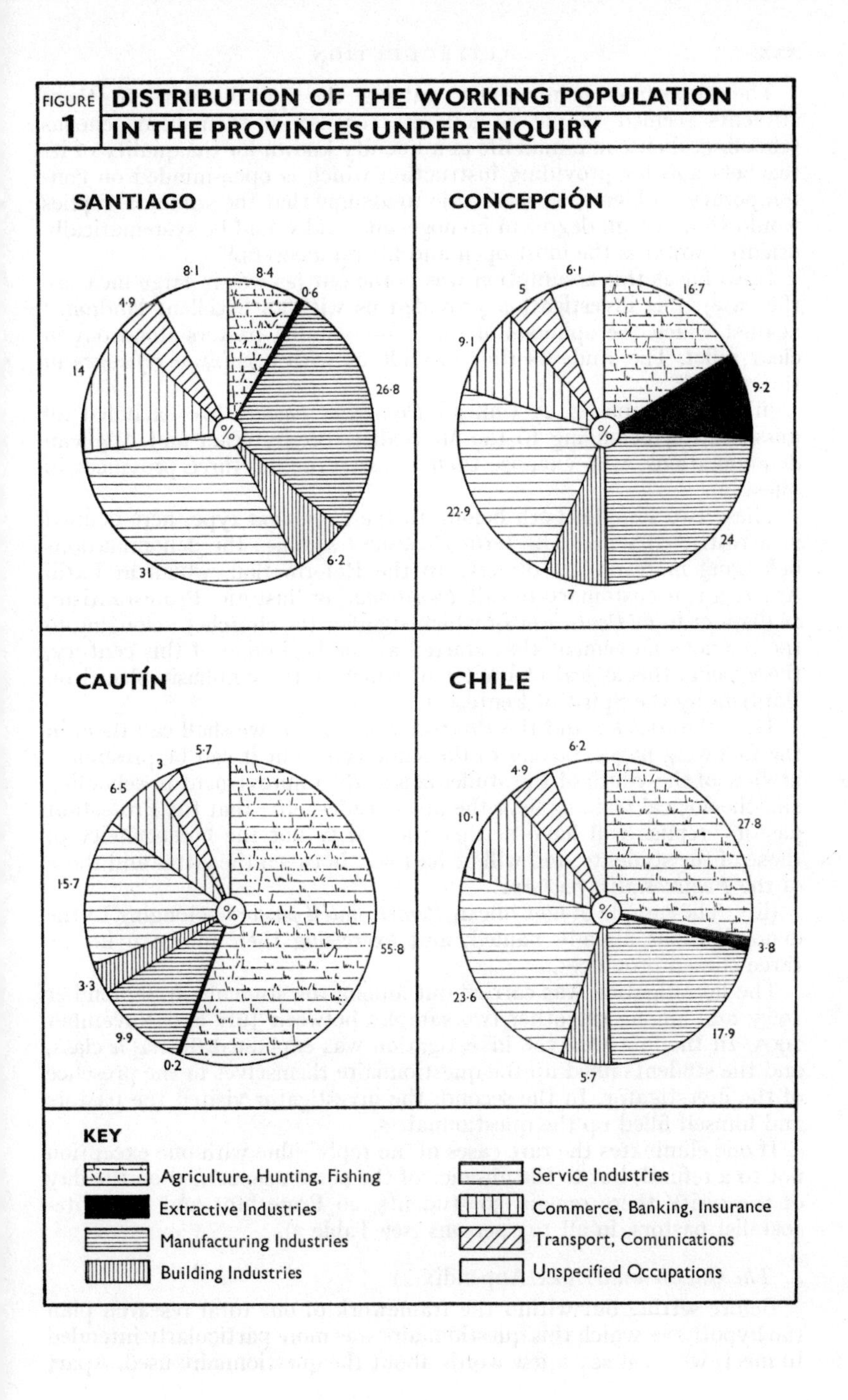
FIGURE 1
DISTRIBUTION OF THE WORKING POPULATION IN THE PROVINCES UNDER ENQUIRY
SANTIAGO
8·1
8·4
0·6
4·9
14
26·8
%
6·2
31
CONCEPCIÓN
6·1
5
16·7
9·1
9·2
%
22·9
24
7
CAUTÍN
5·7
3
6·5
15·7
%
55·8
3·3
9·9
0·2
CHILE
6·2
4·9
10·1
27·8
%
3·8
23·6
17·9
5·7
KEY
Agriculture, Hunting, Fishing
Extractive Industries
Manufacturing Industries
Building Industries
Service Industries
Commerce, Banking, Insurance
Transport, Comunications
Unspecified Occupations

The important point about putting the questionnaire to these students seemed to me as follows: because of their homogeneous schooling, their communal life in a Faculty known for the quality of its teachers and for providing instruction which is open-minded on contemporary problems, we were able to assume that the students' replies would show a high degree of homogeneity and would be systematically oriented towards the most open and liberal answers.[19]

In so far as this assumption was borne out (as was in large measure the case), this investigation provided us with an excellent landmark against which the opinions of the Pentecostalist pastors stood out in clear relief. The students thus provide us with a *point of reference* in this work.[20]

(ii). The sample of 27 Chilean *Protestant pastors* (we excluded all missionaries) belonging to the Methodist, Presbyterian and Anglican denominations, who exercise their ministry in the three provinces in question.

These two samples both belong to the *Protestant* type, here defined in a restricted sense. The term *Protestant* signifies the denominations belonging more or less directly to the Reformation, which in Latin America it is customary to call '*traditional*' or 'historic' Protestantism, as distinct from *Pentecostalist* which signifies the churches belonging to the religious movement that started at the beginning of this century, the specific theological character of which is the emphasis placed on Baptism by the Spirit of Pentecost.

Thus the *students* and the *Protestant pastors* (as we shall call them in the following pages) belong to the same type, but it can be presumed, in view of the youth of the students and the improvement in schooling and theological training over the last decades, etc., that the Protestant pastors' replies will have neither the clarity nor the homogeneity of those of the students, and will be half way between the latter and those of the *Pentecostalist pastors*.

(iii). The sample of 66 Chilean *Pentecostalist pastors* belonging to the denominations already named, and exercising their ministry in the three chosen provinces.

The investigation was carried out among the students in September 1965, and among the other two samples between July and November 1965. In the first case the investigation was explained during a class, and the students filled up the questionnaire themselves in the presence of the investigator. In the second, the investigator visited the pastors and himself filled up the questionnaires.

If one eliminates the rare cases of 'no reply' (due with one exception not to a refusal, but to the absence of the person concerned on the day of the visit), there remain 36 students, 26 Protestant and 61 Pentecostalist pastors, in all 123 persons (see Table 3).

4. *The Questionnaire* (see Appendix 2)

Before setting out within the framework of our total research plan the hypotheses which this questionnaire was more particularly intended to meet, we must say a few words about the questionnaire used. Apart

Table 3. Composition of the Samples

SAMPLE	NUMBER ON LIST	ABSENT*	REFUSED TO REPLY	QUESTION-NAIRES COMPLETED
Sample 1:				
Students	38	2	—	36
Sample 2:				
(*a*) Anglicans	5	1	—	4
(*b*) Presbyterians	4	—	—	4
(*c*) Methodists	18	—	—	18
Protestant pastors	27	1	—	26
Sample 3:				
(*a*) Igl. Met. Pent.	28	1	1	26
(*b*) Igl. Pent. Chile	11	—	—	11
(*c*) Misión Igl. Pent.	11	2	—	9
(*d*) Igl. del Señor	3	—	—	3
(*e*) Igl. de Dios	13	1	—	12
Pentecostalist pastors	66	4	1	61

* These persons were absent on the day of the enquiry, had moved away, etc.

from certain questions of fact (age, social and religious origin, etc.) and test questions (designed to define, for example, the degree of general knowledge), we asked for the *opinion* of the interviewee. The method of observation-participation enabled us to find out whether the opinion expressed actually corresponded with the interviewee's actions (the problem of the correspondence between thought and deed).

So as to be able to quantify the results easily, and also to be able to reach an understanding in depth of the replies, we used the method of *closed replies* (yes/no) or of a *choice* of replies (a series of stereotyped answers of which the interviewee has to choose one), and left a blank space in which the person could explain his reply.

5. *The Hypotheses Underlying the Questionnaire*

This investigation by means of a questionnaire, we must repeat, was only one of the methods employed in our research, and complements the other methods. After a first phase of direct observation, it seemed worth while to us to obtain a measurement of the pastors' opinions on certain phenomena. The investigation showed the existence of certain dominant features which a second series of observations and depth interviews enabled us to analyse and to integrate into a total description of the Pentecostal social system.

This is why the following pages do not have the appearance of the report of an investigation. The report was made in manuscript and it is here integrated into a wider perspective, being one of several sources of information.

(i). The choice of the three samples was related to the hypothesis which we shall formulate in the form of a question:

Are the Pentecostalist pastors differentiated from the Protestant pastors by their 'sectarian' opinions and attitudes? If so, up to what point?

The term 'sectarian' is used here in its general sense and signifies a desire to break (cf. the false etymology: *secare*) as much with society as with other churches—a desire which cannot be without influence on their conception of the pastoral ministry and its function.

(ii). The differentiation within the Protestant type between two samples, one of *pastors* and one of *students*, enabled us to define the evolution of Protestant thought in Latin America.

(iii). Each sample is composed of *pastors of a number of different denominations*. We are compelled to ask: Was it legitimate to group them together under one type? The systematic use of cross-checks in relation to the denomination makes it possible to remove this doubt; with one exception—pointed out in the text—these cross-checks brought no noticeable difference to light. On the contrary, as we shall see, the variations occur as a function of the types. Analysis therefore justified our typology.

(iv). Finally, the *choice of three provinces* (in the case of the two samples of pastors), constituting well differentiated socio-economic backgrounds, enabled one to ask questions about the influence of that background on the pastors' opinions.

This problem can be settled here. Apart from some questions,[21] the trends which appear have the same significance, whatever the province. Within the framework of this particular country and this questionnaire, it would seem that the different socio-economic backgrounds have no significant influence on the pastors' opinions. Even in those places where significant differences appeared, a detailed analysis of them will show that it was a question not of a modification of the specific Pentecostalist ideological views but simply a modulation of them.

6. *The Value of the Results*

The lack of differentiation both between provinces and between denominations in each type enables us to reopen the question of the value of our investigation, particularly—since that is where our interest centres—so far as the Pentecostalist pastors are concerned. Is the validity of the results restricted to the pastors of the denominations investigated and to the provinces sampled, or, since identical results were obtained no matter what the province or the denomination, could one not legitimately risk inferring that the same applies to all the pastors of organized Pentecostal denominations in Chile?

Other arguments, qualitative like the one we have just put forward, lend support to this last hypothesis: we were never able to discern, in our visits to other denominations and from our numerous discussions with their pastors, any signs of important differences. Observation produces an impression of uniformity in their organizational schemes, their beliefs and the elements of their doctrine, a uniformity which is in strange contrast with the multiplicity of Pentecostal denominations.

Personally we are convinced that this same questionnaire, given to a statistically representative sample of Chilean Pentecostalist pastors, would confirm our results, but we leave the reader to give his own answer to the question. For the sake of convenience, we shall speak of *Chilean Pentecostalist pastors* when we refer to our sample. The reader will know to which denominations they belong and in which part of Chile they work. If it seems preferable to him, he can himself make the necessary reservations.

4. CONCLUDING REMARKS

(*a*) To avoid possible confusion, let us here define the use we shall make of certain terms. *Protestants* and *Protestantism*, used in a general sense, refer to all the Christian Reformed religious movements.

In a restricted sense, they refer to the 'traditional' or 'historic' Protestant denominations, i.e. created before this century and foreign in origin, in contrast to *Pentecostalism*, created in this century and (generally) national in origin.

The term *denomination* signifies a particular organized religious movement, which has been given a name and has a controlling body. In addition, in sociology this concept has a distinct content and signifies a definite type of religious organization. In this latter sense, we shall write it in inverted commas ('denomination').

In Chile, the terms *mission* and *corporation* are often synonymous with denomination. We shall use the second in this sense, but we shall reserve the concept 'mission' for foreign organizations carrying on missionary activities in Chile.

The *congregation* is the local church, with its principal place of worship and its chapels, its pastor and council. The term congregation is specially valuable in the case of Pentecostalism and Methodism, which are organized on the 'congregationalist' model, in which all the local churches are quite autonomous and rank equally with one another. As a synonym, we shall often use the term *community*.

Perhaps it is necessary to emphasize the fact that the terms *sect* and *sectarian* (which we would be tempted to put in inverted commas as E. Léonard did) are used here without any reference to theological content and without any value judgment. We shall define their *sociological* content in the following chapters, but let us say at the outset that we are borrowing these terms from Troeltsch. They relate to a form of religious organization, the existence of which, in the eyes of the researcher, in itself speaks for their validity.

(*b*) One final point must be made clear. Following upon the historical monograph by Father Ignacio Vergara, we are putting forward here an overall description of Chilean Pentecostalism, and a sociological theory concerning it, which can be integrated into the sociological study of religious movements. But we do not aspire to any sociological imperialism: on the contrary, ours is not the only possible viewpoint, and we invoke the complementary nature of this with the historical and psychological approaches, among others. Nor do we claim to challenge (because we are dealing with a totally different level of reality) Pentecostalist theological theory, or rather theories.[22]

Part One

BIRTH AND DEVELOPMENT OF PENTECOSTALISM IN CHILE

CHAPTER I

From a Foreign Introduction to a National Protestant Movement

I. THE SPREAD OF THE PROTESTANT MOVEMENT IN THE NINETEENTH CENTURY

BEFORE Protestantism could spread into Spanish America the chains had to be broken which the metropolitan power had forged, imposing her law upon the area and isolating it from the rest of the world. As long as the Spanish standard waved over South American shores, only corsairs and pirates would venture upon its coasts to pillage and to hunt down the ships of His Most Catholic Majesty, which came to fetch home spices and gold. And whenever an Anglo-Saxon or Dutch pirate was taken, the gallows awaited the heretic, who the populace were astonished to see had human form. Only revolution and independence could weaken the monopoly of the Catholic Church, and—though this factor must not be exaggerated—it is true that some of the liberators and statesmen such as San Martin and O'Higgins on the Pacific coast, or later, in Mexico, Benito Juarez,[1] saw a chance of using Protestant support as a counter to the Roman hierarchy, who during the revolutionary period had played an obscure game.[2]

In Chile the independence movement sprang up in 1810 and won success eight years later, and in 1821 the arrival of the first 'colporteur' (as missionaries were then called) is recorded. This was Mr. James Thomson, a Baptist working for the British and Foreign Bible Society, who had already distinguished himself as a teacher in Argentina. He had been introducing the Lancaster school method, and was called to Chile by Bernardo O'Higgins himself. Under this system, the more advanced pupils are entrusted with teaching the younger ones, which develops their sense of responsibility and also obviously permits a most economical use of the teaching staff. Thus right at the outset one of the characteristics of Protestant evangelization appears: it is effected through the intermediary of education. A year later, having been invited to Peru by San Martin, James Thomson was accorded Chilean nationality as a mark of gratitude. But it would seem that Catholic opposition was at the root of his departure, and Thomson's work was to disappear without trace.

One of the unvarying ambitions of English missions was to evangelize the Patagonian Indians, and expeditions were organized which were both scientific (Charles Darwin, the naturalist, took part in one of them) and missionary. In these attempts one person in particular stands out: Allan Gardiner, a sea captain, who from 1838 onwards devoted himself entirely to missionary work among the Indians. Lack of success did not discourage him, and his adventures drew him farther and farther south. His supply ship being delayed, he died of cold and hunger with seven companions in Tierra del Fuego in 1851, without having been able to establish relations with the Indian peoples, who were particularly suspicious and hostile.

Gardiner's son followed in his father's footsteps, with the same courage and the same lack of success. In 1859 an expedition to the southern regions was almost totally wiped out by the Indians. The second Gardiner then attempted a mission to the Lota miners, but poor health compelled him to leave Chile for Australia in 1870. Twenty years later, W. Reade Gardiner, grandson of Allan Gardiner, wanted to resume the family task but died of typhus shortly after landing at Valparaiso. No matter how unsuccessful these attempts were, they did inspire people to continue the work; in 1894, at the Jubilee of the foundation by the first Gardiner of the Missionary Society for South America, the Araucan Mission was established in England, and itself began to create lasting work in the Indian country around Temuco, which still exists today under the name of the Anglican Mission.

Thomson and the Gardiners were the forerunners; but the first to establish firm foundations, and by his personality to dominate Chilean Protestant life for half a century (1845–89), was David Trumbull. A graduate of Yale University and Princeton Theological Seminary, this Congregationalist answered the call of the Foreign Evangelical Union, sailed for Chile and started work in the port of Valparaiso among foreign seamen. It seems that the first Anglican worship was held in Valparaiso in 1837, and the first service in the Reformed tradition was held ten years later, in the printing shop of the newspaper *El Mercurio*—the first concrete sign of tactical support for Protestantism by liberal circles and freemasonry. Then Trumbull turned his energies to the building of a church, and he succeeded in spite of the Catholic clergy's opposition. But he had to submit to two restrictions: to build a high wooden wall along the road, which hid the façade of the church, and to be as quiet as possible, so as to avoid all scandal! As a founder of churches and schools, Trumbull's reputation grew beyond the confined circles of Protestantism to the point where Catholic congregations were praying for his conversion! A famous controversy arose between him and the ecclesiastical ruler of Valparaiso, Monsignor Casanova, concerning the cult of St. Isidor, patron saint of rain. This literary jousting (*La Voz de Chile* published Trumbull's articles) was inscribed in the rolls of the liberals' anti-clerical struggle, and earned the missionary the esteem of some of the Chilean *élite*.

The expansion of missionary work, which had at first been done among the foreign elements and now spread to the people of the country, demanded reinforcements. Some help came, but only drop by drop, since the Foreign Evangelical Union was not in a position to assure further development. However, it was still under its patronage that the first two Chilean Protestant churches which worshipped in Spanish were founded. The first was established in 1868 in Santiago, and we are told that it 'had four Chileans on its list of members';[3] the second was organized in Valparaiso in the following year. 1871 was the year in which the first Chilean pastor was ordained—José Manuel Ibañez, probably the first Latin American to be ordained. The greatness of Trumbull, when he saw the need for help and the Union's inability to supply it, was to surmount the obstacle of denominational divisions and to agree to serve under the Board of Foreign Missions of the Presbyterian Church in the U.S.A. This transfer was made in 1872, the year in which the Presbyterian Church as such entered Chile and inherited the work of the Union. The Presbyterian Church set up presbyteral government in 1883 and, with the Anglican Church and the Union Church, was the first Protestant church to be legally incorporated.

Trumbull particularly distinguished himself in journalistic battles which he waged for the recognition of the rights of Protestants. When he arrived in Chile, heretics had no freedom of worship either in private or in public; marriage was the monopoly of the Catholics, and the Roman Church had charge over cemeteries (under the Constitution of 1833). Not until 1865, when J. J. Perez was President, was an interpretative law passed introducing freedom of worship 'within private property', and permitting the founding of private schools 'for the instruction of the children' of the dissenters.[4] The only cemetery available to them was in Valparaiso, and this was due to the personal intervention of Bernardo O'Higgins, who braved Catholic opinion (1819). The bodies of foreign dissenters who died in Chile had to be transported to the port, or, if the deceased's family had no means, surreptitiously buried or thrown into the sea. Not until 1853 was a law passed giving foreigners the right to their own cemeteries. And another thirty years passed before a law was passed authorizing civil cemeteries (1883). Finally in 1884 Parliament legalized civil marriage.[5]

The Methodists came to Chile as late as 1877, when Bishop William Taylor travelled from Panama through to Chile, founding a whole series of missions. His method was to establish schools as screens for missionary activity. It was hoped that these institutions would remain economically independent (the school being intended to finance the mission), but this proved impossible and the work was taken over by the Methodist Church of the United States (1897). The Methodist Church was proud to have in its ranks a fiery preacher, Juan Canut de Bon, a former pupil of the Jesuits, who became a legend, and whose name today is used to designate Protestants: *canutos* is a term used derisively by adversaries, but with pride by Protestant church members.

Other denominations were introduced into Chile. The Lutherans (1846) came only by way of immigrants, never establishing any missionary work. The Baptists entered in 1908, and before them, the Christian and Missionary Alliance (1897), a sort of Presbyterian revival movement.

Leaving aside the case of the Lutheran immigrants, four major characteristics mark this period in which Protestantism was introduced in Chile.

First, and in the case of English missionaries chiefly, evangelistic work could be carried on only among the pagan Indians. Up to and including the Edinburgh Conference (1910), the Anglicans refused to look upon Catholic Latin America as a mission field.

Secondly, the first missionaries took their chief task to be the spiritual care of Protestant foreigners living in Chile; the first churches on Chilean territory were intended for them, and the language of preaching was English.

Thirdly, when there arose, especially among North American missionaries, a desire to extend the work to the people of Chile, the strategy employed was to use education, which has been described as 'the veritable Trojan horse' of Protestantism.[6]

Finally, the struggle to obtain official recognition and legal status was an element in the wider struggle being waged, first by the Chilean liberals, then by the radicals, against the conservatism and power of the Catholic Church.

A balance-sheet for this period must also be drawn up. A century after Thomson's arrival in Chile, that is, in 1920, Protestants numbered only 54,000, of whom 17,000 were foreigners and about 10,000 were Lutherans who had become naturalized Chileans. The result is a meagre one. Certainly Protestant colleges trained generations of university students, who were nevertheless not converted. The intelligentsia sympathized with Protestantism, but did not become Protestant; 'most of them remained Roman Catholics for complex reasons, not only social and economic—as Protestants have been too prone to assert—but on deeper aesthetic and religious motivations.'[7] Their sympathy towards Protestantism originated in the struggle for freedom of thought and the separation of Church and State.

We confirm the penetrating judgment of Dr. José Míguez on the development of Protestantism in Latin America in the nineteenth century and the beginning of the twentieth:

> Protestantism was not able in this period to make a serious inroad in Latin American societies. The landed aristocracy was a part of the old society and had a definite place in the 'sacred order'. The intelligentsia felt a certain congeniality to Protestantism, but neither were the forms of the Protestant churches attractive to them nor was their religious interest deep enough to lead to commitment. The Indian masses and the campesinos (peasants) were also part, as subordinates, of the traditional order, caught in a web of relations of dependence which, in turn, constituted their only protection. Also, the Protestant worship and message were perhaps too intellectual and individualistic for them. Protestantism was able to enter only at two points. Through schools and educational centers, it exercised a certain cultural influence in favor of democratic and liberal ideas. On the other hand, it drew some membership from the lower—but not lowest—social groups, mostly in the outskirts of the urban society and in certain rural areas. In fact, it did not touch the structure of society; it merely gathered 'loose dust' off the surface. . . . Protestants were respected, even admired for their honesty, reliability and seriousness, but they were 'outsiders' in society, queer in many aspects, and somehow foreign even in the literal sense of the word.[8]

This was the period of the pioneers, and the history of Chilean

Protestantism is tied up with the life history of several individuals. But that phase, dominated by personalities, was to give way to a new story, in which the individuals involved remained anonymous and the leading role was played by the people. As we shall see, while the first period of Protestantism was linked with the creation of the *Chilean nation* and the success of liberal ideals, the second phase is rooted in the story of the emergence of the proletarian masses, the *Chilean people.*

2. SCHISM, 1909–10

In the first decade of the twentieth century, a spiritual renewal sprang to life in the Methodist congregations of Valparaiso and Santiago. Were there any warning signs of this? Were there any sporadic demonstrations of enthusiasm in other Chilean congregations? The history of the birth of Chilean Pentecostalism is still too little known for a confident answer to be given, but none of the known sources goes back further than 1902, when Dr. Hoover succeeded Pastor E. E. Wilson at the head of the Methodist Episcopal Church of Valparaiso. In his book[9] the new leader says nothing of the congregations of which he had charge before coming to the great port, and he did not come with the reputation for sowing trouble which he afterwards acquired. But the revival of which he was the instrument was only one of the fires lit by the world-wide explosion of Pentecostalism, the latest of the great internal reformations of Protestantism.[10] In the United States at first, then almost simultaneously in Wales, Scandinavia, South Africa and India, sometimes without any connection between them, whole congregations were seized with a new ardour which drew them to seek Pentecostal baptism, the baptism of fire which seals the gift of the Spirit. The Chilean outburst is not one of the chief occurrences nor the most spectacular, but its particular feature is that it broke out in a Catholic country and from its very beginning had only the smallest degree of dependence on external events. The only direct link is Hoover's visit to a 'pre-Pentecostal' church in Chicago in 1895, 'which was living in a state of constant renewal',[11] an experience striking enough for him to quote it as providing a possible beginning for the history of Chilean renewal. But while a wind of spiritual renewal blows through the little church of Valparaiso from 1902 onwards, and even gives rise to ecstatic phenomena and causes a hundred new members to join, it is only in 1907 that the pastor becomes acquainted with Pentecostal doctrine, in the form of a leaflet sent from India by a friend of Mrs. Hoover's, which spoke of a 'clear and distinct baptism of the Spirit, as a complement to justification and sanctification which we had hitherto believed to comprise the whole of Christian experience'.[12] Only now did Hoover embark on a regular correspondence with Pentecostal leaders in Norway, the United States, India and Venezuela.

This sequence of events makes it possible to conclude that Pentecostal propaganda only served to convince a potential adherent, by presenting to this man athirst for God a new mystical experience—

the baptism of fire made tangible by the gift of tongues—towards which to bend the energies of himself and his congregation.

From 1907 to 1909 prayer meetings, vigils (whole nights of prayer in which the core of the congregation took part), witnessings and worship services multiply. These are the years of marching towards the promised land. Meditation is centred on the accounts of Pentecost and the prophetic references to the Spirit, especially in Joel 2. Miracles and extraordinary events are part of the congregation's daily life:

> Laughing, weeping, shouting, singing, foreign tongues, visions and ecstasies during which the individual fell to the ground and felt himself caught up into another place, to heaven, to Paradise, in splendid fields, with various kinds of experience: conversations with God, the angels or the devil. Those who experienced these things profited greatly and generally were changed by them and filled with praises, the spirit of prayer and love.[13]

To this list should be added dreams, premonitions, special revelations—messages entrusted by God to one person to be passed on to another—all the phenomena believed to be the work of the divine power, proof of the presence of the Spirit in the congregation, culminating in the (Chilean) winter of 1909 in a large number of baptisms of the Spirit.

Parallel with the growing enthusiasm were growing troubles with the civil authorities of Valparaiso on the one hand, and the Methodist hierarchy on the other: the neighbourhood was kept awake by the noisy manifestations of the Spirit and the hubbub from the services and vigils in the church or in private houses. The church members themselves were not to be contained within the walls of the church, but, seized by an overwhelming power, would rush out into the street, crying 'Alleluia, glory to God', and give their witness in the public squares.[14] Journalists made investigations and one of them published a series of articles in *El Chileno* with sensational headlines: 'Work of a hoaxer or madman: shouting, fainting fits and blows; Tragi-comic scenes: full details. Denunciation to the Police: the Law intervenes'.[15] One can guess the effect which was produced by these articles—which Hoover called a 'mixture of truth and falsehood'—upon the bourgeoisie and middle-class townspeople of the port, the upholders of Auguste Comte's rationalism and attracted by the remote deism of freemasonry. This journalist accused Hoover of giving his people 'a potion called the *blood of the lamb* which puts them in a stupor and makes them fall to the ground'.[15]

Here one can see a distinction to be drawn between the facts observed by the journalist and the fables he added. The mystique of the blood of the Lamb is an important element not confined to Pentecostalism but found also in Methodism,[16] in German mysticism of the Middle Ages, etc. Pentecostal congregations adopted a number of choruses of the type which underlines the role of the blood of Christ in purification, for example:

> Aleluyah a la sangre del Cordero (thrice)
> Que en la cruz se inmoló par mí

or Aleluyah al Cordero de Dios (twice)
Que dió su sangre en la Cruz (twice)
Por salvarnos de nuestros pecados[17]

During the ecclesiastical action which the Methodist hierarchy later brought against Hoover, one of the facts put forward in relation to the second charge ('seriously imprudent conduct') was to have allowed

> J. S. to perform, in the presence of the pastor, who did not reprove him, what they called 'being washed by the blood of Christ', which consists of a 'washing' in which a person mimes taking blood in his cupped hands from an imaginary source and moving his hands over the bodies of other persons.[18]

Since Hoover in his book does not refute this, it can be accepted as an accurate description. It is even probable that the performance of this rite did produce certain lethargic and ecstatic symptoms in the participants, as the journalist claimed. But to say 'a potion called the blood of the lamb' was really used was an invention, as the blood was imaginary.

The charge brought in the civil courts, however, was in the end dismissed; but it was not just lack of understanding in the wider society that the congregation was running up against. In the ranks of Methodism itself opposition was growing, though muffled and passive at first. The official journal of the church, *El Cristiano*, which chiefly served as a newsletter concerning congregational activities, refused to publish the items sent by Pastor Hoover, in spite of his repeated protests. In September more serious incidents took place. During that month a young woman of English origin, an orphan, who was recovering from a long illness, 'was converted with power and baptized by the Holy Spirit'.[19] This individual, Elena Laidlaw, went to Santiago, where she visited the two Methodist churches, some of whose members were full of enthusiasm about what was happening at Valparaiso and wished to hear her speak. The evidence of those who were present in itself gives us an idea of the conflict which broke loose in Chilean Methodism:

> During the afternoon worship in the Montel meeting, Sister Elena very humbly asked leave to speak during the taking up of the collection. The minister refused. A congregation of 170 to 180 was present, and almost all of them asked that she should be permitted to speak, but the answer was 'no'. The congregation went out into the courtyard to listen to Sister Elena, and afterwards we went into the church again and one brother, filled with the spirit of love, went to embrace the pastor. The latter roughly pushed him aside and they both fell. As he fell the pastor hit his head on the edge of a door . . . and with the blood running down his face he really did look like a madman . . .

Another account says:

> Twelve days ago, I was summoned by Mr. Rice, the superintendent, who asked me to say what I knew of the work in Valparaiso, which I did to the best of my ability, adding what I knew from my own experience. He very cleverly ridiculed this as hard as he could, and then told me his

impressions, gained in the short visit he had paid to that church. He said he had heard nothing but blasphemies against the Holy Spirit and (seen) the most deplorable disorder. He stated that the church was ruled by an unclean woman (Sister Elena), and that all the manifestations were produced by the power of a crude sort of hypnotism.

To go back to the first witness:

In the evening (on 12th September 1909), we gathered at Portales, in the *Primera Iglesia*. The superintendent had squads of police outside the church. Elena asked leave to speak, and the minister (Mr. Rice) told her she could do so when the service was finished. After the blessing the brethren sat down, hoping to hear her, but when she tried to speak to them, the superintendent gave the order for her to be arrested. And then the uproar broke out once more, and to avoid scandal Elena preferred to give herself up voluntarily. The police cleared the church. Almost all the congregation felt they no longer had any ties with the pastors. Some of the brethren offered their homes so that meetings could be held elsewhere than in the churches.[20]

So it was that on the evening of September 12 1909 the two Methodist churches in Santiago lost the majority of their members, who still regarded themselves as constituting congregations and began to celebrate a Pentecostal form of worship. If not legally, yet in fact the birth of the Pentecostal Church as an independent body occurred on that day. But this independence was neither desired nor premeditated, and, until Hoover was forced to retire from the Mission, the new congregations continued to struggle to obtain a hearing by the hierarchy and to win their point. But in vain; the Valparaiso pastor was regarded as an infectious person dangerous to Methodism and they strove to get rid of him, at first by roundabout methods. In October the Board of Missions treasurer wrote to tell him that the Mission was offering him a vacation. On 4th April 1910 there opened in Valparaiso itself the Annual Conference which put on trial the pastor of the largest and most rapidly growing Methodist church in the country. This trial brought into opposition in the first place the hierarchy and the laity, the holders of doctrinal truth as fixed by Methodist *discipline* against those who believed the Spirit blew where it wished, even outside the lines fixed by tradition; then again two mentalities clashed, one which was sensitive to the extraordinary aspects of Biblical narratives, and heir to the old Indian animism; the other, that of the North American missionaries and their followers: the few national pastors, a mentality stamped by nineteenth century rationalism, drawn to religious liberalism and also the masonic *Weltanschauung*. Thus, as Emilio Willems[21] skilfully shows, this was a rebellion of church members belonging to the common people against a church whose religion was expressed in middle-class ideals and cultural forms. In Ernst Troeltsch's terms, we have here the process of a *church* expelling the *sectarian faction* which is developing in its midst. The report of the Disciplinary Commission demonstrates this so well that it is worth quoting some extracts:

First charge: Teaching and publicly and privately disseminating false and anti-methodist doctrines.

(1) During the ecclesiastical year 1909–1910, in the Methodist Episcopal Church of Valparaiso, W. C. Hoover taught on several occasions false and anti-methodist doctrines, to wit: in public worship he declared that the baptism of the Holy Ghost is manifested in visions, convulsions on the ground, the gift of tongues and prophecy.

(2) In the month of September, when A. A. claimed to be prophesying during a service, a brother protested to the said Hoover, who reprimanded him for not accepting this prophecy.

(3) In the home of J. S., while he was in bed obviously suffering from mental derangement caused by the excess of nervous excitement in the services, and while he was unable to speak but could only make unintelligible sounds, the said Hoover claimed that the sick person was possessed by a dumb spirit.

(4) Before members of this Annual Conference, at Valparaiso on Saturday, 5th February of the present year, he declared that in his church some persons had brought messages from heaven, had had visions, had spoken in strange tongues and practised the laying on of hands. . . .

(6) W. C. Hoover has distributed literature which teaches false and anti-methodist doctrines, such as the periodicals 'The Latter Rain', 'Pentecostal Testimony' and tracts published in the United States and in India which teach doctrines of washing of feet, baptism of fire, faith healing miracles, visions, gift of tongues, prophecies, establishing the date of Christ's return, falling into the power of the Holy Ghost, and opposition to organized churches . . .[22]

At that moment, hoping to be able to justify himself in the eyes of the secretaries of the Missionary Society in New York, Hoover agreed to be sent there on leave, and the charges were withdrawn and replaced by an ordinary resolution in which the doctrines he had expressed were declared to be 'anti-methodist, contrary to the Scriptures and *irrational.*'[23]

The two dissenting groups in Santiago had sent a delegation to the Conference at Valparaiso. The delegation was listened to, but that was all, and its cause was never heard by an ecclesiastical court. Then the dissenters of the First Methodist Church in Santiago formed themselves into the *Iglesia Metodista Nacional*, rapidly followed by the second group, and they both agreed to ask Hoover to assume their spiritual leadership. In his own church, the church members urged him not to go back to the United States but to withdraw with them, and on April 17 he took the decision to do so, his judgment being confirmed by a prophecy. At the end of worship,

when prayers were finished, and the congregation rose, a young girl, filled with the Spirit, asked permission to speak. When this was granted she said: 'Tonight we shall eat the Passover: let everyone see if there is blood on the lintel of his door.' And she repeated these words several times. The pastor was completely surprised by this. For him the words were an immediate answer to his prayer, for (1) the girl did not know what was about to happen, (2) she could not have known the pastor's petition, and (3) to speak of the Communion as 'Passover' was strange and out of the ordinary, and carried one's thoughts to the proposed departure, and was regarded as approval of the projected step.[24]

The three schismatic congregations formed a united body of a congregationalist type, and founded the *Iglesia Metodista Pentecostal*, of which Hoover was superintendent until the schism of 1932. By its very name the new denomination stressed the decisive nature of the doctrine of the Baptism of the Spirit, as related in the first chapters of *Acts*, and affirmed its loyalty to the Wesley brothers, accusing the Methodist Episcopal Church of betraying its founders.

Today, seeing the great work accomplished by the Pentecostalists, most of the Methodist leaders regret the schism and explain it as a conflict of personalities. Dr. Hoover's chief adversary, Mr. Rice, was by a coincidence both superintendent of the region and editor of the Methodist periodical *El Cristiano*, and thus had wide powers which he could press into service in his personal battle. It was he who refused to publish the notes sent in by the Valparaiso congregation, and he who, with Bishop Bristol's sympathy, succeeded in ranging the hierarchy against Pastor Hoover. But ten years later Mr. Rice was expelled from the Methodist mission for disciplinary reasons. However, that would not have been enough by itself to explain the causes of the rupture; other missionaries wielded equal power, and if they had been convinced of the validity of the revival effort being carried on by their colleague in Valparaiso, they would have been able to avert the crisis. Even such a man as Pastor G. F. Arms, who continued to regard Hoover as a friend after the schism, exhorted him to obedience. . . . And the paradox is glaring when one learns that one of Hoover's last attempts to justify himself was to send to *El Cristiano* an article composed entirely of quotations from Wesley's Journal, and that the new editor (Rice's successor) refused, claiming that to publish it would be prejudicial to its author's cause! No; over and above the personalities involved, it was a question of the opposition of two ways of interpreting the Bible and of comprehending spiritual life, of two mentalities, of two forms of religious expression. The Methodist Church, born in its time of the spiritual confusion of the 'poor', was not able to respond to the spiritual confusion of the Chilean people. Once more, Protestant denominationalism proved itself incapable of reformation without further division.

Methodism, which was originally a religious movement intended to meet the needs of the common people abandoned by the official clergy and caught in the whirlpool of the rise of modern England, evolved into a respectable denomination attended by the middle classes, having lost its emotional mysticism of the early days, and preserving only a cold piety and a strict moral code. And when, in Chile, a section of the church members engaged in a mystic search similar in form and function to that of primitive Methodism, the church authorities, stamped by theological liberalism and nineteenth-century rationalism, spoke to those people filled with inspiration in critical terms analogous to those which the Wesley brothers endured from the Anglican hierarchy and English nobility. The expressions used are the same in either case (religious fanaticism, grotesque manifestations, scandals, disorders, obscenities, heretical doctrines, hoaxes, hypnotism, magic, etc.), but those who in the former case were the accused are now the accusers.[25]

When a man, out of loyalty to what he regards as his mission, chooses to break with the church he has always served and by the same stroke with his native country, it is worth enquiring into his personality. Hoover had been trained as a surgeon, and this profession does not have the reputation of encouraging mystical tendencies among its practitioners; but perhaps for that very reason he did not practise it. Eye witnesses have described him as being of middle height, slender, there being nothing particularly remarkable about his physique. The gentleness of his voice, the modesty of his behaviour, would not lead one to expect him to have the makings of a *caudillo* (the idiomatic expression for a charismatic leader). Was he one? As will be seen in what follows, Hoover had a clear and authoritarian conception of the role of the pastor; circumstances led him to assume the leadership of the dissenting movement and he proved a good superintendent. But it appears that he avoided any manifestation which would tend toward what is now called 'a personality cult', whereas this trait is characteristic of military *caudillos* and of the great leaders of Christian Pentecostalism. While there is no possible doubt that the birth of Chilean Pentecostalism is due to his influence, once the initial impulse had been given, the movement would doubtless have survived had he disappeared. Had Hoover submitted to the Methodist hierarchy, the two Santiago groups would have continued on their course, and it was indeed under pressure from the members of his parish who had decided to quit Methodism with or without him that he took that step also. His qualities, his intellectual training, and also his prestige marked him out for the leadership of the movement, but he took no steps to seize it for himself.

This doctor, who was certainly intellectually gifted, nevertheless held a dualist and simplicist vision of the world—of the events of 1909 and 1910 he said that it was a 'struggle between the spiritual forces of good and evil'[26]—and in his search for truth he was to meet on his path all the experiences of the great mystics, from trembling to ecstasy, from tears to speaking in tongues, warning dreams to prophetic revelations. This gentle man was capable of tearing up the roots of his nationality, his social origins and his religion, and placing himself at the head of the great renewal of Chilean Protestantism.

In 1959 the fiftieth anniversary of the birth of Pentecostalism in Chile was celebrated by the *Iglesia Metodista Pentecostal* in a mass demonstration which made Santiago aware of the tremendous growth of the movement. The denomination devoted a special issue of its review, *Chile Pentecostal*, to tracing the history of the movement, which unleashed a dispute by the importance it attributed to the role played by the group from the First Methodist Church of Santiago, in order to justify the denomination's claim to the title of 'Mother Church' of Pentecostalism.[27] The other Pentecostal denominations replied in their own journals, pamphlets were issued,[28] and while the debate has died down, the latent conflict is there still.

The preceding narrative will have shown that the three groups should be jointly considered 'Mother Churches'. Though that in Valparaiso was the last to break with the Methodist Mission, the process orginated there. Certainly the group which broke away from the First Methodist Church of Santiago was the first to constitute an autonomous body, but the group from the Second Church can also claim the honour of having been led by the first Chilean Pentecostal pastor, Victor Pavez T., since it was he who, having been assistant pastor before the rupture, was from the outset recognized as the shepherd of the group, whereas the other group did not know whom to appoint to that post, and even went so far, according to Oyarzun,[29] as to sound Mr. Weiss of the Christian and Missionary Alliance.

Thus was Pentecostalism born in Chile. It is the offspring of a Methodism which, while it had been powerfully evangelistic at the start, after its conquest of the United States and its assimilation into the middle classes, transferred its efforts to the plane of social welfare. 'Go teach the nations' that was how Methodism translated the text of Matthew 28: 19, and this motto was inscribed over the entrance to the Methodist Missionary Society in New York. The dissenters rediscovered and reinforced the purely missionary calling of Methodism, which had never been completely lost but at the turn of the century had been expressed as a puritanical, ostentatious piety combined with a liberalist theology. Pentecostalism rooted itself in the pietist tradition, but, cut off from the mother church—which in concrete terms meant, from the source of finance and leadership—it had to invent the means of assuring its own survival, create its own ministry, at the same time giving up social work, dear to Methodism, for the lack of financial means. This sacrifice was made willingly, so great was the desire for a consecration entirely to 'spiritual things'. The *Iglesia Metodista Pentecostal* became the first truly national Protestant denomination, both financially and in its leadership (with the one exception of Dr. Hoover). Therein lies the principal internal reason[30] for its future success.

If this religious movement must be given a definition, let us use the description 'charismatic'. For the theologian, following St. Paul, the term *charisma* means the particular gifts which God through His Spirit implants in believers. The sociological definition owes much to theology; it is an extraordinary gift which a person has (or at least which church members recognize in him), a gift which constitutes the source of his power with other people.[31]

It is indeed a question of charisma, for all the work and the expansion of Pentecostalism rest on belief in the gifts of the Spirit, both as the source of the leader's pastoral authority and of the missionary authority of the most humble of its members:

> When the Spirit fell upon us with power, the baptized persons, men, women and children, felt themselves compelled to rush into the street and to shout out loud (about their experience), to visit their friends and neighbours, to travel to other places, with the sole object of calling men to repentance and letting them know by their testimony that such a sublime experience was within the reach of every one of them today, as it was in the time of the Apostles.[32]

CHAPTER 2

Social Change in Chile and the Pentecostal Explosion[1]

CUT off from the missionary society, with no professional pastors, with no external financial help, the young Pentecostal movement was able to transform these disadvantages into major opportunities for giving new life to Protestantism in Chile and for setting off a religious revolution which had profound repercussions. In this chapter we shall describe the history of Pentecostal success, its *numerical and geographic expansion*, which has, moreover, not yet come to an end. Then we shall try to formulate a preliminary answer to the question, 'Why did it achieve this success?' giving in evidence the *external factors* which favoured the extraordinary growth of Pentecostalism. That is to say, we shall take an overall view of Chilean society and *situate* the Pentecostal phenomenon within the framework of the evolution of Chilean society. We shall try to discover correlations, coincidences and parallels between the economic, demographic, political, social and religious developments on the one hand, and the development of Pentecostalism on the other. In short, we shall maintain the following thesis, the theme of which is already a classic one in the sociology of 'sects':

> *Pentecostalism appears as a communal religious answer to the confusion of large sections of the population, caused by the anomic character of a society in transition.*

Here the accent will fall on the description of the social anomie, as an introduction to Part II, in which the content of the religious response will be analysed.

It is hardly necessary to underline the fact that this attempt at synthesis—capturing the essence of half a century of Chilean social development and placing this religious movement within it—is somewhat hazardous and hypothetical. The project's very breadth prevents one from expecting the exposition to be completely satisfactory; by involving both an all-embracing and a historical sociological study, it is subject to a dual risk. Moreover, we encountered various technical problems, the chief of which was the lack of precise information about the past, even the recent past, of Chile. While historical works abound, they are generally written from the classic political point of view, of little use to the sociologist, while in the field of the economic and social history of this 'last outpost of the world' (B. Subercasseaux) the ground has hardly yet been broken. This has led us at some points to make dangerous extrapolations.

Nevertheless we are convinced that no explanation of Pentecostalism in itself can be given, nor a sociological description, until one has first established its place diachronically in the society within which it is developing, and with which it maintains a whole complex of dialectic relationships.

Only the analysis of external factors makes it possible to understand the attraction which the internal characteristics of Pentecostalism exercise over the common people. At the same time, it is only by this preliminary examination of the setting out of which it has come that we shall be able to understand the social and cultural forms which this religious movement has borrowed and renewed.

1. NUMERICAL GROWTH OF PROTESTANTISM, 1909–60

Numerical information on Chilean Protestantism comes from two kinds of sources: on the one hand, missionary atlases and statistical surveys; on the other, official population census figures. As is shown in the first two tables, graphically contrasted in Fig. 2, rather contradictory results are obtained, depending on which source is used. It is therefore necessary to analyse these sources critically, using three complementary approaches. First we ask what methods of enumeration are used in each case, so as to establish where there are gaps; then, comparing the two curves for a given date, it may be possible to say where the error has arisen; finally, the curves should be capable of interpretation.

Table 1. Progress of Protestantism between 1916 and 1961, according to church sources*

YEAR	NUMBER OF PROTESTANTS	SOURCE
1916	6,293	*Christian Work in Latin America*, N.Y., 1916
1925	11,591	*World Missionary Atlas*, N.Y., 1925
1938	99,460	J. I. Parker, *Statistical Survey of the World Christian Mission*, N.Y., 1938
1949	264,667	*World Christian Handbook*, London, 1949
1952	370,016	*op. cit.* London, 1952
1957	370,428	*op. cit.* London, 1957
1961	834,839	*op. cit.* London, 1962

* Taken from P. Damboriena, S.J., *El Protestantismo en América Latina*, vol. II, p. 16.

Damboriena's figures are based on five different sources, in which the census criteria appear to vary greatly; the earliest, for example, only includes Methodists and Presbyterians and omits Lutherans, who alone numbered more than 10,000. The second omits the Lutherans and also the Pentecostals, who were by then numerous enough to have been taken into account. Thus up to 1925 the number of Protestants is underestimated, and we prefer to use the census figures, which up to that date are higher, since the census figures can by no means overestimate the *evangélicos* (see below). Lastly, since the war the only religious source is the *World Christian Handbook*. The editors generally apply for information to national councils of churches, which in turn

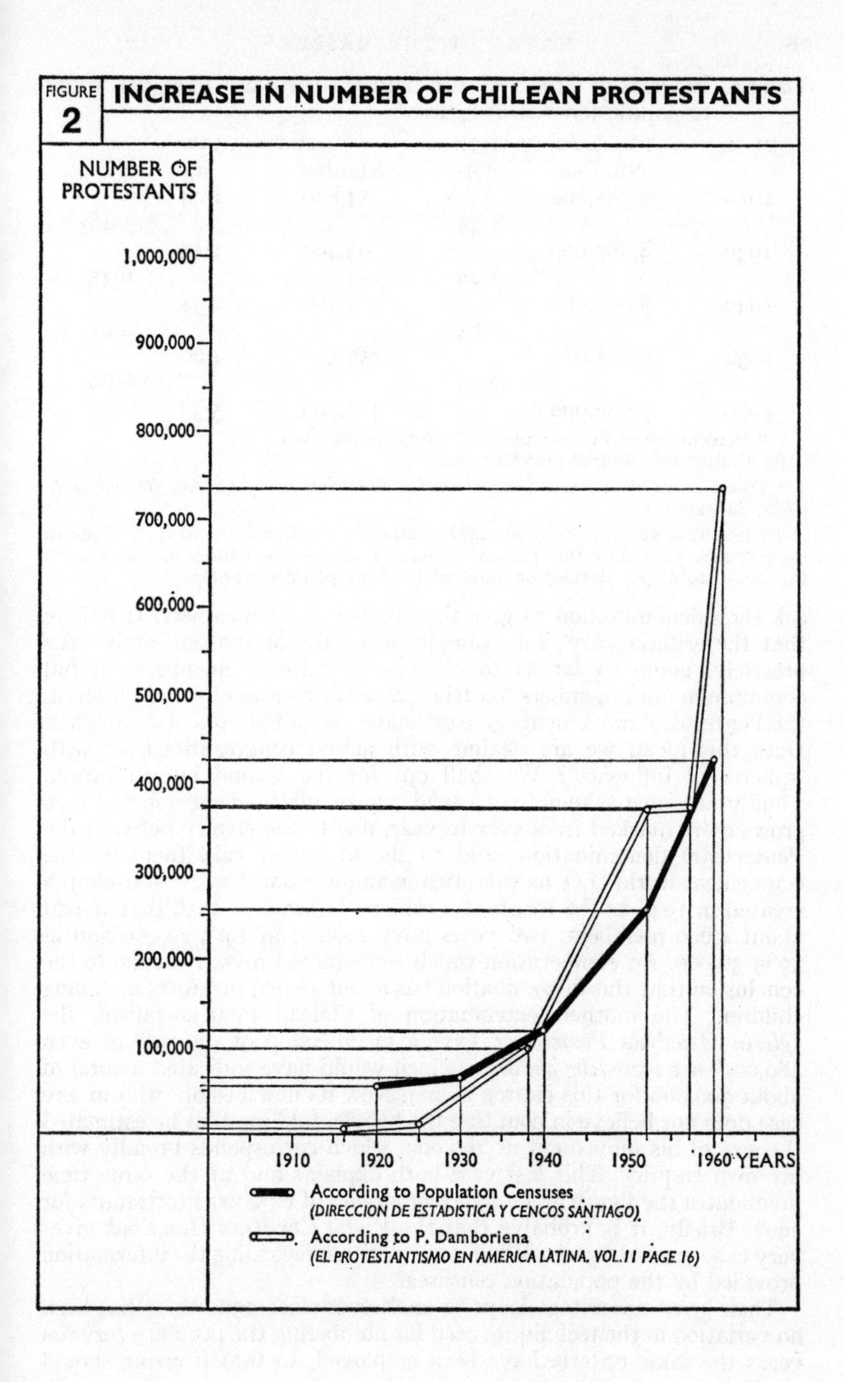
FIGURE 2
INCREASE IN NUMBER OF CHILEAN PROTESTANTS
NUMBER OF PROTESTANTS
1,000,000
900,000
800,000
700,000
600,000
500,000
400,000
300,000
200,000
100,000
1910
1920
1930
1940
1950
1960 YEARS
According to Population Censuses
(DIRECCION DE ESTADISTICA Y CENCOS SANTIAGO).
According to P. Damboriena
(EL PROTESTANTISMO EN AMERICA LATINA. VOL.II PAGE 16)

Table 2. Progress of Protestantism between 1920 and 1960, according to population census figures*

YEAR	TOTAL POPULATION		PROTESTANTS		
	Number	(*b*)	Number	(*a*)	(*b*)
1920	3,785,000		54,800	1·44	
		1·44			1·46
1930	4,365,000		63,400	1·45	
		1·49			6·45
1940	5,065,000		118,400	2·34	
		1·83			6·62
1952	6,295,000		255,500	4·06	
		2·43			6·60
1960	7,628,000		425,700	5·58	

(*a*) Percentage of Protestants in the total population.
(*b*) Cumulative annual growth rate.

* Based on publications of the *Dirección de Estadística y Censos, República de Chile*, Santiago.

To facilitate comparisons, we have computed the figures as at 30th June of each census year. For this reason we have rounded the figures to the nearest thousand (total population) or hundred (number of Protestants).

ask each denomination to give the number of its members. It is here that the criteria vary; for example, while the Methodists reply very precisely, going so far as to distinguish between members 'in full communion' and members 'on trial', and between adults and children, the Pentecostal movements give estimates including up to five noughts. Does this mean we are dealing with actual congregations, or with 'spheres of influence'? We shall opt for the second interpretation. Finally, we must take note of a tendency to inflate membership, which grows more marked from year to year, due to the rivalry between the Pentecostal denominations and to the attention paid them by the ecumenical world. Let us take two examples: one Pentecostal church created in 1946 as the result of a schism declared in 1959 that it had about 4,000 members; two years later 10,000; in 1963 20,000 and in 1965 36,000. An enumeration which I conducted myself led me to the conclusion that this denomination has about 10,000 members including children. The mother-denomination of Chilean Pentecostalism, the *Iglesia Metodista Pentecostal*, gave a membership of 400,000[2] or even 480,000[3] *not including children* (which would have indicated a total of about 700,000 for this church alone). Now its new bishop, who in any case does not believe in counting the people, told me that he estimated the size of his movement at 100,000, which corresponds broadly with my own enquiry. This last case both explains and at the same time invalidates the figure given by Damboriena of 835,000 Protestants for 1961. Briefly, it is probable that the *World Christian Handbook* gives very exaggerated figures. What is the position regarding the information provided by the population censuses?

Their great advantage leaps to one's eye: since 1900 there has been no variation in the techniques used for numbering the people; every ten years the same criteria have been employed, so that if errors should occur they would always be the same errors and the figures would at least be comparable with one another. Protestant detractors of the census put forward four arguments:

(1) Protestants would not declare their under-age children as *evangelicos*, since to be a member of a confessing church one must have reached the age of 14 or 15 and made a voluntary and personal declaration of membership.

(2) Since Protestant denominations proliferate, more than 100 now having been legally incorporated, a Protestant would designate himself by the name of his church, which would engender great confusion in the minds of the investigators, for whom the line of least resistance would be to list them as 'Catholic'.

(3) The investigators are generally Catholic and seek, whether consciously or not, to minimize the Protestant element.

(4) Finally, the Protestants would hesitate to reveal their church affiliation, being influenced on the one hand by remembrance of past persecution, and on the other—and this would be especially valid in the case of the Pentecostal sects—by the fact that counting the people is regarded ill by God, who punished David for his attempt by sending a plague upon Israel (2 Sam. 24).

These four arguments are alike in claiming that the census would minimize the number of Protestants. Of these criticisms, it is clear that the first is the most important, since in Chile as in most other developing countries the age pyramid has a very wide base.

But the last census[4] gives a table by age groups which nullifies this argument. In fact 40·7 per cent. of the Protestants were under 15 years of age, although only 39·7 per cent. of all Chileans are under 15. The average Protestant family is thus a little larger than the average Chilean family.

The second criticism is worth hardly more than the first, for the investigators were told that a Protestant might describe himself in various ways, whereas all the Catholics use the same name.

Let us go on to the third reason for mistakes, to which the Directors of the census told us we should not attach great importance. It may be that the investigator, tired of hearing nine out of ten people reply 'Catholic' and wishing to speed up the number of his returns, in certain cases omits to enquire into the person's religion and automatically lists him as 'Catholic'. But this practice would be unusual and would not greatly affect the results.

The last argument is a surprising one; on the one hand we have observed that the doctrine of submission to civil authority prevails over that of the second book of Samuel, and on the other, are not the Protestants known for their ardent testimony, open-air preaching and their Sunday processions? Are they not by definition confessing Christians? How can their boldness in evangelism be reconciled with the claim that they are afraid to acknowledge their faith to the census investigator?

Before going on to interpret the curve, let us say that the information provided by the official census constitutes the only reliable source.

Certainly it is possible that in distant regions of the country some populations may have been poorly enumerated, but then the error would not affect only the Protestants; it is possible also that the number of Protestants may have been slightly underestimated. *But the census is very close to reality, without a doubt much closer than all the other estimates put forward.*[5]

It would be necessary, too, to define the categories used by the census, which distinguishes Catholics, Protestants, No Religion, and various other religions (Buddhists, Moslems, Jews, etc.) which in view of their small number we can group together as 'Others' (cf. Table 3).

The 'Catholic' answers must be distinguished from the others, for the Catholic Church is still a church of the *multitudes*, whereas the other replies generally arise from the convictions of *confessing* Christians. To call oneself 'Protestant' (or 'No Religion') is to confess a faith (or an absence of faith), whereas those who call themselves 'Catholic' include both practising Catholics and those who attend only at intervals, or indeed in many cases those who no longer maintain any connection with the Church.[6]

Table 3. Distribution of Population by Religious Affiliation (1960)*

FAITH	NUMBER	PERCENTAGE
Catholics	6,572,541	89·1
Protestants	411,530*	5·6
No Religion	343,634	4·7
Others	46,410	0·6
Total	7,374,115*	100·0

* Source: 1960 census. For the slight difference between this and the information in Table 2, see the note to the latter.

The replies therefore have not the same worth, and one cannot compare the 5·6 per cent. Protestants with the 89·1 per cent. Catholics.

The Protestant churches of Chile are all confessing churches; they make a distinction between 'sympathizers', members 'on trial' and members 'in full communion'; those which collect statistics within their own organization only enumerate the last two categories, which constitute the community in the strict sense of the word, sometimes including the children of members also. There are ceremonies which mark entry into the church as a member on trial and, after a probationary period, admission as a member in full communion. The very existence of these hurdles, as we have proved in several cases, prevents mere sympathizers from considering themselves to be *evangélicos* or from declaring themselves to be such when, for example, they are visited by the census investigator. Thus the figure given by the census, by and large, includes only the Protestant community in the strict sense, that is, members included in the denominations' lists, and their children.

To conclude these notes on methodology, we must ask which of the streams of opinion in the 'great family of Reformed churches' is chiefly responsible for their progress. For our needs it is sufficient to distinguish two groups: first, the Protestant churches which descend from the first and second Reformations,[7] that is to say, all of the missionary churches which came to Chile during the nineteenth century; and secondly the Chilean Pentecostal churches created in this century, to which may be added a few and so far not very large North American and Scandinavian Pentecostal missions, together with various indigenous people's churches, not necessarily Pentecostal but belonging to the *Heilsbewegung*. There would be no point in studying the growth of the Lutheran and Anglican churches; the first grows only through natural increase or migration, and the second, loyal to the spirit of the Edinburgh Conference of 1910, has devoted itself until recently to the Anglo-Saxon residents and the Indians. In the Presbyterian Church the number of pastors is decreasing and the number of church members is stagnating; the members of the Methodist Church numbered 4,683 in 1920, 6,869 in 1960—while the country's population doubled, the Methodists only increased by half. Although we do not have certified figures at our disposal, it appears that other denominations, often those closer to the *Heilung* type (Baptists, Christian and Missionary Alliance, etc.) have had a real increase but none of them today has more than 10,000 members. Thus at the moment the group which includes the Pentecostals and the sanctification denominations would, according to Henry P. van Dusen,[8] make up 87 per cent. of Chilean Protestants, which corresponds in broad measure with our own estimate.

Here we can state a sociological law regarding Chilean Protestantism: the younger the church, the greater its numerical growth. Protestant expansion in Chile, quantitatively defined, must be attributed to the 'third Reformation' movements and principally to the Chilean Pentecostal groups.

In 1960 we see that there were 425,700 *evangélicos* in Chile (see Table 2). Does this figure justify the disappointment of so many Protestants, who either dispute the figure or begin to talk of a recession? Should it lead one to the conclusion that the Protestant explosion is an illusion? Far from it.

Let us go back to Table 2 and follow the increase from one census to another. Up to 1930 Protestants increased not much more quickly than the total population, of which they represented 1·45 per cent. (3 Protestants in every 200 people). A good number of them were foreigners: 17,000 out of 55,000 in 1920. It was in the 'thirties that Protestantism exploded: the *annual growth rate* rose from 1·46 per cent. in the decade 1920–30 to 6·45 per cent. in the next decade and is now 6·6 per cent. The break in the rhythm is remarkable; while the rate of growth is below 2 per cent. up to the critical date of 1930, it jumps to about 6 per cent. and stays at that rate almost without variation right up to the present. A rate of 6·5 means that the number of Protestants is doubling every 10–11 years and that today, after thirty years of expansion, for every 200 people there are 11 Protestants. Thus we can understand the warning which Abbé Muñoz gave in 1956 to his fellow

Table 4. Size of Population and Number of (Chile: Distribution by Provinces)

PROVINCE	1920 POPULAT.	1920 PROTES.	1920 %	1920 RANK	1930 POPULAT.	1930 PROTES.	1930 %
Tarapaca	115,901	2,297	2·0	9	113,331	1,271	1·1
Antofagasta	172,330	4,179	2·4	6	178,766	3,107	1·7
Atacama	48,413	731	1·5	11	61,098	678	1·1
Coquimbo	160,256	2,522	1·6	10	198,336	1,190	0·6
Aconcagua	116,914	628	0·5	17	—	—	0·8
Valparaiso	320,398	7,646	2·4	6	—	—	2·3
Santiago	685,358	7,254	1·1	12	—	—	1·3
O'Higgins	118,591	687	0·6	15	—	—	
Colchagua	166,342	288	0·2	20	—	—	0·6
Curico	108,148	116	0·1	24	—	—	
Talca	133,957	208	0·2	20	—	—	0·4
Maule	113,231	281	0·2	20	—	—	
Linares	119,284	291	0·2	20	—	—	0·3
Nuble	170,425	746	0·4	18	—	—	0·5
Concepcion	246,670	2,457	1·0	13	—	—	1·5
Arauco	60,233	337	0·6	15	—	—	
Bio-Bio	107,072	915	0·9	14	—	—	0·6
Malleco	121,429	2,666	2·2	8	—	—	
Cautin	193,628	6,637	3·4	3	—	—	3·5
Valdivia	175,141	6,359	3·6	2	—	—	
Osorno	62,397	1,946	3·1	5	—	—	
Llanquihue	74,809	2,423	3·2	4	—	—	2·7
Chiloe	110,348	352	0·3	19	—	—	1·7
Aysen	—	—	—	—	9,711	184	1·9
Magallanes	28,960	2,076	7·2	1	37,913	1,586	4·2
Antartida							
Chile	3,730,235	54,042	1·4		4,287,445	62,267	1·4

Catholics: 'There is reason for alarm . . . for if the Protestants continue to grow at the same rate, 50 years from now the whole country will be Protestant',[9] all the more so since the figures for 1960 show that the rate is being maintained.

Nevertheless, though Muñoz's hypothesis is mathematically correct, it is sociologically impossible (its author is well aware of this, as we shall see), the problem being not to know whether the Protestants will convert the whole country but to find out at what level they will be stabilized. It is possible to approach this question by observing the distribution of Protestants in the provinces, and analysing the different rates of growth found there.

2. ESTABLISHMENT OF PROTESTANTISM IN THE PROVINCES

While Chile's borders are clearly defined by the Cordillera and the Pacific Ocean, its extraordinary geography extends over 38 degrees of latitude; in the north, deserts rich in copper and nitrate mines; then the area where the population is concentrated—the central valley with the capital, dominated by the vast mass of the Andes, its peaks rising to over 12,000 feet; then, more to the south, the region of great landed estates, completely rural provinces, which bring us to the old 'frontier',

Protestants, according to Five Censuses

1940				1952				1960			
POPULAT.	PROTES.	%	RANK	POPULAT.	PROTES.	%	RANK	POPULAT.	PROTES.	%	RANK
104,097	1,815	1·7	13	102,789	1,522	1·5	22	123,070	3,468	2·8	21
145,147	3,078	2·1	11	184,824	4,417	2·3	15	215,219	8,801	4·1	15
84,312	1,048	1·2	17	80,113	1,378	1·7	21	116,235	3,682	3.2	19
245,609	1,495	0·6	24	262,169	4,072	1·5	22	308,991	7,079	2·3	23
118,049	1,407	1·2	17	128,378	2,613	2·0	17	140,543	3,653	2·6	22
425,065	10,627	2·5	9	498,254	17,615	3·5	10	617,510	26,207	4·2	14
1,268,505	26,767	2·1	11	1,754,954	60,974	3·4	11	2,437,425	107,005	4·4	12
200,297	2,768	1·4	15	224,593	5,260	2·3	15	259,470	8,710	3·4	18
131,248	693	0·5	25	139,531	1,952	1·4	24	158,509	3,705	2·3	23
81,185	713	0·9	20	89,432	2,753	3·1	12	105,802	5,420	5·1	10
157,141	2,081	1·3	16	173,693	5,178	2·9	13	206,154	9,768	4·7	11
70,497	589	0·8	22	72,181	2,053	2·8	14	79,736	3,537	4·4	12
134,968	1,151	0·9	20	146,257	2,766	1·8	20	171,350	6,625	3·9	16
243,185	5,371	2·2	10	251,342	10,630	4·2	8	285,639	18,148	6·4	8
308,241	10,197	3·3	4	411,566	30,598	7·4	3	539,521	64,491	12·0	2
66,107	1,718	2·6	8	72,289	5,076	7·0	4	89,460	13,305	14·9	1
127,312	1,964	1·5	14	138,292	5,360	3·9	9	168,718	11,817	7·0	7
154,174	4,176	2·7	7	159,419	9,232	5·8	5	174,300	13,894	8·0	5
374,659	21,524	5·7	1	365,072	33,672	9·2	1	394,654	38,784	9·8	4
191,642	8,026	4·2	2	232,647	18,256	7·8	2	259,794	27,672	10·7	3
107,341	4,193	3·9	3	123,069	6,573	5·3	6	144,005	10,263	7·1	6
117,225	3,768	3·2	5	139,986	6,147	4·4	7	167,671	9,713	5·8	9
101,706	742	0·7	23	100,687	1,208	1·2	25	99,211	2,156	2·2	25
17,014	211	1·2	17	26,262	541	2·0	17	37,770	1,477	3·9	16
48,813	1,380	2·8	6	56,206	1,010	2·0	17	73,156	2,145	2·9	20
								202	5		
5,023,539	117,502	2·3		5,932,995	240,856	4·1		7,374,115	411,530	5·6	

the River Bio-Bio, across which the Indians were thrown back by the *conquistadores,* who never succeeded in conquering them. Towards the sea lie the coal mines; inland, this was the country of the pioneers where, until the end of the last century, the government's authority did not run and only cunning, daring and strength counted; still farther south, the lake region where the Cordillera becomes lower and is carved into little volcanos; here are the three 'German' provinces, the richest agricultural region of the country, brought into production since the middle of the nineteenth century by German immigrants.

Last of all, beyond Puerto-Montt where road and railway end, there lies the 'country of twilit night' (B. Subercasseaux), the great frozen expanses, till finally the Cordillera sinks into the sea.

In this many-faceted country, Protestantism has (so far?) not been evenly spread and has established itself in very varying fashion. In Table 4 one can follow the growth of the number of *evangélicos* in each province, and their relative importance compared with the total population, from 1920 up to 1960. The maps which follow illustrate the present situation and also, by means of the graphs inset, the growth in relative size of the Protestant body.[10]

One fact can first be established: throughout the country from 1952 to 1960, Protestants were on the increase. In each province, their growth

MAP
3
GEOGRAPHICAL DISTRIBUTION OF PROTESTANTS IN 1960
COMPARISON OF PROTESTANTS AND ATHEISTS FROM 1920 TO 1960
1920 1930 1940 1952 1960
12
8
4
%
TARAPACA
ANTOFAGASTA
ATACAMA
COQUIMBO
PERU
NORTH
BOLIVIA
ARGENTINA
SOURCES :
C.N. DE POBLACION
KEY
50 0 100 200 300 km.
Protestants
No Religion
2 – 4% Protestant
4 – 6% Protestant
6 – 8% Protestant
8–10% Protestant
+10% Protestant

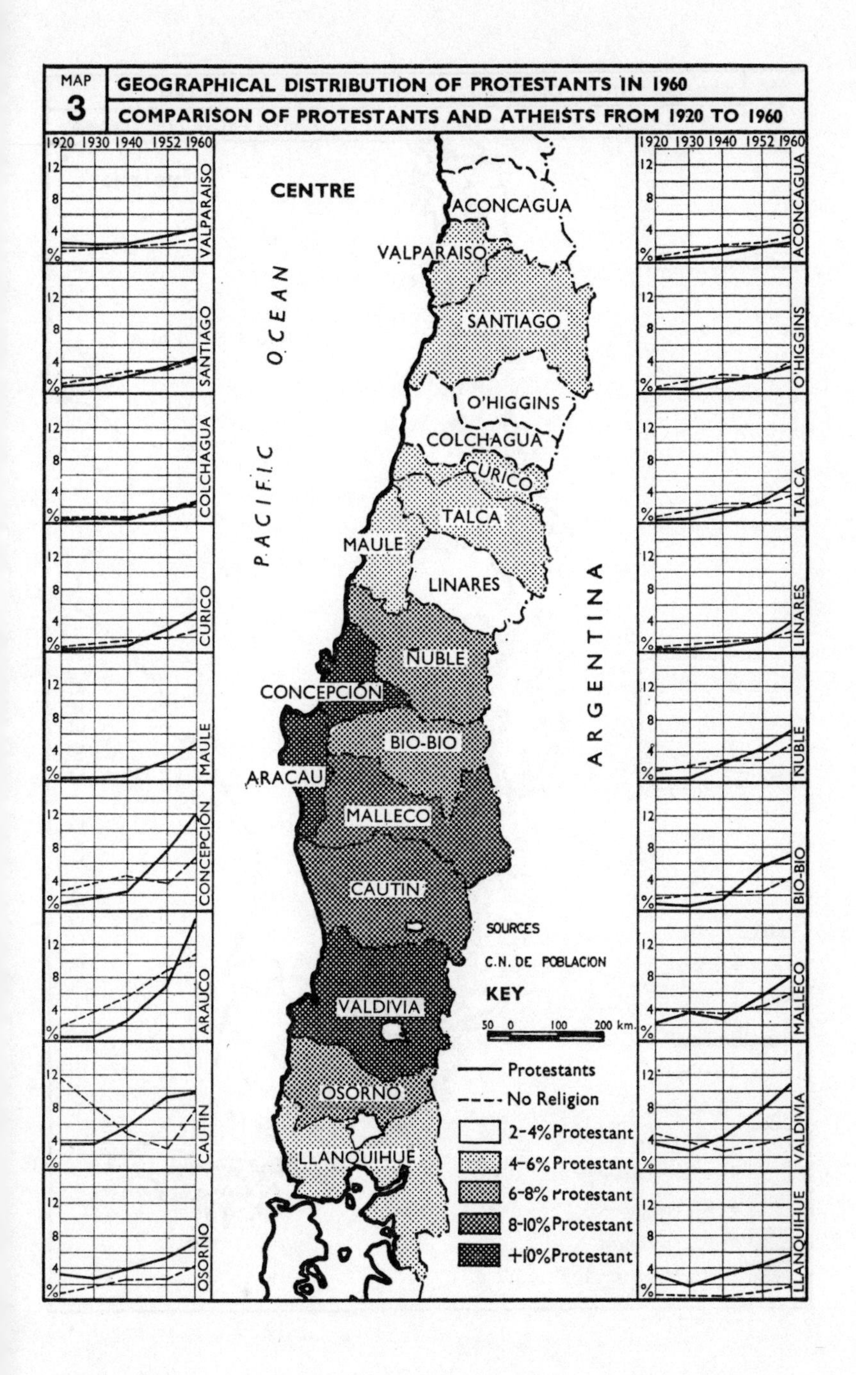
MAP 3
GEOGRAPHICAL DISTRIBUTION OF PROTESTANTS IN 1960
COMPARISON OF PROTESTANTS AND ATHEISTS FROM 1920 TO 1960
1920 1930 1940 1952 1960
VALPARAISO
SANTIAGO
COLCHAGUA
CURICO
MAULE
CONCEPCION
ARAUCO
CAUTIN
OSORNO
ACONCAGUA
O'HIGGINS
TALCA
LINARES
NUBLE
BIO-BIO
MALLECO
VALDIVIA
LLANQUIHUE
CENTRE
PACIFIC OCEAN
ARGENTINA
ACONCAGUA
VALPARAISO
SANTIAGO
O'HIGGINS
COLCHAGUA
CURICO
TALCA
MAULE
LINARES
NUBLE
CONCEPCIÓN
BIO-BIO
ARACAU
MALLECO
CAUTIN
VALDIVIA
OSORNO
LLANQUIHUE
SOURCES
C.N. DE POBLACION
KEY
50 0 100 200 km.
Protestants
No Religion
2-4% Protestant
4-6% Protestant
6-8% Protestant
8-10% Protestant
+10% Protestant

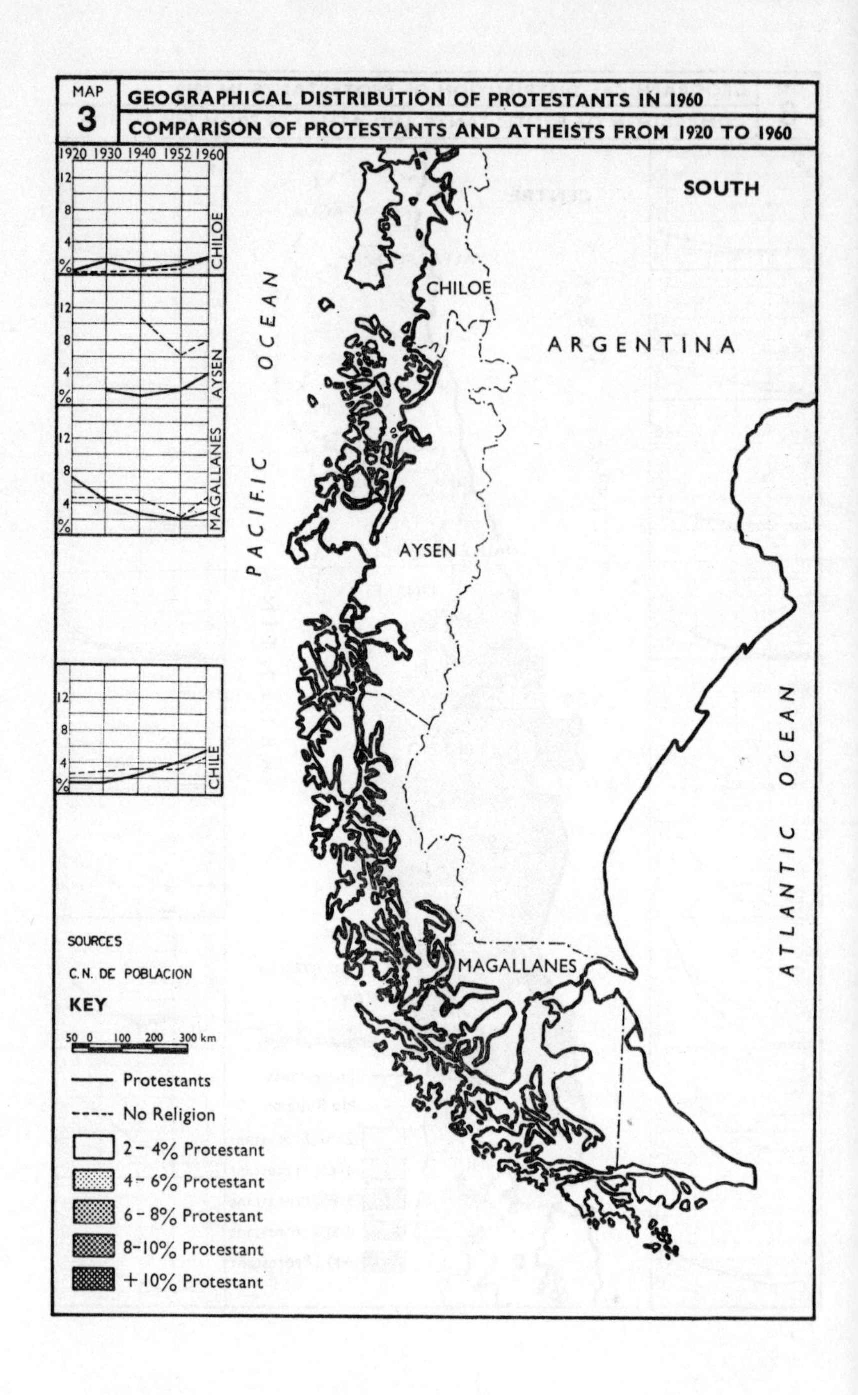
MAP
3
GEOGRAPHICAL DISTRIBUTION OF PROTESTANTS IN 1960
COMPARISON OF PROTESTANTS AND ATHEISTS FROM 1920 TO 1960
1920 1930 1940 1952 1960
12
8
4
%
CHILOE
AYSEN
MAGALLANES
CHILE
SOUTH
ARGENTINA
PACIFIC OCEAN
ATLANTIC OCEAN
SOURCES
C.N. DE POBLACION
KEY
50 0 100 200 300 km
Protestants
No Religion
2 – 4% Protestant
4 – 6% Protestant
6 – 8% Protestant
8–10% Protestant
+ 10% Protestant

was more rapid (generally much more rapid) than the growth of the population.

The graphs make it possible to distinguish three types of growth curve:

(1) First the curve like a saucer; the Protestant minority decreases for a decade and then is stabilized; then grows steadily, but up to now has never exceeded about 4 per cent. (the average for Chile is 5·6 per cent). This curve is common to the provinces at the two extremes of the country: in the north, the four provinces nearest the Peruvian frontier, Tarapaca, Antofagasta, Atacama and Coquimbo, and the three southern provinces, Chiloe, Aysen and Magallanes.

(2) At the other extreme, the curve with an increasingly steep slope, a curve of accelerating progress; this relates to 8 of the 9 provinces in which the proportion of Protestants today is the highest: Arauco, Concepcion, Osorno, Valdivia, Llanquihue, Malleco, Bio-Bio and Nuble. Cautin should be treated by itself, for expansion there is much slower, to the point of being only a little higher than that of the total population in the last decade.

This second category can be subdivided into two groups:

(*a*) The provinces where even in 1920 a certain number of Protestants were established: in Valdivia, Osorno and Llanquihue at that time more than 3 per cent. of the population was Protestant, and these provinces were recognized to be those which received German immigrants. In Malleco, the Protestant minority was over 2 per cent.

The presence of a German Lutheran minority for several decades has certainly assisted today's expansion, even though this minority has not itself sought to make converts. The population is accustomed to having neighbours of another creed, and will have been more tolerant, then more receptive to the 'new' Gospel. But there are two reasons why this factor should not be regarded as the sole explanation: first of all, in Magallanes and in Antofagasta the Protestant minority had already attained a certain size in 1920 and yet did not develop in the same way as in the Lake Provinces. Secondly, as we shall see, there are provinces in which the Protestants were non-existent in 1920 but are very numerous today.

(*b*) In four provinces, Arauco, Concepcion, Bio-Bio and Nuble, the number of Protestants in the population was 1 per cent. or less.

(3) The other ten provinces present an intermediate curve, more or less flattened. The boundary between the categories is naturally an arbitrary one; in particular, the three provinces of Curico, Talca and Maule tend towards the preceding type.

This classification makes it possible to see the direct relation of three factors: geographical situation, classification according to the present-day percentage of Protestants in the population, and the growth curve. In fact the following results are obtained:

1. The four southern provinces and the three northern provinces, which stand at the bottom of the table, and have saucer-shaped curves.

2. The central provinces, which have intermediate curves and stand in the middle of the table. If one wished, one could make a special category for Curico, Talca and Maule, middling provinces which occupy the tenth, eleventh and twelfth places respectively in the table, and present a curve with a more marked slope.
3. The key zone for Chilean Protestantism, the eight southern provinces (excluding Cautin), which are at the top of the table and have curves showing accelerated growth.

This division of the country into geographical zones should not lead one to believe that each has a homogeneous socio-economic milieu. In each zone there are some regions predominantly rural and others predominantly urban. If one took all the provinces and tried to establish a correlation between the crude standards of rural or urban location and the proportion of the population which is Protestant, the result would be negative.[11] Chilean Protestantism is neither specifically rural nor specifically urban. The same ambiguity appears in studying the mining areas; the copper and nitrate mines in the north belong to the first group, the coal mining areas to the third. Moreover, what is the common denominator of the mining provinces of the great north and Magallanes, where they raise sheep? Thus in each geographical zone there is a diversity of social milieux and cultural backgrounds (here again, Curico, Talca and Maule are the exception, for they have a homogeneous rural milieu). Any attempt to find an overall explanation for Protestant advance must avoid hasty generalizations and start by looking for more exact criteria. Perhaps in a sociological analysis of the *rural areas, urban centres and mining zones*, one or two of the keys to the problem will be found.

Before we begin, let us consider a double hypothesis put forward by Father H. Muñoz. According to him, '. . . in the new areas Protestants have an initial easy success among the group containing the most ignorant and unsettled people. Once this group has been explored, they come up against a natural barrier. God grant it may be so.'[12]

A distinction must be made between the two sides of this statement; on the one hand is the idea that Protestant success in a given geographical area will be the greater, the more recent its penetration into that area is. On the other is the more general claim (which is, moreover, almost a tautology) that at a given moment Protestant expansion will come up against a natural barrier.

Let us take the first hypothesis, and consider in each province the percentage increase of Protestants between 1940 and 1952. Interpreting it mechanically without reference to the rate of growth of the provincial population, Father Muñoz finds plenty of indications to support his theory. But the number of Protestants varies too much from one province to another to make the rates which he uses comparable with one another (cf. Table 4). For example, a rise from 100 units to 400, i.e. a growth of 300 units, corresponds, according to Father Muñoz's method of calculation, to a growth rate of 300 per cent.; a rise from 30,000 to 45,000 units (growth 15,000) gives only a growth of 50 per cent. Now one can see that, in the question in which we are interested, to gain 300 or 15,000 persons presupposes quite different 'infrastructures' and methods of propagation. Can one speak of regression and decline in the rate of increase in the second case? At all events, not without making a closer analysis. One cannot interpret these rates without reference to the real numbers they represent. Thus it seems to us that a technical error is to be found at the basis of this author's reasoning. Let us also examine the case of two places where Protestantism has been long established: Santiago and Valparaiso. Father Muñoz says that the latter 'in the last century was an English-language port and therefore Protestant. It was the gate by which Protestants entered Chile and, in a sense, the whole Pacific coast. It was also the starting point of the Pentecostal movement. . . .'[13] To say that Valparaiso was a Protestant port seems rather far-fetched; if the town had had a Reformed majority, the figures for the province would show for 1920 a higher rate than 2·5 per cent! However, on one point Muñoz is right; Pentecostalism did indeed start there. But in spite of that, it never attained the same degree of popular support there as it did, for example, in Concepcion. Growth in Valparaiso is slow, as in Santiago, nevertheless it is remarkable that in neither case can one speak at the moment of a natural barrier; since 1930–40 Protestantism has been growing steadily and today constitutes more than 4 per cent. of the population.

The theory of a natural barrier which will, one day or other, halt the Protestant advance is more tenable than the other and may be admitted without argument. The problem then will be to know whether we can foresee with the information available where this barrier will be, and whether signs of a slowing down of the Protestant advance are already noticeable. Now it is only in the province of Cautin that a levelling off is noticeable, and this is also the province upon which Father Muñoz relied for his first hypothesis. In 1920 Cautin stood third in rank regarding the proportion of Protestants, and from 1930 to 1952 was the capital of Chilean Protestantism, but now the advance there is weakening, to the point of being hardly greater than that of the total population. Are there no more 'ignorant and unsettled' people there, to use the author's own words? One must wait for the 1970 census to answer this question. Certainly Pentecostalism touches hardly any but the common people, and some of them are resistant to it. Thus the potential clientele of Protestantism is not inexhaustible. But it is still very large, and it must not be forgotten that in the more distant parts of the country the Protestant offensive is only just beginning. The graphs seem to show that only in the last decade has Pentecostalism taken over from 'historic' Protestantism, which is in decline or at least stagnant in those provinces. For example, in the province of Magallanes there were 2,076 Protestants in 1920 (which put it first in the table, with 7·2 per cent.), of whom 1,700 were foreigners. In other provinces, including those to the south of Colchagua, progress is accelerating. Thus taking all the evidence together, we cannot say *for the moment* that there is a natural barrier, nor try to place it at any particular level (we must remember that the proportion of Protestants varies between 2·2 per cent. in Chiloe and 14·9 per cent. in Arauco). It seems rather that Protestant expansion will continue for the next two decades. But let us not try to prophesy: in sociology probabilities are often the reverse of truth (Leon Brunschvicg) and the dialectical interplay of social phenomena is so complex that the sociologist ought to refuse to predict the future, however plausible his argument may seem. Let us not forget that Roman Catholicism has within it enormous capacity for reform. In Chile, in particular, a new wind is blowing through the Roman Church.[14] The political victory of the Christian Democrats (in the presidential elections of 1964 and parliamentary elections of 1965), to the extent that all or part of their programme is realized, may indirectly lead to the reconquest by the Roman Catholic Church of its disaffected members. Let us be content, then, with a more modest result: a very positive report on the health of Chilean Protestantism, which underlines its widespread strength.

3. SOCIAL CHANGES AND PENTECOSTALISM

The significance of the curve of the growth of Protestantism as a whole (Table 2 and graphs) is clear: at the turn of the century it was insignificant and stagnant; in the 'thirties it launched out, and has developed in a surprising way, without faltering, right up to the present.

If Pentecostal preaching met such a response, it is because (in market terms) it supplied a demand which was caused by the slow transition from a traditional and seignorial type of society[15] towards a secularized, democratic society. This development, which began in the last century, was not linear at all, nor is it yet complete.[16] There are changes of rhythm, blockages, ruptures and regressions. For all that, the movement which signifies the crumbling away of one form of society and the rise of another is no less real, and the transitional phase will be all the more painful because it is chaotic and confused, and tomorrow's happiness cannot always be foreseen. The broad outlines of the process must be described here, before we show that the change of rhythm in the spread of Pentecostalism occurs in those very years when Chilean society reaches its paroxysm.

In the last century, Chile had made a good start. The copper and nitrate mines in the north (annexed by Chile during the Pacific War, 1879–81) were developed; the coal-mining industry was established in the Concepcion region; virgin lands were brought into cultivation, thanks to the influx of immigrants, leading to a blossoming of agriculture in Chile which enabled her to export wheat even to California and Australia; railways were created; the country seemed prosperous and in 1887 conducted 13 per cent. of Latin America's export trade, whereas it had only 5·4 per cent. of the continent's population. Annual exports earned her more per head of population than in the U.S.A. (185 francs as against 147 francs).[17] But this enchanting picture, already darkened by the very unequal division of income, is only fleeting and Chile was to become 'a case of frustrated development', to use the words of the economist A. Pinto Santa Cruz,[18] one symptom being the constant devaluation of the currency. Between 1875 and 1935 the peso went from 43·8 to 1·5 pennyweights of gold, and the U.S. dollar, worth 25 pesos in 1935, was worth 4,500 in February 1966. Prices rose at a parallel rate, and multiplied twenty-one times between 1951 and 1960, but wages did not follow suit; between 1953 and 1961 agricultural wages lost 41 per cent of their real value.[19]

The chief social phenomena accompanying this economic stagnation were internal migration, explosive urban development unconnected with industrial development, and the fact that the mass of the lower classes were kept at, or fell back to, a marginal level.

The Chilean has always been a migrant. When the copper mines were being developed, he went up to the north and populated that region, which had previously belonged to Bolivia or Peru; the people of the Isle of Chiloe emigrated to the southern provinces and took work there as shepherds; the Concepcion mining area drew farm workers from the interior. Since the turn of the century, however, migration has followed new channels, and people have been sucked up by the towns, or rather, by the megapolis, Santiago. While the population of the country trebled between 1885 and 1960, that of the province of Santiago increased sevenfold, and today it represents one-third of the total population. From 1952 to 1960 330,000 persons have moved from one province to another, and 79 per cent of them settled in the province of Santiago.[20] The remainder went to the cities of Valparaiso, Concepcion, and, to a lesser extent, Antofagasta and Valdivia. This represents a tremendous movement towards the capital and a depletion of the countryside; in 1875, 73 per cent of the population was rural, compared with 39·8 per cent in 1952. According to O. Dominguez—and here one can point to the close relation in time between migration and the development of Pentecostalism—round about 1920 'the movement of rural populations into the urban areas developed a definite, accelerated rhythm. By that date, the exploration of virgin territories was complete, and agriculture had reached a level of employment and productivity which has been maintained without change up to very recent times.'[21]

The large-scale agriculturists have been unable to adapt themselves to the requirements of modern production—although up to the 'thirties they enjoyed very favourable conditions (foreign markets, abundant credit and even the permanent devaluation of the country's currency)—and the result of this failure is that today, although the fertility of its soil is the wonder of agronomists, Chile has to import 30 per cent. of its foodstuffs.[22]

Thus internal migration was chiefly caused not by the attraction of work and social improvement offered by the towns but by the crisis in rural society. On the one hand, the growth of the urban population is 'the reflection of inflexible employment conditions in agriculture and mining',[23] and on the other, unlike Europe and North America, urban expansion has been neither preceded nor even accompanied by a comparable development in industrial activity. As Table 5 shows, agriculture and mining employed in 1960 only 23,400 persons more than in 1952. Although employment in secondary industries increased by

23,800, in service industries and commerce employment rose by 93,500. To take a longer period: while employment in the service industries almost trebled between 1940 and 1960, employment in manufacturing increased by only 50 per cent.

Table 5. Working population (in thousands), by class of industry*

	INDUSTRIAL GROUPS	1952	1960
0	Agriculture, hunting, fishing	629·1	662·4
1	Mining industries	101·0	91·1
2–3	Manufacturing industries	405·1	428·9
4	Construction industry	101·8	135·8
5 & 8	Services	489·7	563·1
6	Commerce	220·9	241·0
7	Public transport	95·0	117·9
9	Unspecified activities	76·2	148·5
	TOTAL	2,118·8	2,388·7

* For 1952, *Cifras comparativas* . . . (undated), and for 1960, *Caracteristicas básicas de la población* (1964), p. 54, Dirección de Estadísticas y Censos, Santiago. The classification used is that of the United Nations (Series M, N*4, Rve. 1).

These figures enable us to discern a dual movement; on the one hand, within the city itself, a vertical mobility due to the disproportionate growth of the public sector, which transforms one part of the population into 'white collar' workers and encourages the development of a middle class. On the other, a horizontal mobility, which has produced on the outskirts of Santiago a belt of *callampas* (literally, mushrooms; *bidonvilles*) in which live the *inquilinos* (agricultural workers) who have been forced to leave the land. A great number of them wander about in search of employment, working in ill-defined callings in order to live, among them itinerant traders and small craftsmen.

A state of 'permanent economic crisis' (Pinto Santa Cruz), a decline of rural society, the rise of a rather unproductive middle class, uprooting of the working classes: these are the broad outlines of the first half-century, which was violently shaken by the crisis of the 'thirties (here we come back once more to the date from which Pentecostal expansion starts), which was felt very deeply in Chile as its effect was augmented by the crisis in the nitrate mines which till then had been the principal source of overseas currency for the country—nitrates were now being produced artificially overseas. The former structure of Chilean society (the *hacienda*) is rejecting the farm workers, and industrial development does not feature in its new structures, so that society in Chile may now be described by the old concept of *anomie*, dear to Emile Durkheim.

According to that grand master of French sociology, anomie is the result of a gap in the regimentation of the individual in society, the concept being related to a characteristic of society itself: the structure of that society, in the security of which the individual used to find support, is in a state of 'rupture', which in turn involves the loss of the consensus that regulates the normative orientation and existential definition which give meaning to the life of the individual or group.[24] R. K. Merton, who has revived the concept and made it one of the keys of the functionalist theory, defines it as a lack of adjustment between the goals and objectives in force in a society and the means which are available to groups and individuals for achieving those goals.[25] Durkheim's definition will suffice for our purpose, and the preceding pages have shown how far this concept is applicable in Chile. The working classes, forming broadly two-thirds of the population, live according to the pattern of social organization which used to be provided for them by the *hacienda*, the basic institution in Chile's traditional life. It consists of an extended family structure, upholder of a family, a name; in it a group of families live together under the *hacendado*'s rule, which is paternalistic, both oppressive and protective; his authority, according to Medina Echavarria, rests on belief in the unlimited power of the chief, and also on the belief that he would not fail to protect each one of the members of the social unit should a crisis occur. 'The pattern of authority created by the *hacienda* is widespread, and extends to all relationships of command; the persistence of this popular image is embodied in the figure of the *patron*.'[26]

This social organization—without a doubt open to criticism, yet providing a certain security—is lost for those who are rejected by the countryside and become stranded in the slums (*bidonvilles*); in areas where extractive industries have been established, it has disappeared entirely, and finally, with a boomerang effect, it is in decline even in the country districts, since belief in it is dying. The result is a general spread of social anomie among the working classes, who live in an uprooted state while still nostalgically regretting the lost father-figure.

But the concept of anomie, and the assertion that here we have a society in a state of anomie, are not sufficient to establish any relation with the rise of a religious sect; it is further necessary that individuals living in such a society feel it to be unregulated and are troubled by it. As Bryan Wilson[27] stresses, anomie must be experienced and keenly felt; the individual must feel a resulting frustration, so that the social protest against it begins to stir and social rebellion murmurs. The *social history of Chile* reveals the process by which the Chilean people became aware of their misery and the social disorder, i.e. the transition from the sociological state of anomie to the psychological state of frustration.[28] The first attempts at organizing labour were made towards the end of last century, and at the opening of the present century the first notable strike occurred: in 1903 at Valparaiso, in 1905 at Santiago, the next year at Antofagasta, and in 1907 at Iquique the populace showed that they were no longer willing passively to accept their wretchedness. These dates are written in red in history, for the brutality with which the workers were repressed breached their ranks: 2,000 were killed at Iquique. In 1919 a demonstration was summoned by the Federation of Labour to protest against the unemployment caused by the beginning of the nitrate crisis, and it was supported by about 100,000 people.

Trade unionism grew, but at the start it hardly touched agriculture. The following years were marked by a succession of strikes and massacres of the demonstrators; that moment was the real beginning of the class struggle. 'In 1920 there occurred one of the country's most dramatic conjunctions of political and social events. The post-war crisis, growth of the labour movement, and petit bourgeois agitation, frantic speculation by the governing classes, and inept government, produced a political climate which had profound repercussions, ending in the fall of the oligarchic government.'[29]

In the presidential election, victory went to the candidate of the middle classes, who were backed up by the working class, but the new president (A. Alessandri P.) proved to be a better demagogue than administrator, and very soon disappointed the lower classes. There then occured—for the last time in Chilean history—a series of military *coups d'état* which led to the seizure of power by Colonel C. Ibañez del Campo, and there was no return to legality until 1932, when Alessandri was again successful in the elections. It was at that time that the Communist Party was finally organized, followed in 1933 by the Socialist Party, which also claimed to stem from Marx. The appearance of the working classes on the political stage reached its first high-point in 1939 with the formation of a popular front government. And today there are only two large political groups, the Christian Democrats, who hold power and look upon themselves as centre-left, and the *Frente de Accion Popular* (F.R.A.P.) which includes both Communists and Socialists. The 'historic' parties (liberal and conservative) and the radical party collapsed in the 1964 and 1965 elections.

The account given in the preceding pages shows that *the 'thirties were not only a significant landmark in religious history, but marked a stage in the whole historical development of Chile.* As regards the infrastructure, it was the period when the current of migration took its final shape, as a consequence of agricultural decline and relative stagnation in mining, which brought about urban development unbalanced by proportionate industrialization. Monetary devaluation, which till then had been gradual, accelerated together with the inflationary process, which was further accentuated under the brutal impact of the world crisis. These phenomena had their repercussions upon the superstructure, leading to the collapse of the traditional organizational system, and so uprooting whole populations physically and morally. Then the popular conscience awoke; from 1920 onward, the masses were organized in trade unions on a national scale, at first lending aid to the political rise of the urban middle class. This upsurge of the class struggle entailed repeated military intervention in the government of the country. Finally in the following decade the proletariat organized its own means of political expression and action in the two Marxist parties.

At that date (1920), what was the situation of Pentecostalism? Till then its growth was due mainly (but not entirely) to the groups which left the Methodist Church, all over the central area of the country, to join the new movement. It consisted of twenty-two congregations, whose places of worship were to be found from Santiago to Concepcion,

Temuco and Valdivia; according to one observer[30] the *Iglesia Metodista Pentecostal* then included more than 10,000 people, and constituted the biggest Protestant denomination in the country.

In 1925 an event occurred which greatly assisted its growth: between two *coups d'état* Chile passed a new *Constitution*, which separated Church and State and guaranteed freedom of conscience, belief and worship. For Pentecostalists, this was the end of the period of persecution, and to their evangelistic zeal was added the seal of legality. Each church member took part in the task, and the message, centring round the tidings of salvation, of which the terrestrial pledge was the healing of the sick, was proclaimed in the streets and public squares by men of the people, speaking the language of the people and addressing brothers of their own class. '*Chile para Cristo*'—'Chile for Christ'—was the watchword and the overriding goal, which Pentecostalism considered to have been prophesied by one of the founders of the movement.

By proffering the certainty of salvation, security within the congregation, and a certain type of human dignity, Pentecostalism canalized the strivings of a large proportion of the working classes. Its rise is parallel to that of the Marxist-socialist movements. They, like it, were born of the same want and the same need, both were nourished by the same rebelliousness and struggled by and large for the same clientele, but giving them very different orientations. To paraphrase a famous saying, one may say that Pentecostalism 'is, on the one hand, the *expression* of real misery, and on the other a *protest* against real misery. It is the sigh of the creature who has been overwhelmed, the feeling of a heartless world, as well as the spirit of an age deprived of spirit.'[31]

However, though present-day research in the sociology of religion places certain European sects of past centuries in the middle of a very tenuous chain leading from religious communities to Marxist communism, is it not a paradox to find one protest which is purely religious and spiritual and another purely social and political being born on the same terrain and developing in a parallel manner? The more so, since, contrary to nineteenth-century Europe, where 'Christianity hesitates between ecclesiastical renewal and reforming sociology . . . [and where] Communism hesitates between semi-religious milleniarisms . . . and the stern rationalism of conscience and class war',[32] Pentecostalism condemns the world, and puts a distance between the world and itself, transferring human hopes to a divine world beyond, whereas Chilean Communism is from the outset Marxist and atheist. This confusion of eras and superimposing of one stage on another is one of the characteristics of the developing countries. Without claiming to exhaust the subject, one can stress the fact that traditional Chilean society, on the level of collective mental states, is characterized by its religiosity, or even its magic mentality, 'primitive' in the Levy-Bruhl sense of the word. Observers underline the 'popular religious sensibility' (I. Rosier), 'the thirst for God' (I. Vergara) of the Chilean people. Certainly they are becoming disaffected towards the Catholic Church, which suffers from a lack of priests, and was too closely allied with the oligarchy to be able to satisfy the proletarians,[33] but their religiosity is demonstrated in the hundreds of popular rites, beliefs and superstitions.

Furthermore, if one looks for the key geographical zone for Chilean Protestants, it will be found to cover very exactly the former Indian territory. The Araucans are still animist, the half-castes (and a large majority of Chileans are half-caste) keep up some of the religious practices, evidence of which is seen along the roadsides in the innumerable *animas* (souls), little stone hillocks or niches where candles burn. It was these religious energies which Pentecostalism was able to divert, by unconsciously reproducing a peculiarity of the region. There the division of functions in the Pentecostal congregation reproduces that of Indian society, the pastor and elders corresponding to the *cacique* and heads of families, while the *machi*, both prophetess speaking in tongues and healer, is parallel with the Pentecostal body of prophetesses who usually perform 'difficult' cures. This division of function according to sex becomes less rigid the farther north one goes, once the 'boundary' of the Bio-Bio river is passed.

From this study of the external factors which favour the expansion of Pentecostalism, we may conclude that *to follow its evolution* (while taking good account of the religious factors) *is to reconstruct the history of the dislocation of social organizations and the history of the acknowledgment of their disarray by the human groups dependent on them.* Chilean Pentecostalism, as all observers agree in noting, touches almost exclusively the lower classes, and we have confirmed (see page 28) that it is neither specifically urban nor specifically rural. We have put forward the hypothesis, to which we now return again, that one must try to distinguish between the different milieux (urban, rural and mining). Pentecostalism was born in the suburbs of great cities (Valparaiso, Santiago, Concepcion), in the heart of marginal populations of the peasant class; then it spread to the rural areas of the south, centring on Cautin Province. Here an analysis of the landholding system would perhaps make it possible to grasp the reason for the different growth rhythm of this sect in rural areas. Cautin Province, formerly Indian territory and only seized from them at the end of last century, is divided into small or medium-sized farms, at least according to Chilean law.[34] Now the smallholder (*minifundio*) will suffer from the effects of the agricultural crisis long before the *latifundio*, and land tenancy here has proved very unstable since the beginning of the century; many families have sold their holding and moved to Temuco, which was a small town at the beginning of the century, and now has 80,000 inhabitants but no industry. The Provinces of Curico, Maule and Talca we have placed in a separate category, because they form a homogeneous rural milieu, and Protestant growth there has been accelerating over the last two decades. In them, by contrast, the *latifundio* is predominant, and the awakening of popular conscience has been much slower, since the *hacienda* resisted all attempts to form trade unions. It is only quite recently that the agricultural workers have organized, semi-clandestinely, having lost their faith in the *hacendado*, disputing not only his power but also his right to possess the land of which he works only a fraction, and that in an unsatisfactory manner. The recent Pentecostal 'rural type offensive' (Muñoz) can be regarded as a similar movement in these provinces.[35]

Let us turn to the towns. Protestants are certainly very numerous in Santiago and Valparaiso, but on account of the enormous concentration of population in these centres, their relative importance is below the average for Chile (Table 4: 4·2 per cent. and 4·4 per cent. respectively, compared with the 5·6 per cent. national average).

To grasp the meaning of this, it would be necessary to divide into more precise categories those two-thirds of the population known as the *working classes*. It would appear perhaps that the bulk of the Pentecostal forces come above all from the most marginal of this social class: people without fixed employment, no vocational training, small artisans and itinerant traders, etc. (of course there are many exceptions), first-generation migrants. A limited enquiry carried out in a district on the edge of Santiago, where the land has been divided into lots of 100 sq. metres and sold to industrial workers at a very low price, showed that the members of the Pentecostal congregation who have settled there were neither owners of the plot which they occupied (but caretakers or tenants), nor workers (but artisans or traders). The congregation was not representative of the neighbourhood, its members are the 'marginal' members of the neighbourhood.[36] Does the relatively low proportion of Protestants in the capital suggest that, once a migrant becomes integrated into the urban milieu, his resistance to Pentecostalism increases?

The Province of Concepcion is also predominantly urban. The growth curve of Protestantism there is almost identical with that of the neighbouring province, Arauco, in which there are no towns, and in which the population today contains the highest proportion of Protestants in Chile (Concepcion takes second place). The coal mining area covers these two provinces and gives them some common characteristics. Strongholds of Communism, they are also bastions of Pentecostalism. The miners come from the hinterland, which is agricultural and Indian country; their wages are low, and bear no comparison with the wages at the copper mines where the employees constitute the workers' *élite* (is this the reason for their greater resistance to Pentecostalism?). The coal is difficult to extract, and its quality makes it impossible to use in smelting unless it is mixed with American coke. As a result, production is stationary, for foreign markets for Chilean coal are not available and an endemic state of crisis rules in the area, aggravated by the fact that almost one-fifth of the population has no definable occupation, being unable to find any openings.

In Part I we have covered first of all the birth of Pentecostalism, then traced its numerical growth and geographical expansion; we have tried to show that this sect gives religious expression to the rebellion of the masses in face of the anomie of Chilean society; we then put forward the hypothesis—for which we still have to provide supporting evidence—that the success of Pentecostalism in a given social milieu is in correlation to the collapse or wearing down of social organizations, and consequently of the values which give that society direction.

Now we should like to suggest a hypothesis which will guide the remainder of our investigation and which concerns the internal factors on which the rise of Pentecostalism is founded:

> Pentecostalism offers the population an attractive substitute society, because it relates back to the known model and at the same time renews it. In our opinion, *the success of this sect*, following upon the repeated checks suffered by the older missionary denominations, *rests on the continuity/discontinuity relationship which unites Pentecostalism with society and the environing culture. It is because Pentecostalist society seems from some viewpoints to be radically different from Chilean society, and from other viewpoints very similar to it, that this religious denomination has provided a possible and effective answer to the needs of the people.*

In introducing this continuity/discontinuity relationship into the study of South American sects, we are making variations in, rather than contradicting, one of Emilio Willems's theories: 'The more pronouncedly the internal structure and inherent value system of a Protestant body deviates from those of traditional Latin American society, the more attractive it has proved to be to the masses.'[37] Willems approaches the problem from the viewpoint of social mobility and rightly stresses the egalitarian character of Pentecostal society. Since power is distributed on the basis of *charismata*, the source of which is divine, each of the members has the same chance of ascending in the hierarchy and attaining both pastoral and administrative responsibilities—something which is clearly not the case in the Methodist, Episcopal or Presbyterian denominations, in which vocation can be pursued only through the channel of higher education, a fact which moreover excludes vocations which occur late in life. But the analysis should not stop at the problem of mobility only; let us take up Willems's example again. Though the Pentecostalist pastor and elders are distinguished from the body of church members by neither social origin nor educational background, once they rise to power, they exercise it in a way which is inspired by the model close at hand, the *hacienda*. The Pentecostalist congregation is organized like a large extended family (Willems has himself pointed this out) whose undisputed head is the pastor. The latter amply fulfils the pattern of the ideal *patron* of their dreams; he is the incarnation of the father-figure who has been lost—or rejected, because he has been found to be unjust. The pastor is the person who protects, who finds work for the unemployed, who gives counsel. Often very authoritarian, he nevertheless ensures the protection of the congregation, and it is possible to have faith in him, since he is the depository of God's gift, the person whose election is marked by His baptism. Pentecostalism both offers equality of opportunity (rupture) and also recreates the old seignorial form of society by fulfilling its ideal of protection and trust in vertical human relationships (continuity).

Since our review so far has been essentially diachronic, this is not the place to follow up this argument, but as we bring to light the interconnected levels of Pentecostal society, there should be revealed at each stage the dialectic of rupture and continuity, which places this sect among the factors that carry on the form of traditional society, while at the same time being radically different from it. Such is the task awaiting us in the following parts.

APPENDIX TO PART I

Protestantism and Atheism

In 1955 Father I. Vergara wrote: 'The most profound division that a country can experience is the division between faiths.'[38] This opinion, which has a medieval flavour in our universe of social pluralism, is the basis on which he builds a reasoning that leads him to regard Protestantism as a decisive stage in a road which is leading man towards atheism (and communism). This line of reasoning, which has several variants, is broadly speaking as follows:[39] Protestantism shatters the religious unity of a nation and introduces both the idea and the possibility of choice. As soon as two 'positive' possibilities are open to a man, a 'negative' possibility can also be introduced: the confession of an absence of faith. From this arises the consequent chain of religious change: the father is Catholic (non-practising), the son Protestant and the grandson atheist. To support this theory, 'cases' will be quoted—such and such a Deputy is a Communist, of a Methodist family; and also 'figures'—for example, the rapid growth in the number of atheists in the provinces of Concepcion (which is true, however, only for the years since 1952) and Arauco.

We can neither confirm nor refute this theory, but we can show that it expresses only personal opinions and not scientific knowledge, that it may be true in isolated cases but that it would be wrong to generalize and turn such a statement into a law.

Table 6. Persons with no religion and Protestants (1920–60) (percentages)*

YEAR	ATHEISTS	PROTESTANTS
1920	2·6	1·4
1930	—	1·4
1940	3·3	2·3
1952	3·2	4·1
1960	4·7	5·6

Source: Censos de Población.

* Percentage of the total population.

We should first of all point out that a particular form of atheism became established in Chile long before Protestantism. The struggle for national independence had its ideological foundations in the French Revolution (and the American War of Independence). Free thought, linked with Masonry, was introduced at that time. At a later date Positivism (Auguste Comte) found a very fertile soil throughout South America. Tables 6 and 7 show that up to and including 1940, the number of those 'with no religion' is greater than the number of Protestants.

Table 7. Persons with No Religion according to Four Censuses (Chile: Distribution by provinces)

PROVINCE	1920 No.	%	1940 No.	%	1952 No.	%	1960 No.	%
Tarapaca	7,194	6·2	6,738	6·5	4,338	4·2	4,960	4·0
Antofogasta	12,387	7·2	11,648	8·0	13,572	7·3	13,670	6·4
Atacama	2,750	5·7	8,404	10·0	6,716	8·4	9,398	8·1
Coquimbo	2,562	1·6	13,315	5·4	11,484	4·4	21,275	6·9
Aconcagua	719	0·6	2,525	2·1	3,260	2·5	4,635	3·3
Valparaiso	4,712	1·5	9,245	2·2	12,407	2·5	19,735	3·2
Santiago	9,671	1·4	34,694	2·7	56,287	3·2	101,165	4·2
O'Higgins	797	0·7	4,620	2·3	4,411	2·0	10,275	4·0
Colchagua	723	0·4	1,070	0·8	1,940	1·4	3,635	2·3
Curico	566	0·6	1,315	1·6	1,680	1·9	2,914	2·8
Talca	1,209	0·9	3,632	2·3	4,699	2·7	7,287	3·5
Maule	1,818	1·6	724	1·0	792	1·1	2,328	2·9
Linares	741	0·6	1,835	1·4	2,935	2·0	4,678	2·7
Nuble	2,393	1·4	6,667	2·7	7,113	2·8	14,201	5·0
Concepcion	6,829	2·6	14,046	4·6	13,704	3·3	36,779	6·8
Arauco	1,196	1·9	3,764	5·7	6,334	8·8	9,721	10·9
Bio-Bio	1,780	1·7	2,962	2·3	3,029	2·2	6,838	4·1
Malleco	4,695	3·9	5,244	3·4	6,663	4·2	10,139	5·8
Cautin	22,413	11·6	18,283	4·9	11,474	3·1	30,938	7·8
Valdivia	8,266	4·7	5,045	2·6	8,068	3·5	11,799	4·5
Osorno			2,774	2·6	3,324	2·7	5,945	4·1
Llanquihue	931	0·7	599	0·5	1,515	1·1	2,902	1·7
Chiloe	59	0·1	620	0·6	956	0·9	2,061	2·1
Aysen	—	—	1,824	10·7	1,621	6·2	3,034	8·0
Magallanes	1,386	4·8	2,297	4·7	1,405	2·5	3,318	4·5
Chile	95,797	2·6	163,891	3·3	189,717	3·2	343,630	4·7

In Table 7 and Map 3, in which we have shown a graph of the numbers of those 'with no religion' by a broken line, it seems that even today, in the provinces belonging to the first group (cf. page 24 ff.) those 'without religion' make up a bigger group than the Protestants. In Chile ideas start spreading from Valparaiso and Santiago, and take some time to reach the extreme north and south of the country, and this fact should further tend to show that atheism was established earlier than Protestantism. In the first group of Provinces, one can see a decrease in the number of those 'without religion' from 1920 to 1960 (at least in percentage terms), and one might therefore put forward the opposite hypothesis and suggest that Protestantism slowed down the expansion of atheism. We must state at the outset that this claim could not be upheld any better than the opposite opinion.

Well-founded indices give strength both to the one theory and the other. Professor C. Munizaga of the University of Chile found in the course of an enquiry (not yet published) among the heads of family in the town of Chiloe that all of the few Protestants among them belonged to the most numerous social classes, whereas almost all those 'without religion' belonged to the so-called middle classes, in which 20 per cent. of the heads of family gave this reply. This observation agrees with what is known of Positivism and free thought; they are ideologies of the middle class. Thus in some parts of the country at least, particularly in the southern and northern areas, atheism would be more especially a phenomenon of the middle classes. In this case it would be difficult to establish a parallel between Protestant faith and atheism, since Protestants and atheists rub shoulders with one another without recognizing one another, because of the difference in their respective social milieux.

But then, what is the situation in Arauco and Concepcion? We have seen that this coal-mining area is particularly sensitive to Pentecostalist preaching, and on the other hand it constitutes a bastion of Communism. But is this discovery sufficient to establish a causal relationship in which the antecedent would be Protestantism and the consequence Marxist atheism? *A priori* it would not; furthermore, history shows us that the rise of the Communist Party precedes rather than follows the spread of Pentecostalism.[40]

It is clear that any attempt to establish a causal relationship between Protestantism and atheism would require a full and exact investigation. However, this deterministic outlook seems to us too simple and to be already contradicted by too many factors. Much more fruitful would be the theory which links the great expansion of atheism and that of Protestantism to the entire Chilean social phenomenon, and which asks whether either of them is not dependent upon the anomie of this society. This is moreover the trail which we have been following in the preceding section.

The material we have at our disposal allows us to make one final check: can one say today, in the provinces of Chile where the proportion of Protestants is high, that the proportion of those 'with no religion' is also high (and conversely)? On the basis of the figures for 1960, distributed according to provinces, the statistical association tests prove negative.[41] In simpler terms, this means that one cannot establish as a general law any relation, of whatever kind, between the atheist minority and the Protestant minority.

Part Two

THE PENTECOSTALIST CONGREGATIONS

CHAPTER 3

The Life of the Congregation

I. THE PROCLAMATION OF THE GOSPEL, CONVERSION AND INTEGRATION INTO THE COMMUNITY

THE chief instrument for the propagation of Pentecostalism is *open-air preaching*. If a 'worker'[1] is sent to a remote region of the country where his denomination is not yet established, or if a retired man leaves the city to return to his native village and discovers no churches there, then he will serve his God, praying and going into the streets to proclaim the Gospel there. All the persons we met who were not brought up in a Pentecostal family attributed their first contact with the movement to this type of activity. In so-called 'pagan' territory, a man will begin on his own, or accompanied by his wife; later the faithful invade the village in little groups and occupy strategic points: the *plaza de armas*, the station, coach stops, busy cross-roads. The group sings, accompanied by local instruments—guitars, mandolins, banjos; and the foreign visitor receives quite a surprise when, attracted by the lively, syncopated rhythms, he draws near in the hope of hearing authentic popular folk music, and finds he is listening to old Protestant hymns, such as Luther's famous hymn, *Ein' feste Burg*, which is very much in fashion. Although Chilean Pentecostal music is inferior to what can be heard in the popular Brazilian churches, and has so far produced nothing original, the way the music is transposed and the choice of instruments make one forget its foreign origins.

In between the musical interludes one of the church members steps forward from the group and addresses the passers-by. The sermon we reproduce here was given one night by a young man who—in a real baptism of fire—was preaching for the first time. His companions, standing back in the shadows, were murmuring prayers for the message to reach his hearers:

> Friends, I want to tell you that the Lord who came to save us, died on the cross and that we are really the cause of the Lord's death. And then, my friends, how can we make amends for it? There is no other way to repay the Lord except to do His will. But how can we do the Lord's will? It is very easy, friends: the Lord Himself while He was on earth preached this Gospel for three and a half years. In that time He told His disciples: 'Go into all the world and preach my Gospel, testify to it to all the Gentiles, testify to it to all creatures. Call them to repentance.' In that time the Lord was with His disciples, but He will come again. He has not told us when, but He has told us the signs which will precede His return: there will be earthquakes, hunger, sickness. Now, friends, today we see the Word of God being accomplished as never before, for today we see all these things coming about. And I tell you: accept this

Lord with all your heart, if you want to be saved, for He has said: 'I go to prepare a place for my children, so that where I am, they may be also.' The Lord freely offers us salvation, my friends; God has the power to save us. Often, men and women try to attain their own salvation by their own means; a man will go astray in trying to make himself like God, or seeking to appear before Him. Friends, the Lord is Spirit and Truth, He is everywhere in the earth, and wherever anyone calls to Him, He hears their cries. Now, why try to make oneself like God, why not go straight to Him? I invite you, friends, to cry out to this God. He who humbles himself before the One who will forgive his sins, will find his life transformed, if he really does it with all his heart—for God looks right into his life, He knows his thoughts. You might be able to deceive me, but you cannot deceive God, who knows your personal lives as He knows mine. So I invite you to know the Lord in spirit and in truth, and you will feel in your lives the presence of God. God will be in you and you will give up your vices. Often, friends, a man thinks himself too young to serve the Lord and to accept the Gospel. Often he says, 'I like the Gospel, but it is not time yet.' A man will always wait for the next day, and then he gets old and says, 'I am too old, why should I accept the Lord?' Friends, the Lord is waiting for you with open arms, whether you are old or young. But perhaps you are afraid? Afraid because you are covered in sins? Then you must learn that the Lord is ready to take them away and to forgive you, and to give you salvation. I invite you this evening to make the decision. Come with us to the church; there the Gospel will be preached and you will understand better. May the God of peace protect you![2]

At the beginning, preaching used to provoke noisy gatherings; arguments broke out, and sometimes counter-demonstrations were organized. The originality of the message, both in matter and form, excited an immediate reaction. Today, most of the time people hardly slow down as they pass by, since it no longer has the attraction of novelty. Is this a sign of decline? We think not; simply this method no longer has the same penetration, but it is still the means of making first contacts, and the most effective method of propagation. Passers-by no longer stop, because they know what is going on; it is the *Canutos*, and they are, as I was able to verify, familiar with the essence of the message. Other, more personal meetings, with friends, relatives or Pentecostal neighbours, will revive the phrases and words gleaned in the streets: pardon, saviour, love. . . . Other persons will take over from the anonymous preacher heard once and furtively, and thus the 'Gentile' will be challenged continuously with the Pentecostalist message.

Analysis of the sermon—which we have quoted because it uses the most frequently repeated themes—enables one to understand why the Pentecostal message used to provoke, and still does provoke, such a reaction in the Chilean people. From the point of view first of form, the Gospel leaves the four walls of the churches to spread about the city, to confront the ideologies of the slums and penetrate that culture of the poor revealed to us by Oscar Lewis.[3] Secondly, it is no longer the priest—the man paid to speak about God—who talks to the people and transmits the message, but the cobbler, miner, seller of *empanadas* (meat or cheese fritters), in short the people one meets every day.

He who speaks might be one of the passers-by, and the passer-by might well be a preacher one day. The Word of God is no longer the monopoly of specialists, to the great offence of the bourgeois and educated people, who are shocked not only by the language of the Pentecostalists but above all by their pretension in wanting to speak about God. 'These men,' said a teacher, 'do not even speak in Castillian but in slang; sometimes they don't even know how to write, and can hardly read. And they quote epistles of St. Paul so difficult that the theologians, who have been working on them for two thousand years, have not got to the bottom of them. By what authority do they teach?' But what scandalizes the *élite* is just what touches the people. Even if the message is coloured with the dialect of Canaan or with slang, it is listened to because it is transmitted in the language of the farm labourer (*inquilino*) and the Chilean 'Cockney' (*roto*), by men who are living the experience they speak of, and live it in the midst of a social situation and in problems and difficulties which are shared by those to whom they are speaking. He who preaches is brother to him who listens, they belong to the same social class and share the weight of the same problems of making a living. If the Gospel here is literally good news, it is because it offers an answer to the human and social confusion of the people. To these uprooted crowds, reduced to a marginal state of existence by the social system which is destroying whatever confidence remained in those who formerly held the power, Pentecostalism announces a Lord who pardons and loves, a Lord just as powerful as the land-owners, the mine managers or the trade union secretaries, because He is God, a God who desires to be called Father and who treats the most wretched of men as His son.

In the Pentecostalist message, the declaration of divine omnipotence is not an abstract theological postulate, but a truth experienced by faith. The power of God is not only proclaimed in hope. The Holy Spirit daily testifies to it by gifts and miracles. A Kingdom beyond this world is preached, which will break through in the imminent future, the existence of which is guaranteed as from this moment by the conviction that one's sins are pardoned, and is often confirmed or made visible by a physical sign, healing. A powerful God is above all a God who heals. Innumerable conversions have been preceded by a cure (whether real or imaginary is impossible to verify) obtained through prayer and the laying on of hands.

Sickness, accidents or unforeseen difficulties are the most propitious times for conversion, for they bring to a climax the state of confusion and insecurity in which the masses vegetate. Here again, reading *The Children of Sanchez* gives one an authentic description of the Latin American proletariat. In the biographical stories we have collected, nearly half the people concerned link their conversion with a cure, not necessarily miraculous, since sometimes it was due to a doctor, but always attributed to God, 'who saved me when the doctor thought it was impossible'. Nevertheless, what strikes one about these stories is precisely the description they give of the life of the poor and its recurring features: first, the breakdown of family life—the person questioned is perhaps an illegitimate child, or knows only one of his parents, or has seen his father living with several women; secondly, the father's unstable employment, with the resultant economic insecurity; thirdly, a bad family atmosphere which produces a feeling of abandonment and drives one into loneliness—no friends, or friends 'who are only good for drinking and stealing', no confidants and no one able to give support.

One can thus understand the emotional shock which those who were converted underwent when they heard the message of salvation which offered to change their existence completely and to transform their living conditions:

> The open-air preaching had an influence on me, and one day I felt an inner need to go to a service. I went there on Sunday afternoon, and when I went in I saw that it was a prayer meeting, and I knelt down too. Beside me was a 'sister' calling on God for pardon, and so I too had need to ask for pardon. I was fifteen. Then I felt something happening in me; I felt repentance and began to weep and to ask Him to forgive my sin and transform my life. And I heard a voice—but not the voice of anyone near me—which spoke to me and said, 'Your sins are forgiven you.' And at the moment my life changed completely, to such an extent that when I left the church, I felt that everything had changed, that the streets and trees and houses were different. It was a very poor district, with some houses in ruins and unmade streets. But for me everything was new and transformed. . . .

The experience of conversion is always marked by a feeling of change, both physically and in one's sensations. Some people speak of a lump or a weight having left them; perception of one's environment is altered and one leaves the church relieved, liberated and weak, sometimes to the point of fainting.

A social catharsis accompanies the individual's catharsis; to the wonderful experience of conversion is added integration into the community (congregation). When an initiate is asked what most pleases him about his church, he replies unhesitatingly, '*el companerismo*', the fact of being surrounded, having friends, spiritual brothers—in short, forming part of a social cell. The man who formerly lived in isolation on the fringe of a brutal society over which he had no hold and was helpless to change finds himself taken charge of by the Church, called 'brother' and integrated right away in the common task. In this process of the individual's integration into the religious community lies the principal social function of Pentecostalism, its *disalienating function.* The term 'alienation' is here used in its original meaning, with no ideological camouflage: alienation is what makes a man a stranger. The general transformation of society has alienated him (made him a stranger) from the extended human groups. The individual has been left incapable of sharing, either politically, economically or socially, in the progress of a society which has thrown him out into its shadow zone, and he becomes a stranger in it and by the same token a stranger to himself, since he can no longer govern his own destiny nor direct it towards the ends he aspired to, or is sometimes even unable to provide for those for whom he is responsible in the eyes of the law.[4] The family, the social cell which philosophers, jurists and theologians regard according to natural law as the basic unit of all society, is going through a crisis, which is illustrated dramatically by the rate of illegitimacy and the number of irregular unions.

In rescuing the individual, Pentecostalism brings to him a human dignity refused him by society. This dignity is symbolized by the title of *hermano* (brother) awarded immediately to the convert. Here this title is not like the empty formula inherited from bygone days, used by pastors in Europe when they address their audience at the beginning of a sermon; in Pentecostalism, the sign and what is signified coincide completely. Calling a person 'brother' indicates that he belongs to a community, between whose members there is solidarity, which is organized on the model of the family, where blood ties are replaced by ties of a common spiritual sonship in relation to one Lord and Father, and which is discovered by each of its members through a similar experience, that is, conversion.

Can one be surprised, then, that these great 'spiritual' families develop stronger and more effective ties of solidarity than those of the consanguineous family? Such ties are first developed directly, as mutual help within the congregation is set going, but above all they develop indirectly, through the moral—and consequently, economic—reinstatement of the family, where blood ties are reinforced by the participation of each member of the family group in the religious community.

The words of integration are accompanied by actions: the visitor is introduced to the pastor by the person who has brought him to the service, and he is introduced to the assembly. After the pastor has spoken, the church members can guess whether the person is moved by curiosity, or is a sympathizer or a brother. In the first two cases, the visitor will be surprised to hear his neighbours praying expressly for him, that God will open his heart and save him. From the moment of his first contact with the community, the sympathizer finds himself to be an object of interest and surrounded by human warmth; he finds that other people attribute to him an importance which he himself never suspected, and learns that God (the one who saves!) is interested in him! Men and women confided to me that they wept the first time they attended a Pentecostal service, 'not because of the beauty of the ceremonial—oh, no, it is not as beautiful as with the Catholics—but because people spoke to me, the pastor shook my hand, and I was able to sing and pray with them'.

This is in contrast to South American Roman Catholic parishes—or indeed European Protestant parishes—which through their stability and internal structuration have become unsuited to welcoming converts. In the Pentecostal congregation, the initiate finds he is immediately given a place which carries rights and duties in the different departments of the organization—young people's department, men's and women's departments. As soon as they are sure of his conversion, they will ask him to declare it during a service of witness, where he will describe, as the formula goes, 'how God worked in him for salvation'. A little later, in a brief ceremony, he will be received as a *miembro probando* or member on trial, and then he will share in the first grade of the hierarchy. Then the congregation begins to make greater demands on him. Before that, he participated 'by proxy', through the intermediary of the members who brought him and acted as his sponsors; now he must himself assume the duties of a member: to contribute financially by tithing and to give the best part of his spare time to the church. But the initiate interprets these duties as signs that he really belongs to the group and shares the common responsibility; just as he needs the group, the group needs him; he is somebody!

2. THE THREE DIMENSIONS OF THE CONGREGATION'S WORK

If one excludes the social and charitable activities which have only recently begun to find a place in the congregations, either through the influence of organizations foreign to Pentecostalism (e.g., food distributions organized by Church World Service), or else as a result of the maturation of some of the denominations (sewing groups, some hospitals, a few children's holiday camps), collective activities fall into three types:

evangelism —the conquering community
spiritual life—the praying community
education —the teaching community

These three activities are all organized around the same focus: adoration of God the Saviour and witness rendered to Him.

The Conquering Community

The departments of men, women and young people are subdivided into sections for pedestrians, cyclists and—in some city congregations—motorists. Each section is allotted a territory to be evangelized, according to its means of locomotion. At week-ends, the swarm of colporteurs and preachers descends on the towns and villages. It is at these times that the observer is made aware of the spreading of Pentecostalism—the preachers' voices, with their urgent, chanting pitch, follow him on his walks; as one voice dies away another replaces it, and when the speaking finishes, songs are heard, the words of which form a new challenge. When the time for worship approaches, the groups of pedestrians join up and form a procession which grows at each cross roads till it stretches more than a hundred yards. At the head the musicians lead the singing, and in the intervals voices are raised making their final appeals, 'Remember thou thy Creator in the days of thy youth, before the evil days come . . .' (Eccles. 12: 1). The conferences attended by all the officers of the denomination are occasions for mass demonstrations; behind the banners of the corporation (denomination) come the musicians, then the pastors, always in dark clothes and carrying Bibles, and finally the church members who have often come from a great distance to see all the leaders and share in the closing worship. These processions do indeed suggest the idea of a conquest or a crusade. Faces lined by a difficult life, and also often by alcoholism—sign of a life that is past—glow with the flame given by the great certainties: 'We are out to conquer Chile', ' "Chile for Christ" is our aim'. 'When I first preached', said a pastor from La Serena, 'ten years ago, there were about five of us. Now there are thousands, and we shall go on growing.'

The Praying Community

Worship is the climax of the community life; it lasts two hours or more, and may be daily. The churches, wooden for the most part, and recognizable by the particular outline of the roof which hangs over the porch, and by the name of the denomination written in large letters on the pediment, are not masterpieces of popular art. One can recognize the influence of the style imported by the missionaries in the last century. The entrance leads into a large rectangular hall with a dais at the back. In the centre of this is the pulpit on which the Bible rests; behind it are seats for the dignitaries and important visitors, surmounted by a huge tableau in strident colours, copied by some artist from North American reproductions, representing the Bible or a Bible story. (Only once, in a little country chapel, did we see a fresco painted on the wall itself, naïvely depicting the Creation in a manner derived from the unknown artist's own inspiration. It made us regret that Pentecostalism has so far not developed its own art.) In these impersonal church buildings which, were it not for the picture and the Bible, might be taken for trade union halls, the members enter, kneel to present themselves before God, and take their seats: women with babes in arms, old men with their grandchildren, and men—a great many men. The striking thing in Pentecostalist congregations is that all age groups and both sexes are represented. Three polls enabled us to confirm that a healthy congregation constitutes a good sample of the age pyramid and sex distribution of the Chilean population, in contradistinction from attendance at Mass, to which go only women, old people and children. (A comparison of Pentecostalist and Catholic processions gives the same result.) The presence of infants and children gives the ceremony a degree of colour as well as background noise. But nobody is disturbed by them, and in any case they could not be left behind at home on their own. As people enter, they greet one another and smile, then men and women separate and go to the side reserved for them; the musicians, after praying at the foot of the pulpit, take up their places on extensions at right-angles to the platform, and tune their instruments. Time is passing but nobody is in a hurry.

At a signal from the person responsible for the service, the orchestra plays the tune of a hymn and the people rise. They seldom sing well, but they sing at the tops of their voices, tapping out the rhythm with their feet or clapping their hands. The orchestra on its own repeats the chorus, and in the hall, following the lead of one of the faithful, the famous salutation of the Chilean Pentecostalists rings out, the triple '*Gloria a Dios*', followed by spontaneous individual exclamations of 'Alleluia', 'Amen', 'Gloria'.

The pastor likes to arrive a little late, and it is always interesting to observe his entry, for it reveals certain traits in his personality. Here is someone debonair and smiling, shaking hands and greeting people; here one who is imbued with his role, advancing up the central aisle with head held high and looking neither to right nor left, accompanied by some of the elders and visitors. In certain denominations a somewhat pompous ritual has become established; like the bishop who enters only after the ceremony has begun, he comes with hat on head and a cape on his shoulders, three councillors following him, one carrying a large Bible. When they reach the platform, one elder takes the hat, one the cape, and the third hands the Bible to the bishop, who then takes his seat.

After the singing there follows a period for self-abasement; the faithful kneel and the leader speaks only to mark the beginning and end of prayer. Each person improvises his own prayer and speaks aloud; a general hubbub is heard, with words and sounds, sighs, groans, shouts and tears. Some scraps of sentences are intelligible: 'Lamb of God . . . thank you for saving me . . . thank you for your blood . . . oh, save us . . .' After ten or fifteen minutes the leader ends with this ritual phrase: 'In the name of the Lord Jesus, Amen.'

The people rise, except for some who continue to pray. This is the time when letters of introduction (*las credenciales*) are presented. Following apostolic practice, which has been transmitted to Pentecostalism through the Methodist Church, the church member who is travelling must ask his pastor for a letter identifying him and giving the reason why he is away from home (private journey, removal, a mission entrusted to him by the congregation, an evangelistic journey commanded by a vision, etc.). When he arrives in a place, the Pentecostalist finds out whether a church of his own denomination exists there. If there is one, he is certain to find food and shelter; if there is none, he will go to a church of another group, and with few exceptions will be welcomed there as a brother.

The letters are examined by the pastor, and the visitor will be introduced to the congregation; later he will have to speak. For important visitors there is special treatment. They have the right to sit on the platform; and while this honours the stranger, he is also shown to the church members because his presence is the sign of the important place taken by the movement. Generally the pastor will ask him to preach instead of himself, to 'bring us a message'; whether the visitor is a pastor or not matters little, for every believer is a preacher!

The whole ceremony unfolds without a time-table or any strict plan. Certainly the broad scheme is always the same, but variations are constantly introduced. If the pastor thinks that the moment for preaching has not yet arrived, there will be more praying or singing. Gradually the atmosphere warms, the Spirit is manifested and inspired dancers rise. Their neighbours move back to give them room; those who are inspired sing and dance and the excitement mounts; sometimes a few collapse on the ground and show symptoms of ecstasy; others are seized by fits of laughter or of trembling or weeping. Sometimes but not very often—except in certain small congregations which make a particular habit of seeking spiritual gifts—there are demonstrations of glossolalia, unformed sounds and babblings, as well as better constructed phrases. Glossolalia may take a prophetic turn; then the 'language of angels' is explained either by the inspired person himself or by an 'interpreter'.[5]

The congregation is then collectively seized with a frenzy, which is, however, controlled and canalized by the pastor and a few elders, the former speaking to and calming his flock. There follows the reading of Bible passages, as a prelude to the sermon. In some denominations the custom is for the Bible to be opened at random—or rather, under the guidance of the Spirit; generally, however, the pastor has already chosen his text or at least the theme of his sermon. This will always have a didactic aim; it leads to an action, the point of it bearing on what should or should not be done. A good Pentecostal preacher is well worth hearing, for he has a genius for communication; his preaching is not a lecture but a dialogue; the speaker challenges his followers, and asks for their approval, which they show both by a barrage of stereotyped phrases: 'It is so', 'Yes, amen', 'Alleluia', 'Glory, glory', and also by repeating whole sentences after the pastor, the better to assimilate them and to remember them when they return home. The eager looks, foreheads creased with the effort of concentration, heads nodding approval, should be seen, as well as the joy which breaks out when once again God's love and man's salvation are affirmed.

The good preacher knows how to speak in images and find anecdotes which will illustrate an idea better than abstract language, and will enable the hearers to identify themselves with the people in the stories. Once a pastor—a wonderful preacher—was telling the story of a prisoner he had been visiting. He told of the guilty man's astonishment when he assured him that God loved him also and wished to save him; the prisoner could hardly believe it, but having been convinced, his doubt was transformed into wonderment: 'I, I too, can be saved!' And the faithful laughed happily at this story; each of them understood what the prisoner had felt, each lived in the latter's situation to the point of *being* him, for the faithful had also been through the same experience in slightly different contexts, and had felt this wonderment tinted with incredulity.

On another occasion, in a little country chapel, the sermon dealt with 'the Good Shepherd', and the congregation repeated the pastor's phrases: 'The Lord is a good shepherd . . . I am his sheep . . . I have a good shepherd . . . He goes with me wherever I go'. At the end of the service, one could not help being moved at the sight of these peasants returning homeward, after bidding the pastor farewell with an embrace, disappearing into the night, certain that they were not going alone.

One should not judge hastily the accesses of emotion which accompany worship in Pentecostalist churches. Before making any other interpretation or any value judgment, theological or otherwise, one must recognize that they permit people to participate in a direct and personal way in religious manifestations and in the congregation. They are forms of participation, they are the languages of those who have no language, the means of expressing their experience of encountering something greater than themselves; they are the thankful demonstration of the individual's liberation accomplished through the activities of the Pentecostalist congregation.

After the sermon, another period of prayer is followed by the collection. Here too, the observer is struck by the procession of members, whose clothes are often in tatters, and their shoes patched, sometimes made of the remains of old tyres, their faces showing signs of a deficient diet, and they come to place on the offertory table, some 50 pesos, some 100, some even more. There is the symbol of the devotion which Pentecostalism engenders in its members, and the secret of its financial autonomy.

Just before the close comes intercession for the sick; those who desire it advance to the podium, where they kneel and wait for the pastors or an elder to lay hands upon them. The visitor thus sees before him a real court of miracles. At the same time the names of those too ill to come to church are collected, and prayers are said for their healing. Then it is time for the final blessing and after countless handshakes and embraces, everyone departs. The congregation leaves, but the next day they will come together again for another service.

Services have several variant forms. One may include a number of testimonies by converts, or by church members cured of an illness or a vice. Another will include a particular rite, such as receiving new members, presentation of children, baptisms, etc.

At certain times the nucleus of the congregation, being urged by the desire for the baptism of fire, will undertake vigils or chains of prayer, whole nights being spent in praying for the Holy Ghost, or teams of people pray for set periods continuously for several days on end. If the objective is not to receive the baptism of the Spirit, it will be to obtain some other spiritual benefit or the healing of a sick person, or again deliverance from some threatening event foretold by a prophetess.

The practice of long, exhausting spiritual exercises is at the basis of all *revivals*, either Methodist or Pentecostalist. This was the way taken by Pastor Hoover's congregation, at the beginning of this century, seeking for the baptism of the Spirit. This baptism, however, was not thought of as an end in itself, but in the last analysis as a point of departure, as the *bestowing of a capacity for action*, which was evangelism. Just as the coming of the 'tongues of fire', according to Acts 2, was the starting-point of the Christian missionary movement, so the mystical experience of the coming of the Holy Ghost in the Pentecostal congregation inaugurates its campaign of conquest, and constitutes the starting-point for its apostleship.

On the other hand, especially in the coal mining area (the Provinces of Concepcion and Arauco), where mushroom churches abound, we found several of these where their activities were restricted to the sole function of prayer and worship, and vigils and chains of prayer followed one another continuously. Prophecy and tongues took precedence over instruction through preaching and over the Bible, and efforts to evangelize had practically disappeared. These congregations were stagnant and sinking into quietism, totally inward-looking, the rare recruits being attracted to them during sickness by the hope of a cure. Such a reduction of congregational life to one single spiritual activity is not rare, but affects only the fringe of the Pentecostalist movement, and in Durkheim's terms constitutes pathological degeneration, since in the heart of Pentecostalism spiritual experience must lead to evangelistic activity—*Chile para Cristo.*

The Teaching Community

Of the three dimensions of congregational activity, prayer, evangelism and teaching, the last is the least well defined. Teaching what? A catechism, that is, teaching given in a systematic manner on the principles, mysteries and dogma of the Christian faith? That would presuppose that Chilean Pentecostalism had a structured theology, emanating from an intellectual *élite* capable of abstraction and conceptualization—an *élite* which so far does not exist. No, their teaching will deal not with dogma, but with a number of beliefs, and with the learning of Bible verses regarded as essential; above all, it will concentrate on moral teaching. Pentecostalism teaches how to believe and live, not how to think. The church member will receive an armoury of precepts, commandments and prohibitions, which describe for him the content of the Christian life by demarcating its frontiers.

The Christian is a 'being apart', one of the elect who is recognizable by his way of life; he does not drink or smoke, does not visit theatres or cafés, does not swear. He goes to services, pays his tithe, gives his time to the church, respects his wife, brings up his children worthily, keeps his house clean and pays his debts. He submits to authority and is industrious in his work.

It is difficult to define precisely the content of the teaching, because of the absence of any catechetical handbook (except in the North American Pentecostal denominations); it is no less difficult to particularize the form this teaching function takes, because instruction is carried on through the services and evangelistic activities. Apart from what is taught in Sunday Schools, which precede Sunday worship and are attended by both adults and children, the church member learns what he should believe and do by his participation in the services and missionary activities. Teaching is based on imitation of the leaders during the course of sharing in congregational life. Only the Sunday School (also preaching, with a different emphasis), inherited from traditional Protestantism, offers some analogy with what is commonly called teaching. But here again it is a matter of teaching not in ideas, but in a way of living, based on the exemplary character of Bible personages and on Bible stories. The public—if one can speak of a public, since nobody comes as a spectator—is divided into small groups according to age and sex, and the 'teachers', who would be better described as 'group animators', relate the Bible text and encourage an exchange of reactions, which takes the form of testimonies, examples taken from experience, and illustrations from daily life.

3. NOTE ON THE INDIVIDUAL'S INTEGRATION INTO THE PENTECOSTALIST CONGREGATION

In a stimulating article, W. S. Landecker investigates the possibility of measuring the integration of an individual or a small group into the *social whole.*[6] The author puts the question in general terms, thinking of the rural migrant moving to an urban centre as much as a new worker entering a business, but his approach will enable us to define the process by which a sympathizer is absorbed into the Pentecostalist congregation, which is a social group with voluntary association.

For the author, 'a typology of integration can be developed on the premise that for sociological purposes the smallest units of group life are cultural standards, on the one hand, and persons and their behaviour, on the other'.[7] From these three elements, cultural norms, individual behaviour and a network of individuals, Landecker draws four types or levels of integration: (i) the cultural level, i.e. consistency of the norms of culture; (ii) the normative level, or conformity of the group's (or individual's) behaviour with that of the cultural leaders; (iii) communicative integration, or intensity of the communication network between individuals, and (iv) finally, the functional level, i.e. the interdependence of the group's members in the division of labour and exchange of services.

(i) Anticipating what will be said when Pentecostalist theology and morality are dealt with, it is clear that the cultural models in the sphere of Pentecostalism form a highly coherent whole. From the reading of the Gospel springs the message of regeneration and sanctification of the individual, a message which is codified in a collection of norms which govern individual behaviour. The communication of beliefs and norms is achieved more specifically in the course of sermons and in the Sunday School; instruction has a very pronounced moral aim; it is a matter not so much of transmitting a certain knowledge, but of inculcating the image of Christian man, 'the portrait of the "new man"', to which the believer should conform; thus (ii) the normative integration is at its maximum (helped by the importance placed upon congregational practices), since the church member must make visible his status as a believer. All deviant conduct is interpreted by the group as the sign of a 'fall', of loss of one's standing as a believer, and so the individual who does not conform to the cultural norms is immediately excluded from the community. (iii) Communicative integration is achieved as soon as the sympathizer is introduced to the congregation. In effect, though the latter is not always a face-to-face group, since it may contain several hundred or thousand members, nevertheless it always consists of a gathering of primary groups, and each member belongs to one of these cells. There are no isolated persons in Pentecostalist society, unless it is a question of relapsed persons who are under the ban of the group. (iv) Functional integration is more difficult to discern, since the congregation has no direct economic function as regards the individual. Would it be possible to interpret this level in relation to the role played by each person in the group? We shall see, when studying the hierarchy,[8] how offices are distributed. In the lowest echelons, those of ordinary members, it is difficult to speak of functional interdependence or reciprocity, since all have the same tasks: sharing in religious observances, hearing instruction, evangelistic activities. All these activities form part of normative rather than functional integration, since attendance at worship and taking part in the proclamation of the message both derive directly from the cultural norms of Pentecostalism. It seems difficult, therefore, to speak of functional integration, since, apart from the hierarchic system,[8] there is hardly any social division of labour; everyone does the same thing. Thus one could not interpret this lack as an index of poor or deficient integration, since it is inherent in this type of group, in which community work requires hardly any specialization or exchange, but rests on the repetition of the same kind of activities. Putting this aside, the Pentecostalist congregation presents a high degree of integration of its members. On account of the authority of the norms, which are regarded as being of divine origin, and the weight of the controls exercised by the group, either the individual is completely integrated, in the sense of the first three levels, or else he is not a member of the congregation.

4. PASTORAL WORK

In our investigation of the three groups (Pentecostalist pastors, Protestant pastors and theological students),[9] the questionnaire used included a multiple question on the pastor's activities. The replies confirm the description of community work in the Pentecostalist congregations which we have given, work which is almost exclusively confined to the domain of religion. As we shall see, in the Pentecostalist tradition the pastor's field of work is very much more restricted and better demarcated than it is in the views of the theological students. There is no doubt that these differing definitions of the content of the pastoral ministry are linked with different understandings of the content of the Gospel, but for the moment we shall leave this problem in parentheses, for it will be dealt with in Part III.

Here is the text of the questionnaire:

Q. Here is a *list of activities* which, depending on one's viewpoint, may or may not be included in pastoral work. In your opinion, which of the activities listed

(1) enter into the pastor's *regular* work?
(2) may enter *occasionally* into pastoral work?
(3) are definitely excluded from pastoral work?

1. Visiting sick church members.
2. Social work: establishing schools, polyclinics, children's homes, etc.
3. Preaching in church.
4. Speaking about political elections in the sermon.
5. Intervening on behalf of a church member with his employer.
6. Visiting hospitals and prisons.

Table 1. The Pastor's field of action (T = 100%)*

ACTIVITIES	SAMPLE	PASTORAL WORK		EXCLUDED	N.R.
		REGULAR	OCCASIONAL		
3. Preaching in church	A	100	—	—	—
	B	100	—	—	—
	C	100	—	—	—
13. Leading special ceremonies	A	97	3	—	—
	B	100	—	—	—
	C	98	2	—	—
1. Visiting sick church members	A	97	3	—	—
	B	100	—	—	—
	C	98	2	—	—
6. Visiting hospitals and prisons	A	86	11	—	3
	B	92	4	—	4
	C	93	7	—	—
9. Preaching in the street	A	42	53	5	—
	B	42	50	8	—
	C	97	3	—	—
11. Finding work for unemployed brethren	A	61	33	3	3
	B	61	35	—	4
	C	93	2	5	—
7. Instructing Sunday School Teachers	A	89	11	—	—
	B	96	—	4	—
	C	91	2	7	—
5. Speaking to employer on behalf of church member	A	33	58	3	6
	B	46	39	15	—
	C	47	30	23	—
2. Social services: schools, clinics	A	42	50	—	8
	B	38	50	12	—
	C	34	33	33	—
8. Collab. in solving general problems	A	78	22	—	—
	B	81	15	4	—
	C	35	21	44	—
10. Representing Protestant Churches	A	44	44	3	9
	B	46	46	8	—
	C	26	28	46	—
14. Speaking on social problems in sermon	A	47	39	14	—
	B	46	23	27	4
	C	8	13	79	—
12. Intervening in defence of trade unions	A	42	47	8	3
	B	19	42	35	4
	C	11	9	80	—
4. Speaking on pol. elections in sermon	A	28	58	8	6
	B	23	35	42	—
	C	10	7	83	—

* A = 36 students; B = 26 Protestant pastors; C = 61 Pentecostal pastors.

7. Instructing the Sunday School teachers.
8. Collaborating (with non-Protestants) in problems in the region which are of common interest, e.g. the fight against illiteracy, establishing co-operatives, etc.
9. Preaching in the street.
10. Representing the Protestant Churches at official ceremonies of the municipality or central government.
11. Trying to find work for unemployed church members.

12. Taking a stand against the authorities and intervening in defence of trade unions in cases of conflict.
13. Conducting special ceremonies: Holy Communion, Baptism, reception of members.
14. Speaking in the course of preaching on social problems, e.g. wages, working conditions, etc.

The activities listed can be grouped under three headings: (a) *Religious* (covering the three functions described above: praying, teaching and conquering)—items 3, 6, 7, 9 and 13. (b) *Charitable*, or all activities designed to help primarily the congregation or some of its members—items 1, 2, 5 and 11. (c) *Socio-political*, implying the congregation's, or the pastor's, involvement in the manifestations and problems of society—items 4, 8, 10, 12 and 14.

An overall study of Table 1 brings us to one initial conclusion: while the number of *students* who excluded such and such an activity from pastoral work was only a very small minority (a maximum of 14 per cent.), in the case of the *Protestant* pastors the proportion was 42 per cent., and rose to a definite majority (83 per cent.) among the *Pentecostalist* pastors. In other words, in a general sense, all the listed activities, according to the theological *students*, enter into the work of the minister, while the *Protestants* are divided on certain points, and the *Pentecostalists* define the field of pastoral work much more strictly, rejecting some of the items on the list.

The difference in the extent of the pastor's duties, according to the views of the three samples, stands out clearly when one examines the proportion of students, Protestant pastors and Pentecostal pastors who exclude one or more activities from the list.

Table 2

	(A)	(B)	(X)
Pentecostalists	7%	93%	4·3
Protestants	35%	65%	2·3
Students	69%	31%	1·5

(A) Percentage of persons who think all the activities enter into pastoral work.
(B) Percentage of persons who exclude one or more activities.
(X) Average number of activities excluded by the persons included under (B).

Whereas almost all the Pentecostalists (93 per cent.) reject some activities, and this is also true of 65 per cent. of the Protestant pastors, 69 per cent. of the students think all the activities mentioned form part of pastoral work.

(*a*) Five activities (3, 13, 1, 6 and 9) are unanimously accepted by the Pentecostalists, and four (3, 13, 1 and 6) are likewise accepted by the other samples. Of these five, only one is not directly religious—visiting members who are ill (1)—but it certainly enters into the universal conception of the pastoral ministry.

The difference in attitude between Protestants and Pentecostalists should be noted in regard to *preaching in the street* (9). For the latter

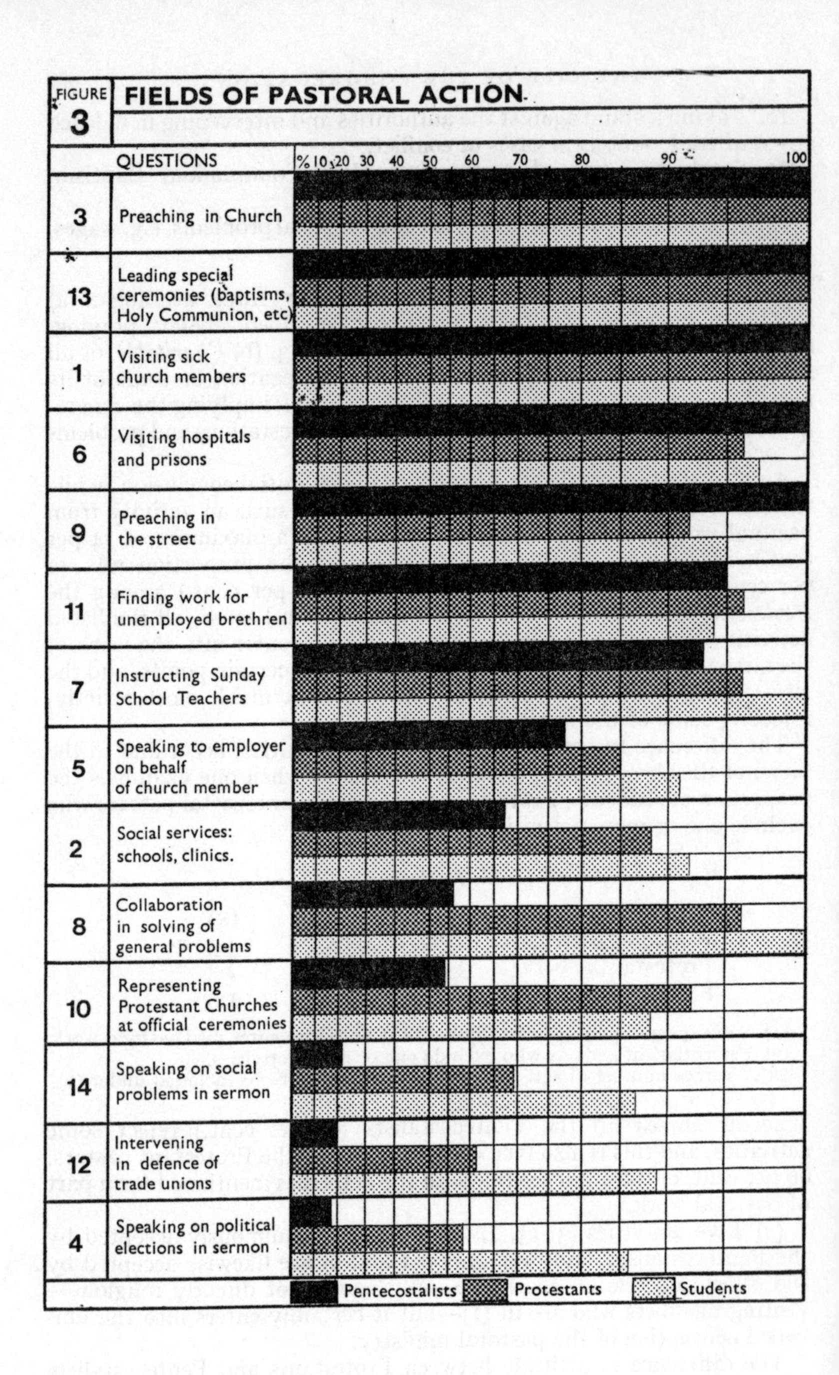
FIGURE 3
FIELDS OF PASTORAL ACTION
QUESTIONS
% 10 20 30 40 50 60 70 80 90 100
3 Preaching in Church
13 Leading special ceremonies (baptisms, Holy Communion, etc)
1 Visiting sick church members
6 Visiting hospitals and prisons
9 Preaching in the street
11 Finding work for unemployed brethren
7 Instructing Sunday School Teachers
5 Speaking to employer on behalf of church member
2 Social services: schools, clinics.
8 Collaboration in solving of general problems
10 Representing Protestant Churches at official ceremonies
14 Speaking on social problems in sermon
12 Intervening in defence of trade unions
4 Speaking on political elections in sermon
Pentecostalists
Protestants
Students

this activity is part of their regular duties; for the Protestants it is rather an occasional task. In addition, the replies of the Protestant pastors and students do not coincide with their deeds: we have never seen a Methodist or Presbyterian minister preaching in the street!

(*b*) Two activities follow (11, finding work, and 7, instructing the 'teachers'), on which the three samples are almost unanimous. It is as well to remember that the Pentecostal pastor's office assumes the function of an employment bureau more often and more obviously than among the Protestants. This is one of the marks of congregational solidarity in Pentecostalism, a further index of which is given in the fact that its pastors place more importance on defending their members (item 5) than on establishing social institutions (item 2).

These two groups of activities on which the Pentecostalists are unanimously or almost unanimously agreed cover all the religious activities in the list and three of the charitable activities, but none of the socio-political activities.

(*c*) The two remaining activities of the charitable type are accepted by two-thirds to three-quarters of the Pentecostalists. However, for many of the Pentecostalist pastors, the establishment of social institutions is a dream impossible to realize at the moment 'since we have no money', as one interviewee stressed, 'and besides, in Chile no Protestant school or hospital exists on national support; they are always financed by foreign missions'.

(*d*) At the bottom of the list come the five socio-political activities, and here it is possible to make a distinction according to the degree of involvement they imply:

(i) The Pentecostalists are divided in their opinions on two activities (8 and 10), which presuppose a compromise with society, without however requiring the taking of a political position.

While a small majority favour these activities, the discontinuity between word and deed must be stressed, for it was very unusual to see pastors participating on municipal occasions, or sharing in the solution of social problems concerning their area.

(ii) Finally, four-fifths of the Pentecostalist pastors refuse to speak on politics or social problems or to intervene in disputes (14, 12 and 4). One can also see that a strong minority (between a quarter and a half) of the Protestant pastors agree with their Pentecostalist colleagues in rejecting Christian participation in the political sphere, whereas for nearly all the students Christian love leads one into precisely such participation.

5. REMARKS ON PENTECOSTALIST AND CHILEAN CULTURE

The description of the life of the Pentecostalist congregation leads to the problem of the relation between Pentecostalist culture and the environmental culture. We have already shown that this religious movement is to be understood as one of the elements in the historical development of Chile in the twentieth century. Now we wish to ask whether an imported, and therefore foreign, culture is developing within the movement, or whether it is inspired by popular culture, merely transforming its meanings and sometimes modifying its manifestations.

Culture, according to Clyde Kluckhohn and William H. Kelly, is a 'historically derived system of explicit and implicit designs for living, which tends to be shared by all or specially designated members of a group'.[10] This definition clearly indicates the source of a cultural system: designs for living, a collection of ideas, values and norms; but it overlooks one element, which in this case is the most important one, i.e. the material means which act as vehicles for these designs. For Joseph H. Fichter, culture is 'the total configuration of institutions which men have in common in society',[11] and by *institution* he means 'a schematized segment of the type of life'[12] of a group, of which two important characteristics are 'intentionality' (the institution's objective being to satisfy a social need) and permanence.

It is clear that there is a considerable divergence between the collective designs for living of the surrounding society (in which a series of sub-cultures exist, which it was not possible for us to study) and those of the Pentecostalist congregation, which draws them from the Gospel, read in the light of Pentecostalist tradition. But our concern is to show what are the cultural vehicles (institutions or material means, depending on the author) which give the guiding ideas material form, within Pentecostalism, and what relation they bear to the institutions of the cultural context.

In the sociology of Christianity such a study assumes a decisive role because, from its inception, the members of this religion have asked themselves what should be their relation to socio-cultural systems. When it was agreed to summon the Council of Jerusalem (Acts 15), there lay behind the circumcision question another important contest which can be summarized in the question, 'Did a pagan need to become a Jew in order to be able to become a Christian?'

After becoming a nation, Israel had developed a body of concepts and norms which ruled the life of the people in its religious and secular aspects; at the time of the Jewish diaspora this culture became a rallying sign and a mark of identification; the proselyte who acknowledged his faith in Yahweh consented at the same time to a Jewish acculturation; in other words, he agreed to assimilate Jewish culture.[13] It is to this that the Judaeo-Christians referred when they alluded to the Law of Moses (Acts 15: 5) and the text precisely tells us that they belonged to the party of the Pharisees, who are known for the very fact that they fought to preserve Judaism from the 'blemishes' of Hellenism. For them, faith in Christ gave new value to Judaic culture, since it gave to the referends in Judaic culture a fresh interpretation. At the same time Judaic culture took on a universal value: to believe in Christ, one had to become a Jew. Thus two conceptions of Christianity were in opposition over the question of rituals. In Bonhoeffer's terms, one asks whether it is a question of faith or religion. In more sociological language, are the referends (the 'designs for living') which are included in the Christian kerygma inseparably linked with a unique series of expressions (cultural vehicles, institutions)—and does this conjunction (referends + expressions = meanings) alone bear the name of *Christian culture*? Or on the contrary, can the Christian message penetrate, and simultaneously regenerate, any cultural system which will serve it as a vehicle? And will there then be no culture which is either Christian or anti-Christian? At the time of the Council of Jerusalem the question was, 'Can the Christian Church exist outside Judaism, or is it only a Jewish sect?'

The consequence we know: Paul carried the day and his great work was indeed to bear the Gospel into the Graeco-Roman world, demonstrating that Christian belief could be clothed in the most diverse garments. (And some idea of the varieties possible can be gained by comparing the Ethiopian Church with the Calvinist tradition.)[14]

If one applies this schema to Latin American Protestantism, one is driven to two conclusions, which deserve a fuller analysis than the rudimentary sketch which is all we can attempt here.

In the first place, traditional forms of Protestantism (such as Methodism, Presbyterianism and Anglicanism) have—unconsciously—fallen into the Judaeo-Christian heresy, in which moreover they are still swimming, in spite of several bouts of conscience. Conversion to Protestantism implies acceptance of a foreign cultural system, since missionaries show themselves to be totally incapable of separating the Gospel from the clothing which has little by little muffled it up in the West.

Secondly, Chilean Pentecostalism—also unconsciously—has effected a metamorphosis of Western Christianity, by its own spontaneous acculturation, while at the same time it has profoundly altered and renewed what Kluckhohn calls the 'designs for living' of the surrounding milieu. In the following chapter, this process will be illustrated in an examination of the organization of Pentecostalism, its conception and use of authority; here we shall be content with quoting from William E. Carter, who gives a series of pertinent examples of the cultural substitution effected by Pentecostalism:

> . . . not only has Pentecostalism known how to meet a felt need; it has known how to fit its ritual into the culture, while yet maintaining its unquestionably unique identity. For example, its church buildings may be on deserted side streets. But it follows the traditional pattern of religion in the plaza, by constantly holding open air meetings there. It rejects the traditional saint's day processionals, but it preserves the basic idea that one should process in religion. One sees immense groups processing from the evening plaza rally to their Pentecostal temple, singing songs that are accompanied by guitars and that come straight out of the popular music of the masses. It instructs its members to refrain from the frequent evening visits with friends in the neighbourhood bar. But it offers, in its place, nightly, informal services with one's friends at the local temple. It retains extended, private prayer, but it dictates that this should be done in a clearly audible voice. It rejects miraculous healing through the saints, but it claims that divine healing may be easily had by direct prayer to God.[15]

Without a doubt, this integration of Pentecostalism with Chilean culture, with which it enjoys a relationship which is one of both rejection and continuity (either it rejects an institution and replaces it by a new one which fulfils the same latent function, or it borrows the institution and gives it a new meaning) is due to the fact that the original leaders, apart from Hoover, were direct participants in that culture, and that, as Carter remarks, they were at grips with a *problem* (how to survive as a religious group, in their own society) and not preoccupied, like the missionaries, with the application of a *programme*, predetermined and remote-controlled from abroad.[16] Here one can put one's finger on the reason for the ineffectiveness of imported forms of Protestantism and the success of Pentecostalism!

CHAPTER 4

Organization, Authority and the Hierarchy

I. AUTHORITY IN THE PENTECOSTAL CHURCHES

BEING the offspring of Methodism, which they opposed on account of its conception of individual and congregational spiritual life, and not on organizational questions, the Pentecostal Churches will naturally be organized according to the canons of the mother church.

The Methodist Pattern

Whereas in the Middle Ages life was governed by the rhythm of the great religious festivals, under Methodism and its derivatives life is regulated by conferences; in fact the sinews of the Methodist Episcopal Church consist of a set of conferences (see Fig. 4) with, at the summit, the (quadrennial) General Conference, which is in fact if not in law 'the legislative body of the Methodist Church of the U.S.A.',[1] and its missionary appendages suffer under its preoccupation with national questions. At the national level, the highest authority is held by the Annual Conference, to which belong the whole body of pastors and one layman from each pastorate. This body elects the executive: the *Junta General*. In the congregations (local churches), quarterly conferences are held. Liaison with the Annual Conference is assured by the District Conferences, the principal task of the latter being to prepare for the former. At the Annual Conference, chaired by the Bishop, the ordination of new ministers is agreed and pastorates are allocated, a very important function as the Methodist ministry is itinerant. In practice this means that a pastor's life is a gradual migration from the country towards secondary towns, and then to the large centres, Santiago and its two principal churches being the ultimate goal. When that point is reached, one is sufficiently influential for itineration to cease! But this system has the great advantage of enabling the Church to make provision for the country charges. The Annual Conference also appoints the District superintendents, who will constitute the formidable Bishop's Cabinet. The electoral system practised in the congregation is based on the principle of the single list. Whereas in Presbyterianism lists of candidates are invited for vacant posts (and if need be, the lists can be supplemented by appeals) and all members in full communion take part in the election, in Methodism a committee consisting of the pastor and elders pre-selects the candidates, not only for the parish council but for all posts; the list thus drawn up must be agreed to by the superintendent before being submitted to the approval of the participants in the quarterly meeting. Since there is generally only one candidate for each position, this approval is no more than a formality. The obscurity of

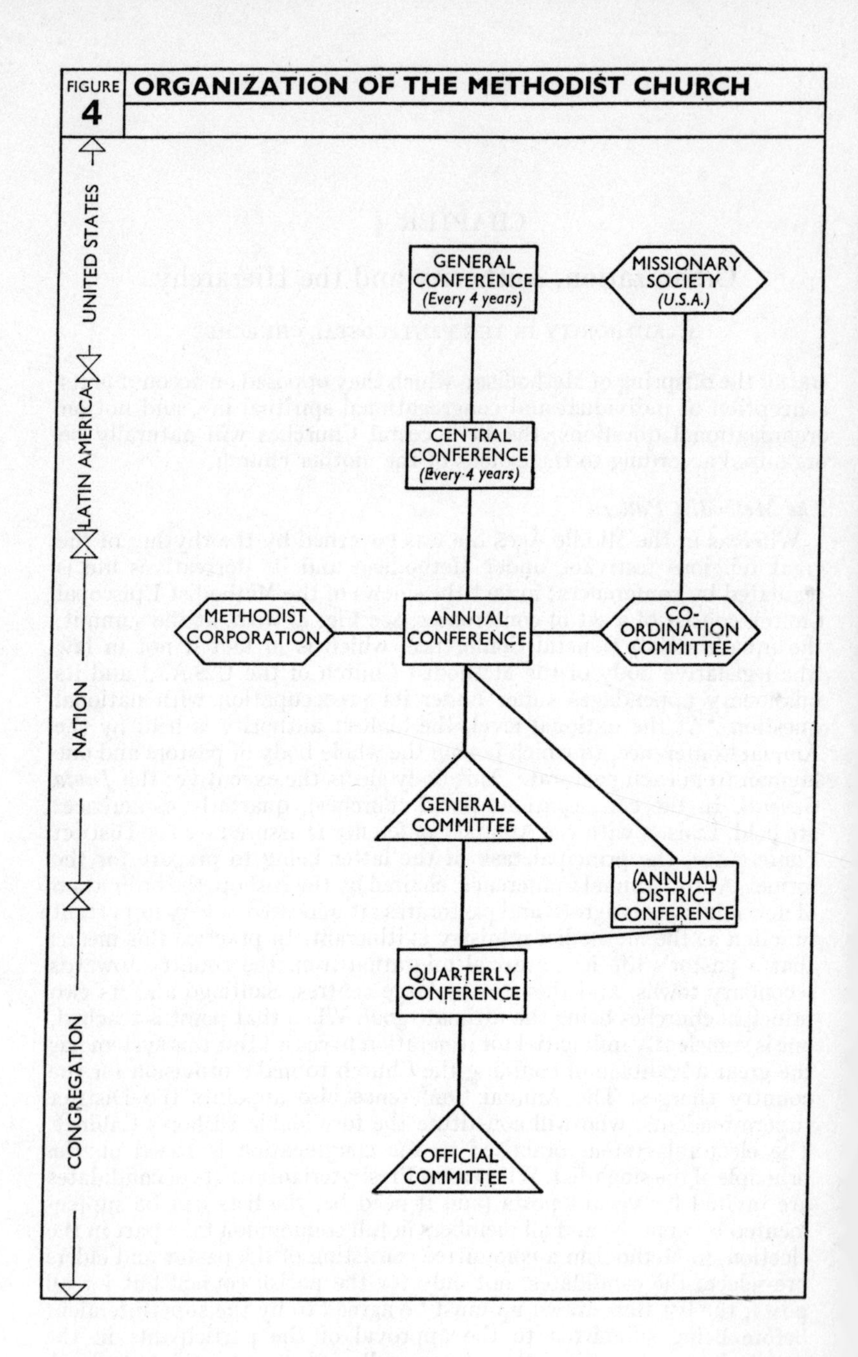

FIGURE 4 **ORGANIZATION OF THE METHODIST CHURCH**

the system is clearly shown in the replies of Methodists in our investigation among the pastors:

Table 1. Electoral system in the Protestant denominations
Question: How is the Junta selected?
(1) By all the members in full communion?
(2) By a chosen group?
(3) By the pastor and elders?

DENOMINATIONS	(1)	(2)	(3)	N.R.	TOTAL
Angl. & Presb. n = 8	88	12	—	—	100
Methodists n = 8	17	50	33	—	100
Pentecostalists n = 61	11	8	71	10*	100

* According to these persons, it is not men but the Holy Spirit who chooses the composition of the Junta.

In fact the Methodists interviewed did not reply in homogeneous fashion, but ultimately more than four-fifths said the junta is chosen from above rather than elected from below. In Methodism the influential members hold the power and one can guess that they transmit it to others like themselves; thus conspicuous innovations in the running of a congregation are ruled out and they short-circuit the 'diffusion of the *élite*'.

Pentecostalist Organization

Conferences also signpost the Pentecostalist year, but the system of decision making—in Methodism already oriented downwards from the summit to the base—is sharply accentuated by the fact that an electoral system is rejected altogether (except in extraordinary circumstances caused, for example, by the death of the leader of the denomination, and the need to find a successor). The council of elders is not elected but recruited by appointment, the pastor, after consulting the council, nominating the new member. The stability of councils is remarkable; there are some which have consisted of the same people for twenty years. For a new appointment to become necessary, an elder must have died, or moved away, or have been in dispute with the pastor and excluded from the congregation.

Parallel to this decision-making circuit, which is vertical and one-way, the allocation of power is rigidly stratified. In the Protestant denominations, as Table 2 shows, the executive consists of the court of elders, of which the pastor is an ex-officio member. Among the Pentecostalists the pastor directs the church and is only *advised* by the junta.

With a few exceptions (as in the *Misión Iglesia Pentecostal*) the junta only 'assists the pastor', who in the last resort makes decisions on his own. Thus the maximization of pastoral power is accompanied by minimization of the power of the council, the composition of which

Table 2. The authority of the congregation

Question: Who directs the church?

DENOMINATIONS	JUNTA	PASTOR & JUNTA	PASTOR	TOTAL
Protestants n = 26	15	77	8	100
Pentecostalists n = 61	2	54	44	100

depends moreover on the pastor who, in the traditional phrase, 'chooses those who have shown themselves to be the most capable and worthy'. Is this pastoral absolutism? Yes and no. A Pentecostalist would assert that election is the act of God and the pastor does no more than recognize and confirm the divine choice.

The Methodist model has facilitated the transition towards a more authoritarian and personal system. Between the Methodist congregation and the Pentecostalist congregation there is not discontinuity but evolution, by the elimination of an electoral system which is in fact only a sham, and by the transition from a paternalistic 'oligarchy' to a paternalistic 'dictatorship'. But it is important to note that this oligarchy and dictatorship are both *voluntarily* accepted by the church members. If Chilean Pentecostalism had been the offspring of the Baptists or Presbyterians, where all the membership in full communion holds sovereign power, such a natural evolution would hardly have been possible, but it could be that, in that situation, the co-existence of a democratic system and the doctrine of charismata would have created an organizational crisis and a revolution.[2] In short, in this evolution Pentecostalism naturally inclines towards the model present in the traditional society, where the chief—whether he be the *cacique* (Indian chief), the *hacendado* (landowner) or *caudillo* (military leader)—is surrounded by advisers (heads of families, trusted men or lieutenants) but he alone holds the power.

In the Chilean Pentecostalist system, all the pastors participate in the Annual Assembly, each accompanied by an elder. The Assembly will reappoint the Directorate of the organization, which consists exclusively of pastors, or if necessary elect new members to vacant places. All the pastor-presbyters (the highest ministerial grade) together form a special body which has control of everything relating to doctrine and the ministry. Though the Directorate has more power than the junta has at the local congregational level, since legally it is the executive body of the denomination, it is usually dominated by the strong personality of the leader—the superintendent or bishop. Just as the pastor is the soul, the 'sociometric star' of the congregation, primarily because he himself created it, in the same way the entire body is incarnate in a leading person with a charismatic halo, who is one of the founders if not the sole founder.

Men like Hoover and Umaña in the *Iglesia Metodista Pentecostal*, like

E. Chavez in the *Iglesia Pentecostal de Chile,* are not just the bearers of a title, they 'are' the denomination—their relationship with it can be described by the concept of 'corporate personality'—and they fulfil the three functions of authoritative roles: they *represent* their movement, they *legitimate* their authority because they know themselves to be called, and they constitute its chief *source of decision.*[3] The fact that these leaders are usually appointed 'for life' will not surprise us. But note: this power structure applies only so long as the chief is also the creator of the movement; as soon as the problem arises of choosing a successor and filling already existing posts, the balance of forces changes in favour of those who claim to be the agents of continuity, the Directorate of the denomination, or the junta of the congregation. The history of Pentecostal communities then enters upon a second phase, which we shall examine later.

2. ACCESS TO THE MINISTRY AND CONGREGATIONAL ORGANIZATION

Power in the Pentecostalist congregations is the monopoly of the pastors. But, in the case of Pentecostalism, who is a pastor? Where are they recruited? How are they prepared? How do they enter the ministry and how do they exercise their ministry? We now wish to deal with the question of power and the directorial functions in a dynamic perspective, for the picture which has just been given might lead one to believe in a rigid and stratified society in which the masses passively submit to the rule of a small ruling class. In that case the Pentecostal communities would be a faithful reflection of the social context to which they belong, a context which—particularly in the rural areas—is marked by polarization into two classes, one a dominant minority and the other the dominated majority. But Pentecostal society presents other characteristics which modify the analogy: the socio-cultural identity of its pastors and laymen; the sub-division of responsibilities and personal participation of each member in the primary function of the congregation, which is evangelization. This is the function around which both the local congregation and the hierarchic allocation of privileges are organized.

(a) *The Parameters of Two Types of Pastor*

Comparing Protestant and Pentecostalist pastors, three criteria differentiate the types: *age, degree of education* and *religious origin.*

More than three-quarters of the Pentecostalist pastors have passed the age of 40 (57 per cent. are over 50), have at best finished primary school and spent their youth in a family totally ignorant of the Protestant faith. At least half of the Protestant pastors are under 40, have completed their secondary education and grown up in a Protestant family.

Of these three essential differences, to which we shall return, the first two (age and education) can be explained as a function of the method of ministerial training prevailing in the two systems. In the Protestant churches the pastor is required to have had a higher educa-

Table 3. Age of pastors

TYPE OF PASTOR	UNDER 30	30–39 YEARS OLD	40–49 YEARS OLD	OVER 50	TOTAL	ACTUAL
Protestant	23	27	15	35	100	26
Pentecostalist	3	15	25	57	100	61

Table 4. Degree of education

TYPE OF PASTOR	INCOMPLETE PRIMARY	PRIMARY COMPLETED	3RD YR. SECONDARY	COMPLETED SECOND.	UNIV. DEGREE	TOTAL	ACTUAL
Protestant	—	15	27	15	43	100	26
Pentecostalist	56	22	15	5	2	100	61

Table 5. Religious Origin

TYPE OF PASTOR	PROTESTANT PARENTS	ONE PARENT PROTESTANT	NEITHER PROTESTANT	TOTAL	ACTUAL
Protestants	58	15	27	100	26
Pentecostalists	16	5	79	100	61

tion, but there is nothing to prevent a young man of 24 who has successfully passed through a theological seminary from being appointed pastor. In the Pentecostal system, on the other hand, there is no educational requirement, but the man who has a vocation must submit himself to a practical apprenticeship which will last a number of years.

It will not be surprising if he is a convert, for the Pentecostalist movement is barely half a century old, is basically missionary, and besides, the age of the pastors in itself makes it improbable that they could belong to the second or third generation.

In contrast, the Protestant system of training for the ministry discourages vocations among adult converts, because of the educational and theological requirements. In our sample, the few Protestant pastors who came from non-Protestant backgrounds were generally converted during adolescence, i.e. young enough to follow the path leading to entry into the ministry.

Though the differentiation in the basic characteristics is easy to understand, it provides us in turn with an important explanatory proposition. The Pentecostal movement is led by *presbyters*, 'elders' in the etymological meaning of the word, in the sense that they have been in the Church for a long time and have had a long life. Now an elderly man is more concerned for the preservation of customs, norms and values than for their reformation; he prefers preservation to renewal; he is the guardian of the tradition which nurtured and formed him. We shall see that the young and vigorous Pentecostal movement is thus subject to the drag of a dictatorial tradition. Besides, the convert—a man who has experienced a radical change of orientation, and transition from a milieu with little or no religious connotations to a society of believers—such a man will be strongly concerned about missionary activities, whereas a man 'born in the Gospel' would confine his function more willingly to the tasks proper to a pastor. The former will look for expansion, the growth of the flock; the second will aim to nurture it better, to encourage its spiritual growth. A missionary tradition will be in opposition to a tradition of succouring the *élite*.

One last criterion, that of socio-occupational origin, gives us two sets of information (see Table 6 on next page).

First, both types of pastor are recruited chiefly from the lower classes, and thus provide two routes for social mobility, though with differing importance. The Protestant path of entry to the ministry permits individuals to better their position not only within their denomination but also on the ladder of society at large, since Protestant pastors belong to the social category of university men. Of course the status of the Protestant pastor is somewhat ambiguous, partly because of his very small income, and partly because Protestantism is regarded as a movement which is foreign, on the fringe, and intended for the proletariat. But it is nevertheless true that this status is raised on account of one objective and recognized factor: his university training. The position of the Pentecostalist pastor is even more ambivalent. His prestige is highest within the Pentecostal movement—where the highest distinction is to serve the Lord—but since the movement is itself on the fringe of Chilean society, the pastor's status in that society will depend entirely on his personality and the way he models his role in relation to the social context. Liston Pope's remark, 'The sects substitute religious status for social status',[4] is absolutely true in the case of Pentecostalism, whereas for a Protestant one of the elements in the pastor's religious status makes his status recognized also in the wider society.

Secondly, whereas 47 per cent. of Pentecostalist pastors come from rural backgrounds (categories 2, 3 and 9 in Table 6), more than one-third of the Protestants come from the urban lower classes (categories 4 and 5). The fact that nearly half the Pentecostalist pastors come from peasant families makes it possible to postulate that the models provided by traditional society will to a certain extent (which needs to be defined) recur in Pentecostalism.

(b) *Access to the Ministry*

'Preparation through study' for the Protestant ministry contrasts with the 'preparation in the streets' of the Pentecostal pastor. Of course, the original leaders had been trained within older churches, but the opinion which Methodists often express, that 'we provide leaders for the Pentecostal movement', is no longer true today. Only 11 per cent. of the pastors in our sample had belonged to another Protestant denomination. Today Pentecostalism recruits and trains its own leaders.

The Methodist pattern

The first clue to the Pentecostal ladder is found in the Methodist type of congregational organization and in its lay hierarchy. The latter is a function of an organization which looks upon itself as a missionary unit, dynamic, ready to expand or even to divide into two, according to the circumstances. In the mission field, the unit is not the parish (geographical criterion) but the congregation (confessional criterion),

Table 6. Socio-occupational Origins, by Categories

	MIDDLE				LOWER						
	UPPER TO MIDDLE	MIDDLE TO LOWER								TOTAL	ACTUAL
	(1)	(2)	(3)	(4)	(5)	(6)	(7)	(8)	(9)		
Protestant	4	12	—	15	23	23	4	15	4	100	26
	(4)	(27)			(69)						
Pentecostalist	5	11	8	5	8	20	5	10	28	100	61
	(5)	(24)			(71)						

(1) University graduates, industrialists and business men, men of independent means.
(2) Small landowners.
(3) Owners of plots of land; middle grade agricultural officials.
(4) Government employees: primary school teachers, police officers, etc.
(5) Employees.
(6) Small tradesmen and independent craftsmen.
(7) Soldiers, seamen and police.
(8) Factory and mine workers.
(9) Agricultural workers.

which uses of a main church building where large-scale meetings are held, and also a number of chapels (which may be places such as barns, a room in a private house, etc.) dispersed throughout the district. These chapels are modestly called 'branches' (*locales*) or sometimes by the picturesque name of *avanzadas* or 'outposts' in infidel territory. One or other of these chapels may grow considerably as a result of the evangelizing zeal of its officers, and will in its turn create a number of 'outposts'. If expansion is not just the result of passing enthusiasm but is maintained over a long period, the 'branch' may be transformed into a church, by the appointment of a committee and a pastor. It then becomes a new congregation, quite independent of that from which it sprang (Fig. 5).[5]

This organization depends on the mobilization of the lay members into a hierarchy. At its base there are a large number of teachers and local preachers. The first are entrusted with the duty of teaching in the Sunday School; the second have been given the right to lead the services and preach the Gospel at them. Each branch, like each church, has its preachers and teachers. The 'outposts' are each in charge of a 'guide', a true lay-pastor, since he directs a group belonging to the congregation, while at the same time carrying on his secular occupation. His powers are nevertheless restricted, for he is under the pastor's direction, and some tasks—celebrating the sacraments and rituals—are the exclusive prerogative of the pastor. The guide is generally also one of the elders of the congregation.

In some cases one also finds assistant pastors (deacons) who either assist the pastor, or assume charge of a particularly large chapel which is shortly to be constituted a congregation. Up to this point the hierarchic line is continuous, and the active and zealous worker would be

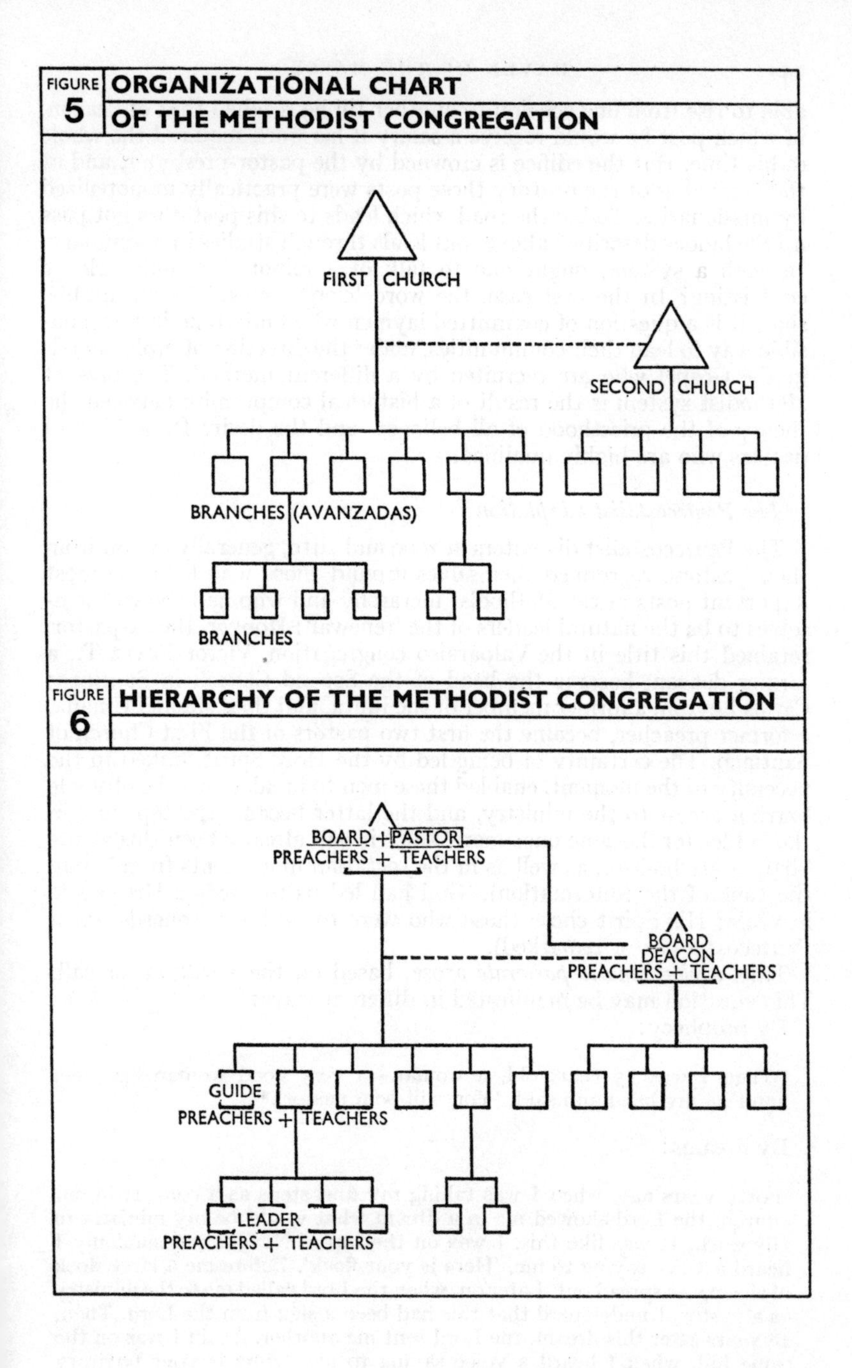

FIGURE 5 ORGANIZATIONAL CHART OF THE METHODIST CONGREGATION

FIGURE 6 HIERARCHY OF THE METHODIST CONGREGATION

able to rise from one echelon to another till he reached that of deacon, in which post he would receive a salary if his work required the whole of his time. But the edifice is crowned by the pastor-presbyter, and at the beginning of the century these posts were practically monopolized by missionaries. Today the road which leads to this post does not pass up the ladder described above, but leads through studies in a seminary. In such a system, ought one to talk of a minor and major clergy co-existing? In the first case, the word 'clergy' would be unsuitable, since it is a question of committed laymen who undertake in a responsible way to lead their communities, under the direction of professionals in the Gospel who are recruited by a different method. The present Methodist system is the result of a historical compromise between the theory of the priesthood of all believers and the desire for a body of pastors who are highly qualified.

The Pentecostalist adaptation

The Pentecostalist dissenters in 1909 and 1910, generally cut off from their pastors, regrouped themselves around those who held the most important posts in the Methodist hierarchy and who had shown themselves to be the natural leaders of the 'renewal': Hoover, the ex-pastor, retained this title in the Valparaiso congregation, Victor Pavez T., a former deacon, became the head of the Second Church in Santiago; Carlos Leyton, a former member of the junta, and then Manuel Umaña, a former preacher, became the first two pastors of the First Church of Santiago. The certainty of being led by the Holy Spirit, linked to the necessity of the moment, enabled these men to break down the obstacle barring access to the ministry, and the latter became the top rung in the ladder (or 'became once more' since it had already been this at the birth of Methodism, as well as in the sectarian movements from before the time of the Reformation). 'God had led us to become His people in Chile; His Spirit chose those who were to be the shepherds' (as a Pentecostal pastor remarked).

Thus a *charismatic pastorate* arose, based on the vocation, or call. This vocation may be manifested in different ways:

By prophecy:

'When I was 15 years old, a woman—a very good woman—put her hand on my head and said, 'You will be a pastor'.[6]

By dreams:

'Forty years ago, when I was taking my first steps as a convert in our church, the Lord showed me in a dream what would be my ministry in His work. It was like this. I was on the top of N. Hill and suddenly I heard a voice saying to me, 'Here is your flock'. Before me a large flock of sheep was spread out. Later on, when the Lord called me to the ministry as a pastor, I understood that this had been a sign from the Lord. Then, 18 years after this dream, the Lord sent me another. Again I was on the same hill, when I heard a voice saying to me, 'Here is your territory (*campo*)'. And from the top of the hill I saw a large part of the American continent. Today I understand that the Lord was showing me my territory as a bishop, and, as we have work (i.e. missions) in Argentina, Paraguay, Bolivia and Chile, I can see clearly that this dream was from God.'[7]

By means of a vow:

'My pastor had sounded me out with a view to being presented to the Annual Conference as a worker available for establishing a new vineyard. I was hesitant myself, because I was in a good profession and was making a good living. Then my wife fell seriously ill and the doctor was unable to cure her. Then I prayed to the Lord and told Him that if He would save my wife, I would give up everything to help to further His work. The very next day my wife was able to get up, and I understood that the Lord had sent me this test, because I had resisted Him.'[8]

Or, more simply, by the slow growth of the certainty of being called.

Nevertheless, before he is able to make his vocation his profession, the Pentecostalist will have to mount the principal rungs of the lay hierarchy, and the ladder is long; he starts soon after his conversion as a preacher in the streets, where he will show the strength of his convictions and the quality of his testimony. It must be noted that in this way all converts, women included, share in this earliest type of ministry; at the beginning they each have an equal chance, being equally responsible for the missionary effort. The hard-working church member will afterwards be put in charge of a Sunday School class and, if he pleases the leaders, he may be entrusted with responsibility for creating and leading a new 'outpost'. That is where he will be able for the first time to demonstrate his charisma; success will be the necessary proof and sufficient proof of his calling, since people are convinced that it is not the man who makes conversions, but the power of God which dwells in him. Thus a vocation which does not bear fruit cannot be of God. This *schema* has moreover a more general import:

The will of God is always fulfilled, and it is thus that one can recognize true dreams, prophecies or vocations.[9]

At this stage, the convert may be able at last to proclaim his vocation, and his pastor will propose his name at the next Conference as a 'worker', the lowest of the lay grades leading to the pastoral hierarchy. If he is accepted, he will be 'sent to a new vineyard' to establish a new branch. He will start work—as we were told many times—'praying and going down into the street and proclaiming the Gospel there'. Here we see the strongest root of the power and prestige enjoyed by the Pentecostal pastor of today among his members: he himself has called them and gathered them, it is he who was the 'instrument of their salvation'.

If the 'worker' establishes a branch, then he will be appointed 'pastor on trial', then pastor-deacon, the first truly pastoral grade, since one is admitted to it by ordination (which has a symbolic and not a sacramental significance).

As a man ascends the hierarchical ladder, so he progressively abandons his secular occupation. Whereas in Brazil the majority of the

Pentecostal pastors have a subsidiary occupation, which provides them with a livelihood, the majority of the Chileans—in the two principal denominations this is the rule—are paid by their congregations, which devote the tithes to this purpose.[10] It is probable that at the time of the schism in 1909 the movement, stamped with the Methodist pattern, would not even have envisaged that its pastors would be able to provide for their own support. However, the breakaway from the mission deprived the congregations of all external financial help. Manna no longer came from the United States. It was then that the practice of tithing was revived, and the way in which it is kept up witnesses to the enthusiasm and devotion of the church members. The tithe—we shall return later to this question—is considered to be the 'property of the pastor, whether it be great or small, for covering his expenses and his needs' (interview with a leader), the general expenses of the church being covered by collections. As the pastor himself comes from the ranks of the congregation, his needs are similar to theirs and, starting from there, a rapid calculation leads to the conclusion that, if the members really give a tenth part of their own income, ten families would be sufficient to ensure that the pastor would have an income equal to the average income of those families.

In the *Iglesia Metodista Pentecostal* it is estimated that 50 per cent. of the tithe is paid; one pastor told us, 'One must not make too strict a law of it, in the first place so as not to discourage members who are still weak, and secondly because some families are really too poor to be able to pay it'. But even so, twenty families (which would represent an average congregation of 100 people) would be able to assure the pastor's salary. The practice of tithing was the secret of Pentecostal financial autonomy—a situation which the Protestant denominations in South America have to this day never really achieved. Another advantage is that the success of a candidate for the pastorate can be checked on the financial level; he must be able to give up his occupation, in order to devote himself entirely to his new duties. If he achieves this, he can be ordained.

In the Pentecostalist system, access to the ministry thus depends on vocation, and the demonstration of this vocation in a channel which induces a process of natural selection (one can guess what human qualities are necessary) which is interpreted as being supernatural.

> 'We take the men who seem to us to be the most suitable, and we send them into the country; if the work produces results, then they are called to the ministry; if it has no results, they are not called and they go back home,' explained a superintendent.

The leaders, taking as their basis the doctrine of the necessary fruit of the gifts bestowed by the Holy Spirit, are in a position to supervise the charisma, and to command an organization which is both healthy and dynamic, since the congregation will have a licensed pastor only if it is able to contribute to his needs, and since the aspiring pastor must gather round him a sufficient number of members to achieve his goal. No congregation—no pastor; no pastor—no congregation!

Every Pentecostalist, we have stated, shares in the collective ministry of the congregation. Every ordinary member is required to devote his free time to the work; the pastors are the authentic expression of the congregation, and the thing which distinguishes them from the mass of members is not their social origin or their way of living or their intellectual attainments, but simply certain qualities they have as leaders of men.

In the new situation created by Pentecostalism, some men who would probably have remained 'in the ranks' are revealed as natural leaders.

This is the great difference between the Pentecostalists and the Protestant pastors, who constitute an *élite* caste on account of their intellectual training. This is also what makes it difficult to consider the Pentecostalist pastor—no matter what authority he holds—as a *cleric*, a concept which would be contrasted with that of the *laity*, whereas in fact he is simply a church member who has reached the top of the ladder, while the whole community continues to bear the evangelistic ministry.

There is one variant of this pastoral ministry, where the charisma is subject to no control other than that of a minimum degree of success. This is in the small, ephemeral churches (mushroom churches) whose members are grouped around a personality; they have generally originated in some schism but have not succeeded in achieving a sufficient size to become organizations with legal status. These congregations, which are innumerable and impossible to count because of their precarious existence, often comprise only a few families, twenty or so members, and the pastor has to continue to carry on a supplementary occupation. On the death of the pastor, the group disappears; either its members scatter, or it fuses with another larger movement. The problem of these 'pastors', who have been the cause of evangelical churches multiplying, should be studied at the same time as the problem of schism.

The manner in which future pastors are trained is inspired by the example of the first four centuries of the Church, before any seminaries were founded. It is comparable to the 'training at the anvil' which master craftsmen used to give their apprentices. The apprenticeship is carried out in the setting of collaboration between master and pupils; the latter listen and observe the master, whom they will *imitate*, and the quality of their training depends on the quality of the master. It is clear that for the Pentecostalist pastor intellectual training (which in any case is hindered by his lack of school education) will be neglected in favour of practical training: how to preach, how to conduct services, how to organize the congregation and its missionary work, and also how a pastor should behave, how to fulfil his role, how to speak, dress, greet people. Imitation (that concept dear to G. Tarde) has a primordial validity, as is shown in the following conversation between an investigator and a pastor on trial (aged over 60; he was only just beginning his pastoral career) in the *Iglesia Metodista Pentecostal*:

Pastor: 'I have learned well what the Gospel is; I know what it is.'
Investigator: 'And what is it?'
Pastor: 'I come from the Jotabeche Church; my pastor was the Bishop, Brother Umaña. *He* knew what the Gospel was. The teaching there was better than anywhere else, on how things should be done, how one ought to preach, or lead the ceremonies. And I learned everything there.'
Investigator: 'And why is the teaching there better than anywhere else?'
Pastor: 'Because it is the mother church, the first in the mission, and the person who founded the mission was there, our Bishop who had revelations and particular gifts.'

Analysis of this passage underlines the role of a tradition which is oral rather than written, where the nearer one is to the source, i.e. the founders, the nearer one is to the truth which has to be transmitted and which consists in not only a message but a whole system of norms, values and customs that rank as revealed truths. Imitation validates tradition which, reinforced by the doctrine of the Holy Spirit, may take precedence over Scriptural authority.

In the sociological perspective, which is the one we are adopting, whereas analysis of the power structure sheds light on the *parallel* with the social context, study of the recruitment of leaders stresses above all the *differences*, since Pentecostalist society offers new possibilities for social achievement and responsible integration. In this, Pentecostalism opens a serious breach in the rigid stratification of Chilean society, providing the model of communities in which, *a priori*, each member has the same chance of one day reaching the summit of the hierarchy.

3. MODELS FOR THE PENTECOSTALIST PASTOR AND THE EXERCISE OF AUTHORITY

While examination of the *distribution* of power emphasizes above all the continuity between Pentecostalist society and Chilean society, study of the route of *access* to power shows a discontinuity. What is the situation in regard to the *exercise* of authority?

In every town and village in Chile, at the end of the afternoon and the early evening, the traveller will see men passing by with the lined faces of miners or farmers, often showing signs of Indian blood, dressed in dark clothes with a black tie, and wearing hats. A Bible in their hands, they walk along, from time to time greeting others whom they pass. These are the Pentecostal pastors and elders going to their church. From the Peruvian frontier to Patagonia, they all have the same way of walking, the same manners. The observer who follows them into their churches and sees their activities and converses with them will often have the impression of finding himself confronted by copies made from a single pattern. The Pentecostal pastor plays a role which half a century of history has to a large extent congealed, a role transmitted to him by his former pastor and which he in turn will pass on to those whom he sends out to the conquest of fresh souls. But where did this role originate? What model inspired it? What margin of freedom does it allow to those who fill it? Today the role determines the man, from which arises the identical pattern of behaviour followed by the pastors and the similarity of the image of a pastor held by the church members. But not so long ago men were creating this role, and we must try to grasp its genesis.

According to its critics, Pentecostalism favours the development of *caudillismo*, 'the bane of our Latin American countries'. Foreigners agree with the critics and regret that 'the Latin American mentality is so ill-adapted to democratic customs, even within the churches'.[11] The term *caudillo*, the Spanish equivalent of the German *Führer*, cannot properly be applied to the pastor, since it means above all a military and political chief;[12] but taken in a parabolic sense, it relates to a charismatic and authoritarian leader, and the Pentecostalist pastor does belong to this type. But before we attribute the emergence of a pastoral *caudillismo* to a peculiarity (which is partly true), we must recall that in Chile (which was considered a pagan or idolatrous country) Protestantism was created out of the activities of missionaries, and that however much it has been nationalized, it is still descended from a foreign operation.

(a) *The Missionary Model*

The missionary comes as the bearer of truths which he aspires to share with others. He has a message, a revelation to communicate. From the first he thinks of himself as different and ultimately superior, even though he is truly humble, since he enjoys a privilege which others do not have and to which they cannot attain except through him. It is vain for him to claim to be simply a messenger, a lieutenant of some other person who himself is the Lord; the missionary is nevertheless the one who speaks and takes the place of that other person, and the path leading to that other person passes through him. He does not consider himself to be more than the humble representative of the Master, but those who listen to him look upon him as the one who makes the presence of the Master real. Whatever may be the missionary's personality or the distance he has put between himself and his own culture, whatever the respect he may acquire for the culture of the country in which he is working, however far he may go in demythologizing the Gospel, in his effort to differentiate the Good News from its socio-cultural vehicles, the earliest relationship established between him and his hearers is a one-way vertical relationship going from the one who knows to the ones who must learn, from the one who is in possession to those who must take possession, from the evangelist to the evangelized, in short from the master to the disciples, since out of this relationship a community will spring up.[13] Of course the missionary is not the founder of a religion, and so not exactly a master in Mensching's sense, but the relationship which unites him with the converts goes far beyond the ties between a doctor and his pupils, which 'are oriented towards objective realities',[14] i.e. some kind of instruction, in which it is of secondary importance whether the pupil does or does not believe. In the case of the missionary, it is not primarily a question of a doctrine, but of salvation, of which the only witness and guarantee is the missionary himself. Thus the relation which is established between himself and his hearers is oriented towards the *person* of the missionary; 'it is his personal life which constitutes in its breadth and depth the point of contact'.[15] Jesus called men to follow Him; the missionary proclaims the Lord and Saviour, Jesus Christ, which means in practice that, at least for a time, His representative must be followed.

Before speaking of the atmosphere of authoritarianism in mission fields, it is essential to establish that, however perfect it may be, *missionary work* by its very nature cannot avoid creating *a body of authoritarian relationships*, around which the nascent community will be organized.

But the thing which could have been avoided has not been avoided either; until very recently vocation was the only important factor for going to distant countries in order to proclaim the Good News. One cannot make a complaint against the first generation of missionaries, for social science and historical criticism were then in their infancy and could not help them. The result was that the missionaries set out to proclaim the Gospel, but at the same time they spread abroad a society and culture which they believed to be Christian. There were exceptions, but we must acknowledge that Africa, Asia and Latin America are still waiting for Christians who, like St. Paul, will know how to transpose the message into the local cultural system. But analysis of this phenomenon is today a commonplace, so let us leave it and pass on. For our purpose it is more important to state its effect: *the reinforcement to an extreme degree of authoritarian relationships*. The missionary is not only the person who proclaims the Gospel; he also holds the secret of 'how to do it': how to preach, how to organize Christian society and create its hierarchy, how to behave, how to speak, dress, live as a Christian. He is a walking Christian encyclopedia. If he is convinced (and most of the time he is) that the society in which he is working bears the mark of sin and paganism in all its parts, he will try to create a Christian society, and will hustle those who listen to him out of the one and into the other. The neophyte is set at loggerheads with his social group, then cut off from it, and, totally disoriented (converted!), he will have only one support on which he can thoroughly depend: the missionary. The result of missionary activity will be, as an I.S.A.L. working group declares, 'the impressive uniformity of Protestantism in Latin America, where it has created a common Protestant sub-culture at the expense of isolation'.[16]

Missionary authoritarianism provides both the precedent and the inspiration for Pentecostalist *caudillismo*. Even in our own day, however much it may be disputed, the missionary is a figure who is watched and imitated. This is particularly striking in the North American Pentecostal missions (*Iglesia de Dios*, *Asambleas de Dios*), which, like the Chilean denominations, are directed towards the masses. We have seen a Chilean pastor going into a service solemnly carrying a camera, because missionaries are never without one. We have heard church members in a congregation led by a North American speak with a slight English accent and use the verb *ser* in preference to *estar*, because the pastor does not know the use of these two forms of the Spanish verb 'to be'. Even for an independent Pentecostalist, the foreign missionary is a personality who is observed and imitated.

The figure of the missionary, that is the man who introduced Protestantism to Chile, is not the only model for the Pentecostal pastor, but it is no less decisive on that account, since the first Pentecostalists were the children of Methodist missionaries.

When Pastor Hoover writes, 'This church was able to show that a church which had been *faithful to one pastor* could be faithful to his successor',[17] he is acting a role already clearly defined, paternalistic and authoritarian, and his historic destiny was to incarnate the transition from missionary to pastor, since he was both the one and the other.

(b) *Biblical Imagery*

Of course the missionary will try—especially if he is a Presbyterian or Baptist, less so if he is Methodist—to educate his church so that it will one day be able to govern itself, by means of an elected council. Will he, by this attempt at democratization, be breaking the authoritarian mould which his presence alone made inevitable, or will he not be falling into the paradoxical situation of imposing from above—that is in an authoritarian manner—a form of democratic government? This ambiguity was emphasized by the I.S.A.L. document already quoted:

> The introduction of a democratic concept of government in ecclesiastical institutions, within a society which is accustomed to authoritarian habits in religious affairs, produces some quite dramatic situations of cultural conflict—conflict between the democratic theory introduced by the missionary and his paternalistic and authoritarian habits, he being regarded as the incarnation of the truth and tradition in religious affairs . . .[18]

There is another legitimate question which South American believers do not fail to ask: Can a certain democratic electoral system be raised to the rank of *the* Christian system of ecclesiastical government? It is acknowledged that the importance of the laity in the Reformed tradition is largely due to the political and religious roles (the two were often combined) played by the bourgeois at the time of the Reformation, just as the egalitarianism of the Anabaptist communities in the sixteenth century and the English sects of the eighteenth century was nourished by the communistic views of the masses who were in rebellion against the social cleavages of their day. Ecclesiastical democracy bears the stamp of the process of the churches' acculturation to their day and their geographical region.

There is another aspect: the missionary and the Pentecostal pastor are two variants of a model found in the Bible, which (inspired by a stable, agrarian society) speaks of shepherd, father, master, patriarch, and puts forward a relationship of love, naturally, but an imperious love. The titles of pastor (shepherd) in the Protestant tradition, and the Catholic abbé (father, papa: these three words have the same etymology), suggest roles which can be included in the framework of paternalistic relations and the Pentecostalist will find in his naïve reading of the Bible the legitimation of his pastoral role; is it not literally nearer to the scriptural sources and thus more faithful than that of the Presbyterians and Baptists, and does not the Pentecostalist system (with its pastors, elders, church members and gentiles) reproduce more faithfully the Biblical relationship between Jesus, His disciples, the believers and the 'race of unbelievers'?

(c) *The* hacendado *Model*

This rapid phenomenology of the missionary shows that the Pentecostal pastor has imitated the missionary manner of exercising power, rejecting only the democratic mask, a procedure which he can legitimate with Biblical examples.

Both the missionary pastor and the Pentecostal pastor are figures of 'leaders', the second of which should be regarded as heir to the first. Though they are opposed to one another in their manner of organizing the church, it is just because (whether they wish it or not) they are the bearers of two different cultures and, by the same token, their systems of reference are different. The missionary, bearer of Western democratic values, imposes a formal democracy which from the outset moves with squeaking wheels, first because he puts himself above the system, which in turn is a foreign body introduced into the cultural context, and finally because, in developing countries, to practise formal democracy accentuates the social stratification by in fact restricting authority to those with the most education. The relative failure of Protestant missions is due to their incapacity for identifying themselves with the cultural context, and the fact that they are appendages of foreign societies. It was the luck of the Pentecostal pastor, though nourished on missionary milk, to have been the rebellious son who was given his freedom and had to survive by his own efforts. Since he is also the bearer of a culture—in this case the surrounding, national culture in which the model of authority is provided by the figure of the *hacendado*—he will borrow certain features from the latter and also fulfil certain of his functions.

According to J. Medina,[19] the *hacienda*, the great landed estate, not only gave to Latin America its predominantly rural character but also forged that character at a deeper level, 'that of its social—or if one prefers, its human—substance'. It created a social structure in which customs were crystallized around three beliefs:

> Belief in the warm value of human relationships, belief in the support which should not be lacking in any moment of crisis, belief in the unknown and therefore unlimited power of the chief.

As we have already shown in Part I, the harsh passage from a stable to a dynamic society, from authority based on tradition to authority based on law, with all the social changes which that implies, has produced a crisis affecting the model of authority which rests on the relationship of protection and obedience, and produced also a loss of faith in it:

When these beliefs collapse, substitute ideas—intellectual orientations—must be quickly constructed from one's own experience. Where shall one rediscover the trust of one's peers and good will of one's neighbours? Whom can one rely upon in illness, in the difficulties caused by a spell of unemployment or in the face of the vagaries of authority and unintelligible laws? Above all, where shall one again find counsel to guide one in the agonizing chaos of a confused world? The best contemporary observers in Latin American countries place the emphasis on this phenomenon and all agree on one word—uprootedness—to describe the psycho-social state of large groups of people, both rural and urban.[20]

This can all be summed up in one single problem:

The vacuum created by the extinction or deterioration of traditional paternalism, the painful gap produced when an institution collapses before its replacement is ready. The *customs* of the old paternalism provide a support—limited, perhaps, but none the less real—against psychological anxiety; today's public and semi-public *organizations* —state, municipality or trade union—yield help which from the sentimental point of view is cold and impersonal, but more effective, because it is calculable and foreseeable. On the road from the one to the other, not always short, lie nothing but anguish and despair,[21]

and also, the author adds elsewhere, nostalgia for the father who has been lost or rejected.

These quotations describe both the model, the trial it is undergoing and the persistence of its image. Pentecostalism has come on the scene at the very time of the 'road between'; it puts forward a reconstitution of the great family represented by the *hacienda*; it validates personal relationships by giving them a brotherly dimension and an elating finality—the service of God; it reaffirms the principle of mutual aid and support; and for the deteriorated image of the *hacendado* whose tyranny was no longer counterbalanced by the protection he gave, it substitutes the image of the pastor, the protective father, who dispenses salvation, the source of whose power is not unknown but acknowledged by each, since it comes from a God who is regarded as present, active and all-powerful.

By breathing into the image new values and goals, Pentecostalism has provided a new, vigorous legitimation for the persisting image of the *patron* in South American society; the pastor, a new personality in Chilean society, fulfils a function which social change has not eliminated but left vacant, to the great peril of the masses.

The missionary, Biblical imagery, and the *hacendado*—there are the three models which affect the creation of the Pentecostal pastor's image in Chile. He owes his existence to the missionary, but, stamped by his own culture, he has pruned the foreign elements from the model he inherited, and has created an authoritarian role which Holy Scripture justifies. One may say that the Pentecostal leader performs his role according to the Chilean tradition of authority, but he himself will, with justice, claim to be following the Biblical tradition.

The missionaries, their disciples and the national Protestant pastors are differentiated from the Pentecostal pastor by their *manner of exercising authority* on the one hand, and on the other by their *system of pastoral training*. Here the terms continuity/rupture may need to be reversed, depending on whether one is speaking of the Pentecostalist congregation or the Protestant congregation. In the latter, the aim is to allocate power according to a foreign pattern (rupture with the cultural context); in the former, power is exercised according to the canons of Chilean tradition (continuity). On the other hand, in Protestantism the possibility of reaching the summit of the hierarchy, the pastorate, can only be grasped during adolescence, and pastoral training introduces the candidate to a defined social stratum which separates him from the lower classes to which the body of believers belong. Here Protestant society is reintroducing a watertight social stratification separating clergy from laity, which is not unlike the stratification of the traditional rural society, where the small number of leaders and property owners stand over against the proletarian masses who live under their direction (continuity).[22] As for Pentecostalism, it breaks down all caste systems, eliminates all barriers within the hierarchy, and, though the pastor performs the role of *patron*, this role has been made potentially accessible to every member (discontinuity). Making a comparison, as has just been done, from the point of view of the exercise of power and the chances of access to power, between our two types of religious society in the context of the global society (Chilean society), the following table is obtained:

EXERCISE OF POWER		SOCIAL
AUTOCRATIC	DEMOCRATIC	STRATIFICATION
Traditional Chilean society	Protestant Community	Watertight
Pentecostal Community		Without barriers

And by the same token one can grasp one of the reasons why Pentecostalism corresponds more closely to Chilean needs than classic Protestantism, since it perpetuates the traditional pattern of power while opening up access to the functions of leadership.

4. THE LIMITS OF THE PASTOR'S AUTHORITY AND THE PROBLEM OF SCHISM

The western observer, accustomed to a society in which democracy exists by law side by side with a socio-economic stratification that hinders it from being applied in practice, is overwhelmed by Pentecostal society. He discovers in it, to begin with, a strict hierarchy in which each echelon has its own representative symbols and its own, well-defined, portion of power, always being exercised by the higher grades over the lower ranks. But he finds, too, after closer study, that the chief leader, the pastor-*caudillo*, is the expression of his group, with which he is completely identified both through his social origins and his educational level; he is the guide, naturally, but he is also the model to which everyone can—if God wills—one day attain. Pentecostal society thus seems to be organized in a hierarchy but to be without class.

Power (taken here in the most usual sense) is the capacity which person A has to make B do something which he would not have done without A's intervention.[23] Since the time of Hegel and his famous pages on the dialectic of master and slave, it has been known that even the most absolute power has limits. The definition of Pentecostalist society—a community in which members associate voluntarily—gives the contours of the leaders' power; if a pastor is in conflict with the leader of the denomination, if a member disagrees with his pastor, each of them has the possibility of leaving the denomination or congregation respectively. In a strictly congregationalist system, in which each congregation is totally independent of the others, the superintendent (bishop or president—his title may vary) has no direct authority except over the congregation of which he is pastor; his hold over the other congregations depends on his authority over the pastors who are their immediate leaders. The goal of the Pentecostal denomination being to save souls, the national leader's prestige will be proportionate to the number of his supporters, and similarly the power of a pastor in relation to his superintendent will depend on the number of members he represents. Contrary to general opinion in Chile, the supreme leader of a Pentecostal denomination does not make decisions 'as seems good to him'; quite the opposite, and the more important a decision is, involving the whole movement and having repercussions in every congregation in the country, the more the leader will take his pastors' views into account. Though his pastors unanimously look upon the Roman Catholic Church as the incarnation of heresy and paganism, a leader of great prestige may certainly take it upon himself to pay a visit to the Cardinal Archbishop of the Roman Catholic Church (as happened in August 1965), provided no decision will result from such a meeting. (And again, in spite of the circumspection surrounding that visit, it aroused a certain amount of internal unrest.) Paradoxically the wish to preserve the unity of the movement exercises such pressure that a majority vote is not sufficient; decisions must be unanimous. Pastor Theo Tschuy, who established the *Ayuda Christiana Evangélica* relief office in Chile, gives the following description of the method of decision-making in the upper echelons of a Pentecostalist organization:

> When I had a request to make to the *Iglesia Metodista Pentecostal*, the bishop summoned his cabinet. I would present my business and he opened the debate, letting his pastors speak without ever intervening directly. When my presence was no longer required, all the necessary explanations having been given, I was allowed to leave, a time having been appointed when the answer would be given me. Out of curiosity, I tried to find out how a decision was reached, and since I knew each of the members of the *Directorio*, it was easy to enquire. I found that a decision was always based on the general consensus of opinion. If a consensus was not reached, but the bishop felt that it could be, he would ask me for more time. If not, his answer was negative. (Interview with Pastor T. Tschuy.)[24]

This search for unity is fundamental, and if the 'leader' does not respect it he risks a schism or at all events repudiation, as in the following case, in which it was moreover Bishop Umaña, the man with the highest prestige in Pentecostalism, who was involved. Several prophecies were in circulation concerning him, one of which said that he was the man who would bring about the unity of the Christian churches.[25] When the Second Vatican Ecumenical Council was first announced Bishop Umaña made the following statement to the press:

> I consider the Pope's initiative very positive and opportune. In the first place, the representatives of all the churches will be able to discuss on an equal footing, and thus we shall know what are the objectives pursued by the Roman Catholic Church and what are the consequences of this invitation. In any event—and here I speak for myself—I am in favour of an agreement between all the churches on unity, each preserving its own rites and ceremonies . . . (July 2, 1959).

In spite of their cautiousness, these words aroused an outcry within the denomination, and the newspaper published a statement:

> Although our bishop is the highest authority in the Church, his statement has no validity without the signatures of the Directorio of the mission, for it is not a single individual but a corporate body which rules the church in Chile . . . (*Chile Pentecostal*, May 1960).[26]

We were able to verify the existence of this consensus when important decisions are to be taken. At the beginning of April 1965, the *Comunidad Teológica Evangélica* in Santiago was inaugurated. In the creation of this institution for theological training, some of the Pentecostalist denominations have been active participants. However, there was a suspicion that the decision came from the national leaders who, perhaps, without being followed by their pastors, saw in this *Comunidad* a means of extending their prestige beyond the bounds of their organization. The sample in our investigation included three Pentecostalist organizations which were members of the *Comunidad* and one which was not, the *Iglesia Metodista Pentecostal*. As Table 8 shows, the pastors of the first three are in favour of the introduction of a theological school, while the I.M.P. pastors are divided.[27]

Table 8. Pentecostalist Participation in a Theological Seminary

Question: Do you think that for training its pastors your denomination should choose the system followed by the 'historic' churches, that is, establish, or share in establishing, a seminary, where future pastors would spend several years taking courses?

	YES	NO	TOTAL
I.M.P. n = 26	46	54	100
Others n = 35	91	9	100

This analysis leads to a clear result: the Pentecostal leader, though he is a charismatic leader, is not a despot. *He cannot be one*, on pain of finding himself at the head of a body of absolutists. He may be very influential and persuasive, but cannot do without the freely-given consent of his subordinates. This limitation makes Pentecostal church government much more truly collegial than it appears. So long as a minority is opposed, even though it is small, a decision concerning the direction of the mission can only be deferred, and this is exactly what is happening today regarding membership of the I.M.P. in the World Council of Churches.

What has been said above concerning decision-making at the highest level is also true at the congregational level. Here the pastor has immediate control over the central church, but relations with the members in the 'outposts' are mediated through the guides. Here, too, it is necessary to seek for a consensus; even though the elders are only the pastor's advisers, and even though the committee does not proceed by voting, the pastor must wait until he has convinced his assistants before committing himself. This process is not a derivative of western democracy, nevertheless it merits the adjective 'democratic'. As Theo Tschuy stresses, it is a transposing of a custom of Indian society, in which the *cacique* also depends on the agreement of each of the heads of family (which is the reason for the custom of holding palavers) if he wants to avoid splitting the clan.

This description ought to dispel (at least this is our hope) the prejudice of Chilean Protestants, proud of their 'advanced' method of government, in regard to the Pentecostalist organization. This prejudice is, moreover, only a transposition of the prejudice which governs the attitude of the members of so-called civilized nations towards the culture of so-called 'primitive' countries. It is the prejudice of the old-time missionary in a pagan country. Without stressing the fact that only the Pentecostalists have an organization adapted to the cultural and social context, let us correct what we said at the beginning of the chapter concerning the diffusion of decisions and orders. Naturally decisions are taken at the summit and transmitted to the base, but the base influences the first echelon of the hierarchy, and the latter has a certain weight and power with the second, and so on. The power of a small branch's guide, of a pastor, a bishop, of each member of the hierarchy, depends on the freely given recognition of the members, who can always withdraw it from him and challenge his authority. The foundation of the Pentecostalist congregation, of which one becomes a member by conversion, is the conscientious participation of every one.

But how do the Protestant denominations (which are also voluntary associations) differ from the Pentecostalist? First of all, in that their existence depends as much, if not more, upon foreign aid as upon the national members. To take an extreme situation, the Methodist Church in Chile would not contain more than a very small number of members, if the Missionary Society did not maintain a whole series of institutions (schools and hospitals, etc.), and parachuted in missionaries to give the church a fresh start. In other, less extreme, cases, the lack of national pastors, stagnation of congregations, the tiny number of members, even while a missionary society is offering substantial help in men and money, proves that the Methodist or Presbyterian member's participation in his church does not have the same quality or intensity as that of the Pentecostalist. Here again we think one of the keys to the rise of Pentecostalism is that this movement allows everyone the feeling of participating in the exercise of power and in the vitality of the movement.

One final piece of retouching must be done to this picture. While the pastor's power is recognized by a sort of social contract in which individuals are integrated in a hierarchized whole that extends beyond themselves, and while that power may be exposed to pressures or be questioned since it is not guaranteed by any law, it is not on that account any less real or effective. Pentecostalism substitutes for an authority originating in tradition an authority with charismatic legitimation, it symbolizes the old image of the 'patron' by replacing faith in obedience by obedience to the faith, and in doing this it gives new life to the *relationship of dependence* which is the primary axis of a nascent community. The disciple of the man who has revealed God to him will lose his critical faculty with regard to his master, who provides him with an example, an ideal and a goal. For as long as empathy exists between church members and pastor, the latter remains the centre of a network of personal relationships tinged with affection, and his authority will not be exposed to any challenge. The pastor's secret will be to know how to maintain and extend his network of loyalties, his aim being not to destroy the almost worshipful confidence of his disciples in him through imposing a decision, but to make them share the new outlook which he wishes to impart to the community (concerning ecumenical affairs, theological training, etc.), convincing them of its value and urgency, presenting it as the product of a divine revelation, or else by a more rational process setting out the benefits which would result for the community from such a decision. To the leaders belong the initiative, the explanations and finally the execution, while the congregation's part is limited to agreeing to the initiative. The decision-making circuit starts from the summit and comes back to it, but even if the role of the disciples in this process is only a passive one, this control does function, as is borne out by the leaders' patience in regard to projects they have at heart, for, as one of them said, 'the time is not yet, my people would not understand'.

Having analysed the questions of authority and of the way it is exercised, we may now turn to two connected problems, that of the succession and that of schism.

The Succession

Up to this point our observations have been concerned with the first phase in the history of a Pentecostalist denomination or congregation, in which the community forms around a man who proclaims the Gospel to it. The power of this man rests on his creative activity; his members are indebted to him for what they are. But what happens when this supervisor disappears? The very existence of an organization which is pivoted on the *Annual Conference* and an embryo form of administration, the *Directorio*, determines the process of succession. During the early stages the lieutenants with the highest prestige, who are members of the *Directorio*, rally their troops, look for ways of extending their spheres of influence by creating a network of clients and by emphasizing the part they played with the late leader. In the churches, particularly in the central church, prophecies erupt, often contradictory. But it is plain that all those who will be responsible for choosing the new leader invoke the authority of the Holy Spirit and await a clear sign from Him. Even if ultimately the Annual Conference proceeds to an election, this will only take place once the result has been assured, a result which will demonstrate that a general consensus has been reached. Here again the seeking of a consensus is fundamental, for two reasons. On the one hand, this alone can bear witness to the pastors' loyalty to the Holy Spirit's will, which could not have two candidates, and on the other, it is the only way of avoiding the division of the movement into two or more parts. The time required for the choosing of a successor may extend over a year or more. In these proceedings the profane and the sacred are intermingled; acts of utter humility and devotion, mixed with rather despicable bargaining; the almost commercial competition of those with ambitions, against the disinterested acts of a pastor with no personal ambition who tries to bridge the gap between rivals and bring to their minds the seriousness of the denomination's position.

At the beginning of 1965 the question of a successor to Bishop Umaña was decided only two days before the Annual Conference. There were two candidates in the lists, one of them being considered the spiritual heir of the late bishop. Local congregations were eager to know who was to be their bishop and were asking for a decision. It seemed that this candidate would win the day, but no consensus could be reached. A schism might then have occurred, for a minority was violently opposed to this person whom they considered unworthy; among other doubtful acts, this man, who was a rich merchant as well as a pastor, was thought to be using part of his personal fortune to 'convince' electors. In the week before the election this pastor was gaoled on the charge of misuse of government money.[28]

His arrest routed his supporters and was interpreted as the work of the Holy Spirit, who thus indirectly showed whom He had chosen. The other candidate, Pastor M. Mancilla of Temuco, was accordingly appointed bishop.

The new leader succeeds to a post and rank which are absolutely identical with those of his predecessor. However, one suspects that the role he inherits and the corresponding authority will undergo a profound change. We have said that the power of a leader is upheld by the prestige which the person has gained as founder of a movement or a congregation. The original chief established the institutions and appointed the men who run them; his successor is appointed by these men and institutions. The founder asked for their assistance; the authority of his lieutenants derived, in part at least, from his authority.

But now it is the body of disciples who ask one of their own number to administer the movement, and the power of the man elected is an expression of their power. One man created a role and a movement; his successor will find himself supported in that role by the movement. The secretary-general succeeds to the charismatic leader; this is the process which Max Weber described as *'die Veralltäglichung des Charisma'*.[29]

In the congregationalist system of the Pentecostals, the congregations enjoy total autonomy in relation to one another and their unity is cemented not so much by a common name as by a founding chief whom they all recognize. The allegiance of a local pastor to the denomination is in the last analysis his allegiance to the person of the original leader and not to the impersonal idea of the denomination; the unity of the movement, all through the first phase, rests on the fact that the founder has created a network of personal loyalties, so much so that nearly all the pastors in charge are his own disciples or his disciples once removed.

When the founder disappears, the unifying bonds of loyalty to one man disappear, and are replaced by the notion of a confederation of churches. The real inheritor of power is not so much the man appointed in place of the late leader, but rather the body of pastors as a whole; the future of the denomination will depend on the way in which the man chosen will feel the role to which he is succeeding to have been profoundly altered because of the very manner in which he is succeeding to it. If he tries from the first to reproduce the founder's model, and to act as if he wielded the latter's authority, then the denomination will disintegrate.

The first task to occupy the new bishop will be the consolidation of the movement's unity, which has been deeply shaken by the struggle for the succession. To go back to the example given above, this is exactly what the new bishop of the *Iglesia Metodista Pentecostal* did. An honest and intelligent man, and also an astute strategist, for almost a year he listened far more than he spoke, and travelled about to make himself known in the congregations, seeking to know and to win them; he was the mouthpiece of the pastors rather than their director, an advocate of compromise rather than the instigator of decision-making.

However, let us not assume that the process of succession will congeal into the pattern by which, after a first stage called the birth or growth stage, in which the organization depends on the leader's web of personal relationships, there follows a stage in which the organization is directed by an increasingly impersonal bureaucracy. This would be to forget that Pentecostalist psychology puts a value on personal relationships. For the leader finally to establish himself as such—which is what is expected of him, in a contradictory and unconscious way—one must be able to call him *'mi obispo'* (*my* bishop). In the suggested scheme, we have omitted the time factor and considered only the moment at which the man chosen takes possession of his charge. But he does not lose all charismatic characteristics, for though it is men—his equals—who have raised him to his new office, they regard themselves as the interpreters of God's will, even though some of them are damming up their wish to question this divine seal and end by rallying to the majority! Thus the electors choose the new bishop, but their choice is directed by God; the chosen person is in the end God's anointed, and not the anointed of the pastors. In addition, as time passes, the new leader will again build up around himself a new network of personal loyalties. Old pastors will disappear, others will be appointed, the *Directorio* will be renewed, the founder's image fade as the face of the new bishop gradually gains sway, and he will resume the rank of charismatic leader.

Of course something new will have come into existence; a tradition of succession will have been created which puts value on the body of pastors in relation to the leader; from then on there will be no one-way dependence, whatever prestige the new leader may acquire through his personal successes in maintaining the unity of the denomination and enabling it to continue to expand.

At the level of the local church (congregation), evolution is the same in almost every detail. It is not the junta who nominate a new pastor, but the denomination's *Directorio* after consultation with the junta. The successor may be one of the congregation, or come from outside; the latter solution has the advantage that it nips in the bud any internal rivalries in the congregation. At all events, until the congregation's dynamism (the turnover of membership due to population movements and the increase of the work) enables the pastor to acquire a margin of freedom, he will have to come to terms with the junta who, in this transitional phase, are the bearers of tradition and thus the inheritors of authority.

The process of succession thus means that the role of the advisers (whether in the *Directorio*, Annual Conference or junta) is strengthened, at the expense of that of the leader. The function of the assistants is regularized and receives the sanction of tradition, and a relation of interdependence is created between the assistants and the leader. Over and above adherence to one person who embodies the unity of the congregation, there dawns the idea of adherence to a more abstract concept: the Church (the denomination). Naturally this is not a matter of the theological concept of the Church, but the birth of a feeling of belonging to a religious organization which cannot be reduced simply to the names of several heroic personalities. Control of the organization rests more heavily upon the charisma—which causes certain moral deviations characteristic of the early stages to disappear—and the latter still retains its primordial role while at the same time its manifestations are canalized into patterns of behaviour which have been first invented (or inspired by external patterns), then crystallized by tradition, and finally made normative by the organization. But (we must insist) this germ of an evolutionary process must not be shut up in an unreal, rigid pattern portraying the transition from the dynamic, spontaneous sect to the 'denomination' which is directed by bureaucrats, and ceasing to expand numerically. On the one hand, since its inception Pentecostalism has had available solid organizational elements,[30] and on the other, though manifestations of the charismatic phenomena appear today in traditional patterns, and are subject to the organization's control, the large Pentecostalist denominations of Chile continue to be characterized by their dynamism, their trend towards growth and expansion and their charismatic character.

Schism

Schism has been a constant feature of Chilean Pentecostalist history. Today there are about eighty legally registered Pentecostal denominations, not to mention the multitude of mushroom-churches with no legal status. Of these, only about twenty cover any large area of the country; the rest feature only on a provincial or local scale. The two most important, the *Iglesia Metodista Pentecostal* and the *Iglesia Evangélica Pentecostal*, number half the total Pentecostalist membership. The fate of the schismatic groups is generally not known, and our information on the subject is very patchy. In 1932, when the unity of Chilean Pentecostalism was disrupted, it was not a matter of a fringe group breaking away from the movement but an internal struggle which divided the church into two equally large fractions. Thus it seems hardly appropriate to use the term 'dissidence' in describing the creation of the *Iglesia Evangélica Pentecostal*, unless it can also be applied *mutatis mutandis* to the break between the Western and Eastern Churches. In fact Pentecostalism split into two branches of equal strength. The fact that they are today by far the largest in the country underlines the adventure on which dissident groups usually embark. Though some of them are successful in attaining growth and recognition as national denominations of the second rank, most of them vegetate and attain only local importance and even risk becoming ephemeral bodies which will disappear on the death of their leader.

Within the larger denominations, the ever-present possibility of schism exercises a check upon the power of the pastor or the general superintendent (or bishop); its threat prevents the charismatic leader from becoming a tyrant, by forcing him always to seek for a consensus. When the leader becomes a despot and infringes the rules of the game by substituting force for persuasion, imposing his will instead of explaining it, then the chances of a split increase. However, it seems that in fact schisms due to a leader's arbitrary and despotic action are not numerous and, as far as we know, only the creation of the *Misión Iglesia Pentecostal* (in 1952) might have been due mainly to such a situation.

In order to arrive at a consensus, it is further necessary that the leaders truly desire it and accept compromise as the price of maintaining the unity of the movement. It can be admitted that the principal leader will put the preservation of unity very high in his scale of values, since in the last analysis his prestige in the outside world is proportional to the size of his denomination. But with some pastors, to whom Pentecostalism has revealed a new path to social success, anxiety about unity is not allowed to interfere with their aspirations; having achieved several rungs on the ladder of the hierarchy, they see their chances of promotion disappearing, the top of the pyramid being already occupied. To reach the top, therefore, they must challenge the authority of those who occupy it. At this level, it is real attempts at a *putsch* that one is observing, which will end if successful in the eviction of the supreme leader, his place being taken by the insurgent, and if unsuccessful in the rebel's expulsion. In either case schism is almost inevitable, since in order for such a struggle to take place the two rivals must already have numerous partisans whose destiny is linked with that of their chief.

One example will serve to illustrate the eviction of a leader. In the 'thirties, the *Iglesia Metodista Pentecostal* was still governed by Pastor Hoover, the founder of the movement, a splendid patriarchal figure with a long beard. A group of ambitious men took advantage of the wave of nationalism which swept over Chile and attempted to evict this last survivor from the missionary era. The struggle was harsh and ugly, and the weapons employed (slander, insinuations about his private life, an attempt to have Hoover expelled from Chile) do not redound to the protagonists' glory. Here there was no longer any question of seeking a consensus and when Hoover's adversaries succeeded in gaining a majority, they expelled him along with the eight pastors who defended him. The latter, followed by most of the members of their respective congregations, founded the *Iglesia Evangélica Pentecostal* (1932).

A second example illustrates the reverse situation. Here, too, it is very difficult to separate *a posteriori* rationalizations from deeper motivations, and to know whether the issue over which the conflict was fought was the one really at stake or only served as a pretext. However that may be, within the *Iglesia Metodista Pentecostal* four pastors initiated an attempt at reform and for a while seemed to be triumphant, but in the end they were overthrown and expelled (1945–46). The most outstanding of them, a magisterial figure, an excellent preacher, a pastor in Curico with a great reputation, founded a new denomination, the *Iglesia Pentecostal de Chile*. This title emphasizes the aim of the new branch of the movement: that is, to be the source of Pentecostalism's regeneration. In the editorial of the first issue of this church's newspaper, Pastor Chavez recounts the events which led up to the schism and emphatically attributes to his group's actions the significance of a spiritual renewal:

> Then (shortly before the rupture) one saw the sorry spectacle of a decadent Christianity. On all sides one heard the same cry, 'We are marching towards inanition'. But the merciful God who watches carefully over His little flock would not let the tree wither and, improving the ground by causing new ideas of Reform to germinate in the hearts of His children, He caused a new burgeoning, thanks to His revivifying rays.
>
> The renewal of faith and baptism led to the birth [of a church]. The fervent desire to serve God with clean hands brought purification, and in this worthy town of Curico, the bud was transformed into a new branch which is growing, filled with healthy vigour, up and up to become the dense foliage of Christ's tree, the *Iglesia Pentecostal de Chile*.[31]

But this prose filled with imagery gives no indication of the content of the reformation being proposed by those in opposition. Another article in the same paper gives some details, to which we have added others gained in the course of interviews with the person chiefly concerned. The two chief points at issue were:

1. The absence of a general fund, and thus the absence of control over the use of money.

2. The title of bishop, which Pastor Umaña had assumed a short while before, and his appointment for life; these were to be replaced by the rotation of the office of superintendent, thus establishing the equality of the pastor-presbyters.

It is not necessary to doubt the sincerity of those who proposed these reforms, but it is difficult to believe that they were not moved to act by deeper and more subjective motivations, camouflaged under a pseudo-logical mental cover. In fact, doubt is cast on these proposals for reform by the fact that, in 1965, the *Iglesia Pentecostal de Chile* was still without an official Treasurer, just as the *Iglesia Metodista Pentecostal* had been 20 years before (though today this post does exist and operate in the *I.M.P.*), and that since its creation the office of superintendent has always been held by the same person, who has been appointed for life (in the rules, one is told, but not in the statutes), and that finally there is talk of introducing the title of bishop in the *Iglesia Pentecostal de Chile*!

In the two cases quoted, the conflicts brought into opposition men who each represented thousands of church members. But tensions may also arise on a more modest scale, within a single congregation, for example between a pastor and a 'guide'. The path for ascending the hierarchy is that of obedience and submission to the pastor. To have any chances, the individual must accept the role of disciple, for the Pentecostal system makes it impossible for two antagonistic leaders to co-exist. If a gifted, ambitious member does not accept the patronage of his pastor who, when he thinks the hour has come, will put forward his name to be sent to a new territory; if, for example, because of differences in temperament, he sees that he does not enjoy the pastor's confidence, then he will be tempted to try his luck and, followed by his own members, will found a small church. It is this process which lies behind the multiplicity of mushroom churches, generally without a future but being created unceasingly, in which the charismatic tradition of Pentecostalism is maintained in its pure state. It is a fertile soil for the growth of strange customs, moral deviations (arising from literal readings of some Old Testament passages); in these congregations good men and charlatans rub shoulders, and it is hard, if not impossible, to distinguish the one from the other, for the former may follow the practices of the latter, and the charlatan may share the honest man's good conscience. Generally the pastor of one of these ephemeral congregations owes his status not so much to his qualities as a leader of men as to a special and miraculous gift—such as the man, for example, who preaches in a strange tongue, which he himself is responsible for interpreting, or the man who has a reputation as a healer. The very structure of Pentecostalism prevents it from regulating its pastorate and defining its frontiers, so that on the fringe it is mingled with animism and spiritualism.

At the end of the day the root of schism is to be found in the struggle for power and the rivalries between individuals, rather than in the charismatic leader's overstepping his rights. The old adage which says it is better to be a large fish in a small pond than a small fish in a large pond is still valued, if one really cannot triumph in the large pond!

However, though divisions are caused more by psychological than sociological factors, that would not detract from the latent function of schism which we indicated above. Schism is generally *produced* when an irreconcilable conflict of personalities occurs, but its possibility limits the Pentecostalist pastor's power and makes him keep this side of tyranny. Contrary to widespread belief, the charismatic leader is not and cannot be a tyrant, so long as he moves within associative communities, since he does not have the instruments necessary for exercising tyrannical constraint.

5. CONCLUSION

The study of power in Pentecostalist society brings in question the adequacy of certain classic concepts such as those of clergy and laity, democracy and dictatorship. Is Pentecostalism clerical? Its pastors monopolize power, just as much on the local level as in the denominational organizations. The pastor's function puts him at a distance from church members by endowing him in their eyes with a high reputation, and the manner in which he exercises command is manifestly authoritarian. However, nothing in the pastors' social origins, recruitment or training separates them from the mass of church members; and even their ordination, whether from the symbolic or administrative point of view, confers on them no particular *power*. (The young congregation built up by an ordinary 'worker' will call its guide 'pastor', and pay him the same respect as if he were ordained.) The gradual abandonment of secular activities by the candidate-pastor highlights the fact that he, far more than any clergyman, is only a layman who specializes to the point of giving all his time to his church. If one takes into account the whole range of intermediate ranks from ordinary convert and street-preacher up to pastor-presbyter, then it seems quite impossible to polarize Pentecostalist society into laity and clergy. Besides, at what point does the clerical state begin? When a member is put in charge of a territory, or when he is ordained? Whereas a clerical society tends to reduce the laity to passivity, in Pentecostalism the neophyte from the outset is, one might say, a member of the *laos*, in the proper sense of the term, a member of the People of God, one mobilized for the service of the Lord and of His Church. We can therefore get rid of the cleric/lay alternative, which assumes that socially and hierarchically two groups stand opposite one another, their status being divided by a very rigid boundary, which is manifestly not the case here, even though the Pentecostalist hierarchy's highest posts do carry with them a halo which endows their holders with considerable prestige.[32]

Similarly, the democracy/dictatorship alternative is hardly appropriate, for the Pentecostalist leaders derive their power neither from themselves nor from the church members but, according to their interpretation, from God. Pentecostalism regards itself as a theocracy, the divine choice being transmitted by way of a sort of natural selection. In this sense, and using an expression in vogue, an authentic 'democratization of the directorial functions' exists which further reinforces the social homogeneity of members. Apart from rare cases of favouritism, the leaders in office are clearly those who are most fitted for the art of government. If we must define Pentecostalist society, then let us call it a voluntary association which is highly hierarchized yet without class distinctions, in which power is exercised from the top towards the base.

Pentecostalism arouses one's astonishment, especially when it is compared with the other types of Protestant society in Latin America, on account of the structural harmony which is apparent. As a society of elected members, the ultimate goal of which is to announce the Good News—a goal not only theoretic but a true source of energy, it has available a flexible, dynamic organization capable both of developing to infinity and of eliminating naturally the branches which wither. It has inherited a paternalistic tradition in human relationships, a tradition transmitted by the Bible and (with variations of meaning due to western acculturation) by the missionary. Pentecostalism has been able to interpret this tradition in the categories of its own cultural and social context, drawing inspiration from the traditional figure of the *patron*, giving it new life and democratizing it. These features make Chilean Pentecostalism an exemplary pattern for Latin American Protestantism.

APPENDIX

NOTES ON THE PART-TIME AND FULL-TIME MINISTRY

The problem of ministerial training is bound up with the question whether the pastor should or should not devote his whole time to his ministry. According to classical theory in religious sociology, with which the names of Max Weber, Ernst Troeltsch and Richard Niebuhr are associated, the type of ministry in a religious movement is a fairly safe index of its degree of evolution, the latter generally leading from the sect, a spontaneous movement with no paid pastorate, to the 'denomination', solidly organized with an official leadership, trained and salaried, which is called a professional ministry.

This pattern calls for modification in particular instances, and in order to understand the evolution of Chilean Pentecostalism itself, it must be noted that, from its creation, it recognized that the pastor in charge ought to give his whole time to his congregation and be paid by them. From this point of view, the road of preparation for the Pentecostalist ministry can be described as the gradual abandonment of one's secular occupation in favour of one's ecclesiastical charge. The existence of a professional ministry is not universal in the Pentecostal movement; in Brazil, even, the pastor generally carries on an occupation which provides him with his livelihood, since in that country the Pentecostalists have not made as strict a rule of tithing as have their co-religionists in Chile. Moreover, their affiliations are all with foreign Pentecostal movements which incline towards the part-time ministry, whereas the Chileans have inherited the Methodist system.

In addition, in some Protestant denominations in South America, especially the Presbyterians, one may observe an evolution in the opposite direction from the classic plan: a good number of Presbyterian pastors in Brazil are carrying on a subsidiary occupation, and the same church in Chile has recently ordained some 'elders' who continue to carry on their occupation so as to supply their own needs.

Our investigation enabled us to ascertain, in the denominations under study, what was the opinion of the pastors on this question, and whether the denomination's teaching is really applied.

Table 9. The Ministry and Pursuit of a Subsidiary Occupation

Question: Do you work in the world as well as in the ministry? (If the reply is negative) Have you worked in the past, after becoming a pastor?

	WORKS NOW	HAS WORKED	NEVER WORKED	TOTAL	ACTUAL
Protestants	8	15	77	100	26
Pentecostals	34	25	41	100	61

Table 10. Compatibility of the Pastoral Ministry and a Secular Occupation

Question: Which seems preferable to you, for the Church and pastoral work:
(1) For the pastor to work 'in the world' as well?
(2) For him to devote himself entirely to the pastoral ministry?

	(1)	(2)	NO REPLY	TOTAL	ACTUAL
Students	42	47	11	100	36
Protestants	12	72	16	100	26
Pentecostals	5	95	—	100	61

(1) STUDENTS AND PROTESTANT PASTORS

With some rare exceptions,[1] the *Protestant Pastors* do not pursue any subsidiary occupation, and believe that this is as it should be:

> The work of the church requires one's whole time. The pastor should not only preach, but also visit members and devote himself to them. And in this way one has time to study . . .

Table 10 shows that on this subject their opinion is closer to that of their Pentecostal colleagues than to that of their younger fellows, the students. Nevertheless, half the pastors refer in their comments to the fact that total devotion is to be preferred, but that the pastor's economic status makes his situation more difficult every day. For many it seems that for the pastor to give himself up entirely to his ministry 'would be ideal, but is no longer possible, for the members are no longer able to pay the pastor a decent salary'. But the sole argument in favour of a part-time ministry is negative: it is this economic argument of too small a salary.

Among the *students*, those who favour and those who oppose a part-time ministry form two groups of almost equal size. The majority of those who defend part-time work generally aspire to a specialized ministry (student work, youth work, an industrial ministry, etc.), and vice versa.

Those who favour a subsidiary occupation refer, like their elders, to the pitifully low level of pastors' salaries, but their vision goes beyond that of the pastors, for they link the question of the time dedicated to the ministry to that of the diversification of ministries and also to the question of the strategy of church work. According to some of them, the full-time pastor lives shut up in his church and is totally ignorant of society. Thus to the economic argument is added the desire to communicate and participate with people and society, as these comments show:

> Economic reasons, and also better identification with the people and the community (i.e. society). In the Bible there is not much said about paid pastors.
>
> It is a form of participation in society.
>
> Two motives for part-time: first, and most important, in this way one can reach areas that the full-time ministry does not touch and moreover the latter underrate the laity. Secondly, pastors' salaries are 'anti-Christian'.

As for the Protestant pastors, our results confirm those of the wider study on the ministry in South America carried out by Douglas Webster, the essence of which is contained in the following passages:

> In a large majority of cases it was specifically stated: (1) that most congregations would prefer a full-time minister; and (2) (the majority, but not so large), that most pastors would prefer to be full-time (p. 33).
>
> Almost everywhere this pattern has arisen through economic necessity, the congregations for the most part being too poor to pay their pastors. It has not been adopted on the grounds of theological, missiological or ecclesiological principle. . . . (p. 29).
>
> In no single case did the enquiry reveal that part-time ministers were part-time in order to be able to evangelize the secular world more effectively (p. 33).[2]

This stern conclusion seems correct to us, with the modification which we shall put forward below. It is clear that the main aim in pursuing a subsidiary occupation, particularly among the Presbyterians but also sometimes with the Methodists, is to improve the pastor's income. It is no less clear that in Latin America the pastor's salary is particularly low: on a par with that of a very minor official. But the denominations which are concerned with this problem ought to ask themselves two questions: first, why cannot the congregations provide a 'sufficient' salary for their pastors? Is it really on account of their poverty? Or would it not be due to a decline in the church members' involvement and devotion to the church? Secondly, how far is the financial claim of the pastors simply the result of a rise in the cost of living, or does it also express a social claim, on the part of people who have studied for a long period?

The modification to be added to Webster's conclusion is that the students *do* introduce theological considerations, and that those of them who support the idea of a subsidiary occupation do so *also* with reference to a new conception of the pastoral task and of Christian involvement in society.

To sum up, setting aside the students, the recent evolution towards a part-time ministry in some traditional denominations seems to be a measure taken as a last resource. It is sanctioned because the situation demands it and no other possible solution can be seen. But this policy sheds light above all on the crisis faced by South American Protestant denominations; they are stagnant, incapable of providing for their own needs without foreign aid, except by makeshift arrangements which are regarded as regrettable.

(2) PENTECOSTALIST PASTORS

One of the peculiarities of Chilean Pentecostalism is, as we have pointed out, the existence of a professional minister who devotes all his time to his congregation and is paid by them.

Note first of all that the rule of tithing is not general. Not to mention the mushroom-churches, in some of the denominations of the second flight, like the *Ejército Evangélico Nacional*, the *Corporación de Vitacura* and the various *Iglesias del Señor*, the pastor-presbyters, and sometimes also the superintendent or bishop, have a secular occupation. While the main reason for this state of affairs is the difficult economic situation, which generally arises out of the fact that the rule of tithing has not been strictly enforced, so as 'not to discourage sympathizers', it may be that the norm is provided by the example of the Apostle Paul, who provided for his own needs by making tents.

But reading Table 9 brings a surprise: even in those denominations which say that a full-time pastorate is the rule, one can see that about one-third of the pastors do have a subsidiary occupation. However, as we shall see, the situation varies from one denomination to another.

The proportion of part-time pastors varies between one-fifth and two-thirds, and these variations are linked with the average size of the congregations. Briefly, one could say that on the one hand there is the *Iglesia Metodista Pentecostal*, with its impressively large congregations, where part-time ministers are the exception, and on the other hand

Table 11. Percentage of part-time pastors, by denominations, and average number of members per congregation*

DENOMINATION	PASTORS WORKING		AVERAGE NUMBER OF MEMBERS PER LOCAL CONGREGATION*	
Igl. Met. Pent.	19%		607	
Igl. del Senor	33	46%	166	102
Misión Igl. Pent.	33		129	
Igl. de Dios	42		56	
Igl. Pent. Chile	64		117	

* This average is valid only for the congregations investigated in each denomination, and one cannot extrapolate this average to the denomination throughout the country. In the case of the *Iglesia Metodista Pentecostal* we have left out of account the huge mother-church of Jotabeche, which is an exception.

there are the other denominations with notably smaller congregations, in which nearly half the pastors work 'in the world'.

How can the difference between rules and practice be explained? The first and clearest clue comes from the competitive spirit existing between the various denominations. We have seen that the definition of 'pastor' is very fluid. Even though he does not have the sanction of ordination, a man is *in fact* a pastor when he is put in charge of a congregation, however small. Naturally, in theory ordination is necessary for him to have a place in the Annual Conference and so, in theory, in the list of pastors of that corporation. But because, in the principal inter-church body of Chilean Protestants, the *Concilio Evangélico de Chile*, the size of each denomination's delegation is determined in part by its number of pastors, it is a temptation for certain leaders who hope to play a part therein to include as 'pastors' members who are in charge of branches or young 'workers' just starting their career.[3]

Some exceptions to the full-time rule can also be explained by the man's desire not to forfeit his right to a retirement pension in the future.

Thus the exceptions to the rule consist almost cntircly of persons who have a pastoral charge but have not yet succeeded in gathering a sufficiently large congregation for them to be able to give up their secular occupation—which is, according to 95 per cent. of those interviewed, the goal to be achieved. The Pentecostalist pastors put forward three types of argument in their almost unanimous defence of the full-time ministry:

1. Work in the secular sphere means wasting time.
2. It also involves the danger of losing the 'spiritual vision' of things.
3. Finally, the Bible commands that one devote oneself entirely to the ministry.

1. 'Why waste time when souls must be won?'
'With a secular occupation, one loses interest in church work'; this is the usual argument.
2. 'One loses one's spiritual balance when one gives oneself to material things.'

'One loses the "spiritual vision".'

3. 'Because the Bible has laid it down so.'
'Because that is the true path of faith.'
'If the pastor believes in the Holy Spirit, he cannot work; God's word says that the just shall live by faith. He must live by the Gospel and have trust in God who will provide.'
'The Spirit commands it.'
'One cannot serve two masters.'
'Because in that case [full-time ministry] God gives an extra blessing, and as the Bible says, "Seek first the Kingdom of God"!'

While on the one hand these comments reveal a clear-cut position on the question—an original position, because it is an exception to the general South American Pentecostalist attitude, at the same time they reveal a conception which is not completely indifferent but very negative in regard to work, which, far from being the place where the Christian vocation is realized (as in the Calvinist tradition), is looked upon as a worldly business and dangerous to faith.

Though exceptions to the rule exist,[4] either because some denominations refuse to have a professional ministry, or are not financially in a position to have one, in conclusion it is important to notice that the full-time ministry is a structural feature of both the organization and the teaching of Chilean Pentecostalism, and has been so from the beginning.

Part Three

THE PROTESTANT CHURCHES IN RELATION TO CHILEAN SOCIETY

PREFACE TO PART THREE

THE dialectic relations which unite the emergence of a religious movement with the socio-cultural evolution of the environing society can be traced along three paths. First, changes in the socio-economic structure and the traditional system of values may have created conditions favourable to the spread of a new religious credo, and in Chapter 2 we have tried to emphasize this. Secondly, the forms of expression of the credo and its concomitant organizations may draw their inspiration to a greater or less extent from the existing Latin American socio-cultural patterns, and we have pointed out the intensity of the process of the socialization and acculturation of Chilean Pentecostalism in Chapters 3 and 4. Finally, the religious movement may in turn influence the development of the environing society. It is this latter theme on which we are now embarking.[1]

From an analytical point of view, the impact of a religious movement on social evolution follows two lines. On the one hand, the denomination is the bearer of a certain conception of society (in theology the term 'world' is used) which regulates the members' behaviour. As we shall see later, the history of Christianity shows that the Church has had not one but several systems of social ethics, sanctioning behaviour ranging from the rejection of society, and the attempt to isolate oneself as completely as possible, to revolutionary political involvement.

On the other hand, apart from the declared social ethic of a religious movement, the latter introduces into society new values and a new style of life which can transform both the attitudes of individuals towards a series of institutions (the family, work, etc.) and their social and economic aspirations (vertical social mobility), and indirectly influence the evolution of the whole society. It will be appropriate to analyse this process and estimate the effect of its impact upon society.

CHAPTER 5

Investigation of Protestant Social Ethics

A. THE THEORETIC OUTLINE

THE social ethic of a religious movement, from a sociological point of view, springs from one of the deeper levels of social reality, the level of *collective ideas and values*. 'To understand the meaning of social surroundings, of *ensembles*, total social phenomena and collective attitudes, to grasp what can be seen showing underneath the models, signs and symbols, one must examine them till one can seize their deepest inspiration, the values which they attempt to realize, and by which they are evoked, as well as the ideas which illuminate and penetrate them'.[2] It must be clearly understood at this point that the community, in declaring that its social ethic is such and such, is *consciously* displaying a collective attitude towards society and culture. Now this conscious attitude, expressed in doctrinaire language from which a system of regulations is inferred, can unwittingly be imposing itself upon a less visible, but equally real, confrontation between a religious group and its surrounding society, at the level of their respective organizations and cultural schemes. By this I mean that a congregation can be teaching its members the need and duty to collaborate in the country's socio-political organizations and at the same time be organizing itself on a model which is completely foreign to that country. The Lutheran Church in Chile serves as an example. Conversely, a religious movement may be sharing deeply in the socio-cultural schemes of a country, and at the same time forbid its members to take any conscious part in the cultural and political life of the country. Wc shall see that Chilean Pentecostalism fits this latter description.

It must be emphasized immediately that the collection of values and ideas making up the social ethic of a religious credo, and therefore governing the form which its members' involvement in society and politics will take, is only one level—relating to the group consciousness of the complex of relationships which the religious community maintains at different grades with the environing culture and society. Having thrown some light on this level, it will be necessary to show how it is connected with the others—and the examples we have given show that there may be a negative correlation—and to look for internal coherence. For, even if one discovers some contradictions, one can claim that in spite of them an overall cohesion does exist, a general equilibrium which, though it may be an equilibrium in tension, binds together the religious community, understood as a total social phenomenon.

The first step in our task is to define the social ethic of Chilean Pentecostalism, and we shall borrow our theoretic outline from that of the sociologist and theologian Richard Niebuhr. In his book *Christ and Culture*[3] he sets out a typology of Christian social ethics. Beginning with Malinowski's definition of culture: 'The "artificial secondary environment" which man superimposes on the natural. It comprises language, habits, belief, customs, social organization, inherited artifacts, technical processes and values',[4] the writer believes he can discern five typical responses of the Christian faith in its co-existence with human culture. At the two extremes there are on the one hand the negative response to culture, which demands a clearcut choice between Christ and culture: this is the type called 'Christ against Culture'; on the other hand, recognition of the basic accord between faith and culture, in which Jesus is regarded as a hero of human society: this is the type, 'The Christ of Culture', illustrated in modern times by the *Deutsche Christen*.

The other three types set their course between these two extremes:

In one case, Christ is 'the fulfilment of cultural aspirations and the restorer of the institutions of true society'; this synthetic type, of which Thomism is an example, is entitled 'Christ above Culture'.

In the fourth type, 'the duality and inescapable authority of both Christ and culture are recognized, but the opposition between them is also accepted', and will be resolved only post-historically. Luther is the example of this model, called 'Christ and Culture in paradox'.

The fifth case is found in the tradition of Augustine and Calvin. Here, 'the antithesis does not lead either to Christian separation from the world, as with the first group, or to mere endurance in the expectation of a transhistorical salvation, as with the fourth. Christ is seen as the converter of man in his culture and society, and so as 'Christ the Transformer of Culture'.[5]

On the basis of this typology, a set of questions was drawn up dealing with the social and political responsibility of the church and the believer, and with the ways in which the believer could be involved.[6]

We have described in our introduction the exact composition of our three samples—Pentecostalist pastors, Protestant pastors and theological students in Buenos Aires—and also the way in which they were chosen. Although our interest lies specifically with the Pentecostalists, we shall give the results obtained from all three samples, as these will enable us to use a comparative method (as has already been done in the earlier chapters) and so to define more clearly the specific opinions of each religious group.

B. RESULTS OF THE INVESTIGATION

1. The Church's Responsibility to Society

The figures in Table 1 underline the fact that Protestants and Pentecostalists hold opposite opinions. While the former are almost unanimous in acknowledging the social responsibility of the Church, two-thirds of the latter reject it.

Table 1. The Church's Responsibility

Question: In your opinion, should the Protestant Church be concerned with the country's political and social problems, and should it make pronouncements about them?

	YES	NO	DON'T KNOW	TOTAL	ACTUAL
Pentecostalist pastors	36	64	—	100	61
Protestant pastors	92	4	4	100	26
Students	100	—	—	100	36

Pentecostalists

(*a*) For the majority of them, politics (in the general sense, encompassing economic and social questions) has nothing to do with the Gospel, as these comments clearly show:

'It would be preaching something alien to the Gospel.'

'It would be *anti-Biblical.*'

'The Church is something different; it has to do *spiritual* work among men.'

'We should not occupy ourselves with those things but with God's work.'

'We should only sow the Word of God.'

'The mission of the Church is to *save souls*; that is the most important thing. Let the politicians do the rest.'

'We are the representatives of God and we should help the afflicted through *prayer*, showing them the path of salvation.'

'There is no ommandment telling us we must take part in politics. We must pray to God to give us what we lack and to show His compassion upon us.'

The basic conception is at once apparent. It rests on the dichotomy of the spiritual and the material, the Church and the world, the spirit and the flesh. The Gospel relates only to the first term in these pairs, and it is through this filter that the Bible is read. According to two of the pastors, participation in the country's problems should only be through the 'medium of prayer' and by the 'saving of souls'.

Others are afraid that involvement of a political nature would bring trouble for the church, and above all might cause believers to lose their faith; 'those that get involved in such things and belong to trade unions or political parties suffer spiritual decadence and end by going astray'.

(*b*) Thirty-six per cent of them nevertheless gave positive replies. Admittedly, this group is cut to 25 per cent if one eliminates those who limit the Church's responsibility to purely social questions, and those who say that this responsibility should be only in exceptional cases, given specially serious problems, for example that of the Chilean-Argentine frontier dispute. (The enquiry took place at the time of frontier incidents in November 1965, when a body of gendarmerie from Argentina stormed a Chilean post in a brief engagement, in which a Chilean lieutenant was killed. This news created a war psychosis in the countryside, and, in the Pentecostalist churches, there were frequent prayers that God should save Chile from the Argentine threat.)

Less than one quarter of the Pentecostalist pastors break the general pattern and say that the Church stands within society and that the believer is also a citizen:

'The Church is a part of society, and because of that, it must take its stand.'
'To fulfil our duty as citizens (we should be concerned . . .)'
'Because of the country's need.'
'We too are at the centre of these problems; we are living with them.'
'We are interested parties.'
'We have a responsibility towards the nation.'
'To learn the needs of those like us.'

This minority, therefore, has a certain awareness of nationality, or even in embryo an awareness of class. But to say that the Church has a responsibility is not to go so far as to advocate the responsible involvement of believers in socio-political, secular organizations, as we shall see later on.

The replies of two pastors who are leading figures give us an indication of the emergence of Pentecostalist political ambitions:

'The evangelical church is beginning to gain ground and might participate in the government.'
'If all of us Pentecostalists united, we should be able to get a man made President, and God would bless the people of Chile in general.'

Protestants

The figures in Table 1 would lead one to believe that the students and the Protestant pastors, who are unanimous in affirming the social responsibility of the Church, have one and the same ethical vision. Analysis of their comments and vocabulary shows that this apparent agreement is illusory and that, as we shall see, the differences are to be explained, not by the 'conflict between the generations' cliché, but rather by a profound transformation in theological thinking.

Protestant Pastors: (*a*) A large proportion (more than half) try, in their comments, to draw a clear distinction between political questions and social questions:

'On social questions, the Church may speak occasionally, but it should not get into the field of politics.'
'Yes, but only those aspects which make it possible to improve the well-being of the Chilean family.'

This group's thinking is nourished on the tradition of the great missionary denominations which came to Latin America to *evangelize* and to *relieve suffering*. (This tradition also led to the existence, in the Methodist system, of departments of evangelism and of social action.) The Church creates schools, colleges, infirmaries and hospitals, etc., in order to alleviate the misery of individuals, and at the same time it refuses to touch the question of the cause of this misery, for then it would have to mix with 'this rotten world'—the political sphere. Or rather, if one asks what is the cause of this misery, the immediate reply is, 'It is the sin of the individual'. So the solution is to convert the sinner:

'The Church must expose sin and offer solutions.'

'In reforming human life, the Church transforms the person and so plays a part in promoting his well-being.'

'The Church's duty is to *change the structure of society by changing people*.'[7]

This is the second presupposition of the Protestant denominations' social ethic (the first being its corollary: to distinguish between social and political questions and accept the former only), and it is also the justification most frequently put forward for the presence of Protestantism in Latin America: by converting the people, we transform the man who, in turn, will transform society, in the same way that the Reformation provided the basis for social and economic transformation in the West, and for its evolution into a capitalist society in which well-being is general. This misuse of Max Weber's arguments ought to be examined.

One can understand that, in this system of thought, there can be only one reason for the Church to become really involved in politics, and that is, to defend the interests of the Church:

'The country's political and social problems affect the future position and the present and future stability of the Church, so it must take a stand.'

'The Protestant Church is affected by these problems, and so it should not be ignorant about them.'

This stand can be called the *trade-unionist*[8] and *egocentric* attitude of the Church. The Church will take no part in politics, except in the early phases to establish its civic rights, and later to maintain them and to establish a certain number of rights and privileges. But this is a consistent position; since the salvation of the world and its happiness will come from the conversion of the individual, everything must be done to enable the Church to devote itself to that task. This line of reasoning lies behind the historic alliance of Protestantism with radicalism and Freemasonry.

(*b*) The arbitrary separation of social and political questions, the belief that conversion of the individual leads to the reformation of society, and acquiescence in political action only in defence of the Church—these three elements still characterize to this day the dominant social ethic of the missionary movements. But a second conception of the Church's political posture must be added: a conception which is, moreover, not in opposition to the first. The Church, 'the light of the world and the salt of the earth' (cf. Mat. 5: 13–14), must give those who are governing their bearings, while at the same time remaining above the struggle:

'The voice of the Church, which gives people their bearings, must be heard.'

'It must give people their bearings and utter the prophetic word, never be partisan.'

'It must point out the great landmarks.'

This conception of the Church as a body producing great directives and norms for political action is not just the product of the Chilean Protestant pastors; it is the most widely-held conception of the role of the Church in regard to society, whether the Church be Catholic, Orthodox or Protestant, whether it expresses its views by means of encyclicals, manifestoes or declarations. We know how vague such proclamations are, so vague that exegetes endlessly dispute over their meaning, and we may well ask whether famine and misery in the developing countries do not urgently demand that more concrete positions be taken, positions which must inevitably take sides if they are to be clearly understood.

(*c*) The last group, ranking fifth in the sample, affirms that our world is God's world, and that the Kingdom of God relates *also* to this world.

> 'Not to do it is the equivalent of fleeing from the responsibilities which are involved for the ambassadors of God's reign.'
>
> 'We live in God's world and we should make known God's plans for His world.'
>
> 'The Church is "the handmaid".'

The Students: the majority support the latter position. In their opinion, the fundamental question is 'to be faithful to the doctrine of the Incarnation'. Without such faithfulness, i.e. if the message of the Church 'is not concerned with the social realities of the individual whom it is addressing, it will fall on empty air'. Their answers are testimony that they reject pietist dichotomy. One must 'buckle to', as one student succinctly put it. They refer to the *mission* of the Church and to its *prophetic function* (5 times):

> 'The Church should take its place in society and in the contemporary world.'
>
> 'The Church is a community within the world, and its dispersed members[9] belong to the world. It must be the prophetic voice.'

The commandment to love one's neighbour is quoted also five times, and interpreted in the sense of refusing to separate the material and the spiritual:

> 'The Church must be responsible for the spiritual and the material as one whole.'
>
> 'These are problems concerning man whom God loves and the world He loves, and for both of which Christ died.'

Thus one can see the outline of a theology which insists on the fact that God was made Man and that the Gospel sees man in his entirety. It follows from this that the Church will use politics, not to defend its interests, but to promote the dignity of man, the creature of God. This difference between the answers of the students and those of the pastors seems to us to be of cardinal importance, for it shows that a generation of future pastors is rising whose socio-political behaviour will rest on a fundamentally changed social ethic, which may in the end bring about radical structural changes in South American Protestantism.

2. Christian Socio-political Responsibility and Involvement

Table 2. The possibility of a Christian's political involvement

Question: Would you say that a Protestant
1. ought to
2. may
3. may, but would do better not to,
4. should not

take part in politics?

	1	2	3	4	NO REPLY	TOTAL	ACTUAL
Pentecostalists	5	7	3	85	—	100	61
Protestants	46	27	8	19	—	100	26
Students	61	36	—	—	3	100	36

Apart from the students, all of whom are in favour of political involvement, it will be seen that more than one quarter of the Protestant pastors and the vast majority of the Pentecostalist pastors are against it, and even forbid it. Here we have confirmation of the results of Table 1. But before going further, let us examine the answers to another question, where we named three (socio-political) organizations and asked if a Christian might belong to them.

Table 3. Involvement of a Christian in Socio-political Organizations

Question: Do you think that a Protestant may be a member (even if it is not obligatory) of
(*a*) neighbourhood associations?
(*b*) trade unions?
(*c*) political parties?

	YES	NO	NO REPLY	TOTAL	ACTUAL
Neighbourhood Association					
Pentecostalists	68	30	2	100	61
Protestants	96	4	—	100	26
Students	94	3	3	100	36
Trade Unions					
Pentecostalists	51	49	—	100	61
Protestants	88	8	4	100	26
Students	94	3	3	100	36
Political Parties					
Pentecostalists	13	85	2	100	61
Protestants	77	23	—	100	26
Students	97	—	3	100	36

The *students* reply to the three questions in a homogeneous and unanimous fashion. For them, the organizations named are 'opportunities for concretely expressing one's love towards one's neighbour'.

The *Protestant pastors* in the main see nothing incompatible in the

Christian's participation in these organizations, although hesitations grow in proportion to the increasingly political character of the organization, so that one-quarter of them forbid involvement in a political party.

This group argues that political involvement, or even trade union involvement, leads the Christian to go astray, or at least reduces his availability to the congregation.

'Such involvement brings credit and honour to a man, who grows proud over it and leaves the strait and narrow path.'
'He will be swallowed up by these organizations.'
'He will be compromised.'

In the eyes of this minority, a believer ought to not take part in the activities both of the Church and of the world. Consequently, the congregation should be organized in such a way that all the available time of church members is taken up in its activities. This is yet another sign of the self-centredness of the churches, which stands out clearly when the weekly activities of the congregation are listed.

If the comments of the Protestant pastors in favour of involvement are compared with those of the students, it will be noted that, as in the case of the responsibility of the Church, the two groups have markedly different ends in view in considering this involvement. For the former, it is a question chiefly of giving one's witness in secular organizations. But the students, without dismissing this objective, see a second dimension in the idea of the Christian as 'salt of the earth'; he should participate consciously in social problems. Here too, the systems of reference differ.

Among the *Pentecostalist pastors* rejection of all forms of participation is much more marked, since 30 per cent of them go so far as to prohibit membership of neighbourhood associations. With three exceptions, those who condemn membership of neighbourhood associations also reject the other two types of activity. If the former is accepted but trade union membership is condemned, then political activities are also proscribed. The determining factor is therefore the degree of 'politicization' in the organization, which enables one to draw the following figure to illustrate the Pentecostalist replies:

Scale of rejection of socio-political activities among the Pentecostalist pastors

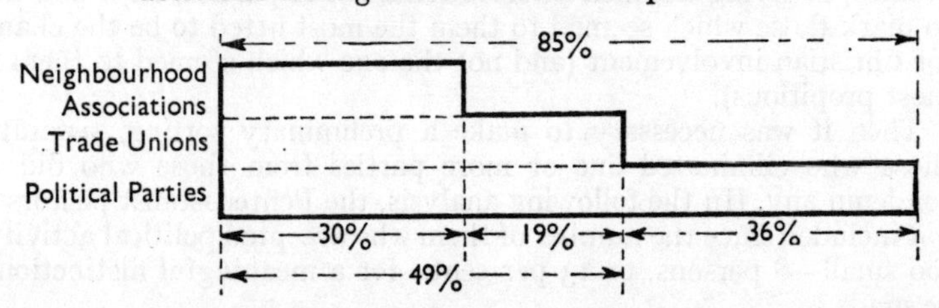

(*a*) Let us first consider those who reject all three forms of activity (30 per cent of the sample):

'They contaminate a man's whole body. We do not belong to such things but to God.'

'They are worldly, not spiritual, things.'

'That is not the Christian's place; his duty is to pray for them.'

'The believer should separate himself from all that.'

'God has brought the believer out of all that.'

'The man who makes himself the friend of the world becomes the enemy of God.'

'It gives the Gospel a bad reputation.'

'It runs away with time that ought to be consecrated to the Lord's work.'

'It is prejudicial to the Christian's spiritual life.'

'These meetings are different from meetings for worship, and one cannot give glory to God in them.'

'We have left the world, and there is no point is returning to it.'

(*b*) Those who accept participation in neighbourhood associations (68 per cent) and trade unions (51 per cent) hold the view that in these cases the chances of compromising oneself are not so great. A minority puts forward positive arguments, holding that this may be the occasion for 'helping one's neighbour', and 'contributing to the common good'. But the majority consider these forms of involvement to be a lesser evil and recommend their flock to keep their distance and not to accept leading positions; 'Well taught by the pastor, the church member will not take an active part.'

Though the attitude of this group is favourable to neighbourhood associations and divided on the subject of trade unions, political activity properly speaking is severely condemned. As in many other countries, the political world is regarded as venal and corrupt, not only by Pentecostalists and Protestants but also by a large section of the population. Nevertheless, corrupt political practices cannot be the explanation why four Pentecostalist pastors out of six would prefer, if it were possible, to abstain from voting[10] (cf. Table 7 below).

In contrast with the Pentecostalists, all the *students* and three-quarters of the *Protestant pastors* agree that a Christian may belong to a political party. But then, what do they consider to be the party policy most compatible with Christian faith? The way in which we formulated the question in the questionnaire makes it possible to give an answer to the opposite question—which do they consider should be excluded?—since, in giving the men interviewed a list of parties, we asked them to mark those which seemed to them the most fitted to be the channel for Christian involvement (and not the one which seemed to them the most propitious).

Then it was necessary to make a preliminary sorting, separating those who eliminated one or more parties from those who did not condemn any. (In the following analysis, the Pentecostalist pastors are not included since the number of them who accepted political activity is too small—8 persons, or 13 per cent—for a meaningful distinction to be made.)

(*a*) The tendency to make no choice is twice as marked among the pastors as among the students (40% and 21%). The reason given for

Table 4. Political Choice: Distribution according to whether or not a selection was made*

	THOSE WHO MADE A SELECTION AMONG PARTIES	THOSE WHO EXCLUDED NONE OF THE PARTIES	TOTAL	ACTUAL	PERCENTAGE OF THE SAMPLE
Protestants	60	40	100	20	77
Students	79	21	100	33	91

* Here only those who agreed to the possibility of party activity are included, i.e. 77% of the Protestant pastors and 97% of the students. Two of the latter did not answer this new question, so 91% remained.

refusing to choose is the same in both groups: political activity concerns only the conscience of the individual, and nobody has the right to decide for another. Some pastors insist on the fact that it is good for Christians to mix with all the parties, so that the Gospel should not be identified with one party's policy.

> 'He can belong to any party; it is a matter for his conscience.'
> 'The Protestants ought to carry the Gospel to hell itself!"
> 'The Protestants should be in the various parties, so that Christianity is not identified with one particular party.'

This group makes a principle of *individual liberty*, and does not think that the Christian social ethic can be more in accord with one political opinion more than another. A correlation must also be noted: *the defenders of individual liberty attribute less importance than do the others to the Christian's political involvement.* In fact, 71 per cent of the students and 63 per cent of the pastors who do not exclude any party, consider that the believer's participation in politics is a possibility but not a duty (cf. the question in Table 2, page 112). On the other hand, 91 per cent of the students and 63 per cent of the pastors who claim that political activity is a duty do make a choice between the parties. One is tempted to believe that those who, while admitting that a believer may be a member of a party, refuse to give their views on party policies, do so less on account of their theological principles (although insistence on liberty of conscience is typically Protestant!) than because they have hardly any interest in socio-political problems.

(*b*) Let us now consider *only the students and pastors who do make a political choice.* These two groups include 72 per cent of all the students, but only a minority (42%) of the pastors.

The *students'* choice is very markedly towards the *non-Marxist left*, as Table 5 shows; the other party policies in general receive mostly abstentions.

This political choice is based—and herein lies the originality of the students' views—on an analysis of the present historical situation in Latin America:

'I think the conservative and centre parties in my country offer no solutions to our problems.'

'The historical situation in Latin America demands a far-reaching revolution in order to achieve social justice.'

'Only the militant left-wing can do it, for it is not compromised either with imperialists or the oligarchy.'

'Being a Latin American, and in view of the situation, the Christian should participate in a revolutionary party.'

Table 5: Political Choice of the Theological Students

Question: Can the believer be a member of a party of one of the following types?

	YES	NO	NO REPLY	TOTAL	ACTUAL
Marxist	19	19	62	100	26
Non-Marxist Left	84	8	8	100	26
Centre (Radical for example)	27	27	46	100	26
Christian Democratic	23	23	54	100	26
Right-wing (e.g. Liberal, Conservative)	11	31	58	100	26

The *Protestant pastors* who make a choice are too few (13 persons = 42%) for analysis to be fruitful. But study of their comments shows that their theological motives differ from those of the students. In fact they justify the elimination of such and such a party's policy by declaring in general that this political ideology is incompatible with Protestant beliefs. Thus, when they reject the Communist party, 'its atheistic ideology' is invoked, and when the Christian Democrats, Liberals or Conservatives are proscribed, it is 'because they are Catholic parties'. Thus one sees a slight tendency emerging in favour of radicalism, 'which has defended liberty of worship and education for the people', or in favour of a Bernstein form of socialism.

This underlines the change in the younger generation's social thought; while their elders reflect upon the problem of socio-political involvement starting from the viewpoint of the Church's interests, the students break away from this attitude and are primarily concerned with the interests of society.

3. *Socio-political Involvement of the Pastor*

Our first question is designed to show whether, in the eyes of those who were interviewed, being a pastor is compatible with participation in a socio-political organization.

Each sample is quite clearly different from the others; however, only a minority of the students and Protestant pastors speak of incompatibility, whereas among the Pentecostalists it is the majority who think this way (almost all of them in the case of trade unions and political parties). According to the *students* the question does not arise, for, in the end 'the pastor is neither more nor less than any other Protestant'.

Table 6. Percentage of pastors who consider their function *incompatible* with participation in secular organizations. (To simplify the table, only negative answers are taken into consideration.)

Question: Do you believe that a Protestant pastor can be a member (even when it is not obligatory) of the following organizations? Answer: *No.*

	NEIGHBOURHOOD ASSOCIATIONS	TRADE UNIONS	POLITICAL PARTIES
Pentecostalists n = 61	52%	84%	95%
Protestants n = 26	12%	27%	35%
Students n = 36	3%	11%	14%

Nevertheless, many of them stipulate that the question is not one of duty but of liberty, which is related to each person's calling and the time at his disposal. He can be an active member 'on condition that he does not neglect his first duty, which is preaching, visiting . . . and activities in the Church'.

Among the *Protestant pastors*,

(*a*) a decided majority, which declines, however, in proportion to the increasingly political nature of the organization, allows that the pastor may be involved in the organizations named:

'I believe in the priesthood of all believers. There is no barrier to laymen and/or pastors being active in these social and political spheres.'

'The pastor is in the same position as other church members: he is a human being.'

Several underline the view that the pastor should involve only himself personally and not his church:

'As an individual he can belong to these organizations, but without compromising his church.'

'As a citizen, yes, but not as a pastor.'

(*b*) A large group—more than one-third —consider their function incompatible with any kind of partisan involvement. According to them, the pastor must devote himself entirely to his congregation, which would be disturbed and perhaps even divided if he were active in a party:

'That would be a bad example to recent converts.'

'He ought to devote himself entirely to the work of upbuilding the church.'

'This might provoke dissension in the church.'

'If he is invited, he can take the opportunity of turning of people's thoughts in the direction of religious things, but he should not take any active part.'

'The pastor should remain at liberty to preach to the church members in all freedom.'

While just under half the *Pentecostalist pastors* allow that neighbourhood associations might at a pinch be a place in which to give their witness, for the majority, participating in a trade union or a party is equivalent to serving two masters:

'The spiritual work of the pastor does not permit it: "let the dead bury their dead".' (Cf. Mat. 8: 22.)

'His mission is to serve God and the Church.'

'He is a minister of God, dedicated to the teaching of God.'

'To devote oneself to spiritual work', 'to be the pastor of souls', 'not to mix up the Gospel (or 'the teaching of God', 'the law of the Spirit') in politics', 'to work for the Church and not the world', these stereotyped answers show the dualism of Pentecostalist thought, the dualism of which we found important traces among the Protestant pastors as well. If the pastor were involved in politics, 'then contaminating influences would appear', and he himself 'would be corrupted and separated from God', who would 'withdraw His grace from his heart'. Beside this dualism there sometimes appeared a quietism reflecting a negative theology of creation and matter: is it not trusting in human powers to take an active part in social or political organizations? Then the pastor 'would be defending his neighbour with his own powers and not those of God'.

Another question, bearing on participation in elections, gives a measure of the Pentecostalist pastor's leaning towards 'disengagement'.

Table 7. Participation in Elections.

Question: If elections were not compulsory, would you vote?

	YES	NO	TOTAL	ACTUAL
Pentecostalists	61	39	100	61
Protestants	92	8	100	26

(*a*) Four Pentecostalists out of ten vote only because they are obliged to. This group pushes to its limits the theology of non-participation in the world. Not to vote would be a release for these pastors, for thus they would be finished with all compromise with the political sphere.

'Then my conscience would not weigh heavily on me any more.'

'No, in order to live an independent life.'

'No, to be completely independent.'

'Why should I go and compromise myself?'

They also mention the false promises of the election candidates:

'We don't know what sort of candidates will be elected, and to vote carries us along the wrong road.'

'The men elected mislead the individual greatly.'

And here again one finds this touch of quietism, this wish to give oneself entirely to a God who would act without man:

'I do not think that for my country the solution is a political one.'
'I dislike giving my vote to men.'
'I have more confidence in God than in men.'
'He who puts his trust in men does not believe in God.'

It is clear that here it is not just a question of disgust with political practices. In any case nowadays the elections are well organized; the inclination to 'make the dead vote' is a thing of the past and the 'magnates' are no longer able to control individual votes directly. (Certainly indirect pressure exists: the parties pay for the journey to the voting station for those who let it be understood that they will vote in their favour, and 'rewards' are given for the services of people who can influence the members of their clientele: great landowners and also—we shall come back again to this later—priests and pastors!) In addition to an aversion for political malpractice, for this 40 per cent of the Pentecostalist pastors it is also a question of totally rejecting politics as such.

(*b*) The majority group unanimously affirm their Chilean citizenship, which imposes a moral duty to perform their civic responsibilities, a duty which 'is prescribed in the Bible: Romans 13'. And again it is an opportunity to give one's support to people who are not enemies of the Gospel:

'We should vote for a man who is not opposed to God's work.'
'A Catholic party might come to power and then what would happen to us?'
'To support liberty of worship.'
'So as to spread freedom, and provided there is a man worth voting for. (In the last presidential elections) my candidate was Duran, but in the end I voted for Frei, so as to resist communism.'

(This last interviewee is referring to the Presidential election in 1964. Duran, a member of the Radical party, was the right-wing candidate, but, following a pre-electoral upset, he withdrew his candidature. That left in the lists only Dr. Allende, the F.R.A.P.* (Communists and Socialists) candidate, and Mr. Frei, the Christian Democrat, who won.)

To conclude this paragraph on the pastor's involvement, let us go back to section 4 of Chapter 3, where the pastor's field of activities was defined; those results agree with what has been shown here: the Pentecostalist pastors, followed by a strong minority (between one-quarter and one-half) of the Protestant pastors, reject activities which have a political flavour.

4. *Indices of Pastors' Knowledge of Socio-Political Problems*

One question gave us an idea of the pastor's interest in national problems, and at the same time constituted a cultural test. We chose

* FRAP = Popular Action Front (translator).

the term '*under developed*', which is heard on the radio and read in the press every day, and we asked for a definition of it. Then we divided the answers into right and wrong. We did not ask for a scholarly answer: a phrase as succinct as 'there is much misery' was sufficient.

Table 8. Definition of 'Under developed'

Question: People say Chile is an under developed country. What does this mean?

	RIGHT	WRONG	TOTAL	ACTUAL
Pentecostalists	59	41	100	61
Protestants	85	15	100	26

Of the Pentecostalists pastors, 41 per cent did not know how to define this term. Most of them admitted not knowing what it was about. Some gave the opposite meaning: 'It means that Chile is a very advanced country.' Others interpreted the term in religious categories:

'Chile is not like the ancient nations where Jesus preached.'
'Chile is given up to idolatry.'
'The Gospel has not yet been preached widely enough.'
'Chile is the most evangelized country of all.'

Another question had to do with a political event which had enormous repercussions: the Dominican Republic, 1965. It will be remembered that in March an insurrection broke out against the military dictatorship in the island, with the aim of a return to the 1963 constitution and the recall of the last elected president, Juan Bosch. After some ups and downs, and just when the insurgents were about to win, American marines landed, according to President Johnson's first version, to protect foreign residents. Later the United States President put forward another reason, since the first no longer justified the presence of tens of thousands of soldiers: the island was about to fall into the hands of the Communists.

Table 9. Opinions on the American landing in the Dominican Republic

Question: Have you heard about the United States' intervention in the Dominican Republic? Do you approve of it?

	DOES NOT KNOW OF THIS EVENT	DOES KNOW ABOUT IT. DOES HE APPROVE? NO	YES	DON'T KNOW	NO REPLY	TOTAL	ACTUAL
Pentecostalists	34	34	17	8	7	100	61
Protestants	15	50	12	15	8	100	26
Students	—	75	8	17	—	100	36

It is a pity one cannot compare these answers with the opinions of larger sections of the population, but in Chile there was no opinion-polling on this subject. It will be seen that ignorance about the event decreases and the tendency to condemn the landing increases from the Pentecostalists to the students. Further, a quarter of the students and a third of the pastors (Protestant and Pentecostalist) either refuse to give an opinion or approve of the American landing. These figures seem high to us, and we would be tempted to think that the Protestant is not as hostile to U.S. politics as his compatriots, and also more responsive to the use of anti-Communist myths. Moreover, in Latin America Protestantism is regarded as an imported product coming from the U.S.A. (which is correct) and we have heard North American pastors who were visiting the Pentecostalist churches slip into their preaching some real political propaganda.

Students: None of them is unaware of the event, and three-quarters of them condemn American intervention, affirming the principle of national self-determination and suspecting the U.S.A. of using a poor excuse to carry out a colonialist policy. The few who approve the landing justify it because of the communist menace, and those who abstain consider it difficult to avoid being the victims of propaganda, wherever it comes from.

The arguments of the Protestant and Pentecostalist pastors add nothing to what the students say, but they show increased receptivity to the interventionist pleading; the U.S.A. 'saved a nation from communism' and 'preserved many lives'.

The important fact is that a third of the *Pentecostalist pastors* are completely unaware of an event which filled the front page of newspapers for several months and continued to appear there from time to time when the enquiry was being made. In addition, not only commentators on radio and television (the latter is seldom found in Pentecostalist homes and only rarely in Protestant homes) but also Chilean politicians and statesmen made statements about it. The educational factor is not enough to explain this ignorance, since we heard the event discussed even in the most humble districts. The investigators were told to ask those who knew nothing about the Dominican Republic whether they read a paper or listened to the radio. The key to the problem was given to us when, almost without exception, they replied:

> 'I have no time for reading the paper; my time belongs to God,' or 'God has told me to read nothing but the Bible.'

The same reply was given concerning the radio, though to a lesser extent, for 'the radio pleases my wife and children, but I don't listen to it myself'.

Once more, this one-third of the Pentecostalist pastors and the 15 per cent of the Protestants who did not know about the bloodshed in the Dominican Republic are a measure of the wish to break away not only from the political world (which is regarded as satanic) but also from cultural life and to live in purely religious categories (as the religious definitions of 'under-developed' show).

The fact that another third of the Pentecostalists (and also a quarter of the Protestants and students) refuse to condemn the landing or even approve it shows that this indifference with regard to the world is in the end a political attitude which favours the *status quo*, in so far as for many the enemy seemed to be, not misery or exploitation, but atheism and the threat to the Church's rights and privileges.

Table 10 shows that the replies on the subject of 'underdevelopment' and on the Dominican question are correlated. The two are thus indices of interest in socio-political questions:

Table 10. Knowledge of the Dominican affair and Definition of 'Underdeveloped'

	PROTESTANT PASTORS		PENTECOSTAL PASTORS	
DOMINICAN REP.	RIGHT*	WRONG*	RIGHT*	WRONG*
Knew about it	91	50	86	36
Did not know	9	50	14	64
Total	100	100	100	100
Actual	22	4	36	25

* *Re* definition of 'Underdeveloped'.

C. SYNTHESIS

1. *The Social Ethic of Pentecostalism*

Of the Pentecostal pastors, two-thirds reject any socio-political responsibility on the part of the Church in relation to the nation; four-fifths exclude from their fields of activity any preoccupation with social questions; 85 per cent forbid church members to take part in politics, and half of them forbid trade union membership. (Those who do permit the latter insist that it should be an inactive membership.) Finally 40 per cent of them would prefer not to vote.

These various traits show that Pentecostalism belongs to Niebuhr's 'Christ against Culture' type, and an analysis of the comments has brought out the polarization of Pentecostalist thinking between spiritual and material, Church and world, Christ and society. Pentecostalism rejects this world, so as to enjoy contemplating the next. There is no possible appeal from the sentence passed upon society: entertainment and sport, when they are not considered 'works of the Devil', are at least 'time lost from the Lord's work'; trade unions and parties are 'places of damnation' and even work itself, because of 'bad companions', is not wholly free from suspicion. One pastor said of his 18-year-old son: 'He stays at home. I do not want to set him to work, for I might lose him.' The world is thus the 'monster' from which 'souls must be snatched', to retire into the refuge of the Church while waiting for the Kingdom of Heaven.

It would be easy for someone who, for example, holds to the Calvinist tradition of Protestantism to condemn this social ethic. However, it is more important to understand the reason for it, and it must be remembered, too, that it is rooted in a Christian tradition which goes back to the early Church and the New Testament texts. Let us begin with this latter point. While one finds traces of this dualism in St. Paul, especially in his setting spirit (*pneuma*) over against flesh (*sarx*), it is in the First Epistle of John that the foundations are found of the social ethic which rejects the world. The following quotation, taken from Richard Niebuhr, underlines the relation between this Epistle and Pentecostalism. In the First Epistle of John,

> Save in two instances (1 John 2: 2; 4: 14) the word 'world' evidently means for the writer of this letter the whole society outside the church, in which, however, the believers live. The injunction to Christians is, 'Do not love the world or the things in the world. If anyone loves the world, love for the Father is not in him' (1 John 2: 15). That world appears as a realm under the power of evil; it is the region of darkness, into which the citizens of the kingdom of light must not enter; it is characterized by the prevalence in it of lies, hatred, and murder; it is the heir of Cain (5: 19; 1: 6; 2: 8–9, 11; 3: 11–15). It is a secular society, dominated by the 'lust of the flesh, the lust of the eyes and the pride of life', or, in Prof. Dodd's translation of these phrases, it is 'pagan society, with its sensuality, superficiality and pretentiousness, its materialism and its egotism'. It is a culture that is concerned with temporal and passing values, whereas Christ has words of eternal life; it is a dying as well as a murderous order, for 'the world passes away and the lust of it' (2: 17; cf. 2: 8). It is dying, however, not only because it is concerned with temporal goods and contains the inner contradictions of hatred and lies, but also because Christ has come to destroy the works of the devil and because faith in him is the victory which overcomes the world (3: 8; 4: 4–5). Hence the loyalty of the believer is directed entirely toward the new order, the new society and its Lord.[11]

The most radical form of this 'Christ against Culture' is found, not in this epistle, but in Tertullian, and, more recently, in Tolstoy. Nevertheless it is the First Epistle of John, which is so often quoted in Pentecostal churches, that offers the greatest degree of likeness to Pentecostalism. In addition to the points mentioned in the quotation, he also restricts the commandment to love one's neighbour to loving one's brother, and while he agrees that Jesus Christ came to expiate the sins of the world, this means, for John as for the Pentecostalists, 'the expiation of the sins of all men, regarded more or less individually'.[12] Similarly, in both cases the aloofness recommended in relation to society does not go as far as a 'rejection of the State or property as such'.[13]

However, to understand the aloofness from the world which is maintained by Chilean Pentecostalism, one must go beyond the level of theological motives, which in our opinion is in part the reflection of more profound attitudes which it serves to cover up. It is at the level of 'collective mental states' (G. Gurvitch) that the root of Pentecostal behaviour appears. We have affirmed that this religious movement expresses a protest against 'a heartless world' (K. Marx); when the pastors assert, 'We have left the world, never to return', what they are expressing is not the outcome of philosophic thinking, but that of a concrete experience—experience of a pitiless society in which misery is the result of all-embracing structures and not of individual laziness.

One should not forget that, for the Pentecostalists as for the majority of Chile's population, the 'world' is above all, and in a tangible manner, the world of wretchedness, sickness and death; the origin of their rejection of it is to be found in their panic fear of the world which has given the new Christian, poor of the poor on the fringe of the fringe, nothing but disappointments and suffering. Once more, if anyone doubts these statements, let him turn to the work of Oscar Lewis, who describes the world of the outcast.

According to Ernst Troeltsch, *separation from the world* is one of the central elements (indeed even the sole variable, according to Benton Johnson)[14] of the sociological definition of '*sect*' and is bound up with a millenarian vision that 'implies a conception of the world which envisages *an end of this world* through the victory of Good over Evil, God over Satan, Christ over Anti-Christ'.[15] According to its understanding of man's share in the coming of the Kingdom of God, the 'sect' adopts one of the two following global attitudes towards society:

(1) If the advent of the Kingdom of God is conceived in a merciless and catastrophic way as the fruit of the Lord's return, to which man can make no contribution other than announcing its imminence, then the congregation will live in a state of passivity as regards society, accepting the latter as a transitory feature in which nevertheless its members find their livelihood, and they will perform no collective activity other than rescuing the greatest possible number of individuals from it by means of preaching the Gospel and by prayer.

(2) The victory is expected to be 'gradual and slow, the way being prepared by human action',[16] and then the rejection of society is accompanied by the wish to transform it radically, and to replace the city of men by the city of God. In that case the sect's activities will be turned towards revolutionary struggle, as was the case with the Taborites, the Münz Anabaptists, some of the eighteenth-century Anglican sects, etc. And if society proves to be impervious, then either there is an evolution towards the first type, or general revolution is renounced in favour of the creation of autarchic congregations (Baptists and Anabaptist groups, and also the Revival congregations of the last century), or again, they emigrate to new territories (the colonization of New England, cf. also the Shakers). In this second type the desire for a break-away far exceeds the limits fixed in the theology of the First Epistle of John and looks towards the creation of a theocracy in this world.

Underlying the expansion of Pentecostalism is a social protest which never, in this religious movement, assumes the form of revolutionary action; the Kingdom of God is still regarded as a transcendent, otherworldly kingdom, of which the congregations are the visible symbol, but they have no relation of continuity with the thing they symbolize. The Reign of God will come from the Heavens; it is radically other and cannot be regarded as a continuation of any human activity. This eschatological conception symbolizes (rather than determines) Pentecostalist socio-political passivity. But where does it come from? One may assume that the Pentecostalists did not originate it and that here they are inheriting a tradition which has sufficient weight to extinguish the revolutionary spark and give a uniquely spiritual warmth to the Pentecostal fire. Pentecostalism being, in Chile, the rebel child of Methodism, perhaps an examination of the social ethic of the Protestant pastors will enable us to find an answer.

2. *The Social Ethic of Protestantism*

The quantitative results of the enquiry in this case are more ambiguous than in the case of the Pentecostalists, but analysis of the comments underlined the distrust of the pastors in political phenomena as such, and showed up three elements in their dominant social ethic: (arbitrary) separation of the social from the political; acceptance of political struggle only in the case of defending the interests of the Church; belief that individual conversion leads to the structural change of society. The characteristic feature of this ethic lies in its individualist vision of religious activities: the Church gathers in, comforts and converts the individual, to whom it then imparts a moral doctrine; it has no contact with society, politics or economic affairs except through the prism of the individual. The furthest it could go, therefore, will be, as a Methodist pastor said, 'to remind the leaders, statesmen and business directors of their responsibilities towards the men who depend on them'.

This social theology is not without some likeness to the Lutheran theory of the two kingdoms, and falls into Niebuhr's fourth category, that entitled 'Christ and Culture in paradox'; the political structures of society, whatever they may be, are recognized and acknowledged to the extent that they, on their side, acknowledge the legitimacy of the presence of missionary churches. But in the end this peaceful co-existence is also based on a dualism: the belief that the Church's only duty towards man is 'religious' (in the strict sense).

The composition of our sample of Protestant pastors is 69 per cent Methodist. The Methodists, therefore, give the tone and the results of the enquiry relate essentially to the Methodist Church from which Pentecostalism sprang. Now it appears that the *ethic of the latter is both a radicalization and a limitation of the Protestant group's ethic*, but there is no contradiction between them, at any rate not on the point relating to the question, 'Why does Pentecostalism have no revolutionary dimension?' posed at the end of the preceding section. The inescapable reply is that the two influences to which it was subject—Methodism and World Pentecostalism—inclined it to apprehend society in this world and the Kingdom of God from the biased standpoint of individualist thought. In his first great work, which counts today as a classic, *The Social Sources of Denominationalism*, Richard Niebuhr stresses that the differences between the English seventeenth-century religious movements and Methodism 'lay in the substitution of individual ethics and philanthropism for social ethics and millenarianism.'[17] According to him, the Wesley brothers 'had substituted for the concept of the kingdom the symbol of heaven',[18] which was as much as to say that they pushed away into a transcendent other world that which their forebears had, partially at least, placed in this world. The author attributes this change to the social origin of the Wesleys, members of the English middle class and holding the individualist philosophy of their background. Wesley 'envisaged sin as individual vice and laxity, not as greed, oppression or social maladjustment. . . . From Wesley the entire Methodist movement took its ethical character. Wesley was more offended by blasphemous use of the name of God than by a blasphemous use of His creatures'.[19] 'Apparently Wesley believed that the justice of a cause was quite secondary in the eyes of God to the personal purity of its defenders.'[20]

It is well known that as North American society was built up and as some of the sects evolved towards the recognized, integrated status of a 'denomination', this individualistic, philanthropic and sentimental ethic of Methodism became general among the Protestant churches of the North American middle classes. Pentecostalism, being born of a deepening of spiritual and religious life, has eliminated philanthrophy from its work; its understanding of the world has been radicalized to the point of seeing it as the place of sin with which there is no compromise; but it has not got rid of the individualism of the missionary societies' philosophy, and, though it lives in more intense expectancy of the Kingdom of Heaven than the traditional denominations, it, like them, conceives it as a transcendent and inexorable event with which man can associate himself only through prayer.

3. *Towards a New Social Ethic?*

While Pentecostalism both radicalizes and strengthens the social ethic which the Protestant missionary societies imported into Latin America, it would seem that the younger generation of Protestant theologians has detached itself from this ethic and adopted a new perception of man and society. Over against the division of man into *homo religiosus* and *homo politicus*, it places the concept of the material and spiritual unity of man in his culture and his society. One student said, 'We South American Protestants have been the victims of a collective alienation. Now we must see that our churches and theology become truly South American.' The great majority of the students think that the proclamation of the Good News is not restricted to proselytizing activities, and, though they think that the work of evangelization in the traditional sense ought to be carried on, it should nevertheless be accompanied by a socio-political involvement, so that the structures of society themselves carry the Gospel by enabling man to live according to just principles. This social ethic, solidly based in Christology (God became Man), belongs to Niebuhr's fifth type.

One can see that, for Protestantism in Latin America, this is a real theological revolution, of which the concrete effects are as yet unforeseeable, but which might enable Christians and Churches to participate consciously in South America's great upheaval. In this new current, instead of wishing to be outside the world and to fight against it, the Church must accept being in the world and for the world; the egocentric movement is giving way to the altruistic movement.

Will this new trend of opinion, being propagated by small groups (some members of the theological faculties; student movements and youth organizations; 'Church and Society in Latin America') be able to overcome the weight of tradition which will act here as the *vis inertia* (F. Engels)? Will it be able to effect in the Churches a real Copernican revolution, since it is in fact a matter of discerning what is their true place?

CHAPTER 6

The Meaning and Consequences of Pentecostal Withdrawal from Society

PENTECOSTAL disengagement from the socio-political sphere, as we have seen, can be ascribed to a continuation of the ethical tradition common to the Protestant missions in Latin America. But even the social work carried on by the missionary societies was renounced by Pentecostalism in Chile, both on account of its radical spiritualization of religious life, and its modest financial resources. On another level, we think it possible to advance the view, in the form of a hypothesis which is at least highly probable, that the attitude of withdrawal from the world is the result of the painful experiences which Pentecostalists have had of society.

Up to now we have treated social ethics as one of the elements in the Pentecostal edifice which it would be possible to isolate. Now we must show that the resulting rejection of society and the attitude of withdrawal and passivity, if not of condemnation, do not arise from one plane only of Pentecostal society (that of collective ideas and values), but underlie its entirety: not only its whole body of beliefs, but its organizational system, its conception of authority and congregational life, etc. Thus we can say that Pentecostalism is built up around its condemnation of a world which will not be renewed until the coming of the Lord (which is imminent but impossible to foretell) and around the mission it has assumed of saving souls from this world and offering them temporary refuge in the congregation.

Pentecostal preaching is aimed at the individual and calls for a free decision. In this first stage, the proselyte makes a conscious and personal engagement; but once this step has been taken, the group dominates the individual and claims from him a total giving of his person to the congregation. To be converted and become part of the Church means for the individual accepting that all his acts be regulated and controlled by the religious community, and that nothing remains to him of the domain in which his personal conscience is the sole judge.

Not only does the community make him participate in all the community activities, but it also decides for him in his private life. Pentecostalism teaches a positive and active morality on everything which concerns the life of the group: taking part in worship and Sunday school, paying tithes, sharing in evangelism, etc. As soon as one enters the sphere of private and family life, obligations (providing a decent life for one's family, showing one's children the 'paths of the Lord', etc.) are paralleled by prohibitions (not to drink or smoke, not to take part in 'worldly pleasures'). Finally, in the domain of one's working and professional life, the morality taught becomes frankly negative and passive: one must be submissive, obedient and respectful to the authorities (whether of the State, one's employer or union), but the golden rule is, 'Thou shalt not take part'. Thus the further a man's life is removed from direct means of control by the congregation, the more the morality that is taught takes the form of prohibitions. The group enjoys a morality of activity and engagement; the individual believer must follow an ethic of non-involvement and withdrawal.

One of the characteristics of sects is that they make a totalitarian claim on the individual.[1] In Pentecostalism, its familial social structure and its paternalistic and authoritarian concept of power imply relationships of dependence which encompass not just various segments of a church member's behaviour, but form traditionally fixed situations which span the whole of the conduct of individuals. The congregation demands a mechanical rather than an organic integration, and while the act of affiliation arises from an individual decision, this decision implicitly includes the resignation of the individual, who renounces his autonomy and becomes merged into the group.

Here the Pentecostal congregation departs from the traditional Protestant congregation, and once again shows a close parallel with the Chilean type of social system, that of the *hacienda*.

The Protestant congregation, in effect, whether it be Lutheran, Calvinist or Anglican, puts as much, if not more, emphasis on the individual aspect as on the congregational aspect of faith and religious life. In the extreme case, a Protestant can live out his faith alone and do without congregational life, by reason of the emphasis placed upon the responsibility of man before God. In the Protestant tradition the solution of problems not directly connected with the parish is a matter for the individual's conscience; if he is asked, the pastor will try to help the church member to see his way clearly, but will not make decisions for him. We have had an example of this attitude earlier (see Chapter 5, section B.2), where 40 per cent of the Protestant pastors declared that political choice concerned every man's own conscience. While Pentecostalism follows the Protestant tradition in calling the individual to be converted, it departs from it in exercising a far more powerful hold over the neophyte, making him subservient to the group.

Like the *hacienda*,[2] the Pentecostal congregation integrates a man into a group; group involvement is reduced to direct, personal relationships of dependence, and the group serves as a buffer between the individual and larger social entities (e.g. the nation-state). Many of the reflections and observations made by the C.E.P.A.L. experts in their analyses of the resistance offered by traditional social systems to change are equally valid for Pentecostalism:

> The awareness of participating as 'citizens' enjoying specific rights and duties, within a national community made up of all the citizens and regulated by impersonal norms, does not seem to have replaced the personal and direct relationships of dependence in the bosom of the local power structures.[3]

Enclosed within the local structure where power is concentrated in the hands of the *hacendado* and relationships are personalized, the individual (*peon* or *inquilino*) has only indirect relations with the nation-state, inasmuch as he is a *client* of the landowner whose political directives he follows; and the landowner alone is effectively a *citizen*, since he is the only one to be directly integrated in the nation and to understand the working of impersonal laws. Thus, until the agricultural workers are offered real and effective protection which will enable them to free themselves from dependence on the *patron*, they will exist politically only as units in the clientele of the *hacendado*.

The political party chiefs quickly realized that, from their point of view, Pentecostal congregations were simply a new incarnation of the traditional social system, and that the pastor played (like the landowner) the role of liaison officer between his group and society. For this reason they approach the pastor as they would the *hacendado*, pointing out to him the advantages which he and his church would obtain if his church members were to give their votes to such and such a party.

This at once shows up one of the ambiguities in the social function Pentecostalism fulfils in a period of change; at the moment when one of the bastions of tradition is disappearing (the familial and paternalistic social system which the great landholdings realized to the full), at that very moment the Pentecostal congregation arises which, without a doubt, fills a void, by enabling the individual to be integrated into a group, organized on the old model, but at the same time making it impossible for its members to participate directly as responsible beings in the modern society which is struggling to emerge. In other words, while Pentecostalism disalienates the individual to begin with, since it allows him to overcome his uprooting and isolation by offering him entry into an organized, protective group, it then in turn alienates itself and 're-alienates' its members, since it looks upon itself as alien to the 'world' and effectively makes its members strangers to society.

Teaching based on severance from the 'world', organization based on personal face-to-face relationships, surrender of the individual to the will of the group, submission to those in authority and above all to the pastor, a community life which is directed towards making as real as possible the break with society, by filling up the whole of the church member's free time—these characteristics define a social system extremely close to the traditional system, and Emilio Willems's proposition, which seems to regard the Pentecostal congregation as a transitional link between traditional rural society and modern urban society, becomes debatable.[4] Willems considers that Pentecostalism has achieved a 'symbolic rebellion against the social status quo' and that 'its basic principles both ideological and organizational are diametrically opposed to the ideological and structural tenets of the traditional society'.[5]

We agree with him in contending that Pentecostalism constitutes a classless society, whereas South American society presents an accentuated class structure. We concede that there is no longer a monopoly of salvation, and that 'access to supernatural powers is directly open to every church member',[6] with the result that the way to the leadership is open to every member. It is equally clear that these organizational elements derive from ideological (theological) characteristics which are in sharp contrast with those prevailing in the Catholic Church and the wider society. These are what we have called the '*elements of rupture*'.

But these characteristics are balanced by others. It seems to us mistaken to affirm 'the internal equality of members of the congregation',[7] for, as we have seen, the members are organized in a quasi-military hierarchy. Similarly, though it is true that, having adopted the congregationalist system, the congregations have equal rank among themselves, it is wrong, *at least in Chile*, to claim that they 'are not subject to a higher ecclesiastical authority'[8] and that they will oppose the accession to power of a leader who has authoritarian inclinations. On the one hand, there is always, in the Chilean denominations, a centralized government, the *Directorio*,[9] with regional superintendents subordinate to it; though they are at the same time pastors of a congregation they are, as it were, officials of the central power, since their charge is to oversee the smooth running of the congregations in their area and in particular to supervise the new pastors (*obreros* and *pastores probandos*).

On the other hand, at any rate so long as the leaders of the generation which founded the denomination survive, it will be dominated by a strong personality, a true charismatic leader in Max Weber's sense. We have shown that one cannot exclude the possibility that this authoritarian system will be perpetuated beyond the first generation.[10] The members of the *Directorio* are selected by the '*leader*' rather than appointed by all the pastors (at the Annual Assembly). Though it is true that 'schism and the formation of new sects is always explained as liberation from an authoritarian and oppressive leadership, and as the return to equality and the untrammelled spontaneity of religious occurrences',[11] it is equally acknowledged that this explanation provides a *rationalization* of schism which does not correspond to the facts, as is proved by the fact that the dissidents reorganize themselves straight away on the pattern of the denomination they have left.[12] It is likewise debatable whether, in large denominations, the 'prophets' who bear inspired messages can balance the power of the pastor,[13] since most of the time the charismatic leader is also the chief prophetic authority (a typical case was the late Bishop Umaña, of the *Iglesia Metodista Pentecostal*, whose prophetic sermons were famous), and when Prof. Willems quotes the case of the *Iglesia Pentecostal de Chile* to illustrate this latter point,[14] he is picking on a case where the schismatics' declared aim, to be more democratic, was only an intellectual disguise, where the denomination is closely linked with the name of an exceptionally strong and gifted personality, and where the prophetic function is reduced to a very small role by comparison with the pastoral function, or else included in it.

Thus, while Pentecostal society is classless, and access to all the posts is open, it is no less clear that power is exercised at all levels in an authoritarian manner, and that the congregation thus reproduces the paternalistic model of the extended family, based, like the *hacienda*, on antithetical concepts: oppression and protection, arbitrary power and mercy, in short, authority and paternalism.

Such are the so-called elements of *continuity* with traditional society which—in this second survey which is centred not on social mobility and stratification within the religious movement, but on the pattern of the hierarchy and the exercise of power—make it legitimate to consider Pentecostalism as a reincarnation of the traditional social structure.

This *disputatio* is not an intellectual game; to a large extent the question of the role played by Pentecostalism in the development of Chilean society depends on the outcome. If one concludes, like Prof. Willems, that Pentecostalism breaks with the traditional social forms, and that the Pentecostal congregation has an egalitarian and democratic character, then it is logical to think it offers man an apprenticeship for life in a 'participatory society'[15] and that it constitutes a link between traditional and modern life. If, as we think is more in accordance with the facts, the Pentecostal congregation is characterized by a 'continuity/discontinuity'—if we may use the expression—in relation to traditional society, if one concludes that the individual must submit to the group, which exercises a complete ascendancy over him,[16] then one would hesitate to consider Pentecostalism as a positive factor in the transitional stage, preparing men for the exercise of responsibility in modern society.

The totalitarian ascendancy over the individual which the congregation exercises not only by its doctrine, but also by its organisational system, its concept of power and its activities, nevertheless has one fault which leads to a permanent confrontation of the 'two kingdoms' in a man's life. The *hacienda* was able for a long time to escape the shocks of contact with overall social change, because it was able to satisfy all the needs of the men who depended upon it. They lived in an enclosed economy, hardly knowing the use of money; for centuries the great landowners had, like states within the State, their own police and army at their disposal. In that situation, the peasant was completely cut off from the world beyond the *hacienda's* boundaries, and the leaders alone acted as intermediaries between him and the nation. Pentecostalism, for its part, has never, in Chile, envisaged creating productive economic communities in order to provide the material needs of its members within the congregation itself. Renouncing its economic function at the outset, it causes its members to live in a permanent state of tension, since it instructs them to retreat from the world without making it completely possible for them to do so. Pentecostalism thus leaves the church member to submit to constant demands ('temptations') from his workmates and from the problems of their working life, to which he cannot be completely indifferent since he shares them.

Professional organizations do in fact enrol believers; in the manufacturing and mining industries, trade union membership is obligatory; in the country areas agricultural workers have for several years been forming organizations, openly or secretly. The party in power (the Christian Democrats) declares its belief in the support and momentum of the masses and urges them to band together in associations of neighbours, mothers, fathers, etc., the official aim of the group being considered less important than the opportunity for meeting, organizing and finding collective means of expression. In the most harmless organization is hidden the desire to raise the individual from his marginal state, and give him the chance of becoming aware of national problems, of sharing in them and having a certain grasp of them. This effort to mobilize the people, which has developed considerably in the last decade, multiplies the pressures upon the Pentecostal church member, who cannot help being divided between his faith and his position as a proletarian worker.

For a church member two responses are possible of which we have seen numerous examples: either obedience to the pastor and the strictest passivity in one's work, or, if a man has a taste for social and labour problems, a conflict between himself and his congregation, which generally leads to a break.

In most cases the church member will follow strictly the rules laid down by his congregation. Being an industrious worker, honest, without vices, he is the worker without problems whom employers appreciate. The rule of submission to authority will in some cases involve him in following a union's orders to strike, but he will never actively participate in the social and economic demands of his companions. One is hardly surprised to learn that the offices of important pastors become employment bureaux which industrialists and *latifondistes* highly appreciate, as these words of a landowner of Curico Province show:

> I like to take on Pentecostalists; they work well, don't get drunk and don't let themselves be taken in by the propaganda of the trade unionists and red politicians, who are trying to spread their lies among my people. With them (the Pentecostalists), there are no problems. When work is finished they go to their services and don't mix with other people. . . . Every time I need more personnel, I telephone Pastor X to see if he can send me anyone.

Over against the employers' esteem for these workers who cause them no trouble is the trade unionists' lack of appreciation. The following is part of a conversation with a leader of the *Central Unica de Trabajadores*:

> The *Canutos*? They follow [trade union] orders but no more. Mind you, I think they have their good points. For example, they don't drink; and alcohol is a great scourge in Chile. But though there are a few exceptions, for us the Pentecostalists are more of a hindrance than a help. If we vote for a strike, they will strike with us, but they will not vote for it. They always on principle bow to the master's wishes, to such an extent that many of them are appointed to be overseers. One cannot count on them to take any responsibility. Or if they do take it, they are always hesitant to act, because they have no idea—how can I put it?—no understanding of society and the labour struggle.

Here, too are some notes made during a conversation with a trade unionist in Lota (Province of Concepcion), who said he was 'a member of the socialist party and sympathetic to the Gospel':

Q. 'What part do the *evangélicos* take in the unions?'

A. 'When it is compulsory they are present, but they rarely intervene. They accept the decisions voted for in the meetings, even if they don't agree with them, and do not try to defend their point of view. For example, in politics, many of them do not have their names put on the electoral register.'

Q. 'But if they wanted to, could they play a part in the unions and in political life?'

A. 'A Communist leader has said to me, "If the *evangélicos* started to be militant, they would be stronger than we are". For myself, I think they would be able to elect a *director* in each union, and a *regidor* (councillor) in every borough in the region. If they had wanted to, they would perhaps have become the Christian Democrats of today. Some of the Protestants have a great gift for public speaking. Every time I talk to the young people, I show them that the *evangélicos* are not playing any part in the social sphere nor in politics, economics or the unions, and that, if they wanted to take an interest in that, without abandoning their religion or the Bible, they would be able to have leaders in each of the parties.'

Q. 'Do you know of any individual cases of Protestants engaged in the unions' struggle?'

A. 'It happens sometimes, and when it happens, the Protestant feels very isolated, loses heart and gives up.'

Q. 'Why?'

A. 'There are two reasons. On the one hand, the union struggle is not easy. If I were an *evangélico*, I would not agree to a brother (as they call them) taking part in the union struggle unless he had the evangelistic mystique and shoulders broad enough to bear it. One has to know how to stand up to the bosses, how to manoeuvre among political opinions, how to avoid the traps which the Communists lay for all trade unionists who are not members of the Party. To be able to hold out, the Protestant needs a solid faith and some training in techniques. On the other hand, the Church does not want him to become involved, and if he does so, then it abandons him. What can he do in those circumstances? As a Protestant he wants to be involved, and his Church lets him down! Usually those who try being involved in trade unions either quickly give up and return to their churches, or they give up attending worship. There was one case which was talked about a great deal a few years ago. Mr. X, of the *Ejercito Evangélico de Chile*. He was a great preacher, and held a good position. Besides his work in Lota-Green, he had a workshop and a fishing boat. He was elected at the first attempt in the miners' union, with the support of the Communists and *evangélicos*. He was told to be careful, that he would take a toss. He answered, "Don't worry, politics won't get me; I am sound, I have faith!" He was even elected *regidor* (municipal councillor) and deputy *alcade* (mayor). Then one day the Communist Party dropped him, and he was not re-elected, and his Church paid him no attention because he was no longer useful to it. Now he has lost everything; he lives in the most abject poverty. He wanders about the streets, dressed in rags. He drinks.'

Q. 'What do you think of this attitude?'

A. 'It is a shame, for if they wanted to, they could do a good job. There is a difference between the *evangélicos* and the others; though they have the same wages, their houses are cleaner; they could do the same in the unions and in politics. *There are a great many* evangélicos, *but since they take no action, or since their teaching forbids them to take action, they are nothing.*'

This last interview shows what usually happens when a church member is a militant member of a union or political party. A pastor in Tomé said:

> I forbid my people to go in for such things. I have seen some young people who took on union responsibilities. Afterwards they no longer read the Bible but studied law and politics. They no longer had time to come to meetings or services; they no longer went out preaching in the open air. They have gone astray.

'They have gone astray'—this expression is constantly heard in the mouths of pastors as a description of those who, being engaged in secular activities, are no longer totally at the disposal of their congregation. As a matter of fact, Pentecostal organization is such that it does not leave the individual—and does not wish to leave him—any chance of other activities. But if a church member does accept responsibilities outside his church, then he begins to question the authority of the pastor and elders:

> Then, when they come to a meeting, they criticize the Church, reproach the pastor for not having officially supported the strikers. They finish up by saying that the Church ought to be in politics, which shows that they have been corrupted and God is abandoning them. Then they must be expelled before they contaminate the members, and create divisions and problems. (A pastor in Concepcion.)

When a Pentecostalist becomes aware of political or union problems, it sets in motion a complex conflict. First the church member comes into opposition with the political prohibition contained in its doctrine; next his new activities diminish his share in congregational life, which is interpreted as a 'sign of spiritual decadence'. Thirdly a personal conflict ensues; one may claim (and the quotation above shows this clearly) that a church member who assumes responsibilities in a union organization will no longer accept the pastor's authority as completely as before. Not only because his act of secular involvement is in itself a challenge to the pastor's authority, but above all because, while he is learning a form of 'collegial' participation with the union leaders (based on discussion, the acceptance of personal responsibility and decisions reached by a vote), he will begin to have doubts about the individual's submission to the group which is implied in Pentecostalism. In Durkheim's terms, when he discovers a form of organic solidarity based on the complementarity and division of functions, he will contest the mechanical fusion of the individual into the Pentecostal body. In the same breath—and the violence of the pastor's reaction in many cases stems from this—the entire hierarchic system and social organization of Pentecostalism are compromised. When a church member no longer follows the rule of passivity, he escapes from the community's ideological ascendancy and from its control; he participates not only in other activities but in other values. He escapes from the *life under tutelage* which, in the last analysis, constitutes the individual's life in the Pentecostal congregation, as in all communities where power is paternalistic and authoritarian. Then the pastor will be struggling not only to preserve the community, but also his own status. He now has opposed to him a member who no longer considers him the 'boss', who thinks he can be the sole judge regarding his secular involvement, and who asks the pastor at least to suspend judgment, since he will not give his approval.

Thus the incompatibility of secular involvement and Pentecostalism is not just an ideological problem, but it permeates all levels of the Pentecostal social phenomenon. A church member's participation in politics naturally has some effect on his norms and moral code, but it also affects his concept of power, his demand for participation and solidarity, and the form which his individual participation should take. In short, the Pentecostal system being what it is, it is correct to state that responsible participation in a trade union comes down to serving two antagonistic masters. The question (theologically speaking) which has still to be raised is that of knowing whether the Gospel really has no political and social dimension, and this drives the Pentecostalist unconsciously to play the role of defender of the old society (the *status quo*) and order, in the face of the mounting forces of progress and modernity.

To a leading Pentecostalist—advocating a form of involvement in politics of which we shall speak again later—who had just been preaching from the book of Amos and had completely omitted that prophet's message of social justice, we pointed out the socio-political dimension of the prophetic books, and asked him if anyone preached on this theme in the churches of his denomination. This was his reply:

> I know that there is a social message, even a political and revolutionary message, in the Bible. Not only in the Old Testament: there is also the Epistle of James. And this message, which is a part of the Gospel, attacks the rich who exploit the poor. There would be a great deal to say on this subject in Chile. But for the time being we cannot do it. Our people are too weak, they lack maturity, often they hardly know how to read. Then what would happen if one preached on these texts? They would not understand; that would create problems and difficulties in the churches. No, we cannot do that. Besides, you know that people mix up "politics" and "*politiqueria*'; the first is the art of governing the people, and the second is the struggle between groups or individuals. And in the Pentecostal churches, there is a fear—a very great fear—of anything political. This feeling of fear is uppermost in our churches, and a ring of spiritual ideas has been created to prevent all contact with the political world. And even to prevent the various denominations banding together in order to form a political force . . . People have the idea that each church forms a privileged people, the people of God, which should live without contact with the rest, who are called 'gentiles'. It is a bit like the Jewish idea at the time of Jesus and the Samaritans.

This pastor is one of the Pentecostalists who is reflecting upon his church in a critical way and is aware of the way in which Pentecostalism cuts down the Gospel. But he justifies the existing state of affairs, advancing the lack of maturity of church members as a pretext.

From the preceding pages an important hypothesis can be extracted for the future of the Pentecostal movement. *The more that real and concrete opportunities for direct participation are offered to the working class by Chilean society, the stronger will grow the tension between belonging to the Pentecostal movement and the awareness of being a citizen of a country.* What will happen then? Before attempting to give a reply, let us first show some of the effects of social pressure on the Protestant pastors' consciousness.

As was indicated in the introduction, the sample of Pentecostal pastors includes all the pastors of five denominations in three of the Provinces. We shall see that pastors' replies to questions relating to socio-political involvement show certain variations, according to the Province to which they belong.

Table 11. Socio-political responsibility of the church, in the opinion of Pentecostal pastors. Distribution by province*

	YES	NO	TOTAL	NUMBER
	%	%	%	
Cautin	—	100	100	10
Santiago	37	63	100	38
Concepcion	62	38	100	13
TOTAL	36	64	100	61

Table 12. Distribution by provinces of Pentecostal pastors who accept church members' involvement in activities of a social and/or political nature (percentages)*

	NEIGHBOURHOOD ASSOC.	TRADE UNIONS	POLITICAL PARTIES	NUMBER
	%	%	%	
Cautin	70	30	20	10
Santiago	63	50	5	38
Concepcion	85	69	31	13
TOTAL	68	51	13	61

* For the text of the questions, see Table 1, p. 108; Table 2, p. 112; Table 8 and Table 9, p. 120.

In these four tables the pastors of Concepcion Province stand out from the others by reason of their better acquaintance with the news and their greater sensitivity to political affairs. Now this province is highly industrialized:[17] textiles in the north, the port of Talcahuano in the centre and coal mines in the south. Trade union membership

Table 13. The definition of 'under-developed' given by Pentecostal pastors, by province*

	CORRECT	INCORRECT	TOTAL	NUMBER
	%	%	%	
Cautin	60	40	100	10
Santiago	53	47	100	38
Concepcion	77	23	100	13
TOTAL	59	41	100	61

Table 14. Intervention of the U.S.A. in the Dominican Republic and the opinion of the Pentecostal pastors, by province*

	HAS NOT HEARD OF IT	KNOWS ABOUT IT; DOES HE APPROVE? NO	YES	DON'T KNOW	NO REPLY	TOTAL	NUMBER
	%	%	%	%	%		
Cautin	40	20	20	20	—	100	10
Santiago	30	29	16	5	11	100	38
Concepcion	15	63	15	7	—	100	13
TOTAL	34	34	17	8	7	100	61

* For the text of the questions, see Table 1, p. 108; Table 2, p. 112; Table 8, and Table 9, p. 120.

is compulsory in these occupations, so that Pentecostal workers are obliged, at least, to tolerate the atmosphere, culture and preoccupations of trade associations. Apart from the town of Concepcion, the urban areas are each situated round a mine or other undertaking; everyone lives on ground owned by the company; not so very long ago supplies had to be bought in the company's stores—at high prices. The industrial environment exercises a constant pressure, and in the end penetrates even the consciousness of the Pentecostalists. Then certain political values begin to be propagated by the pastors themselves when they are directly confronted with work problems, since in that region it is not so rare for the minister to have a secular occupation. There six out of ten pastors think the Church has a responsibility towards society; nearly one-third accept the involvement of their members in party politics, 63 per cent condemned the United States' intervention in the Dominican Republic, and only 15 per cent had not heard of it.

Nevertheless, we should not be deluded as to the significance of these results; the trade unionist whose words were reported above belongs to the coal-mining area and was speaking of the churches in that Province. Most of the questions in our investigation relate to the possibility of socio-political involvement, and not to any concrete encouragement which might be given to it. Lastly, even in this province less than one-third of the pastors authorize their members to take an active part in political parties. It is important to remember what influence the social milieu has on Pentecostal attitudes in regard to types of secular involvement. In Concepcion, where trade union membership is much higher than in the other two Provinces, the *churches are more sensitive to the problems of the surrounding community (industry, mining), because in fact its members participate in them more directly than elsewhere.*

One can easily understand the answers given by the Cautin pastors. This Province is almost exclusively rural and agricultural; trade unionism is insignificant, and the Province provides its inhabitants with only the traditional possibilities of participation, through the medium of social organizations in which there are direct personal links of dependency, be it in agricultural enterprises, the Indian reservations or small-scale industries.

More surprising are the results for Santiago, which are close to those of Cautin. The Pentecostalists in the megapolis and those of the *campo* are thus developing the same attitudes in this realm. Although we were unable to carry out any large-scale investigation, several indications give reasonable grounds for supposing that Pentecostal recruitment in the capital is chiefly among the migrants and the 'marginal', the two terms usually designating the same individuals. Even the term used to describe them, 'marginal', shows that they are unintegrated in the organizations which characterize modern society, and at the same time explains the imperviousness of Pentecostalism in the capital to political preoccupations.

These few indications suggest that when individuals are in fact enrolled in organizations which depend upon emerging modern society, the Pentecostal Church is bound to modify its social ethic. But how far can this process of accommodation go?

Let us look at the problem from another angle. How should one regard Pentecostalism's contribution to the slow and unsteady rise of modern secular society in Chile? The congregations of this movement offer the individual a palliative for his uprootedness, enabling him to belong to and participate in a protective group. But the congregations are organized on the pattern of the declining traditional society. In an era of transition, they are an attempt to restore the past, though with some new features which are closer to the characteristics of modern society—for example, the absence of a rigid and closed social stratification, and internal possibilities of mobility. But its totalitarian ascendancy over the individual makes it more akin to the traditional social structure, trying to cut its members off from the global society. This characteristic, closely dependent upon Pentecostalism's body of beliefs (including its social ethic), makes of it an element in the resistance to change, since it aims to isolate the church member from innovating movements. This is in any case the way in which people not acquainted with Pentecostalism view it, since both the landowner and the industrialist congratulate themselves on the *evangélicos'* detachment, while the trade union leaders deplore it.

At the beginning of Chapter 5 (p. 106) we put the question of the internal cohesiveness of Pentecostalism, regarded as a total social phenomenon. On the one hand, we observed Pentecostalism's acculturation in Chile—which makes it the only form of Protestantism which is authentically South American—which is produced by a curious process of severance from and of appropriation of the classic elements of the surrounding culture (patterns of religious behaviour) and the surrounding society (system of organization, concept of authority, etc.). On the other, we now see that there is a conscious refusal to share in this culture and this society. Is there a point at which these contradictory movements can be reconciled? Yes, and it is to be found in the fact that the Pentecostal congregation is inspired by traditional society (the *hacienda*), not by the emerging modern society. Even though Pentecostalism has spread, thanks to the fact that tradition is being questioned, as soon as certain modern institutions are established and really function, then the totalitarian aim of the Pentecostal community will have to give ground. Does this mean that, if Chile succeeded in its economic and social development, Pentecostalism would mark time and perhaps even regress? Let us beware of making forecasts. Already examples overseas have shown (the Scandinavian countries in particular) that Pentecostalism can have foundations other than economic misery. In the U.S.A. a tendency has been noted for some Presbyterian, Methodist and other churches to be 'pentecostalized', where the members belong to the middle or even the upper classes; in the same country, Pentecostalism continues to exist even when the social status of its members improves. Even in Chile a reading of the indices available to us provides contradictions: while trade unionism in the mining region of Concepcion operates in favour of a preliminary form of social integration, it is none the less true that in this region Pentecostalism is the most lively and dynamic. But trade unionism is only one of the possible indices of integration, and moreover the unions' activities have not eliminated the precariousness of living conditions in the coal-mining area. The latter may be a counterweight to the former.

What is certain is that the growing movement towards enrolling the Chilean people in secular organizations of all kinds will force Pentecostalism to make certain adjustments.

The ideal would be, from a Christian standpoint, for Pentecostalism to alter its political ethic, and aim to form in its members a sense of personal responsibility by offering them an ethic of involvement in national organizations. The believer would join the political parties and the trade unions, and accept responsibilities, by virtue of his Christian faith, which would lead him to participate directly in the transforming of his country.

But a major difficulty then arises: because of the extraordinary cohesion and interpenetration of all the levels of the Pentecostal system, because of the extreme degree of interdependence between organization, social patterns, collective behaviour, the web of social roles and doctrine, it is clear that *any conscious attempt at reform in one particular sphere would by its repercussions rock the whole edifice*. As we have already seen, if Pentecostalism were to adopt a doctrine which recognized the socio-political responsibility of Christians in society, a recasting would be required, which would not be limited to its 'doctrine of the world', but would also affect the status of the pastor, the organization, the way in which the congregations think members should use their time, and so on. A small alteration implies, in the end, transforming the whole of this very closely integrated total social phenomenon, Pentecostalism.

Now there are no symptoms leading one to believe that Pentecostalism would embark on such an adventure. The hallowing of tradition, respect for established norms and the absence of reforming personalities make such a change inconceivable.

Another possibility, which would not in itself affect the structure of the Pentecostal congregations, would be that pastors acquire a positive awareness of political questions and their responsibility in regard to society, and add another dimension to their spiritual and paternal role—that of the political head of their congregation. The congregation would follow its natural leader in politics, just as in the past the workers in the *hacienda* voted according to the orders of the 'patron'. In this way the totalitarian pretensions of Pentecostal organization and ideology would be preserved, and the pastor would play the role of the traditional leader—i.e. that of the mediator between his clientele and the national set-up.

A tendency in this direction already exists in the passive rather than active support accorded to political parties by some pastors of large congregations. Where the political parties are not able directly to influence individuals—that is, where paternalistic social organizations exist, demanding direct, personal loyalty to the 'patron' and so filtering relations between the individual and society—professional politicians have no other course than to seek the adherence of the traditional leaders, the magnates. This adherence may be spontaneous, and it is clear that, since the conservative party represents the interests of the landowners, they will give it their support and that of their clients, so far as in them lies. But there are other 'leaders' with a clientele, whose attitude towards politics is one of indifference: the Pentecostal pastors. Generally they will not give their support at any price either to the conservatives (the party historically linked with the Catholic hierarchy), or to the atheist Communists (although in the coal-mining area they are less antagonistic to Communism than elsewhere). The radical party, defender of liberty of conscience, used to have a good press, and many of the pastors were willing to advise their members to vote for it, in return receiving a pecuniary reward which could be used for decorating the church or constructing a new chapel. At the time of the last presidential elections (1964) when the struggle was between the Christian Democrat party and the F.R.A.P. (Marxist), some pastors leaned toward one candidate and some toward the other. (The choice was difficult, for the one committed the error of offering himself as a *Catholic*, and the other as a *socialist*. Taking all things into consideration, people preferred the black to the red peril.)

One should point out that it is difficult for a party to verify what real support the pastor brings to it, and that we know of only a few cases where the pastor would have intervened from the pulpit to influence his members. The advice is rather given person to person, without great publicity, but without secrecy either, nor with a bad conscience. This is what a young pastor says concerning it:

> Many pastors accept such aid from a party. Not from just any party: it must be one which does not oppose the Gospel. But we are poor churches; our members are very poor, and with this money we can do great things for God's work. Besides, apart from a few unhappy examples, we do not tell the church members that they must vote for one party. We tell trusted brothers that such and such a deputy has given us this help, and that we could help him, and these trusted members repeat this to their close friends. But there is no way of checking, in fact it is impossible to check the votes. And we do not allow the politicians to speak during worship either. Since one has to vote in any case, we might as well vote for a party which helps us.
>
> Personally, nobody has ever asked me anything; that is because I have only recently started work, and so far there are not many members. But if someone were to make me an offer, I would accept. With fear, since I know that it could become a temptation; but I would accept it since I could use the money for my church. Of course, things should not go so far as to compromise the church with one party, and one must know where to stop so that the party cannot give us orders. But I would do it.

This traditional form of political involvement, where the pastor wields his influence over his congregation, might take a more active turn if the dream of a number of Pentecostal leaders were realized and a Protestant party were created, with social-democratic tendencies. This idea is, moreover, semi-officially supported by some foreigners who represent church relief agencies (Church World Service) to whom the establishment of a political force which is neither Catholic nor Marxist would be convenient. From the number of Protestants in Chile, it is clear that, if their votes were directed in a unified way in favour of one party, they would constitute an impressive array. Various factors conspire to stimulate the political ambitions of some leaders. Apart from a certain awareness of the country's needs, there is also a seeking for prestige, manifested not only in this way but also by the desire to build grandiose churches and introduce a decorum into the ceremonial (special ritual and special clothing for the pastors) which would raise Pentecostalism, 'the church of the poor and outcast' to the ranks of a 'respectable religion'. There is also the fact that, being aware of the strength of the movement, some leaders find it humiliating, when they have to present a request to the Government, to have to beg for the support of a deputy or senator. These feelings are mingled in the following words of one pastor:

> In the political realm, I would say that—although we are obliged by law to participate in elections—the churches in general are against all political participation, for fear of losing those who might take part in political activities and struggles. And we have reached the point of sad reality that in Chile, with nearly a million Protestants, we have neither a deputy nor a senator to whom we could submit our requests and who would represent Protestant ideas, the aims of the Evangelical Church, which are to improve the lot of men by means of Biblical precepts and the teaching of our Master, the Lord Jesus Christ.

This awakening of political ambition in certain Pentecostalists is in itself a sign of evolution towards a certain degree of accommodation. But the dream of a party in which the mass of Pentecostalists would participate is still far from becoming a reality, even though it might one day be realized. Moreover, ideas on the subject are very confused. Is it a matter of a *Protestant* social-democratic party, or a Social-Democrat party to which the Protestants would give their support? It seems that the second hypothesis is the right one, since Pentecostalists do not have the people capable of initiating a new political movement with any chance of success. Of course there is talk in Chile of creating such a party, but we should observe that these suggestions come from the dynamic elements of the right wing, which is in a state of collapse and thinks it necessary to find a new guise in order to slow down its decline. Pentecostalism would then find itself once more on the side of order. But the splintering of Pentecostalism and the personal rivalries dividing its leaders make it doubtful whether the Pentecostal population would acquire political unity, the more so since the present leaders of the two principal branches, the *Iglesia Metodista Pentecostal* (which has just severed its links with the radical party) and the *Iglesia Evangélica Pentecostal* firmly refuse to make an alliance with any particular party.

There exists in Chile one denominational leader who also enjoys a certain status as a political *caudillo*—Pastor Victor Manuel Mora, who left the Methodist Church in 1928 to found the *Iglesia Wesleyana Nacional*. He is a rare case, having studied for a time in a Methodist seminary; he was a miner and a trade leader, and took part in the foundation of the Socialist Party. His denomination is established chiefly in the coal mining area, but, to judge by the congregations which we visited, it seems today to be somewhat in a state of stagnation. According to Pastor Mora, every member of his church must be active in the Socialist Party: 'I do not allow anyone to become a member of my church unless he belongs to the Left.'[18] Hence the name *Nacional* given to his church, which signifies that it is in no way dependent on foreign aid, and that it stands 'for the ordinary mining people'. It counts itself faithful to Primitive Methodism (Wesley's Church), but it does contain some Pentecostal features, such as the accent put upon prophecy (it has a 'school of prophetesses') and baptism of the Spirit: 'In the religious realm, we belong to the type called fanatic: we are spiritualist, particularly as regards the doctrines of healing, of which we have daily proofs, and prophecies'.

As far as we know, this is the only case of a denomination with a revolutionary political outlook, a combination due to the founder's own history. But how does he reconcile his faith and his Marxist involvement? In an interview, Father Vergara pointed out the atheism of Marxism to him, and quoted Marx's chief passage on religion to him. Mora replied thus:

> Christianity will never find a rival in Marxism, because Christianity concerns the head, while Marxism relates to the stomach. Besides, we shall never be able to achieve Christian ideals; even Jesus himself did

not succeed, and the proof of it is that they killed him. . . . Communism will come, but it is clear that Christian ideals, as ideals, will survive.[19]

Besides a certain theological liberalism (Christian belief perceived as an ideal), the interesting thing about this position is that it illustrates a way of integrating political responsibility with Christian belief and at the same time preserving the basic scheme of dichotomy: religion is an affair of the spirit, politics of the flesh (or stomach). The difference here is that this is no longer a dualist dichotomy: the flesh is not *a priori* the seat of evil, and on another level politics is just as important as religion: it imperfectly achieves religion's perfect but unrealizable ideal. In conversation with another interviewer, Mora said that the love of Jesus for the poor teaches us the necessity for left-wing political activity. Thus, while the pastor does perform a revolution in the classic Protestant scheme of thought by validating the political phenomenon, he does not succeed in integrating it into the faith in the realm of the spirit. But he is one of the few church leaders to have freed himself from the anti-communism propagated by the Protestant missions and transmitted to Pentecostalism, just as he is the only one who, in his political thought, takes as his starting-point the needs of the people and not the needs of the Church.

Though, on the one hand, the conversion of Pentecostalism into a non-totalitarian Church, teaching responsible involvement of its members in secular society and allowing involvement at the level of social structures, seems to us impossible by reason of the simple fact that tradition plays such a preponderant role; and though, on the other hand, the idea of a massive involvement of Protestants in a single party, under the leadership of pastors assuming the part of political chiefs, seems an illusion because of Pentecostalist pluralism, yet it remains a probability that its expansionist tendency will drive Pentecostalism to accommodate itself empirically to the wider society. That this evolution is already on the way is shown by several signs, such as the political longings of some of the leaders, the relative acceptance of members' actual political involvement in Concepcion Province, and the desire for an honourable social status. But the obstructions—latent or evident dualism, also anti-communism—make it very unlikely that Pentecostalism will change from being a factor favouring the *status quo* and become a motive element favouring change. While the socio-political 'strike' practised up to now by Pentecostalism has made it an a-political force favouring the past and the existing order rather than the future, it might evolve towards a political position on the right-centre. It is clear that if the radical party, now in a state of crisis, were replaced by an a-religious social democracy, Pentecostal votes would preferably be given to it, for fear of the Catholicism of the Christian Democrats and the atheism of the Marxist parties. But in that case, the question would be the following: while the FRAP monopolizes the policy of straightforward revolution, and the Christian Democrats are motivated by the idea of a revolution bounded by democratic liberties, what progressive ideology would form the basis for a shaky Social Democrat party? Could it be anything other than the Right in disguise? And then, anxiety for the defence of the Church taking priority over the defence of the people, Pentecostalism would once again, for the sake of its religious interests, take on a political coloration which went against the class interests of its members.

Conclusion

In Pentecostalism, nineteenth-century Methodism has been changed radically and spiritually, even though at the same time some of its principal 'dogmas' have been preserved and even reinforced, such as the dualism of spirit and flesh, and the imminent but transcendent and ultra-terrestrial character of the Kingdom (situated in the heavens). Pentecostalism teaches its initiates withdrawal and passivity in socio-political matters, limited only by the commandment to be submissive to authority. In its social forms, it appears as a specialized (since it is purely religious) reincarnation of a moribund society, and as the heir of structures from the past rather than the precursor of an emerging society. These components make it in the last analysis a force for order rather than an element of progress, a defender of the *status quo* and not a promoter of change. This is one of the most astonishing elements of Pentecostalism—and in my own judgment most regrettable. It develops in its members, who belong to the Chilean proletariat, a state of mind which causes them to range themselves alongside the conservatives. This is also its point of weakness. In fact, to the extent that organizations of every kind continue to develop with the aim of mobilizing the people and creating attitudes favourable to change, the church member will be more and more divided between his Church and his country, his religious belief and his economic and political interests. The very fact that, with a few exceptions, active trade unionists end by breaking with their Church, which rejects them, shows that this tension operates in favour of secular rather than religious involvement.

In other words—and on this point observers in the years to come must concentrate their attention—will the growing mobilization of the Chilean people check the expansion of Pentecostalism, even to the point of reducing it to a declining force? Will it call forth a change in Chilean Pentecostalism, or will the latter be too bowed down under the weight of its tradition to be able to reform? In our opinion, the shock caused by the awakening of the Chilean masses to political awareness will dominate the history of Pentecostalism in the years to come.

CHAPTER 7

Protestantism, Individual Mobility and Social Change

BESIDES its social ethic, that is, its teaching on society, a religious movement can have on a society an indirect and even involuntary influence. Even while Pentecostalism claims to be uninterested in the political and economic history of the country, the values which it propagates and transmits to its members may have a profound effect on the country's progress and its development. We were told more than once during conversations in Chile that, of course, Protestantism has a very limited social ethic and Pentecostalism has none at all, *but* by teaching industriousness at work, refusal to waste anything and thus a kind of asceticism, Pentecostalism, like all other forms of Protestantism, enables its members to improve their personal position; the children will study longer than their fathers did, and will thus have access to higher occupations. By creating an improvement in living conditions for thousands of families, Pentecostalism works towards the transformation of the whole of Chilean society.

This argument is widespread among the Boards of Mission as well as in Latin American congregations. We met it in our interviews, when some of the Protestant pastors declared, 'By changing the individual the Church changes society'. Protestantism, by the mere fact of holding a body of 'positive ideas' (Rycroft), could have no other result than the remarkable development of Latin America into a democratic and industrialized socicty;[1] 'If only Latin America were Protestant', President Roosevelt once exclaimed, 'everything would be easy'. This profound belief in the social and economic virtues which result from Protestant preaching is also the justification for the a-political or anti-political attitude of the Protestant Churches, and, as is pointed out in a document of the Second Continental Consultation of the 'Church and Society in Latin America' movement (ISAL) 'it is in conflict with the need for social solidarity, which is demanded by the process of national development taking place in our countries'.[2]

This doctrine of the connection between socio-economic progress and Protestantism, which, while not officially taught, appears in missionary journals and is accepted by a general consensus of Protestants, poses two questions that require verification. First of all, is it true that a Protestant improves his situation, and that his children experience an ascent in the social scale? Furthermore, if this first hypothesis is true, what weight has this process of individual vertical mobility in the setting of the global transformation of society? Is it true that, by changing the individual and bettering his economic situation, one transforms society?

Before sketching a reply to these questions by analysing the facts in

Chile, perhaps it is necessary to recall that these beliefs, which have existed in Protestantism since the advent of Calvinist orthodoxy, received a scientific foundation thanks to the studies of the historian and sociologist, Max Weber. Since he is constantly being called upon in support, it would be a good thing first of all to summarize his argument.

I. THE 'WEBERIAN HYPOTHESIS'

Max Weber's study, *The Protestant Ethic and the Spirit of Capitalism*, which introduces his vast *Gesammelte Aufsätze zur Religionssoziologie*[3] is probably the most widely known to the general public, who sum up their recollections of it in the idea that 'Protestantism is the origin of modern capitalism'. In reality, Weber's intention is more subtle, has finer shades of meaning and is also more modest. He first of all seeks to refute 'the doctrine of the more naïve historical materialism, that such ideas' (i.e. capitalist philosophy or again some Protestant dogmas) 'originate as a reflection or superstructure of economic situations'.[4] Weber here alludes partly to the classic thesis of Marxism, in which morality is conditioned by the state of the means of production, but also more especially to a famous passage from Friedrich Engels:

> Calvin's creed was one fit for the boldest of the bourgeoisie of his time. His predestination doctrine was the religious expression of the fact that in the commercial world of competition success or failure does not depend upon a man's activity or cleverness, but upon circumstances uncontrollable by him. It is not of him that willeth or of him that runneth, but of the mercy of unknown superior economic powers; and this was especially true at a period of economic revolution, when all old commercial routes and centres were replaced by new ones, when India and America were opened to the world, and when even the most sacred economic articles of faith—the value of gold and silver—began to totter and to break down.[5]

In opposition to this thesis, which makes religious dogma a mental cover or an *a posteriori* justification of the facts, Weber puts forward two central ideas: on the one hand, it is the spirit of capitalism which engendered capitalist structures (and not the reverse), and on the other, the way was prepared for this spirit of capitalism, in its secularized form, by certain religious values in Protestantism. Note the shade of meaning: Weber never said that Protestantism was the *cause* of capitalism; he shows moreover that other ethical systems can contribute to this *preparation*: in Japan the Samurai code of morals played the role taken by Calvinism in the West. Thus one cannot use Weber to make Protestantism out to be the only source of economic progress and development. Besides, he says:

> We have no intention whatever of maintaining such a foolish and doctrinaire thesis as that the spirit of capitalism . . . could *only* have arisen as the result of certain effects of the Reformation, or even that capitalism as an *economic system* is a creation of the Reformation. . . . On the contrary we only wish to ascertain whether and to what extent

religious forces have taken part in the qualitative formation and the quantitative expansion of that spirit over the world. Furthermore, what concrete *aspects* of our capitalistic *culture* can be traced to them.[6]

Weber's project is thus more modest than the one attributed to him by those who popularize him. Nevertheless, in opposition to a materialist theory (determination of ideas by economic structures) which he calls naïve, he puts forward an idealist theory (determination of economic structures by ideas), and we must trace the links in his chain of argument.[7]

According to Weber, it was impossible for a spirit conducive to the development of capitalism to arise in the Middle Ages, since at that time a subsistence economy, not an expansionist one, ruled and because on the other hand work had no value in itself, apart from enabling one to survive, the accumulation of material goods being regarded simply as a contingent phenomenon, even something to be scorned. For medieval man, the idea of having as one's sole purpose in life the accumulation of riches, not so much in order to enjoy them as to have proof of having done one's job well (which characterizes capitalist man), seemed to him 'explicable only as the product of a perverse instinct, the *auri sacra fames*'.[8] It was thus necessary for new elements to be introduced which alone could explain the discontinuity and opposition between the spirit of the Middle Ages and that of capitalism.

The first element of discontinuity burgeons with Luther who, in his translation of the Bible, presents *work* as a vocation (*Beruf als Ruf*). With the Reformation, one's daily task, not the monastery, becomes the place of privilege in which to glorify God. The Reformation secularizes the cloister, by giving religious value to secular life.

The second element rests on the Calvinist doctrine of *predestination*. It is a question of more than the reformer's own teaching: it concerns its radicalization, effected by the rationalist Calvinism of the seventeenth century. Men being elect or damned for all time, the agonizing question then arises, 'Am I one of the elect?' Now, for Calvinist orthodoxy, election must be followed by visible sanctification, with objective effects, and then Puritan ethics is born: ascetic conduct and a methodical self-examination enable the believer to ascertain his state of grace at any given moment. Thus there flows from Protestantism an ethical code which stimulates man in his profession, drives him to create and produce, and at the same time prevents him from consuming, since, as the parable of the talents (Mat. 25: 14–30) shows, he is only the steward of things belonging to God. This mechanism—high production and low consumption—produces savings, i.e. the capital which permits investment, in short, economic expansion and progress.

The Weberian theory thus means that the Protestant ethic helps in the creation of a *spirit of enterprise and asceticism*, which is exactly the spirit of capitalism, which itself precedes and gives rise to capitalist economic structures.

This work of the great German sociologist had a tremendous effect as soon as it was published. The proof of its importance is that even today, more than half a century later, controversy about him has not died down.[9]

For our purpose the important thing is not to decide what is the relation between Protestantism and the spirit of capitalism, but to point out that the models of economic growth put forward in recent works[10] agree with Weber in affirming that the creation of a productive and ascetic mentality is one of the essential elements in enabling emerging countries to achieve their economic 'take off'. On this basis, South American Protestants have the right to put the question, 'Do our values not contribute to the formation of a spirit of enterprise?'

Nevertheless, modern thought insists on the incomplete character of the Weber model of development, and finally tends to put Weber and Engels back to back, or rather to read them as complementary:

> One of the most serious of these limitations is emphasis on the importance of the motivational factor at the expense of the historical and institutional setting . . . it would be advisable to consider motivation in close connection with institutional structure and its historical development.[11]

Robert Bellah thus suggests that the relation between individual motivation and the structural context does not necessarily fit into a determinist pattern, whether of ideas (as in Weber) or of the economic context (as in Engels). A situation may exist which is propitious for productive activity, without that activity occurring, for lack of the right motivation; it can equally well happen that the spirit of enterprise exists in one part of the population, but the institutionalized occupational channels of social mobility cause individuals to turn towards unproductive activities. In this sense, it is worth reproducing the words of an expert on the problems of development in Indonesia, Clifford Geertz, whom Bellah quotes:

> The extent and excellence of a nation's resources, the size and skill of its labor force, the scope and complexity of its productive 'plant', and the distribution and value of entrepreneurial abilities among its population are *only one element* in the assessment of its capacity for economic growth; the institutional arrangements by means of which these various factors can be brought to bear on any particular economic goal is another. . . . It is for this reason that economic development in 'under-developed' areas implies much more than capital transfers, technical aid, and ideological exhortation: *it demands a deep-going transformation of the basic structure of society* and, beyond that, perhaps even in the underlying value-system in terms of which that structure operates.[12]

Thus the individualist approach dear to Protestantism: 'transform the man and you transform society', has no absolute value. Engels's intuition retains all its worth, for in fact circumstances can exist in which success and failure, riches and misery, do not depend on the individual's effort, but on the conditioning which the social structure effects upon the individual. Let us give an example: does the misery in which part of the Chilean population lives come from the individual's faults of drunkenness, idleness and immorality? Or on the contrary do this drunkenness, idleness and immorality result from the stagnation of the social structures, from the absence of educational prospects and professional mobility, etc.? ISAL had the courage to question the naïveté of Protestant individualism, affirming that our neighbour

> 'appears in a *situation of structural poverty*, which means he is poor not because of his personal inability to overcome poverty, but because of the social structures in which he lives,'

and goes on to call the Christian to

> 'action in society, liberating our neighbour from his structural poverty by changing not only his individual situation but the social structures which made him poor.'[13]

This is exactly the point which must be examined. Even if Protestantism favoured the creation of a spirit of enterprise, will that spirit find the structural channels through which to express itself, and in which to take concrete form in real production, which would lead to a development of the whole society? If that is in fact the case, then Protestantism's great social justification has its *raison d'être*, and its individualism does contribute in the end, indirectly but in reality, to the development of the country. But if that is *not* the case, Protestantism should abandon this argument and re-examine in depth its reading of society. In terms of loving one's neighbour, it cannot avoid the question of political choice since, the individualist solution having reached an impasse, an attack must be launched to reform the fundamental structures. The stakes are high for, as Dr. J. Míguez states, the question will be, without a doubt, to find out whether the Protestant religion is more than just a new form of 'opium for the masses'.[14]

2. INDICES OF THE SOCIAL MOBILITY OF PROTESTANTS IN CHILE

The reply to the question which has been posed requires a three stage development: first of all, do the ideas transmitted by Protestantism and Pentecostalism create among church members a motivation favourable to the spirit of enterprise and asceticism? If this is so, does this spirit bring the Protestants along the road to social and economic betterment, either within or between generations? If the answer is affirmative, does this individual vertical mobility contribute, and how, to the dynamism of the total economic and social development? The first two questions will be dealt with here, and the last will be the subject of the next section.

The lines which follow are certainly not intended to be the last word on this important problem, but rather an introduction. No investigation has been carried out into the social mobility of Protestants in Latin America; no analysis has been done to determine whether Protestantism there retains the same theology of work that it has in the Anglo-Saxon world, and no attempt has been made to integrate an individual approach to the problem of development in a study of the global social structure. Our personal observation has been fragmentary, and our ambition goes no further than to break down the taboos, question certain Protestant conventions, and underline the complexity of the problem which, for apologetic ends, has been simplified to the extreme. It is clear that a scientific study of the subject is one of the conditions for progress in understanding Protestantism in Latin America, and these notes may serve to set the boundaries of the problems.

(1) The people of Chile adopt, in general, a questioning and critical attitude towards Pentecostalism; the bourgeois asks with what authority these uneducated people teach, the trade unionist reproaches them for having lost their class consciousness, the Catholic fears the dissemination of false creeds, and the oligarchy despises this religion of the lower classes. Nevertheless, all the persons we met agree on at least one merit of this religious movement, that of liberating men from various vices, including alcoholism, restoring the family and teaching asceticism. Doctors, nurses, social workers, and also trade unionists, in short all those who know the living conditions in the working-class quarters and on the land, point to the fact that family unity is more stable among the Protestants, that the prohibition of alcohol is an excellent thing,[15] and that Pentecostal homes are better kept and cleaner. The prohibitions which signpost Protestant life (this is just as true for the Methodist as for the Pentecostalist or the Baptist) lead to certain savings and to a better management of the modest family budget. We have often noticed that the Protestant who neither smokes nor drinks has a more intelligent diet and dresses more correctly. Nevertheless (and this is one of the first questions which should be investigated) are the economies resulting from the elimination of certain needs which are looked on as sins, transformed into savings, or are they balanced by new forms of spending? In other words, does Protestant asceticism lead to the building up of a small capital or does it simply lead to a more intelligent use of one's wages?

Perhaps some information on wages will make the alternatives clearer:[16] in the Province of Coquimbo, miners told us that their daily wage varied between 2·5 and 4·0 Eo. The agricultural workers receive in cash rarely more than 1·5 Eo per day. In Santiago our investigation in a poor district revealed that the wages of members of the Pentecostal congregation varied between 70 and 310 Eo. per month; in the coal mining area, no Pentecostalist said he had a wage higher than 350 Eo. per month.

These wages, which have to meet the needs of families in which there are many children, lead one to think that the satisfaction of physical needs, such as the improvement of diet, leaves hardly any place for saving. To this index another argument can be added, related to the monetary economy of Chile: the devaluation of the currency is constant and rapid, and does not favour the creation of savings, but on the contrary encourages the immediate use of money.

These observations make it doubtful whether Protestant asceticism, in the Chilean context, does contribute to the formation of savings and thus of capital.

Following the Weber schema, should we ask whether Protestantism gives worth to the spirit of work, production and enterprise? Is work seen as a vocation, as the place where election becomes visible and bears fruit? Of course we heard pastors make observations such as the following:

> You see that man? He is very rich; he has two businesses. Well, when he was converted, he was a drunkard, good for nothing; his wife had to find the money herself to feed herself and the children. Now he is the richest member of the congregation. God has blessed him!

But much more often, the fear was expressed that riches went with unbelief:

> Those who become rich begin to despise the brethren, and to 'believe in themselves'. They are lost, like those who go in for politics. I know a good example of this. You have seen Brother X. He has a fortune of several million pesos [one escudo equals 1,000 pesos], and has the biggest draper's store in the town. Well, several years ago, before his shop grew to such a size, he began to stop coming to services and was losing his spirituality. Then God punished him; one evening his shop caught fire, and buildings in our town are wooden. So you can imagine how his shop, built of wood and full of material, burnt; one could do nothing to stop it. Then he understood that this was God's punishment. He went down on his knees, in front of his blazing shop, and with tears asked for God's pardon. And then a real miracle occurred: the fire stopped, by itself, and he lost hardly anything. Since then he has been a believer and he pays the whole of his tithe to the church and works for the church. But he is one of the exceptions; the rich are lost; besides, this is what Jesus said of them.

In the setting of an evangelizing Protestantism, the visible sign of election is not material success, but success in proclaiming the message and moral regeneration. Progress is not an essential value, nor is work, which is often regarded as belonging to the sinful world, since in order to go out to work, one has to leave the protective circle of the congregation. You will remember the pastor who was afraid to 'give his son to work', for fear of losing him; in the *bidonvilles* of Santiago we have observed the frequent changes of job among Protestant church members. This was due both to the precariousness of employment and also in several cases to the fear of giving way to the atmosphere of the workshop:

> I was in a shoemaker's workshop but at the end of a month I gave up, for I could not bear my companions. They drink, swear, they belong to the world and wanted to drag me in too.
>
> I prefer to make *empanadas* at home with my wife's help, rather than go to the factory, even though I earned more there. But there I was losing my faith. . . .

Thus, while Pentecostalists are described as good workers, conscientious, raising no problems, it does not seem that they uphold that spirit of enterprise and initiative which characterized the 'conquering bourgeois'[17] of nineteenth-century Europe. Perhaps also as the result of symbiosis with traditional South American culture, which does not see in Work and Progress the *ne plus ultra* of human life, Protestantism does not seem in any appreciable fashion to be introducing a new ethic of work. In Chile work does not acquire a religious worth, but remains in the domain of the world. For proof we turn to those young officials of the Pentecostal churches who only continue to follow their occupation in order to become eligible in a few years for a pension, and who are glad when the due date arrives, from which time they will be able 'at last to give themselves wholly to God's work'. Similarly there are those pastors who state that to follow a secular profession is equivalent to serving two masters.

Thus, contrary to the Puritan ethic of Anglo-Saxon Protestantism in the seventeenth and eighteenth centuries, the Chilean Protestant ethic does not seem to offer any obvious parallel with the pioneer spirit; the fact that the doctrine of sin is not accompanied by a positive teaching on creation leads Protestants to think that God is only glorified in the Church and not in the world, and this prevents them from attaching religious worth to secular activity.[18]

(2) Though at the outset the application of Weber's schema in the case of Chile seems risky, one can nevertheless attempt to modify his hypothesis: by the very fact that it regulates strictly the life of its initiates, Protestantism would make possible a certain betterment in their living conditions, awaken a desire for knowledge, and excite new ambitions for the individual and for his children. Thus it would put the individual on the road to a vertical socio-professional mobility which would cause him to improve his situation, or which would enable his children to mount one or more rungs of the social hierarchy.

This belief is very firmly established, principally in the older Protestant denominations (Presbyterians and Methodists) and there is no lack of cases quoted to support it. Nevertheless, is it an imported idea or a fact which finds confirmation in Chile itself? Is the Anglo-Saxon missionary so far persuaded of the effects of Protestantism on the rise of its initiates that he would, without further enquiry, extrapolate the effect in Latin America? To our mind, so long as no serious overall study has been undertaken, this theory should be followed by a question mark, since it is very true that several factors seem to challenge the assumption.

To begin with, when one notices an inter-generation vertical mobility in Protestant families, one has to remember that it is not necessarily attributable to the religious factor, but may be quite simply due to the evolution of Chilean social stratification. The urban middle class which was born at the beginning of the century and became a political force during the 'twenties, owes nothing to Protestantism for its creation, since the latter's expansion came later. While it is equally evident that young Protestants have had a longer schooling than their parents, this advance can be attributed to the general improvement in the educational level of Chile's population. *A priori*, there is nothing to prove that the advance is greater among Protestants than among the whole of the population.

Observation of Protestant congregations leads one to a second question mark. Of course the central Presbyterian Church and the Second Methodist Church in Santiago are attended by a clientele a large part of which belongs to the fairly well-off middle classes, and of course in some Pentecostal congregations one notices the presence of quite a number of people belonging to the lower middle classes, but, as Ignacio Vergara very rightly points out at the end of a long and meticulous enquiry into the Protestant movements, the history of Protestantism in Chile does not include the name of any 'thinker, sociologist, politician, government man, writer or university professor of note, nor any leading worker in the labour struggle . . .',[19] and we could add, nor any industrialist, businessman or agriculturist of first importance, except of course for some German Lutheran colonists. We know only one Protestant personality who plays a certain part in Chilean society; he is a pastor who is also an industrialist and business man and is the Grand Treasurer of the Chilean Masons.

The foregoing is not intended to deny that the Protestant faith can have an effect on the socio-economic rise of its initiates. But the evidence to support this theory does not stare one in the face, and to verify it requires a meticulous enquiry, the starting-point of which would be to distinguish carefully between what can be imputed to the religious factor and what is due quite simply to the general evolution of Chilean society. What we can affirm is on one side the negative, prohibitive character of the Protestant social ethic, and on the other the lack of evidence of Protestant socio-economic success.

3. INDIVIDUAL MOBILITY AND DEVELOPING SOCIETY

But let us go back to the statement, 'change the individual and society will be transformed'. Let us admit for a moment the idea that the Protestant faith brings about the social and economic rise of the believer, who moves from the masses towards the so-called middle classes, or even further. This advance of a certain number of people is without doubt very fortunate for them. But does it have any advantage for the whole of society? Does it contribute to the development of the country? In other words, does the socio-economic transformation resulting from individual conversion—if this transformation can be verified—justify the belief in an outcome which will transform society? Would this enable Protestantism to stay with its individualist vision and do without either a positive social ethic or direct action related to the transformation of the social structures as well as the individual?

Economic development on a large scale starts with the Industrial Revolution in Europe. This term implies the change from craft processes to industrial processes of manufacturing, the passage from single-piece work to mass production. With the growth of industry, urban development begins, and the movement of the working population, which characterizes the earliest phase of urban development, is the passage from agriculture into industry, or, in Colin Clark's famous phrase, from the primary to the secondary economic sector. The tertiary sector—service industries, administration, bureaucracy—also develops, but in close relation to industrial development. We might say that it is *in the service of* production; it is only in the course of the second phase of the Industrial Revolution, with the appearance of automation and cybernetics, that displacement of the labour force from the industrial into the tertiary sector begins to take place. While it is clear that our *schema* is a simplified one, it is nevertheless evident that the main condition for development is the establishment of heavy industry and manufacturing industries.[20]

Thus, in the development models,

> one generally associates the idea of 'progress' with the process of urban growth and industrialization, and it is supposed that there is between the latter so close a relation that one automatically implies the other.[21]

Now, though this *schema* is broadly speaking valid for the European industrial revolution, in fact in Latin America

> urban growth—particularly that of the chief towns—has preceded industrialization, to such an extent that the middle class and urban proletariat have appeared before the creation of modern productive structures. It is significant that in many countries labour legislation, state control and the centralization of trade union organizations, protection of workers' families, in short social legislation in its entirety—has come before the existence of modern urban industry.[22]

This disequilibrium of the two processes leads to the following conclusion on the part of C.E.P.A.L.'s secretariat:

> It is probable that the low incidence of modern industry in the large cosmopolitan city helps to explain to a large extent the growing disequilibrium of the towns, as well as the weakly expansive character of the modernization process up to 1960.[23]

The result is that the migratory current bringing the country populations into the towns is due 'more to the deficiencies of the agrarian structures than to the attractions . . . of the rising industrial system in the towns. . . . Since it is above all a matter of the "expulsion of impoverished peasants", the result is simply a transfer of rural misery to the towns.'[24] Similarly, it leads not so much to the creation of an industrial proletariat as to that of a sub-proletariat of *bidonvilles*, with ill-defined economic activities.

Table 5 in Chapter 2 (page 32) underlines the stagnation of employment in the manufacturing industries, and the prodigious development of the tertiary sector. Here also disequilibrium is occurring: 'service industries' are no longer closely connected with production but have become the main centre of activity, whether of State bureaucracy or business. Transfers of labour do not take place first between the primary and secondary sector and only then into the tertiary, but directly and chiefly from the primary to the tertiary, whereas neither the capital resources nor the state of technology justify this leap-frogging. Labour in the public sector, which is unproductive, is being increased in an attempt to absorb a fraction of the latent unemployment, but this palliative is absurd, since it contributes nothing to the growth of the national revenue.

These remarks on industrialization and the structure of the labour force lead us to the question of the middle classes. Some authors, transposing European or North American *schemas* to the developing countries, see in the constitution of a middle class the decisive element in economic and social development, both the result and cause of the passage from tradition to modernity.[25] But this idea immediately comes in conflict with the following observation which is called the 'Hoselitz theory': how is it that countries which experienced the greatest forward thrust at the end of the nineteenth century, and which have available not only the most favourable body of social indicators, but also the largest volume of middle-class populations, are precisely the ones which in the last few decades have shown the most symptoms of lack of tone and vital energy, not to say stagnation? The countries Hoselitz has in mind being principally Argentina and Chile, he puts forward the idea that the *quantity* of the middle class weighs less than its *quality*, and at the end of a study of motivation, he concludes:

> . . . in an economy, development of which depends in large measure on private enterprise, if the upper classes are chiefly interested in ostentatious consumption and the middle classes are preoccupied, not with increasing the social dividend, but chiefly with redistributing it in favour of their own members, economic development can only come to a total standstill.[26]

By this remark the economist underlines the lack of feeling for saving and initiative, in short the absence of the 'spirit of capitalism', dear to Max Weber, which characterized the rising *petit bourgeois* of Europe, while the structural conditions are also lacking which would most favour industrial initiative. The C.E.P.A.L. experts end their analysis by qualifying the middle classes as 'the faceless middle class' or, borrowing Nietzsche's phrase, 'domesticated middle classes'. Thus the words of Clifford Geertz which have been cited on p. 149, demanding a transformation of the basic structure of society in addition to a mental transformation, seem particularly pertinent for Latin America.

Our problem is to find out whether, in placing the individual on the track leading to economic and social mobility, one contributes indirectly to the development of society. Study of the structure has led us to distinguish the two channels of mobility. The first governs horizontal movements which mean no improvement of income or social status; it is the passage from country to town, from the cottage to the slum. The second channel certainly leads to promotion, with access to the first layers of the middle classes, and generally entry into the tertiary economic sector. But what we have seen of the middle classes—largely unproductive, participating not so much in the increase of the national product as in its redistribution in their own favour—makes one doubt whether the access of an individual to a post in the State administration, for example, represents an advantage for anyone other than himself and his family. In short, while the affirmation, 'Convert the individual and he will better his personal situation and that of his family', is not without foundation, the basis of the adage which declares, 'Convert the individual and so society will be transformed', is dubious. It is based on the belief in the natural, automatic development of societies, and it is evident that in Europe and North America it had this spontaneous and cumulative character; this is not the case in the developing countries, where a multiplicity of factors (in which the absence of the 'capitalist spirit' is probably not the most important) seems to freeze the possibilities of development and to lead—in accordance with a well-known truth—the poor countries to become ever poorer, in relation to the rich countries which are growing always richer.

Latin American Protestantism thus ought not to disguise the weakness of its social ethic under an argument which is imported, facile but doubtful in all its terms.

4. CONCLUSION

In his speech at the World Conference on Church and Society of the World Council of Churches,[27] Gonzalo Castillo-Cardenas stated:

> Latin American Protestantism . . . has appropriated for its own, without deliberation or theological formulation, but—up to now—by general consensus, the 'doctrine' of individual self-promotion socially and economically, as a natural consequence of the regeneration of the inner man, through faith in Christ.

The role played by this belief seemed to us to merit special discussion. This doctrine is based on the famous arguments of Max Weber, which affirm the coincidence between the Protestant ethic and the spirit of capitalism. Our observations lead us to question very seriously the extrapolation of these arguments to Latin America. Certainly Protestantism leads to a certain asceticism, but here already one can see a difference: asceticism does not seem to lead to saving. Next we have noted that the Protestant ethic, which rests on a dualist vision opposing the Church to the world, does not lead to attributing religious worth to economic activity; it is regarded as a necessity, since one must live, but a regrettable necessity because it is dangerous, since to accomplish it one must go out into the world.

Finally, certain indices show that the economic success of Protestants is not a certainty in the case of Chile, and that an enquiry is necessary to reveal how much is based on imagination and how much on reality. In the last place, we have shown that the individual's social rise does not necessarily and automatically lead to the growth of national wealth and the development of the country.

Even though, personally, we are convinced that the Gospel is not only a message of individual moral regeneration, but includes a political, economic and social dimension, scientific argument does not involve confirming or denying this dimension and passing judgment on the presence or absence of a social ethic in the Protestant churches. But it seems clear to us that, to the extent that the churches believe they have a responsibility with regard to the country's development, they cannot be satisfied with the doctrine of the promotion of individual believers, and they should break with the individualist approach and tackle the problem of society from the angle of joint thinking and action, which would bring together both the structural and the individual problem.

A Haïtian poet has written:

> In truth I cannot myself understand anything of all this. We perform voodoo ceremonies, but nothing comes of it; misery is killing us. We go to the Catholic Church, and misery still remains. Every day the misery becomes more terrible. We turn Protestant, and still nothing changes.[28]

Part Four

THEOLOGICAL AND ECUMENICAL ASPECTS

CHAPTER 8

Ecumenism on Trial

In the history of Christianity, if the nineteenth century is regarded as the century of missions, the twentieth is that of the ecumenical movement. The ecumenical question (an adjective long reserved for specialists, to such a degree that typographers used regularly to alter it to 'economical') assumed an immense popularity upon the summoning of the Second Vatican Ecumenical Council by Pope John XXIII. The question is thus at the centre of controversy; the World Council of Churches, whose work towards unity is well known, is confronted by the International Council of Christian Churches, which accuses the former of being sold out simultaneously to Rome, Moscow and modernism. Signs of the importance which the ecumenical movement has attained are the leading places given to it by publications and learned congresses.[1] This concept, however, has too many meanings to be used without qualification, and for a description, if not a definition, we shall turn to one of the great names of the ecumenical movement. In a speech given in 1953 in the series of Burge Memorial Lectures, Dr. W. A. Visser 't Hooft gave six meanings for this concept:

> (1) pertaining to or representing the whole (inhabited) earth,
> (2) pertaining to or representing the (Roman) Empire,
> (3) pertaining to or representing the Church as a whole,
> (4) having universal ecclesiastical validity,
> (5) concerning the relations between several Churches or Christians of different confessions,
> (6) expressing the consciousness of and desire for Christian unity.
>
> These meanings are given in what is roughly their chronological order. But in most periods two or more of these meanings are found to co-exist.[2]

For our present purpose the second meaning can be either eliminated, since it concerns a bygone age, or amalgamated with the first, since to Roman minds the Empire coincided (almost) with the inhabited earth. Next it must be stressed that the definition which we are told is chronologically the earliest is also the most recent child of the 'ecumenical' concern. Visser 't Hooft asks 'how a word which had at first a purely secular meaning has acquired a specifically and almost exclusively ecclesiastical meaning',[3] but it would be just as important to determine how a concept which had assumed an almost exclusively ecclesiastical meaning has regained its first etymology in Christian thought. It must be remembered that the World Council itself recently held a World conference on Church and Society, where the problem was not so much the unity of the churches as their responsibility, and the responsibility of Christians, in the *oikoumene*, in the sense of the world of men.

This transition, or this enrichment of the vocabulary, has been pointed out in Latin America by that excellent observer Magdelaine Villeroy:

> A non-theological factor in the division of the Church is highlighted by the social involvement of Brazilian Christians, whereas the great ecumenical event of the twentieth century has drawn the attention of Christians almost exclusively to the confessional and theological divisions. Of course, these divisions are a scandal, but many hidden schisms are destroying the internal unity of each denomination at the local church level. . . . These divisions seem to us just as serious as those which were due to the confessional anarchy prevailing in the early days of Brazilian Pentecostalism. That introductory period seems to us to be giving way quickly to a period in which the social question is masking all the other questions. We are tempted to think that it cannot and should not be otherwise. Can faith in Jesus Christ take upon itself all the great human demands? . . . Without a doubt that is the only missionary question for the new generations who feel themselves ill at ease in the social framework of religious experience provided by the principal denominations.[4]

The author goes on to state that for these younger generations 'the "agape" now leads to politics'. The formula is splendid, but perhaps the generalization is too sweeping. A considerable proportion of young people follows uncritically the route taken by their fathers and even in a milieu so sensitive to the socio-political problem as the *Facultad Evangélica de Teologia* of Buenos Aires a minority sticks to the traditional line. Nevertheless, it is certain that the road pointed out by Magdelaine Villeroy is the one taken by the most dynamic and most lucid section of the new generation, the section which is regrouping itself in parallel movements (since they are interdenominational and relatively independent of the denominations) such as I.S.A.L. (Church and Society in Latin America) or the Student Christian Movements (M.E.C.), whose publications, of a quality infinitely superior to the usual missionary literature, are opening breaches in the churches' conformism and in the vacuum of their social thinking.

In the preceding chapters, we have drawn up an account of ecumenism in Chile understood as the whole of relations between men in society, but though we are here limiting the concept to its ecclesiastical dimensions, we wanted to recall the importance of its earliest—and latest—meaning.

Since our perspective is that of an analysis of the state of the search for unity in the Protestant Churches in Chile (and not a historical analysis like that of the General Secretary of the W.C.C.), we shall try to establish in the first section whether there is consciousness of a factual unity—even if it is only unity 'in Jesus Christ'—among the different Christian Churches (cf. the first part of point 6 in Visser 't Hooft's definition); then we shall study the concrete manifestations of the search for this unity (cf. the second part of the same point and also point 5).

I. CONSCIOUSNESS OF UNITY AND FRONTIERS OF THE 'CORPUS CHRISTI'

The concept of *oikoumene* is here taken in the limited sense (which is the one most usually given to it) of the Christian Church in its entirety, or the *Corpus Christi*.

Within Protestantism, it seems to us that, before concern arises for a visible restoration of the unity of the Church, which today is broken, there must necessarily first be a growing awareness that the theological concept of '*Church*' is not to be reduced to that of '*ecclesiastical denomination*' (or *confession*, in the theologians' language), and that other denominations, each one marked by its history and peculiar tradition, all belong to the Church, the 'Bride of Christ', for the same reason as one's own denomination. This idea which, far from identifying a historical and sociological reality (the denomination) with a mystical theological reality (the Church), implies the reverse (establishing the relativity of the former and the value of the latter) has been and still is the starting-point for all ecumenical praxis, whether it be simply in the realm of inter-ecclesiastical collaboration and planning, or whether it seeks to achieve unity by moving forward towards a new, visible incarnation of the mystical Church, beyond the denominations existing today, the form and content of which remain unforeseeable.

This growing awareness is a *necessary condition* for ecumenical praxis. It may be that it is not a *sufficient condition* for producing ecumenical acts: in fact, certain religious groups are satisfied with the awareness of a mystical unity 'in Christ', denying, however, that it ought to be manifested visibly. When we have made that reservation, it appears nevertheless that the first steps in ecumenical sociology should be to deal with the state of this awareness in the various ecclesiastical denominations. By throwing light on this part of a religious group's ideology, as it is actually understood by its members, sociology can provide information on the possibilities of ecumenical action on the part of that religious group, without, however, either saying that the action will be real or stating the conditions under which an ecumenical attitude will be forthcoming.

To go back to our three samples: the theological students, Chilean Protestant pastors and Chilean Pentecostalist pastors. A two-part question was put to them, designed to enable a defining of the contours of the *Corpus Christi* as they see it. The text of the questions was as follows:

Question: Here is a list of denominations or churches; in your view,
(1) Which of the churches in this list are *a part of the body of Christ*, or, in other words, belong to the Church, 'the Bride of Christ'?
(2) Out of these churches and denominations, which are the ones whose members *can be saved*?

The two aspects are quite distinct. From the theological point of view, the first is of an *ecclesiological* nature, and the second belongs to *soteriology*. They are nevertheless interdependent, and one may expect the answers to be 'structured'. In fact, let us examine the four possible combinations:

	1 ECCL.	2 SOTER.	NATURE OF REPLY
1.	Yes	Yes	'Ecumenical'
2.	Yes	No	'Aberrant'
3.	No	Yes	'Mixed'
4.	No	No	'Condemnatory'

The second combination is an aberration. It would certainly seem theologically inconsistent to assert that members of a religious movement are damned and at the same time that the movement belongs to the Church. In fact, out of 119 answers, this pattern appears only twice, both in answers from Pentecostal pastors. These replies were eliminated from the tables, reducing the answers to 117, out of 123 interviews (there were four who refused to answer—one a student, two Protestants and one Pentecostalist).

The formulation of this question was based on the following hypotheses:

(1) The more a denominational type requires its pastorate to have a high degree of cultural and theological training,
 (*a*) the smaller will be the number of condemnations and the number of people uttering condemnations,
 (*b*) the greater distinction will be made between the ecclesiological and soteriological aspects of the question.

(2) Vice versa.

To be explicit, having regard to our formulation of the hypotheses, it is not the educational level (considered as an independent variable) which conditions the reply, but rather the type of pastoral training, inasmuch as it constitutes a structural feature of the denominational type, as we have shown in Part II.[5]

The denominations or groups of denominations named in the list put to the persons interviewed may be placed in four categories:

(1) The *Pentecostal* movements of South America and those related to North American or European Pentecostal missions. This category corresponds to the sample of Pentecostal pastors.

(2) Five denominations which stem more or less directly from the *Reformation*: Presbyterians, Anglicans, Lutherans, Methodists and the Christian and Missionary Alliance (a revival movement in the Presbyterian tradition). Broadly speaking, these denominations correspond to the two other samples (Protestant pastors and students).

(3) Three sects, often considered to be 'Protestant', a description which both they and the Protestants contest: Seventh Day Adventists, Jehovah's Witnesses and Mormons.

(4) The Roman Catholic Church.

From an overall view of Table 1 one fact stands out: none of the samples restricted the *Corpus Christi* to its own group of denominations (see also Fig. 7). In fact, there was a consensus which affirmed that *the Protestant and Pentecostalist denominations constitute the nucleus of the oikoumene.* And the theological basis for this consensus can be found in the remark of a Pentecostalist pastor:

> All the denominations which declare that salvation is in Jesus Christ alone and are faithful to the Holy Scriptures belong to the Body of Christ.

This result is important, since it shows that, in spite of Pentecostalism's sectarian tendencies, it is not exclusivist. However, Pentecostalists make a distinction between the Methodists and Presbyterians on the one hand, and on the other the Lutherans and Anglicans, about

Table 1. The Church and its frontiers(%)*

DENOMINATION	ANSWER: 1. ECCLESIOLOGY: 2. SOTERIOLOGY	ECUMENICAL + +	MIXED — +	CONDEMNATORY — —	KNOWS THE DENOMINATION	DOES NOT KNOW IT
Methodists	A	100	—	—	100	—
	B	100	—	—	100	—
	C	89	7	4	95	5
Christian & Missionary Alliance	A	100	—	—	74	26
	B	100	—	—	100	—
	C	88	12	—	74	26
North American Pentecostalists	A	97	3	—	89	11
	B	100	—	—	100	—
	C	95	5	—	98	2
South American Pentecostalists	A	94	6	—	92	8
	B	100	—	—	100	—
	C	95	5	—	100	—
Presbyterians	A	100	—	—	100	—
	B	100	—	—	100	—
	C	83	13	4	79	21
Anglicans	A	100	—	—	97	3
	B	100	—	—	100	—
	C	56	25	19	55	45
Lutherans	A	100	—	—	97	3
	B	96	—	4	100	—
	C	66	20	14	60	40
Catholics	A	80	11	9	100	—
	B	50	29	21	100	—
	C	13	16	71	97	3
Adventists	A	32	41	27	97	3
	B	57	26	17	96	4
	C	44	16	40	86	14
Jehovah's Witnesses	A	6	45	49	89	11
	B	8	54	38	100	—
	C	8	17	75	91	9
Mormons	A	3	39	58	89	11
	B	12	46	42	100	—
	C	9	21	70	74	26

* A: 35 students; B: 24 Protestant pastors; C: 58 Pentecostalist pastors (refusals to answer excluded)

FIGURE 7

THE CHURCH AND ITS FRONTIERS

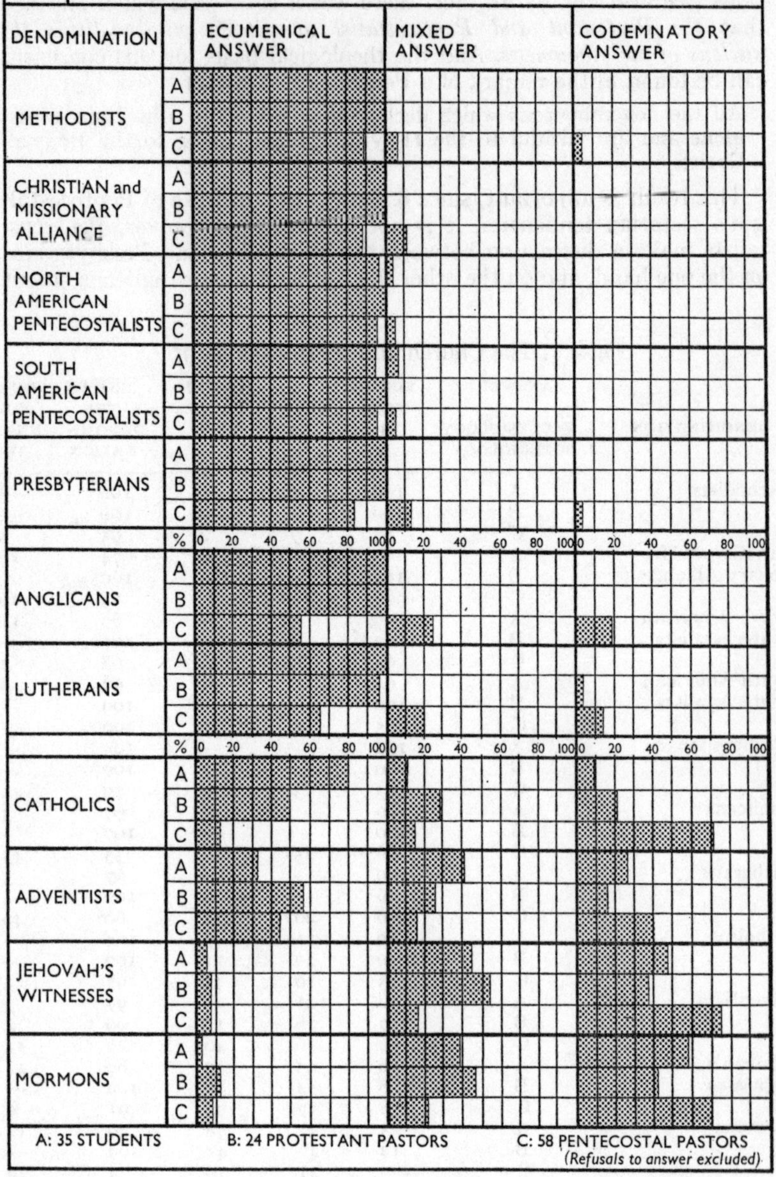

DENOMINATION		ECUMENICAL ANSWER	MIXED ANSWER	CODEMNATORY ANSWER
METHODISTS	A			
	B			
	C			
CHRISTIAN and MISSIONARY ALLIANCE	A			
	B			
	C			
NORTH AMERICAN PENTECOSTALISTS	A			
	B			
	C			
SOUTH AMERICAN PENTECOSTALISTS	A			
	B			
	C			
PRESBYTERIANS	A			
	B			
	C			
	%	0 20 40 60 80 100	0 20 40 60 80 100	0 20 40 60 80 100
ANGLICANS	A			
	B			
	C			
LUTHERANS	A			
	B			
	C			
	%	0 20 40 60 80 100	0 20 40 60 80 100	0 20 40 60 80 100
CATHOLICS	A			
	B			
	C			
ADVENTISTS	A			
	B			
	C			
JEHOVAH'S WITNESSES	A			
	B			
	C			
MORMONS	A			
	B			
	C			

A: 35 STUDENTS B: 24 PROTESTANT PASTORS C: 58 PENTECOSTAL PASTORS

(Refusals to answer excluded)

whom they have reservations: is not Anglican ritual too close to the Catholic? And the Lutherans are 'very materialistic'.

Thus the sometimes violent disagreements between Pentecostalists and Protestants (Methodists and Presbyterians)—the former accuse the latter of a 'lack of spirituality', of 'ritualism and modernism', and above all of not believing in 'the power of the Holy Spirit', while the latter accuse the Pentecostalists of being 'fanatics', 'anarchists in their worship' and of 'believing in false superstitions'—do not obliterate the common conviction of spiritual unity.

Discussion is therefore concentrated on the Roman Catholic Church and the 'semi-Christian' movements (categories 4 and 3). But before going on to a detailed analysis, let us proceed with an overall verification of our hypothesis by counting the condemnations, as well as the number of those who made them (the 'inquisitors').

Table 2. Distribution of 'inquisitors' and condemnations

	INDIVIDUALS MAKING CONDEMNATIONS		NUMBER OF CONDEMNATIONS MADE	
	NO.	% OF SAMPLE	NO.	AVERAGE PER PERSON*
Students	19	54	44	2·3
Protestants	11	46	29	2·6
Pentecostalists	43	74	144	3·3

* Average of those making condemnations. It would be higher among the Pentecostalist pastors if they had known all the denominations on the list. Whereas the Protestant pastors only once put 'Don't know', the students gave this answer 25 times (average, 0·7) and the Pentecostalists 110 times (average 1·9).

Hypothesis no. 1 (*a*) is borne out, if one divides the Protestants and students from the Pentecostalists, since about half the former excommunicate two or three denominations, while three-quarters of the latter reject three or four. Hypotheses 1 (*b*) and 2 (*b*) turn out to be equally correct: take the case, in the first table, of the Seventh Day Adventists, Jehovah's Witnesses and the Mormons. Protestant pastors and students and Pentecostalists are alike, in that only a small number declare these movements to belong to the Church: on the other hand, more of the first group than the second allow that those who profess these 'heresies' have a chance of salvation (mixed reply).

Two observations shall conclude this preliminary survey: first, the fact that the students, in spite of (or perhaps because of) their youth and the fact that their level of education is more uniformly high, do not have a less restrictive view of the Church and salvation than the Protestant pastors. Secondly, speaking in the name of an 'orthodox' doctrine of salvation (one pastor said, a man is a Christian 'if he believes in Jesus Christ the Son of God and has no other written source of revelation than the Bible'), half of both groups display an *inquisitorial mentality*, in that they believe they can deny any chance of *salvation* to initiates of such and such a religious belief.

Students

The 44 condemnations of the 19 'inquisitorial' students relate exclusively to four denominations: Roman Catholic, Adventist, Jehovah's Witnesses and Mormon; they are ranged according to a Guttman type of scale which places the denominations in the above order: all the students who reject the Roman Catholic Church also excommunicate the three others; those who condemn the Adventists also condemn at least the Jehovah's Witnesses and the Mormons, etc. This can be illustrated by the following figure:

Scale of condemnations among Students

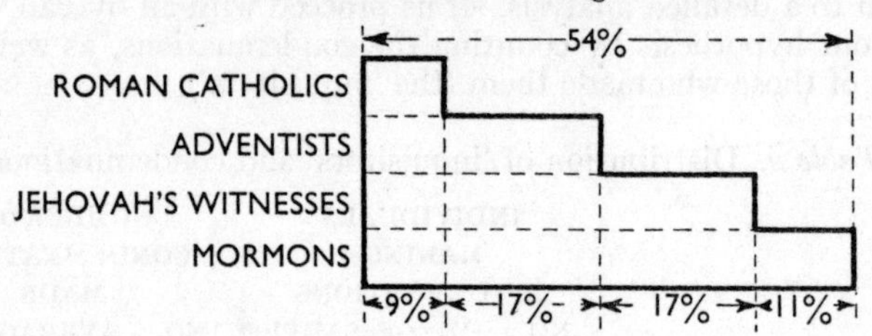

This pattern of replies may seem surprising. Using the language of political science, one could say that, theologically and ecclesiologically, Roman Catholicism lies to the right of the Reformed Churches while the other three denominations in dispute are on the left. Thus one cannot see why condemnation of the Catholics should automatically involve that of, for example, the Mormons. In view of the small number of cases, probably it is no more than a coincidence.

The students are clearly divided from the Protestant pastors in regard to the Roman Catholic Church. Eighty per cent of the students count it part of the Christian *oikoumene*, whereas only half of the pastors do so. It is striking to see that the students are much more favourable to the Catholic Church than to the 'semi-Christian sects'.

Protestant Pastors

As with the students, rejections are concentrated on the same four denominations, and, provided the Roman Catholic Church is set on one side, one can see the same scale appearing.

Scale of condemnations among Protestant Pastors

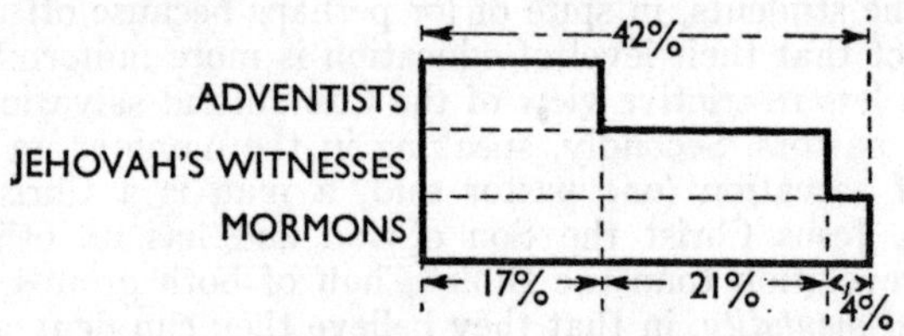

Comparison of the two scales leads one to conclude that the pastors (who, it will be remembered, comprise Methodists, Presbyterians and Anglicans), though less inclined than the students to see in these three movements members of the Body of Christ (particularly in the case of the Seventh Day Adventists), are at least more ready to open to them the door of salvation. Though the students are much more favourably inclined towards Catholicism than towards 'heterodox forms of Protestantism', the pastors maintain their distance equally from both the one and the others. This comes out clearly on comparing their opinions with regard to the Catholic Church and the Adventists: the pastors' distribution of their votes are almost identical in each case, though slightly more favourable to the Adventists. Moreover, there is a cleavage of views: although the majority of those interviewed held the same opinion on both, there were cases in which those who condemn the Catholic Church admit the Seventh Day Adventists to the Body of Christ, and the reverse is equally true.

Pentecostal Pastors

It is worth pausing for a moment to examine the Pentecostal pastors' knowledge of the denominations listed. The Anglican, Presbyterian and Lutheran Churches, which were the first non-Catholic Christian confessions to enter Chile, are much less well known to the Pentecostalists than the Adventists and the Jehovah's Witnesses. Even the Mormons, whose activities in Chile began only a decade ago, are better known than the Anglicans and Lutherans! This is an excellent indication of the passivity of the first group and the proselytizing zeal of the other among the lower classes!

The condemnations here show an original pattern, which may be summed up as follows:

1. The churches of the Jehovah's Witnesses, Mormons and also (with a very slight variation) the Roman Catholics are put in the same boat: those who condemn one of them also condemn the others, if they know them. This applies to three-quarters of the Pentecostal pastors (72 per cent. in the case of the Roman Catholics).
2. Those who commit the Adventists to Hades (27 per cent.) do the same for the three denominations quoted above.
3. Those who reject a church other than these four, condemn them also.

Thus, like the Protestant pastors, their Pentecostalist colleagues hold aloof from both the left-wing (the 'semi-Christian' movements) and the right (Catholicism), but whereas the Protestants make a finer distinction between the question of the *Corpus Christi* and that of salvation, three-quarters of the Pentecostalists pronounce anathemas on both extremes.

The conclusions drawn from this enquiry can be stated thus:

1. All three samples testify to an ecumenical outlook, in that none of them restricts the *Corpus Christi* to the denominational type which it represents.

2. They agree in thinking that the Protestant and Pentecostalist denominations (categories 1 and 2) form the nucleus of the *oikoumene*; Pentecostalists, however, remain divided in regard to the Lutherans and Anglicans.
3. The discriminant role is held by the *Roman Catholic Church*. While four out of five students see in the dominant Church a component part of the *oikoumene*, a still larger proportion of Pentecostalist pastors (87 per cent.) excommunicates it, while the Protestant pastors are divided into two groups of equal size.

This last point merits a brief reflection. More surprising than the fact that the Pentecostalists exclude Catholicism is the favourable attitude of the students, which is a sign of a break with traditional Protestant behaviour in Latin America. Since Protestant missions penetrated this continent in the last century with the aim of announcing the Gospel to a people which the Roman Catholic Church considered to be already christianized, the only result could be a mutual excommunication, the Roman Catholic Church accusing the Protestants of sheep-stealing, and the Protestant missions retorting that the South American people were in fact pagans disguised as Christians. In such a situation, it is clear that a movement centred to such a degree on proselytizing activities as Pentecostalism is perpetuating the long conflict with Catholicism, because the very root of its activity lies in the belief that Catholicism proclaims a completely distorted Gospel. That is why the Pentecostalists declare themselves to be the first to have preached the Gospel throughout Chilean territory, the activities of the Catholic Church being of no account.

While the Pentecostal attitude seems to be in the order of things, there is no information which would permit a non-speculative interpretation of the students' attitude. Does this attitude mean that they do not interpret the Gospel in strict terms of proselytizing activity aimed at man's spiritual conversion, which would lead them to be opposed not so much to Catholicism as to everything which alienates man? Are they more sensitive than the Pentecostalists (or even their elders the pastors who, in the local church, see the petty aspects of relations with the Catholic Church!) to the new trends of opinion in Catholicism—trends which lead to demands that are fairly close to those to which their own thinking leads them? These elements certainly play a part, but are they the only ones, and what weight should one attribute to them? We do not know how to answer such questions. This does not prevent one from saying that it is a fact that the traditional Protestant position is being reversed, and that the intellectual *élite* of South American Protestantism is thus sharing in the ecumenical current.

2. INTER-CHURCH RELATIONS ON THE LOCAL AND NATIONAL LEVELS

In the groups which we studied, there is a clear awareness that the Church (the *Corpus Christi*, the 'Bride of Christ') is a reality which extends far beyond the bounds of one's own denomination. Only one person interviewed confined the Church to the Pentecostal movement, and even he refused to identify the *Corpus Christi* with any organization by name, since he understood it to mean not just his own denomination, but all of the Pentecostal movements in Chile and elsewhere.

With this exception, the Pentecostalists do not claim to have a monopoly of Christian revelation; they are simply convinced that they have rediscovered all its dimensions, and demonstrate its ethical consequences more fully. Considering themselves to be a return to the Primitive Church, Pentecostalists do not deny that other denominations participate in the *Corpus Christi*, although they may have become degenerate through worldly influences, and on this account they may have let revelation be obscured and thus restricted God's regenerative action among them. Even if the charismatic contribution is important in Pentecostalism, even if it introduces a new theological emphasis with its doctrine of the Baptism of the Spirit, and more generally with its doctrine of the Third Person of the Trinity, this religious movement shows itself above all to be a revival which, in Chile, seeks to be on the one hand a return to Wesley, going back beyond a decadent Methodism, and on the other, by reason of the meeting of this nascent reawakening with the Pentecostal volcano, a return to the first century of the Church, going back beyond a decadent Christianity. Whatever may have been the role of some leaders, and the intensity of the empathy linking their followers to them, they have never played the role of new prophets or Messiahs. Even if in a few rare cases the leader tended to identify himself with Christ, this identification was ephemeral and analogical. The same is true of the Pentecostal theological emphases, which are not presented as a new revelation, but as a return to the primitive reading of the Revelation. In this, Pentecostalism is solidly rooted in the Protestant tradition, and even challenges the theology of that tradition in the name of its own criterion: the Biblical texts. Being a return to the source and not a new faith, Pentecostalism does not claim to be the exclusive means of salvation nor to be the only Church, even though it does claim to be the most perfect of the components of the Body of Christ.

But does the awareness of a unity in Christ among Christians of various denominations lead to acts which aim to make this mystic bond visible?

To describe the state of affairs in Chile and the chances of finding a road towards unity, one must bear in mind the road which led to Protestant fragmentation. Each of the Protestant denominations entered Chile with a different motive. The Lutheran Church came only because Germans had settled there, and its ambition never went beyond the wish to satisfy the religious needs of the colonists. The Anglicans came to evangelize the pagan Indians, i.e. to complete a task which the Catholic Church had no more than begun. Presbyterians and Methodists in the nineteenth century were the only ones to consider Chile as a whole as a mission field. Since their efforts to evangelize produced little reaction, and since the denominations in the country were already accustomed to living side by side, the divisions of Protestantism as well as its missionary effort passed unnoticed, though there was appreciation of its schools and colleges! The problem did not really arise until this century, with first the rise of Pentecostalism following a schism which, for once, was not imported; next the fragmentation to the n*th* degree of Pentecostalism, and then the arrival of various violently proselytizing movements, so that today about a hundred denominations exist which have legal status. The struggle for unity, if it exists, can thus be regarded as a continuation of a process of disunity, which, though it seems to be slowing down, has not yet reached a point of stability.

In seeking for the unification of Protestantism, one must first eliminate both the causes of and the value placed on the divisions, which must be examined.

Protestant missions brought their divisions into Chile; Anglicans, Presbyterians, Methodists and Baptists met on nearly all the fields of mission and mutually recognized one another, acknowledging that each was a constituent part of the *Corpus Christi*, though this did not ward off all friction, rivalry and interference. Sometimes agreements were made, such as that between the Methodists and Presbyterians by which they divided up Latin America. Chile is one of the few countries where both these denominations are found, but here too the country is divided into zones of influence. In fact agreement of this type seems to be one of the first marks blazing the trail towards unity, for it implies that, tacitly at least, the two denominations, over and above differences arising from historical circumstances, are both bearers of the same message, the same truth and the same values, since they can be substituted one for the other in the countries to be evangelized. But though on the national level agreement can be made to facilitate the common task, it is doubtful whether these denominations will go beyond the stage of collaboration and grapple with the question of unification. Their dependence, in different degrees, upon foreign bodies (missionary societies) and the value put upon their own tradition makes one think that their unification will be the result of an external process, as their division was.

In the case of Chile, the origin of these divisions goes back to the dark ages and they are the expression of opinions belonging to the time of the Reformation (since, with the exception of Methodism, they do not relate to schisms within Protestantism itself but to various protests against the Roman Church). To those divisions can be added others whose history is within living memory. Methodists today think that the schism of 1909 was in large measure due to Bishop Bristol's lack of understanding and the shady game played by Pastor Rice who was, moreover, expelled from the Methodist Church several years afterwards. It is now acknowledged that Dr. Hoover was making a justifiable claim when he appealed to Wesley against the Methodism of the late nineteenth century, and it is thought that, with a little more social aplomb and brotherly spirit, this *revival* might have proceeded without leading to a division. Moreover, the Chilean Methodists never fail to stress the fact that Pentecostalism is one of their derivatives.[6] But the Pentecostalists for their part do not share this view; for them, the reasons which led to the separation have not disappeared; in fact others have been added, so that, in the words of one pastor, 'If the Pentecostal Church did not exist independently of the Methodist Church, it would have to be created'. The Methodist Church lacks 'spirituality' and 'ardour', which is proved by its numerical stagnation; it is also blemished by 'modernism' and does not believe in the Baptism of the Spirit. It is blamed for its dependence on foreigners. On this point, it must be pointed out that the national and independent character of Pentecostalism was an indirect, involuntary result of the schism, in which only one foreigner played any part. Later the nationalist argument was used in order to get rid of that foreigner (in 1932, in the division of *Iglesia Metodista Pentecostal* from the *Iglesia Evangélica Pentecostal*, the latter remaining loyal to Hoover), but at the start the movement thought of itself as a revival, not a nationalist movement. Nevertheless, without a doubt the national aspect was one of the factors in Pentecostalist success. Finally, over the years, a sociocultural cleavage has been produced. Even though Methodism continues to recruit members among the lower classes, its office bearers belong to the lower middle classes and cultivate an attitude of superiority. How many times have we heard people say, 'Pentecostalists have quantity, but we have quality!' This is the basis on which they claim the right to the leadership of the Protestant movement, which is, of course, radically disputed by the Pentecostalists. There is continual friction and ruffling of feathers, proving that those who consider themselves the *élite* have been unable to find the right attitude in their relations with the Pentecostalists, just because they believe themselves superior. Thoughts such as those which follow underline these conflicts. A Pentecostalist pastor from Cautin Province:

> They (the 'traditional' Protestants) do not respect our customs and our rites. They consider them pagan or I don't know what. For instance, we have had joint meetings when great foreign evangelists have visited the country. Now when we go to the Methodist church, I tell my people, 'They don't have the same customs as us, they do not pray in the same way, but since we are going to their church, we must behave like them; watch what they do and copy them.' But when they come to our church, they do not accept our customs, will not say 'Glory to God', and this shocks my people.

Another from the same Province:

> You know our customs; you know that if anyone is ill, we go to pray in his house and lay hands on him. Once a young man came to look for me because one of his friends, a Methodist, was seriously ill. And I went with him. Some days later, the Methodist pastor came to see me and tell me that I had no right to enter the home of one of his members. I told him that the pastors of other movements often came to pray for one of mine, and that I considered it a good thing, because we all believe in the same God, and our prayers could mean that God healed the sick person. Then he got angry and told me that he did not believe in all these Pentecostal things. You know [this interviewee said smiling], they are, after all, much more sectarian than we are!

A young Methodist pastor from Concepcion Province (it must be noted, however, that he had done a considerable amount of ecumenical work, organizing discussions and Bible study to which all were invited):

> Recently a group of Pentecostalists who formed a little free church with no official status asked if they could be attached to our church. I told them that it would be possible, but it would be necessary for them to give up their 'Glory to God', because that could not be done in our church and was not Biblical.

Certainly this salutation, peculiar to Pentecostalism in Chile, is not specifically commanded in the Bible, but does it not express a thankfulness towards God just as valid as most of the rites peculiar to traditional Protestantism?

Finally one must mention the cascade of schisms suffered by the Pentecostal movement. Here, whatever may be the justifications adduced, the cause is usually to be found, not in doctrinal conflicts or the desire for renewal, but in personal conflicts, illustrated by the old adage, 'It is better to be a large fish in a small pond than a little fish in a large pond'. These movements recognize one another and there is a constant traffic of members from one denomination to another, particularly on account of the large movements of population. A migrant will probably not find a church belonging to his old denomination in the place to which he moves or, if there is one, he may not feel at ease there, not getting on well with the pastor and leaders. He will prefer to visit other congregations until he finds the one that suits him.

The rivalries which cause conflicts between the leaders, and also the total absence of motivations which might lead them to wish for an effective unity, makes it quite improbable that there will be any early unification of the chief Pentecostal movements. Even their union with older denominations will not come about, according to them, except by the conversion of the latter to Pentecostalism, since Pentecostalism is the highest, purest and most faithful form of the Christian faith and the Christian Church. This attitude leads to a call for separation, and some movements, in particular the *Iglesia Evangélica Pentecostal*, even refuse to collaborate in any way with other denominations, for fear of being soiled by contact with them. The value thus put upon isolation rests on the teaching of Hoover himself; we shall quote a large part of one of his writings to which the I.E.P. pastors are constantly referring:

> 'Church' is derived from *ecclesia*, a Greek word which in its turn is derived from two words, *ek* meaning *outside of*, and *kleetos* meaning *called out* or *chosen*. Thus *ecclesia* means *called* or *chosen out of* some more numerous company of people. . . . At first the Church, filled with the Holy Spirit, was pure and separated from the things of this world, but little by little love of money, of pre-eminence, of popularity and pleasure entered in and gradually the Church began to govern its thought by, and act upon, human reasoning and no longer the Word of God, till the presence and power of the Holy Spirit were lost. . . . Then sincere and

fervent souls, who could not tolerate this deviation, felt that God was *calling them to leave* this Church which had been contaminated by contact with the world and compromised with it, and they formed another Church. From this comes the term SECT, which is derived either from *sequi*, to follow, or from *secare*, to cut. This cutting was done to separate the pure from the impure, the things of God from the things of the world. . . .

Following the Waldensians, Lutherans, Presbyterians, Methodists, Salvationists and many others who thus left the bosom of the Church to form another, purer church, we Pentecostalists have also done the same; we are the last to do so, so far.

[Hoover then asks what must be done to prevent the process of degeneration from continuing, which would necessitate further divisions. —*Author's note.*]

When a church leaves another, it is for the same end. Every church originally has a powerful reason for existence. It was a *sect*, or a *cutting off*, if you prefer. This cutting off freed it from all ties which hindered it from being completely and solely obedient to God and from going forward with the Bible as the only light for its path. Let us look again at the Church. If it had remained cut off, removed and separate from other churches, it would have remained, pure, zealous and victorious. In its early years it illumined any place where it entered and its growth was phenomenal, both in numbers and in the power of the Holy Spirit.

But it preached simplicity in clothing, abstinence in one's way of living, and the vast majority of the preachers were working men of little culture. Its meetings were full of life, and took place anywhere, in the fields, the kitchen, living room, stable—what did it matter! . . .

What must we do?

We must understand that we have been called out of the church to which we used to belong—not to form another identical with that which we have left (in that case, why should we have left it?), but to be *separate*, *cut off* from it and from the things which today it venerates. If we have a reason for existence, then that reason calls us to a life of separation, so as to preserve what God has entrusted to us. . . . We must be fanatics, as they call us, and be sectarian, so that this 'worldly spirit which works in the church more furiously than anywhere else' does not embroil us nor deceive us. It is time to learn to preserve the heritage which has been entrusted to us, and this heritage is in greater peril from half-friends than from declared enemies.[7]

This wish for total separation is maintained by only a few of the Pentecostalist denominations, but its continued existence is emphasized by the fact that one of the two giants of the movement, the *Iglesia Evangélica Pentecostal*, remains strictly faithful to it.

The absence, not only of efforts aimed at making a mystic unity visible but even of any real desire for unity, has not prevented the creation of networks, in the form of local, regional and national *Concilios Evangélicos*, for establishing relations between the denominations. Those which were created before the war were usually the work of pastors of good will who wished to establish prayer links, or a body capable of organizing spectacular evangelism campaigns, or again an organization which would facilitate the defence of Protestant interests in the face of the 'common enemy'. A proportion of the denominations (large or small depending on the place) shared in these councils, always represented by their pastor. Although Chileans have usually called these bodies by the name of 'council', it was in fact a matter of 'assemblies'[8] without any power of their own, without finance and with very limited activities, until, after the war, this network was extended so that it could be used for the distribution of gifts of food and clothing, chiefly 'from the people of the United States to the people of Chile', as stated on the labels stuck on the parcels distributed.

At the national level, the Methodists, Presbyterians and Baptists,[9] together with some other less important groups, founded the 'Committee of Co-operation between the Churches'. Concretely, it was a group of pastors in the capital, who regularly met for prayer, Bible study and discussion. Impelled by a visit from John R. Mott, the committee transformed itself in 1941 into the *Concilio Evangélico de Chile*; new groups joined, including several Pentecostal denominations, and its first chairman was Dr. McLean, a Presbyterian, the professor of English Literature in the University of Chile. Its aim was chiefly to organize evangelization campaigns and to distribute religious films.

In 1958, however, this Council assumed an importance which its originators would never have imagined possible, and against which they would probably have protested. In that year *Church World Service*, one of the voluntary agencies in the United States to which the U.S. Government entrusts the world distribution of surplus commodities, was established in Chile and entered into relations with the C.E.C. The latter created a special department, the *Ayuda Christiana Evangélica* (Evangelical Christian Aid) which was charged with distribution on the national level. This department, as we shall see later, rapidly became a 'state within the state', with the result that today the *Concilio* appears to be a mere appendage of its own department.

As an indication of the situation, we may mention that the C.E.C. in 1964 had a budget of about U.S.$6,000 (not including that of the A.C.E.), which came from the following sources: $4,000 from the Committee for Co-operation in Latin America (a department of the National Council of Churches, U.S.A.), $250 from fees from the member churches, and $1,750 from a nation-wide collection (which was not to be made in 1965). Thus the artificial character of the C.E.C. is stressed by its financial dependence upon foreign sources. In fact the story of Pentecostalism's fifty years of existence proves that Pentecostalism in Chile is capable of providing finance itself for activities which it deems to be indispensable.

Three other national councils compete with the C.E.C. The first (*Nuevo Concilio Evangélico Nacional*) brings together a number of small churches of the 'sanctification' type and has a marked political character, since in the last presidential election it supported the candidature of Dr. Allende of the FRAP. This council accuses the C.E.C. of being 'sold out to the dollar' and claims to be the only authentically national council. The second, called the *Concilio Evangélico Independiente*, is at present moribund. As one informant (whose statement we have checked) told us, 'It had a certain degree of success so long as it was able to count on the support of an ex-Senator of the Republic, who generously obtained state subsidies for its churches'. The last (*Concilio Chileno de Iglesias Evangélicas Fundamentalistas*) unites the smaller fundamentalist denominations, and is allied with the International Council of Christian Churches.

Thus in Chile the interdenominational bodies do not seem to be the crucible in which to fuse an ecumenical spirit, if by that one understands a search for a way of overcoming disagreements, so as to create a Church which will be greater than and other than the existing churches. These bodies might rather be described as trade unions, or distribution centres. In this setting, it can be understood that dialogue with the Roman Catholic Church cannot extend beyond small circles of friends. Of course—and that was the prior condition on the Roman side for any dialogue—the Roman Church was aware that it was only superficially established in Chile, and today it accepts the question raised twenty-five years ago by Father Hurtado in his book, *Es Chile un País Catolico?*, which at the time caused a furore.[10] For this reason it no longer accuses the Protestant Church as violently as it did in the past of stealing members from it. However, reading scholarly Catholic journals (it is useless to go through parish magazines, either Protestant or Catholic, since they abound in summary judgments and condemnations) may give one an idea of the approach being made by the Catholic experts to Protestant movements:

First an overall judgment on the relation of religion and society, made by Father Vergara in 1956:[11]

> The most profound division which could be produced in any country is that of belief. This diversity of religious ideas, in a people where religious instruction is one of the most serious problems (79·8 per cent of the State primary schools have no teacher of religion), disorientates the lower classes daily more and more.

The following passages are extracted from an article by Father Prudencio Damboriena. The first refers to the Lutherans and Anglicans, and is of interest because it reveals the author's 'ecumenical' approach:

> Rather than being adversaries of Catholicism, these two groups seem to constitute an excellent terrain in which, by means of carefully established contacts, they could be brought to see more clearly the true face of the Bride of Christ, which is His Church.[12]

One would like to know what the parties concerned think of this. Next, this passage dealing chiefly with the Baptist and Methodist denominations, in which the tone, more than the ideas expressed, is revealing:

> It was above all the middle-class Catholics who, refusing to let themselves be led astray by the siren voices of 'modern Christian education' or very 'up-to-date' juvenile organizations, put a stop to the Protestants' endeavours to work their way in with all the methods already employed (like true Trojan horses) in their penetration into the other Republics. All this is encouraging and constitutes a ray of hope for the future.[13]

For this author, Pentecostalism 'constitutes the truly perturbing element in the Chilean panorama'. In fact, its character as an indigenous movement, economically independent, strongly proselytizing, and even contagious, seems to be an exception by comparison with the other Protestant missions in South America, materially so tied to the dollar, and so poor in doctrinal conceptions and in the power to initiate matters themselves.[14]

He ends by expressing a fear that in several generations from now, when the original *élan* of Pentecostalism will have disappeared,

its members, tired of religious experiments which end in failure, will abandon all religion and become indifferent, or go over to the enemy, even if that proves to be Communism.[15]

In contrast to this picture, in which Protestantism is depicted as a threatening and destructive heresy,[16] there are an article and a book which lead to a dialogue in depth, a meditation on the contribution of the Protestants and above all of the Pentecostalists. The article is signed by Father H. Muñoz,[17] and the author begins by analysing the Protestant view of South American Catholicism. We here reproduce his conclusion, which seems to be pertinent:

This book by Dr. Mackay[18] and the documents of the congresses mentioned above propound the climate in which the Protestant attack arises: they think of themselves as sixteenth-century reformers, and believe in the essential corruption of the Catholic Church; they sincerely wish to preach the Gospel to pagans who are disguised as Christians, and in a very simple way regard the legitimate defence of the Catholic Church as the work of the devil, with the crudest intolerance.

The author makes three remarks on the subject of accusations made against South American Catholicism:

In the first place, it seems to me that the incomprehension and implacability which these judgments show form part of the general incomprehension and implacability of Protestantism against the Catholic Church. Protestant psychology is the opposite of Catholic psychology. Even well-known authors generally proceed in the following manner: they make a caricature of the Catholic doctrinal position; then it is very easy for them to criticize it and even to point ridicule at it. Unhappily—we must acknowledge it—many Catholics fail to avoid the same fault. . . .

The second cause of implacability in Protestant criticism seems to me to be the incapacity of the Anglo-Saxon mind to understand the Spanish mind. . . . The Protestants' criticisms reflect all the antipathies and scorn of the Nordic races for the Latins. . . . Finally, *we must acknowledge with humility that on a great many points they are right*. This is not the place to undertake a critical assessment to see how far they are right. We have not yet any scientific sociological studies, either on one side or the other. We are both basing our positions on mere appreciations made more or less *a priori*.[19]

The book to which we referred is that of Father Vergara, entitled *El Protestantismo en Chile*. In this monograph describing the innumerable Protestant denominations, he isolates the essential features of all the most popular religious movements. This study led its author to make an interesting experiment, since his parish, situated in a popular quarter of the port of Antofagasta, is at many points inspired by the Pentecostal pattern.

In spite of these openings, the dialogue between Catholics and Protestants seems for the moment to be made impossible by their feelings towards one another. It cannot be denied that, for nearly all the Pentecostalist pastors and half of the Protestants (cf. Table 1), Catholicism is not a *Christian* Church, chiefly on account of its hagiolatry and mariolatry. Conversely, the ambition of the Catholics (who often even take their inspiration from certain Protestant techniques: popular preaching, greater participation by the laity, etc.) is to put a stop to the expansion of the 'separated brethren' (to use the terminology blessed by Vatican II) who sow discord among the people. As will be seen in the last section, we agree with Magdelaine Villeroy in stating that 'though ecumenicity to us seems to be linked with the implications of the faith, as a social phenomenon it is linked with historical circumstances which either stifle, paralyse, permit or encourage it'.[20] And in Chile the climate is hardly favourable to its flowering. But, before discussing the sociological aspect of ecumenism, we must examine the impact which has been made on the Chilean churches by their relations with interdenominational and international organizations.

3. THE IMPACT OF INTERNATIONAL ECUMENICAL BODIES[21]

(*a*) In 1955 an agreement was made between the Governments of the United States and Chile, permitting the surplus foodstuffs of the former to be given to the latter. In 1958, to organize the reception and distribution of these gifts on the Protestant side, Church World Service, a Protestant inter-church aid agency, sent to Chile Pastor Theo Tschuy (who remained there until 1961). The *Concilio Evangélico de Chile* created a special branch, the *Ayuda Christiana Evangélica*, which employed the network of local councils and extended it so as to make it fit to carry out the local distribution of the food and clothing received. A little later, Lutheran World Relief became associated with this work. The initiators intended it to be of a temporary nature, corresponding to needs arising from natural catastrophes rather than an endemic situation, but it has increased at a giddy pace since 1960, as is shown in the report made in 1963 by Pastor Kadicsfalvy, who was then associate director of A.C.E.:

> In the month of July 1958 the first cargo of foodstuffs arrived, and we proceeded immediately to distribute them. Up to December 1958, a total of 375 tons of food was distributed among an average of 25,000 persons. . . . There has been a progressive increase up to this year—1963—and our network now reaches 160,000 persons and has distributed, up to the end of June, a total of 17,717 tons of foodstuffs in 5 years.[22]

Before we examine the results of this social work, let us ask what is its cause. Without a doubt it lies in the United States' overproduction of agricultural produce, which could not be disposed of either on the home market, because prices would collapse, or on the international market, because the countries which might be interested did not have the necessary foreign currency. But since the only potential buyers were the developing countries, it was necessary to work out a system of payment in the currency of the buying countries, all the more so since the storage and preservation of surpluses was costing the U.S. Government more than a million dollars a day. The 83rd Congress of the U.S.A. in 1954 passed the famous Law 480 'for the assistance and stimulation of agricultural trade' which regulates the sale of agricultural surpluses to 'friendly nations' and gifts of agricultural produce to, among others, voluntary agencies in the U.S.A. for their work in foreign countries. There were thus two dimensions: on the one hand, efforts to sell the produce, and on the other, gifts to benevolent agencies. It is the latter activity which concerns us; the law states that it must be of such a kind that 'it does not interfere with any sales that might be effected'. The U.S.A. provides for the transport of these products as far as the port of entry into the receiving country, but the latter in turn is responsible for the total cost of distributing them in its territory. The following table will give an idea of the cost which this represented for the Chilean Government and its increase over the years:

Table 3. Chilean Government Subsidies to the Voluntary Distributing Agencies (in Escudos).

	CARITAS*	A.C.E.	O.F.A.S.A.*
1960	439,200	54,800	6,000
1961	709,500	61,900	50,000
1962	902,940	107,800	95,000
1963	878,500	145,900	145,000
1964	1,324,900	301,937	214,000
1965	1,910,041	723,400	283,400

* Caritas, the Roman Catholic organization, working with 'Catholic Service'; O.F.A.S.A. with an Adventist agency.

The total State subsidies for the year 1965 were of the order of one million U.S. dollars (2,916,841 escudos). When it is recalled that the 1964 budget of C.E.C. came to 18,000 escudos, one can appreciate the imbalance between this body and A.C.E., which in the same year received from the State over 300,000 escudos.

The first and chief problem raised by this material aid was that of the close association between the churches' charitable activities and government policy. Put more crudely, were the churches not acting as screens for political objectives? The reply is clear if, as Mr. Vendrell has done, one takes the trouble to read carefully Law 480 mentioned above, from which the following extracts are taken:

It is hereby declared to be the policy of Congress to expand international trade among the United States and friendly nations, to facilitate the convertibility of currency, to promote the economic stability of American agriculture and the national welfare, to make *maxium efficient use of surplus agricultural commodities in furtherance of the foreign policy of the United States*. . . .

It is further the policy to use foreign currencies which accrue to the U.S. under this act to expand international trade, to encourage economic development, to purchase strategic materials, to pay U.S. obligations abroad, *to promote collective strength, and to foster in other ways the foreign policy of the U.S.*[23]

The A.C.E., a department of the C.E.C., thus becomes a pawn in the world policies of a great power, and serves as a propaganda network for the latter. In fact, according to article 305 of this law:

It must be clearly indicated on each parcel or box, and, if practicable, in the language of the place where the goods are to be distributed, that they are presented by the people of the United States of America. . . .

Consequently, in every local distribution office a prominent place must be given to the notice of the Alliance for Progress which reads: 'Gift of the people of the United States of America to the people of Chile'. (In this propaganda campaign they prefer to speak of 'peoples', not 'governments'.)

To this is added the fact that control of the A.C.E. is largely taken out of the hands of the Chileans. At least there is no doubt that this body has two loyalties—and one can guess which one will carry the day, since it is the one on which the manna depends. In effect, the *real* direction of the distribution programmes in a country is the province of the North American representatives appointed by North American agencies.

Given that under the system of legislation and related regulations *the weight of responsibility* for distribution, accounting, supervision and information *rests on the North American representative* of the voluntary agency, the primary object of our inspection was to determine . . . whether the food programme was functioning effectively under the North American representative.[24]

One can guess then at the power which this representative wields, and at the same time the political influence which he might be tempted to exercise among the churches wishful to take advantage of these distributions, if the agencies did not show great shrewdness in their choice of a person.

Our intention is not to accuse the United States of using the Good Samaritan image for political ends. That would be naïve; on the international plane, every plan for aid and assistance is attended by political motivations. We have simply tried to enlighten the churches as to the origin of the foodstuffs which they distribute. It comes not from the people, still less from the churches, but from the Government of the U.S.A., because of the excess national production in that country. Its free distribution is not a result of the generosity of the great people of the north, but only occurs, as the Law states, to the extent that it cannot be sold. It is even probable that these gifts, including the cost of transport, do not cost the U.S. Government any more than the storage of surpluses would do, and it is obvious that the prestige of that nation would suffer considerably if the stocks were purely and simply destroyed. Finally, the churches ought to know that these foodstuffs are used for propaganda ends, as part of the foreign policy of the U.S.A. We repeat, every nation uses charity as a political weapon, and the problem lies elsewhere, in knowing whether the Church of a country ought to agree to serve as a screen for foreign propaganda.

Perhaps, therefore, one should not exaggerate the direct impact of this propaganda. A sort of passive resistance is developing, and often the notices of the Alliance for Progress disappear behind a mountain of sacks and nobody troubles to explain to the beneficiaries the origin of the distributions. All the commissions of enquiry sent by the Agency for International Development (a U.S. Government agency) affirm that most of the recipients did not know the source of the gifts. And those who did know that they came from the United States frequently believed that the donor was a religious denomination.

But it is also necessary to examine the impact of such an undertaking on the churches on the one hand and the people on the other. W. E. Carter, co-author of one of the best sources of information on South American Protestantism,[25] has observed:

> The most consistent signs of ecumenical rapprochement are found in Chile and Argentina. In the former country, Church World Service has played a catalyzing role in bringing extremely divergent groups together, into what has been basically a hand-out program. As a result, open-handed co-operation is taking place between holiness sects and traditional denominations. Reciprocal visits are made; care is taken not to berate the contribution of sects with approaches highly divergent from one's own, local councils of churches are forming, and attempts are being made to look at Protestant denominations as complementary, not as competing. However, the formal structure in Chile is too weak to take real advantage of this unique opportunity. The National Council of Churches represents only one fraction of the whole, and is administered only in the spare time of an ageing Santiago pastor.

It can be seen that in the eyes of this observer, the C.W.S. activities had very positive effects which the churches were unable to turn to account.

Without a doubt, the relief programme of C.W.S. has created a meeting point for pastors of the most diverse Protestant churches. Looking at it optimistically, one could say that a meeting point creates dialogue, and dialogue opens the way to mutual acquaintance, collaboration, respect and finally the overcoming of disagreements. This has sometimes been the case. More often this meeting has given rise to relentless competition, each wanting a larger slice of the cake. Even more often, collaboration has been restricted to the business in hand and even though local committee meetings do begin and end with prayer, the effort put into social service does not spill over into other realms.

One might hope that social action would lead to serious thought about such action. Being aware of the real misery of the people, and of the role they play themselves, which is exclusively one of distributing relief, the officials might go on to ask themselves whether they could not contribute to relieving that misery at the local level and using local means. The very fact of being shocked by endemic undernourishment might provoke doubts about the proposed remedy: instead of continuously distributing foodstuffs, would it not be better to attack the root of the evil, by creating opportunities for work and promoting vocational training? These questions have been raised, but only occasionally and only within the Baptist, Anglican, Presbyterian and Methodist denominations.

Of course, one must not minimize the real relief which this aid has brought to thousands of families suffering from hunger. Even though the food provided is unvaried, it enables the families of the unemployed and those where the father has disappeared to survive in a little less inhuman fashion. But one must also emphasize the dysfunctional character of this form of social service, for many beneficiaries become completely dependent on this manna falling from heaven. Knowing how to make do with very little, the beneficiaries end by being satisfied with their monthly or weekly ration, and acquire a 'pauper mentality' which makes them unfit for all attempts to integrate them into the productive process. They abandon all thought of work. In satisfying the essential physical needs of man, this social aid lulls his conscience to sleep and takes away his wish to be involved, making him forget the real causes of his misery and the steps required to remedy it.

Social action on such a large scale is justifiable in unusual and temporary circumstances like earthquakes, such as that of 1960 which changed the map of southern Chile, or that of 1965 which left 100,000 people without shelter in central Chile, or again during particularly hard winters like that of 1965. But when it acquires a permanent character, it disguises the real problem and postpones the solution, a solution which requires that the consciousness of the masses be awakened. The observation made by Senator J. Gomez in the Chilean Senate chamber, citing Caritas, though the same is true for A.C.E., bears out our own conclusion:

> We are receiving surplus foodstuffs from North America in the form of a loan which our children will have to repay and through free assistance from Caritas which, whatever one may say, will in the long run undermine the integrity of our nation; these two forms of aid conspire together against our own rural production. . . . And to a certain extent they are driving us towards the abandonment of productive work and so degrading us.[26]

A second dysfunction, this time from the ecclesiastical point of view: when the Protestant churches agree to serve as agencies for North American bodies, this reinforces the image which South American society has of Protestantism—a foreign religion serving as an agent for foreign infiltration. Even the Pentecostalists themselves, whose independence and national character have been strongly emphasized, are losing their good reputation. The director of one Pentecostal denomination, after having been appointed an official of the A.C.E., then resigned from the post, thus performing an act of real moral courage (especially as he lost a considerable salary which, moreover, he had been placing at the disposal of his church). The following is his comment:

> We Pentecostalists have existed for fifty years with no external aid. We were free. Now, with C.W.S. and other agencies, we struggle among ourselves, one against the other, to get more gifts and also more money. We are letting the foreigners corrupt us. They are even going to ask for money from the U.S.A. for the struggle against communism!

Even the posts in the A.C.E., which are filled in accordance with ecclesiastical policy rather than the capacities of the candidates, encourage moral laxity! The salaries are too high in relation to Chilean scales, and the Director—who for example has had professional training as an accountant—earns more than one of the Ministers of the Republic. The advantages which A.C.E. affords to its staff and to those who gravitate around it make it easy to understand why the latter are opposed to any querying of the existence of this enterprise.

In local churches, food distribution becomes a proselytizing weapon. Whole groups leave one church which refuses to be associated with the aid programme and join another which does participate; individuals become converts so as to get their ration. There is an organizational catch here; although the statutes lay down that foodstuffs must be distributed to the most necessitous without regard to religious affiliation, how can one avoid a preferential distribution if one works through religious organizations?

Finally, in this survey of ecumenism, we come to the third dysfunction. Far from being the origin of an ecumenical spirit, the presence of A.C.E. has unleashed a veritable power struggle within the C.E.C. It is evident that those in control of A.C.E. have at their disposal a weighty instrument in their ecclesiastical policies. In addition, to foreigners they appear to be the representatives of Chilean Protestantism in general and they are in direct contact with sources of subsidies of all kinds. In fact, they do not represent anything other than their own denomination, and at a pinch a few others, but always an infinitely small proportion of the Protestant population. The fact that international organs think of the C.E.C. as the organ representing Chilean Protestantism, though in fact it is not (in February 1966 only 14 denominations were members of the C.E.C.), helps to confuse the issue.

The United States is at the moment in the process of successfully solving the question of its agricultural surplus, and thus in a few years the problem posed by C.W.S. will disappear. Nevertheless, it seems to us to be an example of the problem created by social aid given by world inter-church movements. To our way of thinking, if aid programmes are not preceded by an analysis of the socio-economic conditions in the countries where they are to be applied, and if the programmes do not simultaneously attack both the cause and the effect—we should like to say, if they do not aim chiefly at eliminating the cause rather than mitigating the effect—we believe that these programmes will be harmful rather than beneficial, that they do not measure up to the Christian search for social justice; that they kill rather than stimulate the churches' social conscience, by offering them a false 'charitable' conscience as a palliative; and that they foment tensions rather than favour the spread of an ecumenical spirit, by creating the illusion of a false unity and false collaboration.[27]

(*b*) It is very difficult to assess the impact of the World Council of Churches on Chilean Protestantism. Some personalities in the ecumenical movement (John R. Mott, for example) stimulated the development of the C.E.C. in the course of their visits. The official work of the World Council of Churches nevertheless got off to a very poor start. After the war, without making contact with the local Protestant churches, it created an office for refugees and put in charge of it a very strict Roman Catholic. In the Chilean context this was a serious blunder. The President of the C.E.C. learned of it, and went to see this official, who told him that he had not known that there were any Protestants in Chile!

After this interlude contacts were resumed on a more serious footing through the work accomplished by Church World Service. The first representative of that organization in Chile was Pastor Theo Tschuy, who afterwards worked in the Division of Inter-Church Aid of the W.C.C. Through his encouragement, two Pentecostal groups became members of the World Council: the *Misión Iglesia Pentecostal,* whose superintendent is Pastor Victor Pavez (son of the first Chilean Pentecostalist pastor), and the *Iglesia Pentecostal de Chile,* directed by Pastor Enrique Chavez, the present chairman of the C.E.C. Each of these denominations claimed to have 10,000 members at the time of their admission to the W.C.C., in the course of the New Delhi Assembly (1961). Even though these two churches are not in the top flight, their participation in the ecumenical movement deserves to be given prominence for, on the one hand, it stresses the W.C.C.'s regard for the latest of the Protestant movements and demonstrates that its spiritual contribution is recognized, and on the other, it shows that Pentecostalism is not necessarily opposed to ecumenical approaches. The relative isolation in which Chilean Pentecostalism existed up to the end of the world war and its independence of all missions have certainly made it easier for these churches to join the World Council of Churches. Had they been part of the world Pentecostal movement, which is known to be fiercely opposed to the W.C.C., membership would not have been possible for them. Besides, we have found that Chilean Pentecostalists do not claim to be the only Church, even though they do consider other denominations to be degenerate; their vision of the *Corpus Christi* transcending all ecclesiastical bodies is a help to the ecumenical approach; but naturally this more specifically theological motivation is just one of a complex bundle of other motivations (the feeling of power which affiliation to a world organization gives to churches that are regarded in their own society with a certain degree of disdain; the possibility of using this affiliation in order to assume a certain 'leadership' within Chilean Protestantism, and finally the economic advantages which may result from membership); in addition, membership of the W.C.C. does not imply that one becomes the champion of ecumenicity at the local level; the Lutheran Church, which is a member indirectly through its international affiliation with other Lutheran bodies, lives in Chile in a completely watertight compartment! The local effects of membership of the W.C.C. by these two churches do not enable one to draw a completely clear picture: the other denominations have not followed them in their approach to Geneva, and there has been renewed activity on the part of the fundamentalist international organizations. We would be tempted to think that the matter is of interest to the principal leaders, since contacts abroad enable them to strengthen their personal position, but that it does not touch the main body of pastors and still less the Pentecostal church members.

Our summing up of ecumenism in Chile would be rather sombre; since it has been manifested indirectly through charitable activities, it has rather the appearance of being a foreign intervention that complicates the Chilean situation, falsifying Pentecostalism's self-propagating evolution and not necessarily directing it towards ecumenicity. Such interventions have caused troubled minds, awakening longings and ambitions, creating what several Chileans themselves call 'the waltz of the millions'. The pseudo-representativeness of the inter-denominational bodies in Chile makes them like the statue in Nebuchadnezzar's dream: they have feet of clay, for, because of the needs of foreign agencies, they have suffered an inflation which bears no relation to the local situation. Ecumenism in Chile, an imported product, has the same artificial character as the missionary churches.

The following anecdote will illustrate the ambiguity of ecumenism: in August 1965 the Rev. Patrick Rodger, secretary of the Faith and Order Department of the World Council of Churches, visited Chile. His Department is known to operate on a small budget and to conduct purely theological and spiritual activities, and he came chiefly to stimulate this work in a country where, on account of the cultural level of the Protestants, theological thought is effected with difficulty. He was received, not so much as the representative of 'Faith and Order', but rather as one of the mighty in the World Council of Churches, the body responsible for administering and sharing out very large sums of money. Thus he was obliged to meet ministers, be present at the arrival of a Church World Service shipment, and stand up to a great many requests for subsidies!

4. SOCIOLOGICAL CONDITIONING OF ECUMENISM

That ecumenism belongs to a particular time and place, 'that it is bound up with historical circumstances which either stifle or encourage it' (M. Villeroy), that it is itself history and sociology, is an undoubted fact and should not shock anyone. That is why we find it hard to understand the arguments of a man like Jaques Ellul:

> The ecumenical trend? Is the ecumenical movement developing out of pure fidelity to the will of Christ to gather in His Church? If that had happened in the seventeenth century, for instance, I would have replied yes without any hesitation. But today? How many secondary, purely sociological motives can one not discover? Christianity is everywhere in retreat, being battered in most countries of the world, submerged under new religions (communism), old resurgent religions (Islam), under secularization. But in all groups threatened by an external enemy the trend is to gather together, to silence internal divisions. A National Front in a country at war is of the same order! Similarly in the world today we see before us a general tendency (bearing a certain universal character) to constitute racial or political blocs: the western and eastern blocs, the Islamic bloc, the Black Africa bloc, the European bloc, etc. Do the Churches not follow precisely the same movement in forming a bloc like all the other great units in the world?[28]

Ecumenism is part of a general movement towards unity and occurs at a time when the whole planet has become the *oikoumene*, the inhabited earth; this we do not dispute and shall return to again. But Ellul seems to believe in a clear dichotomy between divine and human, between the theological and the sociological or historical. It is this dualism which we challenge, from the sociological (and theological)[29] standpoint: theology does not belong to a transcendent and watertight universe, but forms a part of man's world, part of one level of social reality—that of ideas and values—itself closely related to and interdependent upon the other levels of that reality. For a sociological approach, the famous distinction between theological and non-theological factors is a false one, since both kinds belong within the same reality, that of the total social life of man.

Having said that, the sociological approach does not claim to exhaust the religious phenomenon, nor challenge the *theological* value of its message, since it is evident that the theological hypothesis (according to which God works through the psychological or sociocultural process) cannot be either invalidated or confirmed sociologically. This has, moreover, been stated by one of the great names in the discipline:[30]

> Even if one tried to prove that economic or social conditions in a given society gave rise to a desire for salvation, the promises of redemption which a religious message might include would not be invalidated by research into their social infra-structure, provided that the correlation was not conceived in determinist terms but interpreted as a functional relation. . . .[31]

The fact remains that the ecumenical quest, understood not as a return to such and such a form of church (the primitive church, or the catholic church) but as a 'march together of all the Christian churches . . . towards a completely new and original form of church' (R. Mehl), has been created in one precise sociological context, which must be borne in mind if one wishes to understand why Chile does not seem at present to favour this kind of experiment. In his *Sociologie du protestantisme*, Professor Roger Mehl includes a fairly elaborate essay in this new discipline, the sociology of ecumenism, and we shall summarize some of his arguments.

For Mehl, 'the break-up of Christianity, the dissolution of Christian civilization, and the presence of unbelievers are some of the sociological conditions which have made the ecumenical movement possible and have given direction to its work'.[32]

The concept of western *Christian* society is crumbling: the Church has been deserted first of all by the working classes, the unbeliever is no longer the exception on the fringe but, in a forward-looking view, the normal case. This questioning of the churches by society makes disagreements between the churches fade into insignificance, such is the strength of the world's defiance. The West, by its conquest of the world, and since decolonization, by its technological and economic processes, etc., has presided over the birth of a civilization which is universal, but in which culture is not bathed in a specific religion. While the rest of the world was under the political control of the West, the churches were able to maintain the hope of eliminating the non-Christian religions; but today the latter are able to fight against Christianity on an equal footing, and push it back or smother it. At the turn of the century the missionary situation was such that denominations which in their home countries tolerated one another and acknowledged the existence of a *status quo*, on the mission field treated one another in a spirit of competition; if such a situation even then encouraged ecumenical efforts (one may recall the link between the birth of the ecumenical movement and the conferences of missionary societies), then today such competition must for even stronger reasons give way to collaboration or even fusion. At a time, then, when State is divided from Church, a-religious cultures are arising, all institutions are breaking away from their Christian origins and, above all, man is no longer being born a believer, the Church should prove its authenticity by demonstrating that the questions it poses to man are still valid, across all geographical and sociological types. Thus on the one hand there is the radical challenge to Christianity, and on the other the planet-wide dimension of our social universe, and both drive the churches to rediscover the concept of *oikoumene*, the unity of the Church in the whole inhabited earth.

Perhaps one should add here that the evolution of thought, scientific research and historical knowledge have, among those who participate in these fields, dealt a fatal blow to religious fanaticism. As soon as a person becomes aware of the factors which condition Christianity through its history and the multiplicity of its historical embodiments, he can agree to discuss whether the form of Christianity embodied in his own denomination is the only true Christianity. This relativization, itself the result of a historical process, enables him to look forward towards a new form of Church, a search which for instance in the seventeenth century, to take Ellul's example, would have been hazardous, in that particular historical context.

However crude this *schema* may be, it enables us to re-examine the Chilean situation.

We notice first that Latin America used to be regarded by the Roman Catholic Church—and still is in certain quarters, though they are, it is true, diminishing—as a continent in which the whole population was Catholic (with the exception of the Indians of the forests where civilization could not penetrate). Protestant missions considered it a continent of heathens disguised as Christians, and still do so. Without prejudging the value of these postulates, it is clear that so long as they predominate, all ecumenical efforts between these two main streams of Christianity will be rendered vain.

Next, even if unbelief is beginning to widen a breach in the Chilean population (more than 350,000 persons having declared themselves to have 'no religion' in 1960),[33] even though the churches are empty, the popular outlook is not sceptical but religious, as we have shown in Chapter 2. Atheism is a potential challenge, but its threat is not yet strong enough to serve to stimulate the surmounting of inter-confessional disagreements.

In the third place it must be stressed that in Chile the *Reformation* (if one can use that title in a context which is completely different from that of Europe in the sixteenth century) is a recent fact; Protestantism had no weight until this century; far from being in decline, it is conquering; it is Protestantism which is presenting a challenge to society and its culture, and not the reverse. Its rate of expansion gives it a feeling of power, a self-confidence which makes it pay little heed to any questioning.

Conversely, one is compelled to observe that ecumenical relations have developed in those countries where relations between religious forces have been stabilized, where the denominations, if they do not always recognize one another, at least mutually accept one another's presence. Even though the clergy continue to preach in the churches, though the Churches present declarations to the governments and peoples, Christians there are silent, and internal missionary efforts are on the decline.

In Latin America the relations between religious forces are in a constant state of turmoil, Protestants proclaim the Gospel, and even if their message seems patchy, nevertheless its essence is proclaimed and carried forward by each member, who believes in the truth of what he proclaims as well as in his own mission to proclaim it. Here we put our finger on the huge question mark: what does the ecumenical movement signify in a place where religion has become the business of specialists, where the Gospel is no longer proclaimed by those who claim to follow it? Are ecumenical relations possible between very active and silent Christians?

Finally, one must refer to the problem of the cultural level of Chilean Protestants. In the eyes of a man (whether pastor or church member) who has not completed primary school, the faith which he shares, the beliefs he has been taught, the types of organization to which he belongs, the moral code he observes, are genuinely and utterly Biblical and Protestant. This is the Christian faith and this is the Christian Church. Modern theologians' problems seem to him to be monstrosities: the spirit and the letter in his eyes are one, and the fact that two thousand years separate him from the Biblical letter does not remove any of its total and immediate value. That anyone can believe in the Church and relativize his own church, that one can confess God the Creator and yet doubt that creation took place as related in Genesis 1, that to him is heresy and scepticism. His schooling has prevented him from taking part in the progress of thinking and science, and in his eyes thinking and science deny the faith. Chilean Pentecostalists are *fanatics*, in so far as this word means a choice and a radical involvement. Once again one must ask whether the decline in fanaticism does not have a correlation with a lack of apostolic conviction, both of them encouraging the rise of ecumenism?

This rapid comparison makes it possible to see why ecumenism as we understand it in Europe does not find favourable conditions in the Chilean situation.

It may be that the path which modern ecumenism has described is not the only possible one, that other 'ecumenical junctures' may exist; perhaps by the very fact that economic conditions, social structures and religious forces are evolving rapidly, the Chilean denominations will find a form of ecumenism peculiar to themselves which will, at the same time, be a contribution to the international ecumenical movement. But to achieve this, it would in any case be necessary for international church organisms to work with more discrimination and greater discretion in Chile, and take care not to become a parasite restricting the internal dynamism of Chilean Protestantism, but to respect its peculiar genius and its evolution. Is that still possible?

CHAPTER 9

Theological Aspects of Chilean Pentecostalism

IF one takes 'theology' to mean that the beliefs of a religious group and the ways in which its faith is expressed are classified as concepts and considered as a system, then the study of Chilean Pentecostalist theology proves to be very disappointing. Troeltsch said[1] of the sect, 'It has no theology, but a strict ethical code, a lively mythical imagery and a passionate hope for the future'. In Chilean Pentecostalism theology is an imported product, poorly assimilated. There are very few articles in local journals dealing with doctrinal points and published over the signature of national writers; generally they are taken from North American periodicals. The leaders state that they accept 'Pentecostal doctrine', but we are tempted to believe that up to now the experience of the Pentecostal groups has been so alive that they have not felt the necessity to produce elaborate reflections upon their faith and are satisfied with the material provided by Pentecostal foreign missions.

Since the study of journals reveals hardly anything of the specific character of Pentecostal theology in Chile, would the recording of a large number of sermons have enabled one to reconstruct their theology? Two complementary reasons led us to by-pass this approach: on the one hand, the limited time at our disposal and on the other the lack of equipment and/or trained investigators. It would have been necessary to gather a large collection of sermons in order to be able to trace back to doctrine from practical teaching, and we were not equipped to do this.

That is why we decided to restrict our enquiries to some points of theology, the exact content of which we would be able to ascertain either by direct observation or by adding some points to our questionnaire, and we chose some beliefs which, by reason of the emphasis given to them, seem to be particularly characteristic of Pentecostalism; that is to say, the Bible and the conception of the theology of the Holy Spirit; on the one hand its relation to scriptural revelation, and on the other to Baptism by the Spirit, shown in a visible manner through the phenomenon of glossolalia, and other gifts of the Spirit.

The absence of any theological writing belonging particularly to Chilean Pentecostalism (apart from some articles by Hoover and a few others) determined our line of approach. Regard for the subject to be studied compelled us to start from what actually exists, i.e. a collection of beliefs which are manifest in certain practices, and not a theoretical superstructure (as for example, the 'Pentecostal Theology' found in certain European and North American handbooks) which in this case would have no concrete meaning. Starting from the facts we have been able to collect, though they are fragmentary, we shall be able to compare them with the theological statements on which world Pentecostalism seems to agree, and we shall thus also avoid attributing to Chilean Pentecostalism a system of doctrine which it does not possess.

1. THE BIBLE

'We believe in the divine inspiration of the Holy Scriptures (the Bible), which is the word of God and contains all things necessary to salvation. It contains the Old Testament of 39 books and the New Testament of 27 books.'[2]

The Pentecostalists are not afraid to call themselves fundamentalists. 'In Chile', said one leader, 'we are the fundamentalists', and in fact they read the Bible in a literal manner. But though they believe in 'divine inspiration', there is no written text which develops this statement, and this permits a certain freedom of interpretation, as the answers to the following question show:

Table 1. Do you say the Bible is
(*a*) inspired *word for word* by God and the Holy Spirit,
(*b*) inspired in its *substance and ideas* by God and the Holy Spirit, but that men have written it down using the language and imagery of their time?

(a) If the person questioned answered affirmatively to (*a*):
(1) Does this apply to the Bible you have *in Spanish*?
(2) Does it apply to the *original text*, in the language in which the Bible was written?

(b) If the person questioned replied affirmatively to (*b*):
Could the men who wrote down the Bible have introduced *errors* into it (the scientific concepts of their time, or religious beliefs which today are thought to be wrong)?
(3) No
(4) Yes

	(*a*) WORD FOR WORD		(*b*) SUBSTANCE AND IDEAS			
	1	2	3	4	TOTAL	ACTUAL
	SPANISH	ORIGINAL	NO ERRORS	ERRORS		
Protestants	4	—	23	73	100	26
Pentecostalists	25	27	33	15	100	61

Note that the answers all assume belief in the divine inspiration of the Bible, and only deal with its interpretation. While the Protestant pastors tend to choose the widest possible interpretation, the scattering of the answers of the Pentecostalist pastors (with a slight preference for middling solutions) shows the absence of rigid teaching on Biblical inspiration. All told, the interpretations (*a*)1 and (*a*)2, which might be called 'fundamentalist', are held by only half of the pastors, and the other half make a distinction between the spirit and the letter.

The absence of a strictly fundamentalist consensus can be seen in other things. The fundamentalist is characterized by his diligent use of the Bible, regular reading, conscientious reference to the Bible in preparing sermons, etc. What is the case with the Chilean Pentecostal pastor?

Table 2. Frequency of Bible reading

Question: Do you read the Bible—

	EVERY DAY?	TWICE A WEEK?	LESS?	NO REPLY	TOTAL	ACTUAL
Protestants	96	—	—	4	100	26
Pentecostalists	75	21	4	—	100	61

The number of Pentecostal pastors who do not read the Bible daily rises from a quarter to a half if one adds those who read it daily (as one of them said) 'because we have a service every day and I read the Bible there'. As will be seen in looking at the problem of study, some pastors are on their guard against too frequent Bible reading:

'What profit is there in studying the Bible if one does not pray or fast?'

'There are so many words there that a man gets lost in it. It is not good to read it too much.'

'Too much Bible study may be detrimental.'

Thus diligent Bible reading is not the prime characteristic of the Pentecostalists. This, however, is not in any way to prejudge their loyalty with regard to Biblical revelation, which contains 'all things necessary to salvation'. Likewise, preparing a sermon by reading and meditating on a Bible text is not universally practised; furthermore, some consider it a heresy:

Table 3. Preparation of Sermon

Question: Do you prepare for preaching in advance by reading and studying the Bible?

	YES	NO	TOTAL	ACTUAL
Protestants	100	—	100	26
Pentecostalists	77	23	100	61

This last table can be interpreted from two standpoints. Taking the one we have chosen (the hypothesis of Pentecostalist fundamentalism) the assumption is challenged by the 23 per cent. of pastors who do not prepare their sermons (the proportion is increased if one adds the pastors who simply say they think of a text and meditate on it). The answers given by this group make a second interpretation possible:

'One should not prepare; that would be *carnal.*'

'No, since God speaks to us directly and shows us what must be said to the congregation.'

'No, since I know God will give me the words which must be said, in prayer.'

'Because preaching is the *revelation of the Spirit.*'

'I believe that one must be *inspired*, not prepared.'

'We should link ourselves to what the Spirit wants us to say.'

'If we prepared ourselves, the congregation might believe we were attacking them.'

'If we prepared ourselves, some would believe the pastor was attacking them through the Bible. The Lord gives the necessary words.'

For this group, preparation conflicts with inspiration, and prevents the Spirit from acting freely. Here again one sees Pentecostalist supernaturalism. If the pastor does prepare, his preaching becomes 'human' and his reproaches to the congregation come not from God but from the pastor. The Pentecostalist pastor's second loyalty springs from this: his loyalty is not so much to the Biblical word as to the Spirit which gives life to the written word. In this connexion it would even seem that our enquiry, which dealt, as we have said, with *organized* Pentecostalist denominations, has brought to light an evolutionary movement towards greater reliance on the Bible, for it seems that in the past refusal to prepare sermons was the rule (as it still is today in the smaller denominations) and not the action of a minority. A third loyalty can be seen in outline: that towards the tradition of the denomination itself. This should not be surprising, since it is clear that Catholic, Reformed and Orthodox Christians all read the Bible in the light of premisses derived from their respective traditions. In the case of Pentecostalist groups, it is possible to go further and state that knowledge of the Bible—at all events in the case of believers whose cultural level makes them unaccustomed to reading—is transmitted through the instruction given by the pastor and church leaders. What is Biblical is what the denomination teaches and practises. For example, if one asks a pastor of a denomination in which the ministry is thought to be incompatible with secular work why he should not have another occupation, he regularly answers, 'Because it is Biblical'. And the pastor of an organization which recommends its ministers to have another parallel occupation makes exactly the same response. We must acknowledge that both traditions are founded on Biblical texts.

These differences in interpretation do not prevent the Bible from being the emblem and symbol of Pentecostalism: a pastor is known by his Bible, a church by the texts decorating its walls. But we have found that regular Bible reading is done mostly in the church, during worship, and only rarely at home. The level of education is partly responsible for this fact, but it is not sufficient to explain it altogether, since in other places and at other times, in similar populations, Protestant evangelism has created a much more pronounced use of the Bible and Biblical culture than it has among the Chilean Pentecostalists. On the contrary, the fact that certain liberties are taken with the Bible is, in our opinion, to be ascribed above all to the characteristic belief of Pentecostalism: its faith in the Holy Spirit living and acting today in a spiritual, that is, supernatural way. The meeting between Biblical fundamentalism and Pentecostalist spiritualism (which is radically divided from other forms of spiritualism precisely by its faithfulness to the Bible) sets up a tension, since to read the Bible and reflect upon it is to set to work by human means, while the Spirit acts in a superhuman way. While in the organized denominations today there is a marked tendency towards preparing sermons by choosing a text and meditating upon it, this is a remarkable evolution, and we shall refer to it again later. According to the evidence of those who have belonged to the Pentecostalists for several decades, the original position was 'that one must let oneself be guided by the Holy Spirit, for the head swells with study, but not the heart'.

2. DOCTRINE OF THE HOLY SPIRIT

The *revival* which was started by Pastor Hoover took a new turn when echoes reached him of the budding Pentecostalism and he heard of 'a clear and conclusive baptism of the Spirit which was complementary to justification and sanctification'.[3] That is to say, Pentecostalism gave a new *emphasis* to the doctrine of the Holy Spirit, an emphasis which took the concrete form of a privileged *experience* (baptism of the Spirit) but was not limited to the latter. In the Pentecostalists' eyes, 'The traditional churches . . . came to a stop between Easter and Pentecost. They know that Jesus died and rose again, but they lack the *power of Pentecost* which drove the disciples to knock on closed doors (John 21) and made them courageous witnesses to the Gospel'.[4] For Chilean Pentecostalist church members or pastors, the Holy Spirit is above all the life of God—or in their own words the *power of God*—over and within human existence. When they speak of the Holy Spirit, they always allude to the experience of a power, a concrete fact, an intrusion into human life of the divine. The power of God is the proof of God.

One must stress the boundary separating the Pentecostalists' spiritualism from surrounding forms of spiritualism, that is, that their pneumatology is rooted in the Bible. Their whole understanding of the Spirit rests upon their reading of the Bible, in particular the Lucan evidence (Gospel of St. Luke and the Acts of the Apostles). Hollenweger rightly affirms that for the Pentecostalists 'the Acts of the Apostles is the normative rule of the normative primitive congregation'[5] and any deviation from the model is interpreted as a sign of degeneration. Now according to Eduard Schweizer, the theologian, 'the particular point of the Lucan witness lies in the view that a community which is without special power for the carrying out of its missionary mandate is a community without the Spirit'.[6] And Hollenweger adds, 'According to Luke, those who *pray with faith* receive the Holy Spirit, whereas according to Paul . . . *faith and prayer* are a *consequence* of the Holy Spirit's action'.[7]

The importance of the Biblical norm in Pentecostalist pneumatology gives one an understanding of why, whatever the liberties taken in regard to the Bible in the name of the Spirit, Pentecostalist prophecies or revelations have never had more than relative or temporary validity and were not treated as a new Revelation, complementary to the Holy Scriptures.

The great international Pentecostalist denominations (Assemblies of God, Church of God, etc.) have elaborated a doctrine of the Spirit and make a distinction between His gifts (glossolalia, prophecy, gifts of healing, of instruction, etc., cf. 1 Cor. 12) and His fruits (all the signs of sanctification and also missionary activity). In Chile the pastors who were questioned stated that they did not make this distinction, 'that everything is the gift of the Spirit', and we met only one single piece of writing which developed what could be called a 'doctrine of the Spirit', and that was obviously compiled from foreign articles. Moreover, the contents of the article have not been assimilated by the pastors belonging to the author's denomination, who do not believe they should make it the basis of systematic teaching.

> 'Pentecost is for all Christian people. Pentecost is not the monopoly of one evangelical sect. It is for everyone and our most sincere hope is that all, wherever they are, will receive it and each in his post will be useful for the Lord. Do not miss that benediction which belongs to you also. Ask for it in your prayers and you will receive it. Ask for God to give it in His own way; don't impose rules on the Lord. Don't be afraid of emotionalism and don't fall into routine patterns of dogmatic formalism. . . . The Baptism of the Holy Spirit should not be confused with the sanctification of the believer, that is, the fruits of the Spirit. Thus doctrinally in the purely Biblical sense, the experience of baptism of the Spirit is not salvation (regeneration), although it is for the saved; nor is it sanctification (fruit of the Spirit), although to retain this power we must keep ourselves in a state of sanctity; it is a *power of witnessing* . . . "You shall be my witnesses", Acts 1: 8.'[8]

In this setting, baptism of the Spirit appears as a higher level of spirituality, confirming salvation without being necessary for it, but giving assurance of greater strength and effectiveness. Here again the idea of *power* comes in. But when we review some of the *charismata*, we shall see that Chilean Pentecostalism, which has intense experience of manifestations of the Spirit, has so far neither organized them nor in its system of thought reduced them to a set of rules.

(a) *Glossolalia*

The article by Bishop M. Umaña will provide us with a methodological starting-point:

> 'One must distinguish between speaking in tongues as an initial proof of baptism (of the Spirit) and speaking in tongues as a gift given to the Church. . . . Speaking in tongues, as a gift, is not for everyone, but as an initial proof it is for everyone. A person who receives the baptism of the Holy Spirit will speak in tongues, and that will be the proof of his baptism, but it may be that subsequently he will no longer do it, for in that case it would be the gift of tongues.[9]

Thus one can distinguish between two phenomena:

1. Glossolalia as an audible proof of the Baptism of the Spirit. The Biblical foundation for this doctrine is found in Acts 2: 4; 10: 46; 19: 6.

2. Glossolalia understood as one of the gifts of the Spirit. It may then appear in the midst of preaching (1 Cor. 14: 27) or in prayer (Rom. 8: 26).

The Baptism of the Holy Spirit is an ecstatic mystical experience. Here is a description of such an event given by a Roman Catholic observer, which broadly corresponds with what we have seen.

> The candidate, before receiving the Spirit, must pray earnestly, out loud, and ask for conversion with loud cries.[10] The rising and falling rhythm of voices and the exhortations of the preacher excite him. The sight of other brothers beside him nearing a state of trance influences him. And at a given moment, physically exhausted, with a sudden nervous movement he falls to the ground ('he is carried away', in Pentecostal language), his saliva begins to run and he utters unintelligible phrases, or—in a supreme act of possession—he stretches himself out on the ground with eyes fixed on infinity. Some cry, 'The Spirit has laid hold on our brother'. 'Glory to God, Alleluia, glory, glory', others chant, forming a choir around him. The elders approach and lay their hands on him, while the faithful continue to chant alleluias. When he wakens, he is transformed. Then come tears, embraces, and congratulations.[11]

One must point out a paradox here. To seek for the Baptism of the Spirit was the goal of Pastor Hoover's followers and Pentecostalist pastors frequently speak about it, but nevertheless it does not seem to constitute a crucial activity in the Chilean congregations. Only in small denominations and mushroom churches did we attend meetings the sole purpose of which was waiting for the Holy Spirit. Elsewhere, the things which seem to be most sought after are the gifts of the Spirit, which fall upon particular individuals; visiting a congregation again after several months' interval, we noticed that it was the same persons who danced, prophesied or spoke in tongues.

It is also known that in many of the international Pentecostal denominations, one must have been baptized by the Spirit to be able to be appointed pastor. Among the Chilean denominations this is not a hard and fast rule, as the following table will show. In it, for this purpose, we have divided our sample of Pentecostal pastors into those who belong to the *Iglesia de Dios*, which originated in North America (Church of God, Cleveland) and those who belong to national movements.

Table 4. Pentecostal pastors and glossolalia
Question: Have you spoken in tongues?

	YES	NO	TOTAL	ACTUAL
Iglesia de Dios	92	8	100	12
Chilean denominations	49	51	100	49
TOTAL	57	43	100	61

Thus in these Chilean denominations, half the pastors have not had the experience of glossolalia, but this did not prevent them from having a ministerial charge. The criterion for entry into the ministry is success in evangelism rather than this mystical experience. May one say that the Chileans, at this point, are more faithful to the spirit of the Acts of the Apostles, while the North Americans cling to the letter of it, since, as has been shown, the consequence of Pentecost is essentially evangelization, not glossolalia?

The glossolalia-type phenomena observed during times of prayer are generally sighs, groans and various sounds. When they are accompanied by ecstatic manifestations, then a vision or prophecy follows, and incoherent sounds escape the lips of the one possessed. If he has not previously spoken in tongues, he will now be considered baptized. A frequent form of glossolalia takes place during singing or the playing of music. Then the 'Spirit' is manifested in dance. Individuals or sometimes whole groups begin to gesticulate, jump up and down, give nervous jerks and then to circle round. A few types of dance are recognizable. The men generally only hop up and down on the spot, while slowly turning. The women—and according to elderly witnesses, this was the earliest type of inspired dancing—extend their arms and spin round wildly. Or again they may dance with their hands together, palms outwards, in front of their faces. According to one leader, the origin of this type is as follows: the believers, when they saw someone inspired beginning to dance, would cross their arms around their heads to ward off blows. Then this became a form of dance. Either during the dancing or when they collapse exhausted on the ground, the inspired dancers cry 'Alleluia', 'Glory', and begin to babble.

It is to be noted that, while only half of the pastors have spoken with tongues, a still smaller fraction has, in the habitual phrase, 'danced in the Spirit'.

Table 5. Pentecostalist pastors and 'spiritual' dancing
Question: Have you danced in the Spirit?

	YES	NO	TOTAL	ACTUAL
Pentecostalists	44	56	100	61

Within the largest denominations it is acknowledged that the pastors do not dance or speak in tongues. In reality the pastor's function is to direct and to supervise. He must pay the closest attention to all that is going on; he observes the arrival of newcomers and sends one of the elders to bring them to the front row; he notes the appearance of charismatic phenomena and instructs one of the supervisors to channel the effusions, or even to stop a dance or prophecy if he thinks the person possessed is pretending and dancing 'according to the flesh'. This task of leadership makes him preserve a certain degree of detachment towards the contagious manifestations going on in the church. There is only one time during worship when the pastor may truly share in the outpouring of feeling and emotion: in his own preaching. It may then happen that the pastor is affected by the general atmosphere and that words in 'angelic tongues' are intermixed in his sentences, to the point where his sermon becomes pure glossolalia. Then two things may happen: either the phenomenon is interpreted as a manifestation of the Spirit who is thus showing His presence in the pastor but without giving a particular message, or, once the pastor comes to himself again, he announces that he has received a message or a prophecy which he then interprets.

The last of the functions of glossolalia which we came across is as the vehicle of a divine message. We shall return to this in the section on prophecy.

How should glossolalia be regarded? Father Damboriena, whose description of a baptism of the Spirit we quoted above, calls the phenomenon 'ridiculous' and adds that this judgment is shared by many Methodists, Presbyterians and Lutherans. This is a sweeping statement which does not bring us any closer to understanding, and demonstrates the attitude of highly-educated persons towards things which they consider to be 'the indiscipline of the common people'. Hollenweger takes up the explanation given by the Anglican priest Morton T. Kelsey,[12] who interprets glossolalia in terms of Jungian psychology: 'Speaking in tongues seems to him to be an expression of the collective mind. According to Kelsey, for certain people—and not only primitive or uneducated people—it contains a healing function, similar to that of a dream, and ought in no case to be rejected as a sign of illness, as "the shadow of the spiritual springtime of the primitive church" (Behm, in the article "Glossa", TWB I, 726) or as a demonic act.'[13]

Another interpretation is suggested, in my opinion, by the complementary relation between glossolalia and dancing: is it not simply and primarily a question of a *language*? That is to say, a form of expression, participation and lastly communion with the assembly and with the divinity? For the Pentecostalists, are not dancing and glossolalia the language of people without language? The experience of worship, lived so intensely, requires forms of expression so that the worshipper can make manifest his joy and the fullness of his participation. The language he has learned, and which he handles badly except in things relating to his daily life, does not allow him to express what he feels at the very moment when he most feels the necessity to express it. Hence the dancing, shouts, sighs and also speaking in tongues. And here Kelsey seems to us to be quite right in insisting on the dangers which would arise if one were to restrain this collective need to express oneself which liberates the participants and constitutes a form of collective therapy.[14] Finally St. Paul the Apostle was intuitively right when he wrote:

> 'Likewise the Spirit also helpeth our infirmities, for we know not what we should pray for as we ought; but the Spirit itself maketh intercession for us with groanings which cannot be uttered.' (Rom. 8: 26.)

This is how glossolalia is interpreted by J. L. Sherrill, a journalist who, while making an investigation into the phenomenon, ended by personally sharing in it. For him, as for all the great mystics, moreover, 'intelligible language is not sufficient for prayer, and there are things which can only be expressed in silence or in tongues'.[15]

The concepts of 'contagion' and 'imitation' used to explain Pentecostalist charisma are useful but do not exhaust the question. It is a fact that glossolalia and dancing can sometimes be simulated and serve to reinforce the power of one's personality. (Yet even in such a case, it is rarely a conscious pretence.) But these phenomena fulfil important functions of a psychological nature for those who experience them. The famous 'Pentecostalization' of Presbyterian churches and others in the United States, attended by middle-class worshippers, also shows that these emotional manifestations are not to be explained solely by the cultural level of those involved.

(b) *Prophecy*

By prophecy we mean a message which the bearer attributes to God and which expresses His behest (call, command) to those addressed, and which probably (but not necessarily) foretells a future event. The prophet in the Biblical and Christian tradition is not primarily someone who describes the future but the messenger of God.[16]

Prophecy employs three principal channels: dreams (or visions), sudden inspiration (illumination), and lastly utterance in tongues which has to be interpreted. The first and last are the most frequent. For example, a brother visits a neighbouring congregation, gives the pastor his letter of recommendation and asks to speak during the service. He rises, states that God has spoken to him in a dream and has charged him to say, 'You must make a chain of prayer for a week, and send out teams of evangelists every evening. Then the harvest will be great and you will heal many sick people.' The procedure is then as follows: every prophecy must be confirmed at least three times. Either other messengers must come bearing the same oracle, or the same person comes to repeat his call, having seen his vision repeated.

Prophecy in tongues abounds, especially in the south in the region centring on Temuco, that is, the old Indian country, and also on the coast in the coal-mining area. While we were carrying out our participatory observation in the Pentecostalist congregations of Lota, a mining town, we discovered a curious phenomenon of acculturation. One evening in December 1965, we were attending worship in a congregation of about fifty. We noticed a number of women of different ages, whose heads were covered with white veils. When one of them came into the church, whereas most of the other worshippers prayed in their places before sitting down, she went and knelt before a pulpit decorated with a picture of the Good Shepherd, prayed for a long while with sighs and repeated bowing, and then went to her seat. Our first observation, which we afterwards found confirmed many times, was that the pulpit took the place of the altar in the Catholic Church; undoubtedly it was the place set apart for the divine presence. Then, when the celebration began, conducted by the pastor and an elder, these women were revealed as, if I may use this paradoxical expression, the organizers of the spontaneous manifestations. They led the responses and, when the orchestra played, began to dance in turn, whereas usually several inspired people dance simultaneously. Then two of them spoke in tongues, each interpreting her own words, bit by bit. The friend who was with me whispered, 'It is *Mapuche*' (the Indian language). A movement of fear passed through the worshippers, for one of the women announced an earthquake in forty days' time, and added that perhaps the congregation might be able to avert it by their prayers. The pastor then resumed control of operations, begged them to be calm and recalled that the prophecy had to be confirmed. When we left we remarked that none of the men had danced or prophesied.

The next day I had an interview with the pastor of the congregation, and here are the notes written after that conversation:

'Why do some of the sisters have veils on their heads?'

'They are the sisters in "*primera comunion*"' (*Note*: the pastor meant to say, 'in full communion', that is full members of the congregation. Here again, Catholic terminology has often been adopted, indeed with a new meaning.), 'those who have been baptized by the Spirit. In 1 Cor. 11: 15 it says that women who pray and prophesy should cover their heads.'

'Then these are the prophetesses of your church?'

'No, they are simply women who have been baptized with water, after six months of instruction, and who afterwards have received the baptism of the Spirit. Prophetesses are something different. . . .'

'What does the instruction prior to baptism consist of?'

'Well, they must prove that they are well behaved, they must not miss worship, they must pray, and share in the vigils.'

'Do you give them special Biblical teaching?'

'No, not special teaching; they go to the Sunday school and hear the preaching.'

'But you do have some prophetesses?'

'Yes, we have two. We have some young apprentices, but they are not ready yet.'

'Because one has to learn how to prophesy and speak in tongues?'

'Yes, the older ones teach the younger how to do it, with order and discipline. To speak in tongues and prophesy, to capture the grace of God in other languages, that is the greatest gift. Here, besides, prophecies are in the old language of the country, *Mapuche*. This is how the Lord manifests His power.'

'But do the prophetesses know *Mapuche*?'

'Yes, as a rule. We all have some Indian blood! And they translate what they say into Spanish. But a prophecy has to be confirmed, because it is written, I forget where, that there must be two or three witnesses. You were there yesterday, and now we are waiting today for the confirmation of yesterday's prophecy. But it is quite likely that it is true, for this woman has a special gift of clarity. In 1960 she foretold the famous earthquake forty days before it happened. But confirmation is necessary and the church does not remain inactive. God may change His plan; think of Nineveh!'

'Do men also prophesy and dance?'

'No, not with us. I know that, in the Bible, there are some men who do, but I have never known such a thing either in my mission* or in this region.'

* *Translator's note:* 'Mission' means church; see Introduction.

'Do you practise the healing of illnesses?'

'Yes, of course. We should not be Pentecostalists without that. Nearly all of those who are converted are so because they have been cured.'

'But how do you do it?'

'Generally during the service people give us the names of sick people and we pray for them. If they are present we lay hands on them. If not, we go to do it in their homes.'

'Who lays his hands on the person?'

'The pastor, the elders, the prophetesses. If none of them are present, then a member "*in primera comunion*".'

'Do you also perform healing "operations", or do you act as if you were a doctor, in the name of the Spirit?'[17]

'Yes, sometimes, during worship or at the sick person's home.'

'Who does this?'

'Usually a prophetess, with the pastor and elders round her praying. This is in difficult cases, when the sister says to us that the Spirit wants us to do this. But the sister must be in a state of sanctity, she must have fasted two days in the week and prayed a lot.'

'Can a woman be a pastor, or a member of the council of elders?'

'With us it is not so. I cannot remember this happening.'

On the basis of this conversation a social division of tasks in the congregation can be observed. The leading functions are reserved to men; on the other hand the most characteristic gifts are the domain of women: dance, glossolalia, prophecy and also a certain method of healing. Secondly, the Indian background stands out: these women prophesy in the *Mapuche* language, which they already know (it may be noted in passing that this does not trouble anyone), and prophecy is a calling which is passed on by apprenticeship.

One day at Chol-Chol, a little town in the heart of the Indian reservation (or, as the Spanish language bluntly says, *reduccion*), we had explained to us the main features of Indian organization, and a striking parallel was brought out between them and our Pentecostalist community in the division of social functions: the heads of family and *caciques* can only be men. Women have only one special function, that of the *machi*, which is hereditary by nature. The *machi* prophesies during Indian religious festivals and uses glossolalia which a male interpreter translates. The language used by the *machi*, according to one informant, is the Indian language, but spoken so rapidly and swallowing so much of the words or even phrases that the interpreters have to be specially trained. These *machi* are also the clans' healers.

It is clear that the congregation we observed bore the imprint of the Indian model. Should one speak of syncretism? To be able to do that, one would need to know if the meaning attributed to the rites originated in animism. From what we were able to see, Pentecostalism carries out a conversion, if not of the meaning at least of the thing signified, understanding it exclusively in relation to Christ.[18]

Later we tried, too hurriedly, unfortunately, to establish the geographical area in which this rigid division of tasks between the sexes is found, and the type of Pentecostalist congregation where it is found. Broadly speaking it seems to coincide with Indian country, from the

Bio-Bio river in the north down to the Province of Llanquihue in the south. It is also found chiefly in the small denominations with a few congregations, found exclusively in this zone, and above all in the *callampas* churches which abound in this area. In the churches of the large denominations one finds this phenomenon here and there, but to a much less marked degree. Thus it seems, until more ample information can be gathered, that this organization inspired by the Indian context is geographically and typologically limited; it touches a section of Chilean Pentecostalism which is in a minority and has clearly defined characteristics, and should not be extrapolated to apply to Chilean Pentecostalism in general.

Elsewhere in the country a certain degree of sexual dimorphism is to be observed, but this reflects the culture of a social class or even of society itself rather than that of an ethnic group: it is rare for a woman to be a pastor (though this is not impossible): on the other hand the 'gifts of the Spirit' and particularly glossolalia are more often manifested in women.

Prophecy deals mainly with the work of the Church: greater zeal in evangelism, stricter obedience to the pastor, commands to pray that the gifts of the Spirit may abound, etc. Sometimes, as in one of the examples given, it takes the form of foretelling a catastrophe. Again, at the time of presidential elections the 'possessed' break out and sometimes, in the same church, give contradictory prophecies. Finally, prophecy may be addressed to an individual person, aiming to stimulate his conversion, to instil fear into parents who oppose their child's attending the church, to frighten the sinner, or again to entrust a special mission to one of the worshippers.

Last of all, glossolalia in preaching: the pastor speaks to his flock using an 'angelic language', which he may or may not translate. Most of the time this phenomenon occurs at the end of a sermon, when the pastor is no longer acting as supervisor but is the principal participant. One of them thus described this process:

> Sometimes the message which God commands me to deliver is so important that Castillian words cannot express it. Then the Spirit gives me His own words and I speak in His language . . .

In some mushroom churches preaching 'in tongues' is the real source of the pastor's power. Here the latter has what the Pentecostalists call the 'permanent gift': he can speak in tongues whenever he wishes, and by reason of this power he acquires a certain number of adherents. This form of glossolalia does not occur in the large denominations, where indeed it is often considered to be a fraud:

> In the Bible I know of no example of men speaking in tongues whenever they wish. One only speaks in tongues when the Spirit commands it . . .

Glossolalia and prophecy hold an important place in Pentecostalist worship. Nevertheless, if one regularly attends the congregations, by degrees the conviction grows that the manifestation of the gifts of the

Spirit is much more important than the content of the prophecies. Competition between prophets has certainly been the cause of congregations dividing; the visitor is told of great prophecies which were actually fulfilled (and which generally concern earthquakes); warning dreams occur constantly in biographical accounts; sometimes—here we speak of some extreme cases—pastors even claim to have had particular revelations for acting in ways contrary to morality and Biblical teaching.[19]

Prophecies never become transformed into revelations which are complementary to the Bible. Prophecy refers either to a precise event and then dies with it, or (and this is so in most cases) it has no aim other than to affirm the presence and action of the Spirit within the congregation. The importance which Pentecostalism places upon the gifts of the Spirit arises from the fact that these gifts are understood as visible signs or proofs of divine activity. Their value in themselves is quite secondary in relation to their value as testimony to the Divinity.

(c) *Faith-healing*

For the Pentecostalist, God is not an idea but a presence and a power. God saves; He has the power to save, and even more concretely the power to cure, whether it be from the effects of sin or of illness. Countless conversions were preceded by a cure (whether real or imaginary is impossible to verify) obtained by prayer and laying on of hands.

As Table 6 shows, with one exception almost all the pastors questioned confirmed that they have experience of divine healing:

Table 6. Experience of Faith-healing
Question: Has divine healing taken place through you?

	YES	NO	TOTAL	ACTUAL
Pentecostalists	98	2	100	61

Prayer for the sick is an important part of worship. Those who desire it come up to the platform, and kneel, and the elders pray with their hands placed on the worshipper's head.

In a society where there is sickness, and where the medical system, although rapidly growing, is still inadequate and in particular provokes fear among the people, the power of healing plays an enormous part. A priest told me that when a Chilean is seriously ill he sends for a priest and a pastor, the first so as to receive through Extreme Unction assurance for the hereafter, the second in the hope of an extension of his time on earth! Conversion through healing is very frequent and this is the story of such a case, told by a pastor:

> One night—at that time I still had a little workshop and a lorry—a family came looking for me. The mother was quite paralysed in one leg, and they asked me to take her at once to the hospital. My lorry had broken down, and it would have taken me several hours to mend it. I said to them, 'Listen, I will gladly take you to the hospital, but it will take time to mend the lorry. But I also know that we, the Pente-

costalists, can cure your mother.' They would not hear of it, so then I made a bargain with them: 'We will mend the lorry, but while we are doing it, the brothers will come and pray. If by the time we are ready to go your mother is cured, will you all agree to be converted to the Lord?' They agreed. . . . When the lorry was ready and we picked up the mother in our arms, she gave a cry and moved her leg. She was cured. Since then that family always comes to our services. . . .

The Pentecostalist newspapers are full of marvellous tales of healing. In reading them one recognizes a pattern in the way the experience is retold: the person is very ill, but the illness is not exactly defined;[20] doctors have given up the case; then a Pentecostalist group intervenes and the power of God is shown, and the person 'confesses the name of the Lord'.

In some accounts which we collected, the cure is accompanied by prophecies and other supernatural manifestations. Here are two accounts, which we reproduce, less on account of the healings which they relate, than because they throw light, on the one hand on how non-believers regard Pentecostalist communities, and on the other on the supernatural world in which the worshippers move.

The first account:

This happened more than 25 years ago. My two sisters walked in the paths of the Lord. I did not: I played football and drank. I also had to work to support my sisters, and was working at the mine, on the third (night) shift. They asked me to go to the church but I did not want to go. I already had a stomach illness; I had what they call here *el salto del chanchito* (lit. 'piglet's jump') and I was very weak. I could not sleep, or eat, because my stomach was rotting away. One day when we were out walking and went near the church, the two of them took me by the arms and dragged me in. The elder said, 'Come along, and perhaps the Lord will cure you as he cured me'. 'Stupid', I said to her, 'why should He cure me?' But in the end I followed them, so as not to leave them alone. I did not want to go in, for I knew that they danced and jumped about, and all those things, and I did not like that. Besides, one has to kneel, and humble oneself, and I would not. To please them I went in, but I sat near the door and said to myself, 'When they begin to do those things I shall get up and go'. . . . The worship began and after a time the leader said, 'Let us pray'. 'Good,' I thought, 'this is the moment to leave.' They all knelt down, and I tried to stand, but God! I could not. I tried again, without success. I thought, 'What is happening?' Round me some people were dancing, and one of them, whom I did not know, put his hand on my head and then on the place where the pain was and said, 'Listen to me, my son, God wants to save you; you have been ill for such and such a time, and it started in such and such a way' (and he described how it began). 'And the Lord tells me that no doctor can heal you, but I am your doctor and will heal you. This illness prevents you from eating and sleeping'—and I thought, 'How does he know all this?' He finished by saying, 'Listen, my son, the Lord will come Himself to operate on you with His own hands, so that you shall know Him. He will soon take away this stomach pain. . . .' And I went away, thinking, 'How can that be done? Are they sorcerers?' The second night after the service, I was in bed and groaning with pain. I was lying on my back with my eyes closed when suddenly a little old man came towards me from the corner of the room, on his knees, and when I saw him words came to me: 'Save me, save me in your mercy, Lord!' And he got on my bed and put his hands here (indicating his stomach) and did this (indicating a massaging movement) and I gave a cry and he disappeared and I was cured to this very day. The next day I went alone to the midday service. Seeing me, the leader said, 'What has made you come alone?' 'Nothing,' I replied and I sat down. I wanted to see whether the 'instrument' [sic] who had told me the previous time about my cure knew what had happened in the night. During the time of prayer, the instrument gets up, comes over to me and says, 'You see, my son, last night the Lord came to your house, in such and such a shape . . .' and he told me everything that had happened, word for word, and ended up by saying, 'You are cured because the Lord wanted to show you His power and that you should believe. Don't draw back.' This is the first time I have told this story. . . .

The second story:

I had a lung illness and was very weak. The doctor told me I needed a long treatment and perhaps would never leave hospital. But God who is powerful took an instrument, as we say here—a prophet who, during a service, put his hands on my forehead and said, 'You no longer have any lungs, but God will cure you'. During another service, another prophet said to me, 'Listen, on such a day, a Sunday, you will go to the church at the place called El Peumo, and God will heal you'. On that day I went there, and did not know anyone there, but a third prophet came up to me in the church and said, 'My son, I am going to cure you'. He stretched me out on the ground, and tapping my back, he said, 'On this side there is nothing left; on the other there is a little, but I am going to give you new lungs, all pink and lovely. And I am going to operate on you, with pain so that you know I have power'—the instrument was speaking in the name of God—'so that you shall have no doubt and do not slip backward.' And I felt everything he was doing, just as if it were a worldly doctor. He made a cut in my back and I cried out. And he showed me the new lung he was going to give me; 'Do you see it?' Of course I saw it, although it was only spiritual! 'So that you will feel it, I am going to give it to you hot.' And I felt the heat when he gave it to me, and I cried out, 'Ow, Lord, it hurts!' And I felt him sew me up like a worldly doctor, although everything was spiritual. And he said to me, 'I shall bandage you as if you were in hospital. In a week, come back and I will take off the bandage and remove the stitches.' And that is what happened. The three prophets did not all belong to the same denomination, but God works as He wishes. All that is the truth, and since then I do what God tells me to do.

This last account brings us to the subject of a particular ritual of 'healing operations', when the pastor (or the prophetess), dressed in a white overall and surrounded by 'assistants', performs a simulated operation ('spiritual' operation) on a sick person stretched on a table: 'I am opening your abdomen with the Lord's lancet, I am removing the sore with the Lord's forceps,' etc. The congregation sings and prays. This rite is based on a reading of 1 Cor. 12: 9–10 where Paul speaks of the diversity of gifts: 'to another gifts of healing by the one Spirit, to another the working of miracles'. This tradition is read in the context of modern medicine, from which comes the miming of the surgeon's work.

A Catholic theologian sees in the Pentecostalist healing practices a deviation from the sacrament of Extreme Unction:

> The sacrament of Extreme Unction, instituted by Christ to solace first the mind and secondly the body of Christians who are seriously ill, has been altered by this sect and turned from its true sense and meaning. Its members practise ritual anointing and laying on of hands accompanied by prayer, giving them a fundamentally charismatic significance.[21]

One can guess what a Protestant theologian would say of such a statement: to speak of Extreme Unction as a sacrament instituted by Christ, a detour must be made by way of the Church, the trustee of the Revelation and continuer of the work of Christ. From the sociological point of view, healing by faith has nothing to do with the Catholic sacrament, but is culturally rooted in the tradition of healing saints, who are very numerous in Chile and very important in popular belief.[22] Just as they say to the saint, 'Cure me and I will do such and such', the sick person makes a bargain with Christ, 'If You heal me, I will be your disciple'. Pentecostalism does away with the hagiolatry, but conserves the system. Extreme Unction is regarded quite differently, as a preparation for death and the meeting with God beyond death. This sacrament is replaced in Pentecostalism, on the one hand by the belief that healing is possible, and on the other, 'if the time has come', by prayers of intercession by the dying person's bedside. The functions fulfilled by the Catholic sacrament and by faith-healing are therefore totally different.

For Pentecostalism, faith-healing, the sign of God's power, lends value to conversion, to 'life in Christ'; it constitutes—as does, at another level, congregational life—an earnest of the heavenly Kingdom. The Pentecostalist needs a concrete faith, attested by material signs in the form of some vital change. As Hollenweger says, to the Pentecostalist faith-healing is 'the adequate proof of God'.[23]

3. PROTESTANT PASTORS AND PENTECOSTAL GIFTS

Here we desire to record the reactions of the Protestant (Methodist, Presbyterian and Anglican) pastors and the Buenos Aires students with regard to Pentecostal gifts. We wish to do no more than make this information available for the dossier on inter-Protestant relations. The superficial character of most of the replies in any case underlines one fact: a good number of pastors and students have preconceived ideas which do not make for easier collaboration with the Pentecostalists.

Three questions enable us to discern their attitudes:

> Do you think that *dancing* during worship, as it occurs in Pentecostalist churches, *could be* a gift of the Holy Spirit?
>
> Do you think that *speaking in tongues could be* a gift of the Holy Spirit?
>
> Do you think that *faith-healing is possible*?

Table 7. Protestants and Pentecostal Gifts

GIFTS	SAMPLE	YES	NO	N.R.	TOTAL	ACTUAL
(1) Dancing	Students	22	56	22	100	36
	Pastors	19	65	16	100	26
(2) Tongues	Students	61	22	17	100	36
	Pastors	61	21	18	100	26
(3) Healing	Students	75	14	11	100	36
	Pastors	100	—	—	100	26

In this case, refusal to answer shows a distrustful attitude towards the phenomenon being considered, and in the following analysis we can assimilate those cases with the negative answers. It should be noted at the outset that pastors and students react in the same way to the first two questions, but while *all* the pastors believe in faith-healing, only three-quarters of the students do.

If the replies given by each person interviewed to the three questions are studied, it can be seen that they agree in excluding certain combinations. Apart from three untypical cases, the answers fall into the four following patterns:

	(1) Dancing	(2) Tongues	(3) Healing
Group 1 (Believe in all 3 gifts)	+	+	+
Group 2 (Exclude dancing)	—	+	+
Group 3 (Believe only in Healing)	—	—	+
Group 4 (Deny all three)	—	—	—

The logic of the pattern is theo-logic: in fact the most frequently disputed phenomenon is dancing, for which there are no Biblical references, and the one most often accepted is healing, which plays an important part in the Bible. Thus the person who accepts dancing will also accept the other two phenomena. The person who rejects dancing but believes in glossolalia believes in healing. The person who denies glossolalia also denies dancing, but may believe in healing. Finally he who does not believe in healing rejects the other two phenomena.

This structure makes it possible to establish a scale of attitudes, as shown in the following diagrams:

Scale of opinions of students on Pentecostal gifts

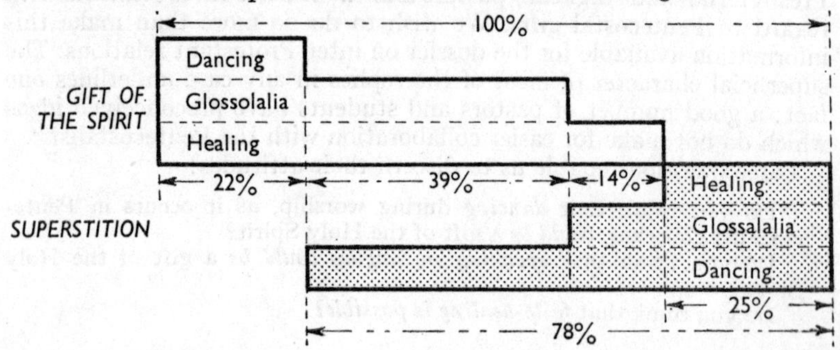

Scale of opinions of Protestant pastors on Pentecostal gifts

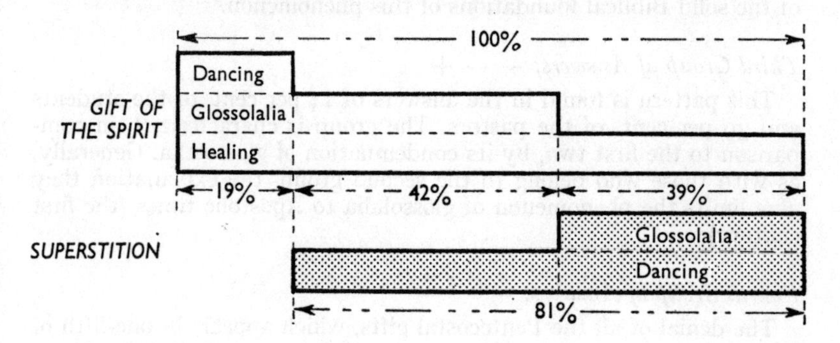

First Group: + + +

About the same proportion of the two samples replied in this way (three positive answers) (22 per cent. of the students and 19 per cent. of the pastors). They alone believe that dancing could be a gift of the Spirit in the same way as glossolalia and healing. Their comments show a certain hesitation, and also the wish to separate divine action from human emotion:

> 'Yes, although there is a lot of distortion and human emotion in it.'
> 'Yes, when it is the fruit of worship and does not arise from psychological problems.'
> 'Yes, but sometimes I think it is the fruit of auto-suggestion, which is attributed to the Holy Spirit.'

The group's judgment on dancing as a gift of the Holy Spirit is, 'Yes, with reservations'. The fact that all the others, that is 80 per cent. of those interviewed, reject dancing throws light on the hesitations of Protestants in regard to Pentecostalist worship. The words of one person interviewed sum up the position of this first group:

> 'I think nobody can put limits on the work of the Spirit, although for many of us this form (dancing) is doubtful and incomprehensible.

Second Group of Answers: — + +

Thirty-nine per cent. of the students and 42 per cent. of the pastors condemn dancing but believe in the other two gifts. Here are some opinions on dancing:

> 'Don't ask silly questions!'
> 'The Holy Spirit is unostentatious.'
> 'God does not manifest himself to man like that.'

It should be noted that only these first two groups, i.e. 61 per cent. of each sample, believe in glossolalia. This may seem surprising in view of the solid Biblical foundations of this phenomenon.

Third Group of Answers: — — +

This pattern is found in the answers of 14 per cent. of the students and 39 per cent. of the pastors. The group is characterized, in comparison to the first two, by its condemnation of glossolalia. Generally, as with those who belong to the second group, the explanation they give limits the phenomenon of glossolalia to Apostolic times (the first century).

Fourth Group of Answers: — — —

The denial of all the Pentecostal gifts, which appears in one-fifth of the student sample only. Here again, they try to limit this gift to Apostolic times, and state: 'God manifests Himself today through medicine.' This minority can be called 'rationalists of faith'.

This brief analysis shows above all how very passionate is the reaction to these questions. Even theologically speaking, it is surprising that nearly 30 per cent. of the two samples deny glossolalia and a quarter of the students dispute faith-healing. It should be noted here that there is a sharp difference between the pastors' reaction and that of the students. All the former believe in faith-healing, while a quarter of the latter tend to consider it as a superstition.

The sweeping style of the comments made by those questioned suggests that the problem posed by charismatic manifestations has hardly been studied at all seriously from the theological point of view, and certainly not from the point of view of psychology or sociology. The replies are often based on prejudices, which themselves strengthen the latent antagonism between the so-called 'traditional' denominations and Pentecostalism. It is clear that the 'ecumenical dialogue' which is so much spoken of between these trends of opinion will have to go through a stage of re-examining the Protestant positions, which are more rationalist than Biblical.

4. CONCLUSION

This examination of certain aspects of Pentecostalist theology has been carried on in a sociological perspective. We have dealt not with their theological truth but their social or psycho-social significance. In other words, we have tried to see what functions they fulfilled in the minds of the worshippers and the congregations. Is it necessary to stress the power of integration, participation and communion which is represented by dancing and speaking in tongues? Or their importance in the process of group therapy which occurs during Pentecostal services? It would be interesting to have a psychologist make a study of this point, but in the absence of a more detailed analysis let us quote the conclusion reached by Bryan Wilson in his study of a Pentecostalist denomination in England:

> The Elim church is something of a curative agency for this social malady (isolation). It can appeal only to certain socio-economic strata, and its activities would be impossible to those of a higher cultural group, but within this range it has latent functions for the 'desocietalized personality' . . . It is (precisely) this intense intimacy and the creation of an in-group feeling which fulfils the latent functions of Elim and similar sects; it makes the individual one of a group, a very immediate personal group, and it is exactly this process which is useful in the resolution of psychological maladjustments.' In a sense the group itself takes over the individual neuroses, and institutionalizes them; certainly, after its own fashion, its function offers very obvious analogies with group-psychotherapy, in which the minister is leader; and the intensity of the services—with spontaneous testimonies (often with every show of deep emotional involvement)—is a near natural approach to the situation offered in psychodrama. The basis of organization is one of sharing a guilt-feeling—sharing a deep-laid sense of sin. Even the function of psychodrama is represented in the Pentecostal group—the individual has release for emotional tension in dramatic form when he is unable properly to enunciate his thoughts, or is afraid to do so: the psychological blockage or the intellectual inability is by-passed in the phenomenon of unknown tongues. There is a type of group free-association, and a group transference—the individual unloads his insecurity feelings into a situation where all recognize his frailty, and do not condemn him for it.[24]

It is essential to call attention to the role attributed to Christ in this sort of group therapy. While the 'traditional' Protestants are inclined sometimes to look upon the rites belonging to the Pentecostal form of worship as 'superstitions', 'non-biblical practices' and to establish parallels (often forced) with certain forms found in popular Catholicism or even animism, nevertheless it is still true that each element in the worship, each emotive or charismatic phenomenon, is explained in terms of Christ's action. While psychological theory attributes curative and liberating powers to the group itself, for the worshippers it is God who is at work in the social group and who makes the liberation possible.[25] The depth of faith of the worshippers, and the importance of the latent psycho-sociological functions fulfilled by their religious practices and forms of worship, should give Christians of other traditions pause to think, and at least prohibit them from making any superficial and hasty judgments.

SUMMARY AND CONCLUSION

A. IS PENTECOSTALISM IN A STATE OF EVOLUTION?

In his study of the evolution of sects, Bryan Wilson puts forward the hypothesis that they

> experience different types of tension which vary according to their own constellation of values, as well as the circumstances of their origin. In response to such tensions, in the attempt at their management, we may expect to find the genesis of processes which cause some sects to develop into denominations, others to wither, some to be exterminated, some to fragment, and some to remain, over several generations, as sects.[1]

If this approach is correct (and we think it is) it is necessary to go beyond Troeltsch's sect/church dichotomy[2] and use a more refined typology enabling one to classify the sects themselves. Naturally, from the Troeltschian standpoint it is plain that the Chilean Pentecostal groups belong to the 'sect' rather than the 'church' type: are they not communities which one joins voluntarily, where membership follows conversion? Do they not correspond to the principal features in Mehl's description:

> The sect regards itself as a movement rather than an institution; that is why it is so often characterized—at least in the early stages—by a fluid, embryonic and spontaneous organization, and usually by discarding the idea of the pastoral ministry as a professional occupation. It refers so often to the pattern of the primitive Church because it considers —not without reason—that the latter was not at all institutionalized. Like the primitive Church, the sect tries to make charisma prevail over function, spontaneity over organization, the prophet over the priest, inspiration over doctrine. In the proper sense of the word it is 'enthusiastic'.[3]

Finally, Pentecostalism is characterized by its passionate opposition to the official church, the Roman Catholic Church, and its undeclared opposition to society, taking concrete form in its refusal to participate in politics.

Having said that, it is necessary to grasp that (going back to Mehl's terms) a sect is never entirely a 'movement' without any of the features of an 'institution', and it is just this combination of two trends at the moment when the sect is created which determines, in part, the ultimate evolution of the sect.

Wilson tells us that a sect can be born through the action of a charismatic leader, or by schism, or by a revival.[4] All three elements were present in the advent of Pentecostalism in Chile, but the predominating element was *revival*. Though Hoover had certain of the characteristics of a charismatic leader, and though a schism enabled the Chilean Pentecostal movement officially to be born, yet it is true that the goal it pursued was that of a spiritual, mystical, and consequently missionary renewal of the Methodist congregations.

Those who formed the first Pentecostalist congregations were all Methodists. They bore the mark of a religious tradition of which they challenged some, but not all, of the elements. Thus it was far from being a sect formed exclusively around a charismatic leader with more or less precise ideas as to his plans, whose disciples came from different religious spheres. The Pentecostalists inherited from Methodism a body of beliefs (which they revised at certain points), practices (to which they added) and an organizational system; they did not need to invent their manner of meeting, but simply to integrate the Pentecostalist contribution with the Methodist heritage, and adapt the latter to its new situation (the break with foreign countries, the absence of seminary-trained pastors, etc.). Thus *though the 'movement' predominates over the 'institution', yet the latter is present from the beginning*. Chilean Pentecostalism had available from the start not only an organization but also a fairly well-developed structuration of the component elements (beliefs, collective practices, system of organization, values, etc.). From the start it was a coherent whole, and the problems posed by the separation from Methodism were rapidly and easily resolved. That pure improvisation and spontaneity were overborne and even canalized by the organization and resumption of old Methodist patterns is shown, for example, in the following fact: the two dissident congregations in Santiago asked Hoover to accept the superintendence of their movement from 1909, i.e. while he was still a missionary and member of the Methodist Church (which he left in 1910). No sooner had the schismatic groups been created than they adopted a federal organization and acknowledged the authority of a man capable of containing within the institutional mould the manifestations of spontaneity. From the start, too, the congregations appointed pastors, whom they paid themselves, and this last feature is in contradiction to the classic model (the ideal type) of the sect.

These elements show that Chilean Pentecostalism belonged from the time of its first appearance to the sub-type which Yinger called 'the established sect', as distinct from 'the spontaneous sect', the latter being capable of further sub-division into 'cult', which indicates a group which is small, unstable and unorganized, and 'sect' in the proper sense.[5] Bryan Wilson has taken up this concept of the established sect and given it a content which corresponds more closely with our problem. The established sect

> is already an established pattern of theory and practice when (new members) enter it; they are not themselves creating a new way of life, and providing for themselves patterns appropriate to their needs, but they are rather fitting and moulding themselves to a given way of life, the terms of which are already laid down. . . . The established sect

provides an objective social environment for the individual, and imposes constraints upon him, for ultimately the moral codes of the group are identified with the behests of God, acknowledged as external, transcendent and impersonal in their authority. The spontaneous sect, which, of course, if it persists, generates the established sect, may ease psychological tensions by encouraging individuals uninhibitedly to express their feelings; but the established sect finds need . . . to discipline in some measure the spontaneous expressions of its members, and to pattern enthusiasm into institutionally approved channels.[6]

Regarded from the standpoint of the typology of religious societies, the events of 1909–10 can be described in the following manner: groups of people who were members of the Methodist Church (which belongs to the sub-type called 'denomination'), finding that their religious needs were not being satisfied, attempted by a revival to transform it into an 'established sect'; then, this attempt at reform having failed, they founded an 'established sect' outside their original church. Till now we have used the term denomination in its usual sense, to define a religious movement which has legal status and thus a name. But since the work of Richard Niebuhr,[7] this word also defines a sub-type of religious society, nearer to the 'church' pole than the 'sect' pole. In the denomination, the spontaneous and charismatic elements clearly have to give way to the institutional schemes and organization; opposition to the wider society fades in the face of the trend to compromise with the 'world', or even the desire to be an integral part of the world. As Yinger says, 'the "denomination" is conventional and respectable; it has gone rather far along the road to compromise'.[8] Nineteenth-century Methodism corresponds well with that description.

To analyse the evolution of Chilean Pentecostalism, it is important to realize that it did not appear in the most pronounced and virulent sectarian form, but belonged to a type in which an organization, a hierarchy and the control of spontaneous manifestations were present from the start. Were a contemporary observer to start from a sketch of the 'spontaneous sect', it is clear that he would conclude that Chilean Pentecostalism would become subdued and move towards the 'denomination' formula. This is the error committed by Roger Mehl in his commentary on the entry of two Pentecostalist Churches into membership of the World Council of Churches (at New Delhi, 1961); he writes that it must 'be clearly stated that old-established Pentecostalist Churches were concerned, much more sober and much nearer to the Baptist faith than to the original, effervescent Pentecostalism'.[9]

As will be seen later, the trend which a sect follows in its later development depends upon the characteristic type of mission it pursues, or in other words, 'on the response of the sect to the values and relationships prevailing in society'. On this basis Wilson distinguishes four types of sect (art. cit., p. 5):

The *Conversionist* sects which 'seek to alter men, and thereby to alter the world'.

The *Adventist* sects which 'predict drastic alteration of the world, and seek to prepare for the new dispensation'.

The *Introversionists* who 'reject the world's values and replace them with higher inner values, for the realization of which inner resources are cultivated'.

The *Gnostic* sects which 'accept in large measure the world's goals but seek a new and esoteric means to achieve these ends'.

Pentecostalism is a good example of the first type, which has preaching the Gospel and evangelism for its *raison d'être*. The clear and unceasing desire to expand ('*Chile para Cristo*') distinguishes the 'conversionist' sect from the other three types, in which the accent is less on recruitment and more on purity of doctrine, and which are satisfied to remain in a small minority (generally these groups teach one of the many varieties of the doctrine of the 'small number of the elect or the saints'). Now it is clear that evangelism continually exposes a sect to the contagion of society, because on the one hand it is sending its evangelizing agents into the world, and on the other, in its desire to grow, it is integrating large bodies of the converted into itself. Thus as Pentecostalism in Chile grows in numbers, its very nature leads one to think, rightly, that it will be subject to an evolutionary process.

While evangelism is one perpetual source of tension with society, there is another which we think will have even more influence on the future of the Pentecostalist groups, to which we have already alluded in Chapter 6. It concerns the movement's anti-political attitude, at the very period when a vast operation is under way to mobilize the common people.

While Pentecostalist preaching is making one appeal to Chileans who belong to the lower classes, another message is reaching them, inviting them, not to prepare for the coming of 'singing days ahead,'[10] but to share in the construction of that future. With the irruption on to the political scene of Christian Democracy, which is, by competing with the Marxist parties, simultaneously stimulating their activities, there are two development ideologies engaged in proselytizing activities among the people. We have given examples of the problems posed by that situation for church members and Pentecostalist pastors.

The evolution of a sect into a denomination has for a long time been expressed in terms of passage from the first to the second generation. With the 'automatic' admission of the children of converts, the institution takes precedence over inspiration, charismatic phenomena disappear and, since the asceticism of the parents has often enabled the children to rise in the socio-economic scale, the latter aspire to become integrated into society and cause the religious movement to lean towards the path of compromise.[11] This *schema* has been criticized, in particular by Wilson, so far as it concerns the latter three types of sect.[12] But even in the case of a conversionist sect like Pentecostalism, it poses serious problems. In particular, so long as the movement is expanding, at what point does the second generation begin? In Chile, where the number of Pentecostalists doubles every 10 or 11 years, and where, in our sample, 80 per cent of the pastors belong to the first generation, it seems that, more than half a century after its foundation,

Pentecostalism is still in the first-generation period, and may be so for a long time to come. To this is added the question of the turn-over of members. It would in fact seem that, round an inner circle of members who remain loyal to Pentecostalism all their lives, there is a large number of people who are converted, become 'members in full communion' and then after a certain length of time disappear. We can give no figures or any estimates, but the hindrances we encountered when we tried to make a study of mobility in certain Pentecostal corporations lead us to think that the problem does exist. During interviews two leaders went so far as to compare Pentecostal denominations to a church with two doors, one for coming in and the other for leaving (both informants added that 'on this point their mission was an exception'!). This religious mobility can be explained partly by the general mobility of Chileans. When he migrates from one region to another, it is not certain that the church member will find a congregation to his taste in which he can reintegrate himself. But this factor does not provide the full explanation for the phenomenon, and it is clear that Pentecostalism suffers from a large number of lapsed memberships. As a result, the rate of conversions is much higher than the rate of growth due to conversions alone[13] and in consequence the second generation will have still less weight in a movement which has a continuous turnover. Finally, it is far from proven that the children of Pentecostalists will remain Pentecostalist. One may allow that they remain loyal to their church until they come of age, but the anxiety expressed by several pastors of old congregations leads one to believe that the integration of the second generation is not without difficulty nor without losses. To the extent that several months of participant observation give one authority to form provisional conclusions, which must sooner or later be verified by a quantitative investigation, we had the impression that in general the members of the second generation had hardly any weight in the congregations, either quantitatively or qualitatively.[14]

If it is granted that, on the one hand, Chilean Pentecostalism is still living in the first-generation period of expansion, and therefore that Niebuhr's theory, right or wrong, cannot be used in Chile, but that on the other hand, its own expansion, like the political mobilization of the Chilean people, is a source of tension to Pentecostalism and makes it probable that this religious movement will evolve internally, moving from the 'established sect' to the 'denomination' type, then we must establish certain criteria denoting these two types, and see if really there is evolution in relation to these criteria.

1. The first criterion would be to discover whether people belonging to the *Directorio* of different Pentecostalist corporations seem to be *professional officials*, that is, officers who are specially set aside and draw salaries, or whether they perform this duty in addition to their pastoral responsibilities.

2. Secondly, we may ask whether a tendency is discernible to give *special theoretical training to pastors*, which would contribute to distinguishing them from lay members.

3. Thirdly, does there exist in certain Pentecostalist leaders a desire to play a role in Chilean society? It is evident that the *presence of political ambitions* among some leaders makes them more inclined to accommodation to and compromise with society.

4. We will start this examination by analysing a fourth criterion, that of schism, which differs from the others in that it does not enter into the construction of either the 'sect' or the 'denomination' models. According to Niebuhr, schism is often the sign of a reaction against a religious movement's evolution towards more fixed and rigid forms, where the 'poor' (taking this concept in the socio-economic sense) have no place. Schism then expresses 'the revolt of the poor' who go off to found a 'sect' corresponding to their needs.[15] As we have seen, such a schema can be applied fairly well in the case of the birth of Chilean Pentecostalism which resulted from the schism of 1909–10.

Does this mean that the later schisms (starting in 1932) indicated each time that Pentecostalism was tending to become 'denominationalized'? Is this a tendency against which a fraction would react by leaving?

On the whole, large-scale schisms are caused not by the wish to remain loyal to the original model, but rather by personal rivalries. Accusations of deviation, abuse of power and degeneration come *a posteriori* to camouflage and justify the real motive, which is the struggle for power. In addition, the dividing line does not follow the socio-economic cleavage line between members, but relates to the 'clienteles' at the disposition of each leader. And finally, an examination of the organizational system and the practices of a corporation following its secession reveals the absence of any important difference between the schismatics and their original church.[16] In these cases schism should not be interpreted in the way that H. R. Niebuhr does.

On the other hand, in the case of small schisms, purely local and affecting only one congregation, another tendency can be seen, that of the sectarian radicalization of Pentecostalism. In Chile Pentecostalism owes its genesis to a 'denomination', and has formed an 'established sect', but thereafter the congregations have seen a succession of small groups separating from them, and constituting 'spontaneous sects' (Wilson) or 'cults' (Yinger) around a leader who has a special charisma (glossolalia and/or prophecy). These little congregations, which we have often called 'mushroom churches', are inclined less towards evangelism than towards the life of worship and mysticism, and their only organization is their leader. On the death of the latter the group is usually disbanded; some members rejoin a Pentecostal corporation of the 'established sect' type; others disappear, still others rally or create a short-lived church. These little groups, in the grip of a perpetual movement of creation and disappearance, form the fringe of Pentecostalism and offer the greatest hold to syncretism, with either spiritism or animism. They are fairly numerous in the south of the country, but their small numbers and instability make them sociologically a marginal phenomenon.[17]

Since schism, in the case being studied, is not an index of a tendency towards 'denominationalization', let us take up again our first three criteria:

1. *Does there Appear to be a 'Central Bureacracy'?*

All the Pentecostalist corporations have a centralized organization, the *Directorio*, but this is composed of pastors who are in charge of a congregation, and not of ministers who specialize in administrative and governmental responsibilities. The *Directorio* is composed of a chairman (who is the superintendent or bishop), a vice-chairman, a treasurer, secretary, etc., but the holders of these offices are not salaried. Though one-tenth of the tithes of each congregation goes to the central organization, these finances are not used for salaries, and only a small part is devoted to 'administrative expenses', which are kept to the strict minimum. This money, rather, is devoted to building churches or to providing a small pension for the widows of pastors, for example, if they have no other means of support. The General Superintendent's (or Bishop's) travel expenses and those of the regional superintendents are covered by collections made in the congregations which they visit.

We know of only one exception to this rule: the present head of the *Iglesia Evangélica Pentecostal* no longer has charge of a congregation and devotes himself entirely to his office of superintendent. He therefore receives a salary from his corporation.

Does this case mark the beginning of an evolutionary change? It seems to us hardly likely that it will be imitated in the coming years, for the leaders whom we questioned on this point were unanimous in wishing to remain at the head of their congregations. This is understandable, since the congregation is the most stable foundation of their own power, their place of assured refuge if they had to give up the office of superintendent, and also a demonstration of their pastoral status.

2. *Is there a Move towards Special Training for Pastors?*

The fact that several corporations participated in the creation of the *Comunidad Teológica Evangélica de Chile* in 1965, which it is proposed shall provide theological and biblical training for pastors and laymen, shows that there is one trend of opinion within Pentecostalism which aspires, if not to procure for itself a pastorate of good intellectual quality, at least to have available a better knowledge of the Bible. The fact that they accept the idea of learning from books, or from teachers in a classroom, and not directly from the Holy Spirit, is a sure sign of change. Now this desire is not peculiar to the leaders of the member corporations of the C.T.E., but is shared by the large majority of their pastors.

Let us first see what is their opinion on the necessity for theology, understood in the sense of training in knowledge of the Bible.

In the two groups, those who have reservations insist that faith, Spirit and feeling are as important as study, literal knowledge and

Table 1. Necessity for Theology*

Question: Some people say that the Chilean churches need more theology (i.e. to know the teachings of the Bible better). What do you think of this statement?

Are you (1) in complete agreement?
(2) in agreement, but have reservations?
(3) in complete disagreement.

PENTECOSTALISTS	(1)	(2)	(3)	NO REPLY	TOTAL	ACTUAL
Members of the C.T.E.	69	23	8	—	100	35
Non-member corporation	42	39	15	4	100	28
Total of Pentecostalist pastors	57	30	11	2	100	61

* In this table a distinction is made between the Pentecostal denominations which are members of the C.T.E. and the one which is not.

intelligence, if not more so. Those who totally deny the statement think that study kills faith and feeling.

But it is a fact that seven out of ten of the pastors of one denomination which participates in the C.T.E. admit a lack of theology in Pentecostalism:

> 'We are very much behindhand.'
> 'There are many things we don't know.'
> 'We lack an overall knowledge of the Bible', etc.

Though this view is less clear in the corporation which is not a member of the C.T.E. (the *Iglesia Metodista Pentecostal*), it does nevertheless exist, since only a small minority declare their total disagreement, while 42 per cent are in complete agreement.

Let us add that there is a marked tendency among the pastors to prepare their sermons in advance,[18] whereas those who remember the 'thirties say that the rule then was to 'let the Spirit speak' and that to prepare in advance was thought to be 'carnal' (as it is still today in the eyes of some Pentecostalists), and we can conclude that there has been a change of attitude in regard to study and theology.

Moreover a three-part question made it possible to discover the Pentecostalist pastors' interest in the introduction of schemes for Biblical and theological training.

From Table 2 it is clear that the corporations which shared in the launching of the *Comunidad Teológica* did so with the full support of their corps of pastors. And though there are still no pastors who have received a special theological training, and it is probable that it will be a long time yet before they constitute a group of any size, at least the desire for pastoral specialization is indeed present.

Even in the *Iglesia Metodista Pentecostal* nearly half of the pastors think it would be good to establish a school of theology for training ministers.

All these signs lead one to believe that the face of the Chilean Pentecostal pastorate will undergo some changes in the coming decades.

Table 2. Desire for special training for pastors

Questions:

1. 'Do you think your church should organize, for example once a year, an *'institute' lasting one or two weeks*, at which pastors would make a special study of the Bible and the problems of pastoral work and of the church?'
2. 'If the leaders of your church organized the preparation and/or distribution of a *correspondence course* for pastors on the Bible and problems of pastoral work, would you use it?'
3. 'Do you think your church should adopt for the training of its pastors the same system as the historic churches, i.e. by *creating a seminary* at which future pastors would study for several years?'

		YES	NO	TOTAL	ACTUAL
1. 'Institute'	A	81	19	100	26
	B	100	—	100	35
2. Correspondence Course	A	58	42	100	26
	B	91	9	100	35
3. Seminary	A	46	54	100	26
	B	91	9	100	35

A = Corporation which is not a member of the C.T.E. (the *Iglesia Metodista Pentecostal*).
B = Corporations which are members of the C.T.E.

Nevertheless two points must be made about the rhythm of such an evolution:

(*a*) In the first place, there are many obstacles standing in the way of the realization of a school of theology in which the Pentecostalists would share. The *Comunidad Teológica*, dominated by Methodists and Presbyterians, has aroused some strong hesitations among the Pentecostalists; in fact the chief Pentecostal corporation taking part in the foundation of the school withdrew at the end of a year. The creation of a purely Pentecostalist school—which they would of course prefer—would not only pose financial burdens, which the Chileans would not be able to bear on their own, but would also run up against the rivalries between the Pentecostalist groups—and leaders!

(*b*) In the second place, even if it were possible to find some method of realizing the project, it is certain that there would be no jump from the Pentecostalist system to the so-called 'Protestant' system[19] of pastoral training, but that in-service training and training in the seminary will be combined, with the former clearly predominating. In fact, though today some young Pentecostalists do attain their baccalaureate, they are still the exceptions and, because of this, a Bible school would provide a popular type of instruction, available to the laity as well as to those who are already on the rungs of the pastorate.

Though it can be said that the evolution we foresee will be very slow, it is no less true that the desire for development shown by the leaders is evidence of their wish to stabilize their churches, to give greater weight to the 'institution' than to the 'movement', or at least to institutionalize the charismatic gifts!

3. *Is there an Awakening of Political Ambitions?*

The desire which some Pentecostal leaders have expressed to have pastors who are better prepared from the intellectual point of view not only reflects their awareness of the theological and biblical gaps, but also in certain cases betrays a reaction against those who say that Pentecostalism is a religion 'for the lower classes'. If the movement had an *élite* who could hold their own with the Methodist or even the Catholic theologians, then it would gain in respectability. This seeking for social standing—a trend latent in every movement from the moment it receives its earliest ratification, that of numerical strength—is also being expressed on a political level in a certain number of cases,[20] and precise goals have already been suggested by some of the superintendents, e.g. an alliance between corporations to elect a deputy or senator; a pact with one political party; the creation of a party, etc.

None of these suggestions has produced an effective result. The chief reason for this is that this awakening of political ambitions is far from being manifested in all the corporations; some leaders of large bodies would oppose this trend with their last breath, and even in those corporations whose chiefs admit having political desires, a large proportion of the pastors are fiercely opposed to politics. We were present at a debate on this subject between one superintendent and his pastors. He was explaining that it was necessary to distinguish between 'politics' (*politica*) which is, 'as a great scholar of olden times said, "the art of governing the people",' and *politiqueria* which signifies more or less underhand dealings. He enumerated the advantages which their churches might gain if they belonged to a party, etc. One group of pastors approved, but another, without even trying to discuss the matter or argue, rejected the idea saying, 'These things are of the devil'. In this case it was clear that to go against their wishes would have been enough to cause a division in that corporation.

We can repeat here what we said at the end of the preceding section: the signs preceding evolution are present here and there, but everything leads one to suppose that it will be slow and irregular.

Examination of the three criteria shows that a clear and simple answer to the question concerning the evolution of Pentecostalism is not possible. Though some corporations seem to be at the beginning of the road leading to a 'denominational' form, others which are just as important and sometimes greater seem to remain identical with the primitive Pentecostalist model, i.e. that of the *Iglesia Metodista Pentecostal* during the twenties. Strategists in inter-church relationships would be wrong, in our opinion, to speculate with any idea of Pentecostalism's 'accelerated and progressive denominationalization'. The present state of affairs leads one to think that, though such an evolution is possible, it will be slow and will extend over more than one generation. But does a study of half a century of Chilean Pentecostalism make it possible for the sociologist or historian to see what are the long-term prospects?

Our examination leads to the following conclusion: If no notable changes occur in the structure of Chilean society[21] Pentecostalism will tend to evolve slowly and irregularly towards the 'denominational' type.

Now, in the case under discussion, it is evident that the reservation we have included makes the conclusion fairly hazardous: what will Chilean society be like at the end of President Frei's term, that is in 1970—only a few years hence? Whether the Christian Democratic experiment will then end in success or failure we cannot judge in advance, but whatever its final outcome may be, it will have set off such a series of reforms of structures, created such a mobilization of the people and raised such hopes, that Chile in 1970 will not be the same as Chile in 1965. It is inevitable that changes in the global society will have repercussions upon Pentecostalism and will affect its evolution, but since we are in no position to evaluate these changes we should be entering the realms of pure speculation if we tried to foretell their effect on this religious movement.

B. CHILEAN PENTECOSTALISM AS A MISSIOLOGICAL EXAMPLE

Is it possible to use a study of Pentecostalism as the basis for wider generalizations on the conditions for the success of a religious mission? And is it even possible, if one can reduce the religious message on the sociological level (and only on the sociological level!) to an ideological category, that the case of Chilean Pentecostalism can tell us anything about the conditions for establishing in a country an ideology which is foreign both to the society and the culture of that country?

Two propositions can be made, one being inadequate without the other and vice versa:

The adoption of a new and foreign religious credo by an important section of the population of a country depends—

firstly: *on the* presence *of problems, needs and tensions of different kinds among the population, to which the religious credo supplies answers and solutions*;

secondly: *on the* translation *of the religious credo and its accompanying socio-cultural system into the social and cultural language of that country.*[22]

Needless to say, we are assuming that there is no legal barrier to the entry of new creeds, as there was in the time of the Spanish Empire.

The first condition relates to what we have called the external factors in Pentecostalist expansion. Though analogies borrowed from economic science are generally ill regarded when it is a question of the things of God, nevertheless it is true that an ideology will find no response and create no converts except where a potential market exists; in other words, only where it can satisfy a need. In Chile we have shown the existence of a need and the satisfaction which the message of Pentecost brought:

need of the Lord, need of pastors, need to lead a life in society, need for Salvation, need for healing, etc. When a feeling of frustration is experienced on a large scale by a large part of the population, it is probable (if not certain) that it is the result of a breakdown in the equilibrium of society, its destructuration and its evolution towards a new state of total equilibrium.[23]

The second proposition seems to us to be just as obvious as the first. It cannot be fulfilled, we should note, unless national adherents adopt the credo completely; they will then be able spontaneously to carry out the acculturation to the country of the whole socio-cultural system, without which the credo cannot continue to exist. Here lies the key to the difference in the effectiveness of traditional Protestant forms of religion and Pentecostalism in South America: both are, broadly speaking, tied to the same credo; both have before them the same potential market. The first, however, affect only very small groups and are stagnating; the second seems like a tidal wave. But whereas the former remain still foreign, the latter is integrated into the country to the point where it seems one of its possible religious forms of expression.

We have here stated *sociological* conditions.[24] Factors of a different order may arise to prevent the missionary societies from taking them into account. A widely accepted argument is to term Pentecostalism syncretism, and so to accuse it of perverting the Gospel. On the same lines, it is thought better to keep the younger churches of the developing countries in a state of tutelage, for without the paternal oversight of the founding churches they might be tainted with the surrounding paganism. People argue, therefore, on the theological level, decreeing, 'This is true Christianity, that is false', laying down a norm. If the sociologist is asked what he thinks of such a statement, he will reply by turning the question: by showing how far what is called true Christianity is imprinted with a given social system—that in which the founding Church lives![25]

To create trust in the national or regional churches, their members and leaders, trust in their fitness to help themselves and to solve their own problems—that, I think, is what the Pentecostal example urges upon us. It is a lesson in modesty—doubly so, in that the religious movement which is gaining the most members is the one which has the smallest financial and intellectual resources, and in that some of the most serious problems and 'temptations' experienced by the Pentecostalist movement in Chile today are the result of the implantation in Chile of international inter-church bodies!

To create trust in the national churches—is that not, at the end of the day, to create trust in God? An Anglican missionary priest who is campaigning for the autonomy of the Indian congregations, made this comment to me:

> Sometimes I wonder whether we missionaries are not trying to make ourselves substitutes for God. We think we are indispensable, and believe that if we left the Indians would relapse into animism. Perhaps they would. . . . But if God creates congregations, will He not give them leaders and everything they need?

APPENDIX I

Theses

Method

I. The dialectic which unites the global society and an emergent religious movement may be approached analytically from three standpoints:
First, changes in the social structure and its system of values will have created a state of affairs favourable to the introduction and spread of the new faith.

II. Secondly, the forms of expression of this faith, and its concomitant organizations and institutions, will to a certain extent take their inspiration from the socio-cultural schemes provided by the global society.

III. Thirdly, the religious movement, having become a constituent part of the global society, will in turn exercise an influence on the future of the latter.

Conclusions

1. Traditional Protestantism was and still is a socio-cultural element foreign to Chile, where it has neither past nor future.
2. The schism which divided the Methodist Episcopal Church and gave birth to a Chilean Pentecostalism was the result of the opposition between a middle-class ecclesiastical hierarchy, dominated by foreign influence, and the body of believers who were nationals of the lower classes; the former inherited a rationalist religious mentality, and the latter a mythical religious mentality.
3. The diachronic and geographic study of Pentecostalist expansion may serve as a pointer to a questioning of the basic institutions of the traditional society, and to a movement towards its destructuration as well as to the consequent upheaval for the lower classes.
4. Pentecostalism offers to the masses faith in a God of love, the certainty of salvation, security in a community, and a sharing in responsibility for a common task to be fulfilled. It thus offers them a humanity which society denies them.
5. Chronologically, the expansion of Pentecostalism and of socialism are parallel, but ideologically they are antagonistic. The Chilean people's social protest receives from Marxism a political, atheistic content, and from Pentecostalism it receives an a-political and religious content. The latter proclaims an imminent Kingdom of God, the former works for an immanent kingdom of men.

6. Pentecostalist society maintains dialectical relationships with Chilean society of both continuity and discontinuity. It builds itself up by a continuous process of borrowing and rejecting from the surrounding socio-cultural patterns; either it adopts the symbol and alters the referend, or it preserves the referend and transforms the symbol.
7. In the last analysis, Pentecostalist society is an avatar of traditional society, the dominant pattern of which it ideally fulfils, rather than a prefiguration of and preparation for the society of the future.
8. Pentecostalism teaches its members a positive, active morality in the life of the congregation; a morality of duty and prohibitions in private life, and of prohibitions and passivity in public life. Its social ethic is dominated by a radical condemnation of 'the world'.
9. In the perspective of a sociology of development, Pentecostalism—like any kind of a-politicism—is an ideology of order and not movement, of conservatism and not change.
10. Some of the Pentecostal *charismata* (dancing and glossolalia) should be understood, apart from any theological interpretation, as the language of men without language, an attempt to express and communicate an ineffable religious experience, an experience in community.
11. The adoption by a large section of a nation of a foreign ideology, whether religious or not, depends, first, on the answer which it provides to the people's problems; secondly, on the 'translation' of that ideology and the cultural system accompanying it into the social and cultural 'language' of the people.

APPENDIX 2

Questionnaire (in Spanish)

1. Ha pertenecido Ud. siempre a la Denominación a la cual sirve hoy como pastor?
   0. S.R.
   1. Si.
   2. No.
2. (Si responde 'no' en P. 1. (Cuales otras denominaciones ha pertenecido Ud.?
3. Está trabajando Ud. en lo material además del pastorado? Si 'no'; Ha trabajado Ud. en el pasado siendo pastor?
   0. S.R.
   1. Está trabajando.
   2. Ha trabajado.
   3. Nuncaha trabajado.
4. (Si responde 'si' a P. 3.) Cuál es/fue esta profesión? (Con precisión. Indicar si asalariado o independiente. Si ha ejercido varias profesiones, indicar la última.)
5. Qué le parece lo mejor para la Iglesia y el trabajo pastoral?
   1. Que le pastor trabaje también en lo material.
   2. Que él se dedique sólo a la labor pastoral.
   0. S.R.
6. A continuación consignamos una lista *de actividades* que pueden estar o no comprendidas en la labor pastoral. A su juicio, Cuáles actividades de la lista:
   1. están comprendidas en la labor pastoral?
   2. pueden entrar ocasionalmente en la labor pastoral?
   3. están excluídas de la labor pastoral?

Lista

1. Visitar a los miembros enfermos.
2. Obra social: crear escuelas, policlínicos, guardería infantil, hogares para niños, etc.
3. Predicación en el templo.
4. Hablar en el sermón acerca de las elecciones.
5. Intervenir en defensa de algún miembro de la Iglesia frente a su empleador.
6. Visitar hospitales y cárceles.
7. Clases de maestros (estudios bíblicos para los maestros de la escuela dominical).

8. Colaborar con otros (no evangélicos) en los problemas de interés común (sociales, económicos, etc.) de la región. Por ej. lucha contra el analfabetismo, creación de cooperativas, etc.
9. Predicación en la calle.
10. Representar a las Igl. Evangél. en los actos oficiales de municipalidades y gobierno.
11. Preocuparse por conseguir trabajo a los hermanos que lo necisitan.
12. Tomar posición e intervenir frente a las autoridades en defensa de los gremios de los trabajadores.
13. Dirigir ceremonias especiales (bautismo, Santa Cena, recepción de miembros, etc.).
14. Hablar en el sermón de asuntos sociales, por ej.: sueldos y salarios, problemas y condiciones de trabajo.

7. Lee Ud. la Bíblia?
   1. Cada día.
   2. dos veces por semana.
   3. menos de eso.
   0. S.R.

8. Prepara Ud. con anticipación su predicación, leyendo y estudiando la Bíblia, o con la ayuda de manuales?
   0. S.R.
   1. Si.
   2. No.

   Si su respuesta es 'no', Porqué?

9. Diría Ud. que la Bíblia
   1. Es inspirada palabra por palabra por Dios y el Espiritu Santo?
   2. Es inspirada en su fondo y en sus ideas por Dios y el E.S. pero los hombres la redactaron usando el lenguaje y las figuras literarias de sus épocas?
      — Si respondiera afirmativamente a 9/1: lo que fue inspirada palabra por palabra por Dios y el E.S.
      1. Es la Bíblia que Ud. tiene en la lengua castellana?
      2. Es sólo el texto original, en la lengua en que fue escrita?
      — Si respondiera afirmativamente a 9/2: Pudieron los hombres redactar la Bíblia original introduciendo errores (conceptos científicos de su tiempo, o creencias religiosas que hoy se consideran falsas?
      3. No.
      4. Si.

10. A continuacion consignamos una *lista de denominaciones e iglesias*. En su opinión, Cuáles de las iglesias de la lista son *partes* del 'Cuerpo de Cristo', o sea, que participan en la Iglesia, 'esposa de Cristo'?
    1. Anglicana.

2. Alianza Cristiana Misionera.
3. Testigos de Jehova.
4. Presbiteriana.
5. Los Mormones.
6. Pentecostal de origen Norteamericano (Igl. de Dios, Asambleas de Dios).
7. Católica Romana.
8. Pentecostales Chilenas (Igl. Metodista Pent.; Igl. Evang. Pentec. etc.).
9. Luterana.
10. Adventista.
11. Metodista.

11. En su opinión, Los miembros de cuales de estas iglesias pueden ser *salvados*?

12. Qué significado tiene para Ud. la palabra *Teología*?
1. El juego de universitarios sin el contacto con la realidad de la iglesia.
2. No dejarse guiar por el Espíritu Santo en las reflecciones sobre la Bíblia.
3. La reflección del hombre sobre su fe.
4. El estudio serio y profundo de la Bíblia.
5. Otra respuesta.

13. Algunos opinan que las iglesias de Chile tienen necesidad de *más teología*. Qué piensa Ud. de esta afirmación?
1. Completamente de acuerdo.
2. De acuerdo con algunas reservas.
3. En desacuerdo total.
0. S.R.

Porqué?

14. Cree Ud. que el Evangélico puede ser miembro (también cuando no es obligatorio).
1. de clubes deportivos.
2. de grupos artísticos.
3. de juntas de vecinos.
4. de sindicatos.
5. de partidos políticos.

Porqué?

15. (Sólo si el entrevistado piensa que el Evangélico puede ser miembro de un *partido político*.)
Ud. cree que el Evangélico puede ser miembro de un partido político. Pero de cuál de los partidos que se encuentran en Chile?
1. Comunista.
2. Socialista.
3. Padena.
4. D.C.
5. Radical.

6. Liberal.
7. Conservador.
Cuál es el criterio a su juicio?

16. Cree Ud. que el *pastor evangélico* puede ser *miembro* (también cuando no es obligatorio).
    1. de clubes deportivos?
    2. de grupos artísticos?
    3. de juntas de vecinos?
    4. de sindicatos?
    5. de partidos políticos?
    Porqué?

17. En resumen, diría Ud. que el evangélico
    1. debe
    2. puede
    3. puede, pero mejor no
    4. no debe
    participar en política?
    0. S.R.
    Porqué?

18. Dicen que Chile es un *país sub-desarrollado.* Qué significa esto para Ud.?

19. Ha oído Ud. hablar de la intervención de los EE.UU. en Santo Domingo).
    1. Si.
    2. No.

20. Si el entrevistado a oído hablar de ello: Aprueba Ud. la intervención de les EE.UU. en Santo Domingo?
    1. Si.
    2. No.
    3. No sé.
    0. S.R.
    Porqué?

21. En su opinión, piensa Ud. que la Iglesia Evangélica debe preocuparse de los problemas políticos y sociales del país y hablar sobre ellos?
    1. Si.
    2. No.
    3. No sé.
    0. S.R.
    Porqué?

22. Si la votación fuera optativa, Ud. votaría?
    1. Si.
    2. No.

0. S.R.
Porqué?

23. Cuántos miembros en Plena Comunión y miembros probandos han, en su Iglesia (congregación)? (Sin los niños.)

24. Tiene Ud. una junta de oficiales o ancianos?

0. S.R.
1. Si.
2. No.

En caso que no, Cuál es el motivo?
(Preguntas 25–27 sólo si hay una junta.)

25. La junta tiene reuniones:

1. Cada semana.
2. cada dos semanas.
3. cada mes.
4. menos.
0. S.R.

26. Cómo se elige la junta?
1. Todos los miembros en Plena Comunión.
2. Un grupo selecto de miembros.
3. El pastor, de acuerdo con su Junta.
0. S.R.

27. Quién dirige la Iglesia (congregación)?

1. La Junta.
2. El Pastor.
3. La junta y el pastor.
0. S.R.

28. Su iglesia tiene un tesorero oficial que no sea el pastor?
0. S.R.
1. Si.
2. No.

29. El dinero del diezmo es . . .
1. el dinero de la Iglesia?
2. el dinero del pastor?
0. S.R.

(Preguntas 30–32 sólo a los pastores pentecostales.)

30. Cree Ud. que su Denominación debería optar, para formar a sus pastores, el sistema de las iglesias históricas, o sea, crear un seminario en que les futuros pastores deban cursar ciertos años de estudios?

0. S.R.
1. Si.
2. No.

Porqué?

31. Cree Ud. que su Denominación debería organizar, por ej., anualmente un seminario o estudio de una, o dos semanas, en el cual los pastores estudiaran especialmente la Bíblia y los problemas del trabajo pastoral y de la iglesia?

    0. S.R.
    1. Si.
    2. No.

    Porqué?

32. Si los dirigen es de su denominación (Conf. anual, Directorio, etc.) organizaran la edición y/o difusión de un curso por correspondencia para pastores, sobre la Bíblia y les problemas del trabajo pastoral, utilizaría Ud. este curso?

    0. S.R.
    1. Si, con seguridad.
    2. Si, quizás.
    3. No.

    Porqué?

    (Preguntas 33–34 sólo para los pastores protestantes.)

33. Generalmente los pastores de su iglesia se han formado en seminarios, donde han estudiado por varios anos. Le parece a Ud. que este sistema responde a las necesidades de su iglesia?

    0. S.R.
    1. Si, totalmente.
    2. Si, en parte.
    3. No.

    Porqué?

34. Ud. sabe que los pastores pentecostales reciben una formación enteramente práctica y que lentamente van ascendiendo los escalones de la jerarquía pastoral. Le parece a Ud. que este sistema (de formación en la calle) puede presentar ventajas y que su propia Iglesia podría inspirarse en él, sobre algunos puntos?

    1. Si.
    2. No.
    0. S.R.

    Explicaciones:

35. Fecha de nacimiento:

    0. S.R.
    1. menos de 29 años.
    2. 30–39.
    3. 40–49.
    4. 50 años y más.

36. Profesión del padre del entrevistado. (Indicar la ultima antes de la muerte o de la jubilición, con precisiones. Asalariado o indépendiente?)

37. Nivel de estudios del padre del entrevistado:
    0. S.R.
    1. Escuela primaria incompleta.
    2. Escuela primaria completa.
    3. Tres años rendidos de humanidades, o estudios comerciales, técnicos, etc.
    4. Bachillerato o humanidades completas.
    5. Título universitario.

38. Religión del *padre* en el tiempo de la juventud del entrevistado:
    0. S.R.
    1. Católico fiel.*
    2. Católico no practicante.
    3. Evangélico.
    4. Otro.

39. Si es respuesta 3 de la P. 38, Cuál es el nombre de la denominación evangélica?

40. Religión de la *madre* en el tiempo de la juventud del entrevistado
    0. S.R.
    1. Católica fiel.*
    2. Católica no practicante.
    3. Evangélica.
    4. Otro.

41. Si es respuesta 3. de P. 40.

    Nombre de la denominación evangélica.

42. (Hacer la pregunta solo si los dos padros del entrevistado no eran evangélicos. Ref, p. 39 y 41).
    A qué edad se convirtió Ud. al Evangélio?
    0. S.R.
    1. menos de 19 años.
    2. 20–29 años.
    3. 30–39 años.
    4. 40 y más.

43. A qué denominación evangélica asistió Ud. después de su conversión?

44. Estado civil:
    0. S.R.
    1. Soltero.
    2. casado.
    3. viudo.
    4. otro.

* Asistencia de por lo menos una vez al mes a misa y práctica de la confesión.

45. Número de niños:

 0. S.R.
 1. 0.
 2. 1–4.
 3. 5–9.
 4. 10 y más.

46. Nivel de educación del entrevistado:

 0. S.R.
 1. Escuela primaria incompleta.
 2. Escuela primaria completa.
 3. Tres años rendidos de humunidades o estudios comerciales, técnicos, etc.
 4. Bachillerato o humanidades completas.
 5. Título universitario.

 (Preguntas 47–49 para los pastores pentecostales.)

47. Ha danzado Ud. en el Espíritu?

 0. S.R.
 1. Si.
 2. No.

48. Ha hablado Ud. en lenguas?

 0. S.R.
 1. Si.
 2. No.

49. Ha obrado en Ud. la sanidad divina?

 0. S.R.
 1. Si.
 2. No.

 Explicaciones:

50. (Preguntas 50–52 solamente para los pastores protestantes.) Cree Ud. que la danza en el culto, como se encuentra en las iglesias pentecostales, puede ser un don del Espíritu Santo?

 0. S.R.
 1. Si.
 2. No.

 Explicaciones:

51. Cree Ud. que hablar en lenguas puede ser un don del E.S.?

 0. S.R.
 1. Si.
 2. No.

 Explicaciones:

52. Cree Ud. que puede haber sanidad divina por la fe (imposición de manos)?

0. S.R.
1. Si.
2. No.

Explicaciones:

53. Provincia del entrevistado.

54. Denominación del entrevistado:

55. *Sexo:*

1. Hombre.
2. Mujer.

NOTES

INTRODUCTION

1. See list on pp. 256-57.
2. To use a term at present very much in fashion in Chile.
3. In this and the following section, I hope I may be permitted to use the first person singular.
4. When I look back on this situation, I am grateful to the C.E.C. and particularly its President, Pastor E. Chavez C, for having received me *so cordially*, for really it must have seemed unforgivable that a research worker sent by the W.C.C. should drop on them out of the clouds one day, when they had received no information concerning him for the previous six months!
5. The following information is based on *Boletin Num.* 10,488 of the Chamber of Deputies of the Republic of Chile, a document of 318 pages entitled: 'Report of the Special Commission set up by the Chamber to enquire into the plans of the "Camelot Plan" and its diffusion in Chile and any other activity of alien organizations which might threaten our sovereignty or interfere in national life.' (1965)
6. *Op. cit.*, p. 10. The *Boletin* is here quoting a passage from the Camelot Plan itself.
7. *Ibid.*, p. 23.
8. A similar affair known as the *Plan Simpático* was unmasked in Colombia.
9. In disguising the source of its finances and the name of the sponsoring organization, the Camelot Plan infringed two of the fundamental deontological rules of scientific research.
10. For a description of this method, see M. Duverger: *Méthodes des Sciences Sociales*, pp. 297–317.
11. The 'observer-participant' participates only because observation demands it. The 'participant-observer' is one who is himself a member of the body being studied and puts his participation above his observation.
12. *God's People*, pp. 146–49.
13. It goes without saying that on the sociological level I neither confirm nor deny the interpretation of these manifestations given by the Pentecostalists. I simply record it.
14. The questionnaire is given in Appendix 2, pp. 226 ff.
15. We have from the outset omitted the pastors of the 'mushroom-churches' which are continually springing up or disappearing, and which are quite impossible to count. We have taken account only of the pastors belonging to denominations which have an estimated membership of more than 7,000.
16. As will be explained later, the membership figures given by the denominations are suspect, and so we refrain from making any estimate here.
17. For the enquiry among the students, the solution was simple, since they were all together in one place, which I was to visit.
18. 'Southern promontory' or 'cone'—Translator's note.
19. All the more so since the questionnaire was drawn up with the Pentecostalist pastors in mind, and simply adapted to the two other samples in places where this was necessary. Some of the questions therefore seemed very simple to the students.
20. For further information, see my *El Estudiante de Teología frente a la Iglesia y a la Sociedad*, where this investigation is set out in detail.
21. Cf. chapter 6, pp. 144f.
22. It is clear that the Pentecostalist pastor interprets his religious movement in a way which differs from that of the Catholic or Reformed theologian.

CHAPTER 1. FROM A FOREIGN INTRODUCTION TO A NATIONAL PROTESTANT MOVEMENT

1. O'Higgins (1778–1842), hero of Chilean independence, and Supreme Director of the Republic (1817–23). J. de San Martin (1778–1850), liberator of Chile and Peru. B. Juarez (1806–76), who fought the French expedition to Mexico, and after the defeat of Maximilian of Austria became president.
   This theory of the 'protection' given by liberal leaders is developed, though in an exaggerated and over-rigid form, in *El Protestantismo en América Latina*, by Father Damboriena, vol. 1, pp. 17–44.
2. See *Historia de la Iglesia en América latina*, by L. Torno *et al.*, vol. 3, *La Iglesia en la Crisis de la Independencia.*
3. J. H. McLean, *Historia de la Iglesia Presbiteriana en Chile*, p. 42.
4. I. Vergara, *El Protestantismo en Chile*, p. 39.
5. R. Donoso, *Las Ideas Políticas en Chile*, p. 173 seq.
6. Father Prudencio Damboriena, *El Protestantismo en Chile*, p. 149.
7. José Míguez, *Latin America*, p. 171.
8. *Ibid.*, p. 172.
9. W. C. Hoover, *Historia del Avivamiento pentecostal en Chile.*
10. On the history of Pentecostalism, see *inter alia*: Nils Bloch-Hoell, *The Pentecostal Movement*; Walter J. Hollenweger, *Handbuch der Pfingstbewegung*, vol. 1; and M. Harper, *As at the Beginning, The Twentieth Century Pentecostal Revival.*
11. W. C. Hoover, *op. cit.*, p. 9.
12. W. C. Hoover, *op. cit.*, p. 14.
13. W. C. Hoover, *op. cit.*, p. 33.
14. These quite spontaneous demonstrations were the origin of 'open-air preaching', a characteristic institution of Chilean Pentecostalism.
15. W. C. Hoover, *op. cit.*, p. 39.
16. Cf. John Wesley's *Journal*, vol. 3, pp. 43–44.
17. 'Alleluia for the blood of the Lamb who sacrificed himself on the cross for me'; 'Alleluia for the Lamb of God who gave his blood on the cross to save us from our sins.'
18. W. C. Hoover, *op. cit.*, p. 60.
19. W. C. Hoover, *op. cit.*, p. 35. It must be underlined that this person did not come in contact with the 'revival' until the month of August 1909, for many have tried to make her out to be Hoover's evil genius and to make her the scapegoat (e.g., A. Oyarzun: *Reminiscencias Historicas de la Obra Evangélica en Chile*, p.50, quoted by I. Vergara, *El Protestantismo en Chile*, p. 112). But Elena Laidlaw came on the scene—where she undoubtedly played an important part as prophetess—at a time when the movement, which had been taking shape since 1902, had reached a point from which there was no turning back.
20. W. C. Hoover, *op. cit.*, p. 36–37. These accounts are accepted as trustworthy by all contemporary authors.
21. E. Willems: *Protestantismus und Klassenstruktur in Chile*, p. 665.
22. Quoted by Hoover, *op. cit.*, pp. 58–59.
23. *Idem*, p. 62—our italics.
24. Quoted by Hoover, *op. cit.*, pp. 71–72.
25. On the origins of Methodism, see H. Richard Niebuhr, *The Social Sources of Denominationalism*, and Sydney G. Dimond, *The Psychology of the Methodist Revival.*
26. Hoover, *op. cit.*, p. 43.
27. *Chile Pentecostal*, September 12, 1959, Santiago.
28. In particular, *Sembrado*, Oct./Nov. 1959, which is the organ of the *Iglesia Misión Pentecostal.* We have seen a pamphlet (which I. Vergara also quotes in *El Protestantismo en Chile*, p. 120) with no indication of origin nor signature which exalts Hoover and violently attacks the Bishop of the *Iglesia Metodista Pentecostal*, though without actually naming him.
29. *Op. cit.*, pp. 51–52.
30. By 'internal reason', we mean it is a reason proper to the religious movement.

Other factors which were external (i.e. arising from the wider society) also played a part (see later).

31. Cf. Max Weber, *Wirtschaft und Gesellschaft*, vol. 1, p. 159.
32. Hoover, *op. cit.*, p. 43.

CHAPTER 2. SOCIAL CHANGE IN CHILE AND THE PENTECOSTAL EXPLOSION

1. An earlier version of this chapter was presented as a paper at the Sixth World Congress on Sociology (Evian, September 4–11, 1966) in the section of the Research Committee on Religious Sociology.
2. *World Christian Handbook*, 1962.
3. R. C. Moore, *Los Evangélicos en marcha en América Latina*, p. 75.
4. It must be pointed out that the 1960 census information on religious affiliation has not been published and we worked from a manuscript belonging to the *Dirección de Estadísticas y Censos*, kindly put at our disposal by Father R. Poblete B. of the Instituto Bellarmino, Santiago.
5. We must point out that we have carried out a limited enumeration of the Protestants in one commune of the Province of Concepcion and that our results agree with those of the census. This discussion was necessary because the figures given by Damboriena are being constantly repeated (as well as those of Vergara in *El Protestantismo en Chile*, among others), while these authors have not examined their sources critically.
6. Father H. Muñoz R., in *Sociología religiosa*, using the parish typology established by Boulard, estimates that for Chile the requirements of that author should be considerably lowered. According to him, a parish in which 20 per cent of the Catholics receive communion once a year should be considered good, and so should a parish in which 10 per cent attend mass on Sunday (*op. cit.*, pp. 13–14).
7. Cf. I. Vergara, *op. cit.*
8. *The Challenge of the Sects*.
9. H. Muñoz R., *Situación del Protestantismo en Chile*, p. 166.
10. The information given according to provinces for 1930 should be regarded with caution, apart from that which concerns the four northern provinces and the two in the southern zone. The curves are drawn on the basis of the percentage of Protestants in the population of the province. We chose this rate for preference, since it makes immediate comparison between provinces possible, by reducing the figures to the same scale. In addition, the increase in this rate from one date to another allows one to speak of 'progress' in absolute terms. If one were using a crude growth rate, it would be necessary first to compare it with that of the population.
11. Correlation tests by rank. Spearman and Kendall confirm H_0 for thresholds equal to or less than 0·10.
12. H. Muñoz R., *Situación del Protestantismo en Chile*, p. 168.
13. *Art. cit.*, p. 167.
14. On this subject, see the Jesuit journal *Mensaje*, especially nos. 115 and 123.
15. By analogy with Europe, the traditional Latin American society has often been called 'feudal'. This term is being disputed more and more, for the *hacienda* (large landed property) does not correspond to a medieval fief. Like J. Medina (*Consideraciones sociologicas sobre el Desarrollo economico*) and others, we prefer to speak of seignorial society, a more general type which includes both the fief and the *hacienda*.
16. This is underlined by the fact that the three countries which are the most advanced from the socio-cultural point of view (Chile, Argentina and Uruguay) are suffering from economic stagnation.
17. Pedro S. Lama, *Boletín de la Sociedad de Fomento Fabrik*, 1887, Santiago, quoted by O. Dominguez C., *Sociología Rural*, p. 31.
18. A. Pinto Santa Cruz, *Chile, un Caso de Desarrollo Frustrado*.
19. O. Dominguez, *op. cit.*, pp. 40–43.
20. Instituto de Economía, *La Migración Interna en el período 1940–1952*.
21. O. Dominguez, *op. cit.*, p. 61.

22. R. Dumont, *Terres Vivantes*, p. 75. Cf. A. Pinto Santa Cruz, *op. cit.*, pp. 84–86.
23. Dominguez, *op. cit.*, p. 61.
24. E. Durkheim, *Le Suicide*, pp. 263–311.
25. R. K. Merton, chapter entitled 'Social Structure and Anomie', in *Social Theory and Social Structure*.
26. J. Medina, *op. cit.*, p. 34, cf. pp. 30–40.
27. Bryan Wilson, *Sects and Society*.
28. In this section we have chiefly relied on J. Cesar Jobet, *Ensayo crítico del Desarrollo económico-social de Chile*, and A. Pinto Santa Cruz, *op. cit.*
29. The struggle in the previous century between the liberals (mining industries) and conservatives (landed proprietors) was quickly replaced by the formation of one single social class, the oligarchy (J. C. Jobet, *op. cit.*, p. 156).
30. W. Browning, *The West Coast Republics of South America*, p. 30.
31. Cf. Karl Marx, *Zur Kritik der hegelschen Rechtsphilosophie* (1844), *Die Frühschriften*, p. 208.
32. H. Desroche, *Les Shakers américains*, pp. 289–90. In this paragraph we allude particularly to this author's work. His latest work, *Socialismes et Sociologie religieuse*, must also be mentioned.
33. In note 6 to this chapter we gave Father Muñoz's estimate of what is a 'good Catholic parish'. This gives one some idea of the degree of disaffection in the Catholic Church. Nevertheless Pentecostal success cannot be explained satisfactorily simply by the dissatisfaction engendered by the Catholic Church. In particular, it does not tell us why Pentecostalism succeeds where traditional Protestantism fails. Cf. the pertinent remarks of E. Willems on this subject in *Protestantismus und Klassenstruktur in Chile*, p. 661.
34. Emilio Willems, *Protestantism and Culture Change in Brazil and Chile*, p. 102.
35. To test the hypothesis, it would be necessary to construct a map of Chilean land tenure. This will not be possible until the publication of the 1965 Agricultural Census.
36. Here again, this is not a matter of an assertion, but a line of research which ought to be followed up.
37. E. Willems, *Protestantism and culture change in Brazil and Chile*, p. 108. Discussion of Willems's theory will be taken up again in Chapter 6.
38. I. Vergara, *Avance do los 'Evangélicos' en Chile*, p. 262. It will be observed that this sort of argument no longer appears in the same author's book published in 1962.
39. It will be found in P. Damboriena, *El Protestantismo en Chile*, and I. Rosier, *Ovejas sin Pastor*.
40. To confirm this it is necessary only to look at the maps presented by Ricardo Cruz Coke in his *Geografia electoral de Chile*.
41. It must be recalled that the demonstration of an association or correlation does not amount to a demonstration of a functional or causal relation. On the contrary, to exclude an association means at the same time exclusion of any functional or causal relation. In the present case, both Spearman and Kendall (correlation tests by rank) have established H_0 for thresholds at or below 0·05.

CHAPTER 3. THE LIFE OF THE CONGREGATION

1. A candidate for the ministry.
2. Sermon given in the station square, Curicó, June 13, 1965.
3. Oscar Lewis, *The Children of Sanchez*.
4. On this problem, see A. Mattelart and M. A. Garreton, *Integración nacional y Marginalidad*.
5. Charismatic manifestations are analysed in more detail in Part IV.
6. Werner S. Landecker, *Types of Integration and their Measurement*.
7. *Ibid.*, p. 333.
8. Following chapter.
9. Here we are using for the first time results from the investigation among the pastors; the method is described and the results and applicability discussed in the introduction, p. xxiv *et seq.*

10. Clyde Kluckhohn and William H. Kelly, "The Concept of Culture", p. 98.
11. J. H. Fichter, *Sociologie*, p. 245.
12. *Ibid.*, p. 223.
13. That the Jews in dispersion were not completely impervious to the influence of their environment, and unconsciously took over elements of Hellenistic culture, does not alter the fact that initiates were required to submit to a cultural conversion.
14. Theologically speaking, the decision of the Council of Jerusalem should have had normative value for matters connected with the relation between the Gospel and socio-cultural systems. The effect on missionary strategy can be seen. It is plain, however, that we are not prejudging the question of the equation of expressions and referends—a question the solution of which presupposes collaboration between sociology and theology. From the sociological point of view, the reaction aroused by a new message depends directly upon the manner in which it is communicated, and thus upon the way in which it uses the means provided by the culture of those to whom the message is addressed.
15. Ivan Vallier (director), *Anglican opportunities in South America*, ch. 5, p. 24.
16. Ivan Vallier (director), *op. cit.*, ch. 5, p. 25.

CHAPTER 4. ORGANIZATION, AUTHORITY AND THE HIERARCHY

1. Mimeographed document by Pastor Raymundo Valenzuela, *La Conferencia Central*, p. 1.
2. When divisions inspired by Pentecostalism occur in these denominations, schismatic members will break with their own system and follow the example of Pentecostalist organizations already in existence.
3. Cf. H. Gerth and C. Wright Mills, *Character and Social Structure*, chap. 14.
4. L. Pope, *Millhands and Preachers*, p. 137.
5. The Jotabeche Church (Santiago), the centre of the *Iglesia Metodista Pentecostal* is a present-day example of a three-tier congregation.
6. Biographical interview with a Pentecostalist pastor.
7. Biographical interview with a Pentecostal pastor.
8. Biographical interview with a Pentecostal pastor.
9. As we have already seen in the quotations above.
10. On this subject, see the appendix on p. 96.
11. Observation made by Methodist pastors.
12. Cf. Raul Cereceda, *Las Instituciones políticas en Amèrica Latina*, p. 73.
13. G. Mensching, *Sociologie religieuse*, pp. 185–201.
14. *Ibid.*, p. 187.
15. *Ibid.*, p. 188.
16. Unpublished document from the 2nd Consulta de Iglesia y Sociedad en América latina. El Tabo, Chile, January 1966. It will be observed that here 'Protestantism' is being contrasted with 'Pentecostalism'.
17. Hoover, *op. cit.*, p. 10. Our italics.
18. Cf. note 16.
19. J. Medina, *op. cit.*, pp. 30–40.
20. J. Medina, *op. cit.*, p. 39.
21. J. Medina, *op. cit.*, p. 39.
22. C.E.P.A.L., *El Desarrollo Social . . .*, Chap. II, *La situación rural.*
23. Cf. R. Dahl, *The Concept of Power*, and also R. König (ed.), *Soziologie*, pp. 112–33.
24. Pastor Tschuy added that the bishop gave the impression of deciding on his own, for he never called for a vote before giving a reply. But, in fact, he waited to ascertain what was the consensus.
25. Bishop Umaña died at the end of 1964.
26. The episode is related by Ignacio Vergara, *op. cit.*, pp. 217–19.
27. In this question, for various reasons, we did not mention the *Comunidad*. On the other hand, the answers provide indications of a certain contemporary evolution (from sect to church) in Pentecostalism, of which we shall speak again later.

28. The State, in fact, makes subsidies to churches for their charitable and social work.
29. Cf. Max Weber, *op. cit.*, pp. 182–88.
30. Since its inception Pentecostalism in Chile has belonged to the type named by Yinger 'the established sect'. In the Conclusion, we shall return to this question and to the discussion of evolution.
31. *La Voz Pentecostal*, Curico, no. 1, April 1947.
32. In this sense, sociologically speaking, traditional Protestantism corresponds better than Pentecostalism with the definition 'clerical', since its pastors are subjected to a very strict process of intellectual selection.

APPENDIX TO CHAPTER 4

1. When this investigation was being undertaken, the Presbyterian Church had not yet proceeded to ordain laymen with no theological training. The 'exceptions' would now be somewhat more numerous.
2. Douglas Webster, *Patterns of Part-time Ministry in Some Churches in South America.*
3. It appears that some leaders, when sending us their list of pastors, enlarged them a little for reasons of prestige.
4. Webster's statement (*op. cit.*, p. 25) that Pentecostalism in Chile has no part-time ministers must therefore be modified.

CHAPTER 5. INVESTIGATION OF PROTESTANT SOCIAL ETHICS

1. This paragraph is paraphrased from Emilio Willems's *Protestantism and Culture Change in Brazil and Chile*, p. 93. Willems puts the question strictly in terms of culture.
2. G. Gurvitch, *La Vocation Actuelle de la Sociologie*, vol. I, p. 105. This author sets out to consider social reality as a multi-dimensional phenomenon, and to distinguish within it ten stages or levels, from the 'morphological surface' and 'organizations' to 'ideas and collective values', and finally to 'mental states and collective psychic acts', with six other layers in between. The aim of this division is to simplify the approach to and analysis of social phenomena, but the author stresses at the outset that the levels form a unity (in which the order of importance may vary) and that therefore they are not autonomous but 'interpenetrate and mutually impregnate one another' (cf. *op. cit.*, pp. 66–118).
3. H. Richard Niebuhr, *Christ and Culture*, Faber, 1952.
4. *Ibid.*, p. 46. Malinowski here calls 'culture' that which others describe as 'the social'. As for Niebuhr, what he calls 'culture' describes civilization.
5. The quotations are taken from pp. 55–56, *op. cit.*
6. Cf. Introduction, p. xxiv f.
7. Italics ours.
8. When we speak of the 'trade-unionist' attitude of the Church, we do not mean to discredit the trade unions' actions, the motive of which is precisely to defend the interests of occupational groups. But we should like to suggest that the Church is not a trade union.
9. The student is referring to the concept of the community 'dispersed' in society by the secular activities of its members. The 'community' is 'gathered' when it takes part in collective activities, e.g. in worship.
10. Voting in Chile is compulsory.
11. H. R. Niebuhr, *op. cit.*, pp. 60–61 in Faber edition. The author refers to C. H. Dodd's *The Johannine Epistles*, 1946, and quotes from page 42.
12. *Ibid.*, p. 61.
13. *Ibid.*, p. 61.
14. Benton Johnson, *On Church and Sect.*
15. H. Desroche, *Les Shakers américains*, p. 60.
16. *Ibid.*, p. 60.

17. *The Social Sources of Denominationalism*, p. 65.
18. *Ibid.*, p. 74.
19. *Ibid.*, p. 67.
20. *Ibid.*, p. 68.

CHAPTER 6. THE MEANING AND CONSEQUENCES OF PENTECOSTAL WITHDRAWAL FROM SOCIETY

1. Bryan Wilson speaks of the totalitarianism of the sect, which is not 'only an ideological unit, it is to greater or lesser degree, a social unit, seeking to enforce behaviour on those who accept belief, and seeking every occasion to draw the faithful apart from the rest of society and into the company of each other' (p. 1); 'its essential totalitarianism consists in the re-organization and re-orientation of the ideals, values and sentiments of its members' (p. 4). Quotations from *Sects and Society*.
2. Cf. C.E.P.A.L., *El desarrollo social* . . . pp. 40–59.
3. *Ibid.*, p. 42.
4. E. Willems, *Religiöser Pluralismus und Klassenstruktur in Brasilien und Chile*, p. 202.
5. E. Willems, *Protestantism and Culture Change in Brazil and Chile*, p. 103.
6. Willems, *Religiöser Pluralismus und Klassenstruktur* . . . , p. 202.
7. *Ibid.*, p. 199.
8. *Ibid.*, p. 199.
9. The tendency towards centralization among religious movements of the Pentecostal type has already been pointed out, e.g. by Bryan Wilson in *An Analysis of Sect Development*, p. 9, and in several places in his work already quoted, *Sects and Society*.
10. See Chapter 4, section 4, 'The succession', p. 88.
11. Willems, *ibid.*, pp. 199–200.
12. Cf. Chapter 4, section 4, 'Schism'.
13. Cf. Willems, *ibid.*, p. 200.
14. Cf. *ibid.*, p. 200.
15. The concept is from J. A. Kahl and characterizes a developed industrial society. Quoted by Willems, 1965, p. 194.
16. Moreover, the totalitarian claim of the congregation over the individual, which is a fundamental characteristic of a sect (see note 1 in this chapter) seems to contradict Willems's argument.
17. See Introduction, page xxvii et seq.
18. Unfortunately we were unable to meet Pastor Mora. The conversation we report here is taken from the work of Ignacio Vergara, *El Protestantismo en Chile*, pp. 140–44.
19. *Idem*, p. 143.

CHAPTER 7. PROTESTANTISM, INDIVIDUAL MOBILITY AND SOCIAL CHANGE

1. Stanley W. Rycroft's very popular work, *Religion and Faith in Latin America*, is an excellent example of this Protestant missionary 'dogma'.
2. Publication entitled *II Consulta latinoaméricana de Iglesia y Sociedad*, p. 20.
3. *Die Protestantische Ethik und der Geist des Kapitalismus* was first published in 1904 and 1905 in the *Archiv für Sozialwissenschaft und Sozialpolitik*, Tübingen, Vols. II and III, and then in the book, *Gesammelte Aufsätze zur Religionssoziologie*, Tübingen, Mohr, 1920. Later editions are all based on the latter text. The quotations are taken from the English edition, Allen & Unwin, 1930.
4. *Ibid.*, p. 55.
5. Preface to the English edition of *Socialism: Utopian and Scientific*, first published in 1892 in London. Allen & Unwin, 1936 edition, page xxi.
6. Max Weber, *op. cit.*, p. 91. Our italics.
7. A more complete résumé is found in A. Biéler, *La Pensée économique et social de Calvin*, pp. 477–93.

8. Weber, *op. cit.*, p. 71.
9. On the historical and theological level, one may consult a recent critique by Biéler, *op. cit.*, pp. 493–501. On the socio-economic level, see Kurt Samuelsson, *Religion and Economic Action*; N. Birnbaum, '*Conflicting Interpretations of the Rise of Capitalism*'; and H. Luthi, '*Calvinisme et capitalisme*', as well as several articles in *Archives de Sociologie des Religions*, no. 15, January–June 1963.
10. See for example C.E.P.A.L., *El Desarrollo social . . .*, pp. 98–102.
11. Robert N. Bellah, *Reflections on the Protestant Ethic Analogy in Asia*, pp. 54–55.
12. Bellah, *op. cit.*, pp. 55–56. Our italics.
13. Second Continental Consultation on Church and Society, January 1966. Report of the Commission on 'Ideology and Belief in a Dynamic Society', mimeographed, page 1.
14. Cf. José Míguez, *Latin America*, p. 179.
15. On the problem of alcoholism, see the excellent study by M. Zamorano and C. Munizaga, *Crimen y alcohol*.
16. At the official exchange rate, U.S. $1 equalled 3·4 Escudos (Eo.) in March 1965 and 4·5 Eo. in February 1966. The national income per head, for the years 1960–62, was U.S. $433 in Chile (in Argentina 551; Ecuador, 188; Switzerland 1,474; Great Britain 1,312; U.S.A. 2,335). The cost of living index, calculated on the basis of 100 for New York (U.S.A.) at the beginning of 1966, is 72 for Santiago (Chile), 93 for Quito (Ecuador) and Buenos Aires (Argentina), 87 for Geneva (Switzerland), and 82 for London (England). Sources: Rate of exchange of the escudo: Chilean press; National income: unpublished U.N.O. document; Cost of Living Index: Bulletin Mensuel de Statistique, U.N.O., October 1966.
17. Allusion to Charles Morazé, *Les bourgeois conquérants*.
18. The preceding paragraphs are manifestly true for Pentecostalism, but also with some modifications for Methodists, Baptists: in short, traditional Protestantism.
19. I. Vergara, *El Protestantismo en Chile*, p. 241.
20. This is based on the two following works: Raymond Aron, *Dix-huit leçons sur la société industrielle*; W. W. Rostow, *The Stages of Economic Growth*.
21, 22 and 23: C.E.P.A.L., *El desarrollo social . . .*, p. 63. Two other C.E.P.A.L. reports should also be consulted: *Problemas y perspectivas de la agricultura latinoaméricana* and *Problemas y perspectivas del desarrollo industrial latinoaméricano*.
24. J. Medina, *Consideraciones sociológicas . . .*, p. 41.
25. For Latin America, see John J. Johnson, *Political Change in Latin America*.
26. Hoselitz has expounded his theories in *Economic Growth in Latin America*, in *Contribution to the first International Conference of Economic History*, 1960. J. Medina, *op. cit.*, reproduces them in summarized form, pp. 82–84. This quotation is from p. 83.
27. Geneva, July 12–26, 1966.
28. Esdras St. Amand, *Bon Dieu Rit*, p. 8.

CHAPTER 8. ECUMENISM ON TRIAL

1. For example:

Robert Lee, *The Social Sources of Church Unity*. The title of this work suggests that it was written in response to H. Richard Niebuhr's classic, *The Social Sources of Denominationalism*.

Peter L. Berger, *A Market Model for the Analysis of Ecumenicity*. This is the most interesting article published on ecumenism; the author interprets the American movement towards unity by analogy with the model of a market economy.

R. Mehl, in his *Sociologie du Protestantisme*, devotes a chapter to ecumenism. We shall refer again to his analysis.

Another index of the importance attained by ecumenism: it was one of the three study group themes in religious sociology at the Sixth World Congress of Sociology, Evian, 1966.

2. W. A. Visser 't Hooft, *The Meaning of Ecumenical*, pp. 5–6.
3. *Op. cit.*, p. 6.
4. Magdelaine Villeroy, *Enquête sur les églises protestantes . . .*, pp. 67–68.
5. Chapter 4, section 2a. Finding out whether the educational level in itself has an influence on the attitude towards ecumenism is equally important, but would require that different samples of church members within a single type of denomination be taken, according to their degree of education. We did not have an opportunity to carry out such an investigation.
6. For example, in a brochure entitled *Methodism in Chile* (no date or place of publication given), one reads: 'In 1909 a group left the Conference to form the Methodist Pentecostal Church which today claims about 400,000 members.'
7. W. C. Hoover, *op. cit.*, pp. 105–10 (written about 1910).
8. The use of *concilio* instead of *consejo* is due to the influence of the English word *council*.
9. The latter withdrew afterwards, because of the relations between the C.E.C. and the World Council of Churches.
10. Published by Editorial del Pacifico, 1941 (Santiago). This book appeared in 1941, two years before the famous *France, Pays de Mission*, by H. Godin and Y. Daniel, whose arguments followed the same direction.
11. I. Vergara, *Avance de los 'Evangélicos' en Chile*, p. 262.
12. P. Damboriena, *El Protestantismo en Chile*, p. 146.
13. *Ibid.*, p. 149.
14. *Ibid.*, p. 149.
15. *Ibid.*, p. 153.
16. Let us again quote the two articles by I. Rosier and M. Veloso, on the same lines, which were published in *Anales de la Facultad de Teologia*, Universidad Catolica, no. 11, Santiago, 1960, pp. 88–137.
17. H. Muñoz, *Visión general del Protestantismo en Latinoamérica.*
18. He alludes to *El otro Cristo Espagnol.*
19. *Art. cit.*, pp. 69–70. Our italics.
20. Magdelaine Villeroy: *Enquête sur les Eglises protestantes dans le Brésil . . .*, p. 67.
21. This section is based on an unpublished study entitled 'La Accion de Church World Service y del Lutheran World Relief en Chile' prepared by Mr. Francisco Vendrell during our collaboration. However, because of the contentious nature of the views here put forward, we would like to state that we personally take all responsibility for them.
22. Mimeographed text, July 18, 1963.
23. (Our italics.) The officers of the *Concilio Evangélico* pursue an ostrich-like policy, trying to make a subtle distinction between the government and the people of the United States. The Director of A.C.E. expressed this outlook at a Church World Service consultation which took place in Santiago at the end of 1965. But he was interrupted by an official of the U.S. Embassy, who held that on the contrary this was a piece of foreign policy which the government regarded as highly important!
24. *Informe de Auditoria n. 97 de la Agencia Intern. des Desarrollo: Programa de Ayuda en Alimentos. Titulo III de Church World Service (CWS) y Lutheran World Relief, Inc. (LWR) en la Republica de Chile* (translated into Spanish and distributed in mimeograph form by A.C.E.), p. 1.
25. *Anglican Opportunities in South America*, ch. V, p. 9. Ivan Vallier, project director.
26. *El Mercurio*, March 11, 1966, p. 23. The Senator here emphasizes an important point: this aid runs counter to all attempts to improve the antiquated agricultural techniques which Chilean landowners employ.
27. These lines describe the situation up to the end of 1966. In 1967 various important events took place, among them the break between Church World Service and *Ayuda Christiana Evangélica*. The C.W.S. ceased all its activities in Chile and dismissed its last representative, John Nichols, who was found to have been trained at the notorious James Hofa's trade union school. But Mr. Nichols stayed on in Chile as adviser to the A.C.E., which appointed a new director and sought the support of other Protestant social agencies in

the United States and Europe. On this question, see John B. Housley, '*Protestant Failure in Chile*'.

28. J. Ellul, *Fausse présence au monde modern*, p. 72, quoted by Roger Mehl, *op. cit.*, p. 185. Since Ellul refers to the seventeenth century, let us quote the paper presented recently to the 6th World Congress of Sociology (Evian, September 1966) by Jean Séguy, entitled *Les oecuménismes du XVIIe siècle et les relations internationales de l'époque*. He shows that the ecumenical movements of that century also bear a 'certain relation to the evolution of contacts between nations in the same period' (pp. 1–2 of mimeographed text).
29. Here we are not arguing theologically but pointing out the docetic accents in Ellul's position.
30. One might also quote the affirmation of an atheist: 'If science does not concede divine intervention as an explanatory cause, it is because the object, God, does not lend itself to any of the scientific modes of treatment: in that sense he cannot have any existence.' (Lucien Sebag, *Marxisme et Structuralisme*, p. 100.)
31. Joachim Wach, *Sociologie de la religion*, p. 430.
32. Mehl, *op. cit.*, p. 185 and the whole of chapter ix.
33. See Table 6, p. 40.

CHAPTER 9. THEOLOGICAL ASPECTS OF CHILEAN PENTECOSTALISM

1. Troeltsch, E., *Die Soziallehren . . .*, p. 270.
2. *Iglesia Pentecostal de Chile, Manuel del Ministro*, p. 7.
3. W. C. Hoover, *op. cit.*, p. 14; cf. our Chapter 2.
4. W. J. Hollenweger, *Handbuch der Pfingstbewegung I, Hauptteil*, p. 79. Our italics.
5. Hollenweger, *op. cit.*, p. 66.
6. Eduard Schweizer, article, 'Pneuma' in TWB VI, 410, quoted by Hollenweger, *op. cit.*, p. 90.
7. Hollenweger, *op. cit.*, p. 90.
8. M. Umaña (then bishop of the *Iglesia Metodista Pentecostal*) in *Chile Pentecostal*, September 1955, p. 4.
9. M. Umaña, *art. cit.*, p. 5.
10. The observer's error will be noticed: for a Pentecostalist (and the simplest church member knows this) conversion and Baptism of the Spirit are two distinct things.
11. P. Damboriena, S.J., *El Protestantismo en Chile*, pp. 151, 152.
12. M. T. Kelsey, *Tongue Speaking: An Experiment in Spiritual Experience*.
13. W. Hollenweger, *op. cit.*, p. 95.
14. Bryan R. Wilson, in *Sects and Society*, speaks of a form of expression needed by men for whom glossolalia is the only public form of language possible.
15. J. L. Sherrill, *They Speak with Other Tongues*.
16. On this subject see G. von Rad, *Theologie des Alten Testaments*, vol. 2, pp. 45–111.
17. See following section; the operations are mimed.
18. This problem merits further examination in connection with studies of popular religious attitudes.
19. In a *callampa*-church a certain amount of licence may become established because there is no control over the pastor. Nevertheless such cases remain isolated. When a similar phenomenon appears in a congregation belonging to a larger denomination, sooner or later the organization brings the disorder to an end.
20. Not because the illness was invented, but because of the lack of medical knowledge on the part of those involved.
21. Father D. Mario Veloso, *Vision general de los Pentecostales Chilenos*, p. 131.
22. A list of the healing saints and their specialities is found in Oreste Plath's *Folklore religioso chileno*, p. 17.

23. W. J. Hollenweger, *op. cit.*, p. 119.
24. Bryan Wilson, *Sects and Society*, pp. 345–46.
25. Cf. B. Wilson, *ibid.*, p. 346.

SUMMARY AND CONCLUSION

1. Bryan R. Wilson, *An Analysis of Sect Development*, p. 4.
2. E. Troeltsch, *Die Soziallehren . . .*, pp. 360–77.
3. Roger Mehl, *Sociologie du Protestantisme*, p. 203.
4. Bryan Wilson, *art. cit.*, p. 7.
5. J. Milton Yinger, *Religion, Society, Individual*, p. 150 ff.
6. Bryan R. Wilson, *Sects and Society*, pp. 9–10.
7. H. Richard Niebuhr, *The Social Sources of Denominationalism*. To avoid all confusion, we use denomination in inverted commas when we use it in the sociological sense. And we prefer to speak of Pentecostalist corporations (not denominations).
8. Yinger, *op. cit.*, p. 150.
9. Mehl, *op. cit.*, p. 203.
10. '*lendemains qui chantent*'—from the farewell letter of Gabriel Peri to his wife before being shot by the Germans in 1941 for Resistance activities.
11. Cf. H. R. Niebuhr, *op. cit.*, esp. pp. 19–20, and also Liston Pope, *op. cit.*
12. Wilson, *art. cit.*; cf. also *Sects and Society* (introduction).
13. On the basis of Table 2 in Chapter 2, one can say that the rate of growth due to evangelism for the last decade equals the rate of growth of Protestants (6·60) less the rate of natural growth of the population (2·43), i.e. 4·17 per cent. per annum. This may be called the net rate of growth through evangelism, the crude rate being higher if one allows that Pentecostalism loses a certain number of members not because they die, but because they 'fall'.
14. From every point of view it would be exciting to make an enquiry into a sample of adult descendants of Pentecostal converts. It would provide information not only about the religious problems of the second generation, but also about its social mobility, etc.
15. H. R. Niebuhr, *op. cit.*, Chap. 2–3.
16. Schism has been dealt with in section 4 of Chapter 4.
17. R. Bastide, in a review of Damboriena's work, *El Protestantismo en América latina*, vol. 2, believes that the 'tiny sects, with a dozen members, whose existence is ephemeral . . . are of no value for a study of Protestantism, and can only interest the psychologist' (A.S.R., 17/1964, p. 171). Though we agree with him in thinking that they have no sociological weight and that a monograph study of them would be of slight interest, their continued existence is nevertheless an expression of an invariable feature of the very nature of Pentecostalism: the temptation to cultivate charisma as an end in itself, and not as a prelude to missionary action.
18. Cf. chapter 9, p. 193 ff.
19. Cf. Chapter 3, section 2.
20. This point is dealt with in detail in Chapter 6, p. 141.
21. This is the famous reservation, 'all other things being equal', which is made when the results of a piece of research are extrapolated in time or space.
22. It should be noted that these two propositions make no claim to be new. It is, however, true that missionary organizations do not always draw the conclusions implied in them.
23. This first condition, and the way in which we have formulated it, will perhaps shock some believers. We beg their forgiveness and wish to stress that we are not speaking of the cause but the condition. In addition we believe that we are only repeating the words of Jesus, who knew that the disinherited of the earth were more receptive to the Gospel than those who had possessions: Mat. 19: 16–22, 11: 19.
24. This is why we believe our propositions are also valid for ideology in general.
25. While our first proposition has points of correspondence with the words of Jesus, the second was held, as we have indicated in Chapter 3, pp. 62 ff., by the first great Christian missionary, Paul the Apostle.

BOOKS CONSULTED

Classification Plan

I General Sociology
II Sociology of Religion*
III Religions a. In Chile
b. In Latin America
IV History, Economics and Sociology a. Chile
b. Latin America
V Miscellaneous

Note: In the period between the completion of this work and its publication, two books on the subject have appeared which unfortunately could not be taken into consideration:

Kessler, J. B. A. *A Study of the Older Protestant Missions and Churches in Peru and Chile* (Oosterbaan & Le Cointre N.V., Goes, 1967), a piece of research rich in unpublished historical material.

Willems, E. *Followers of the New Faith: Culture Change and the Rise of Protestantism in Brazil and Chile* (Vanderbilt University Press, 1967), a broad sociological study, certain preliminary conclusions of which we did know through articles published earlier.

Classification

Alonso, I., Poblete, R., and Garrido, G.
La Iglesia en Chile, Fribourg/Bogotá, F.E.R.E.S., 1963. IIIa

Archives de Sociologie des Religions. II
No. 1 (Jan.-June 1956).
No. 21 (Jan.–June 1966), Paris, C.N.R.S.
In particular:
No. 10 (July–Dec. 1960): 'Socialisme et religion'.
No. 12 (July–Dec. 1961) and No. 15 (Jan.–June 1963): 'Religion et développement'.

Arcos, J.
El sindicalismo en América latina, Fribourg/Bogotá, F.E.R.E.S., 1964. IVb

Arms, G. F.
El origen del metodismo y su implantación en la costa occidental de Sudamérica, Santiago, 1925. IIIb

Aron, R.
Dix-huit leçons sur la société industrielle, Paris, Gallimard, 1962. V

Avalos, R.
Le Chili, Paris, P.U.F., 1963. IVa

Bastide, R.
Les religions afro-brésiliennes, Paris, P.U.F., 1960. IIIb

* Excluding books and articles on Latin America, included under III.

Classification

Bates, M. S., and Pauck, W. (ed.)
The Prospects of Christianity throughout the World, New York, Ch. Scribner's, 1964. IIIb

Bellah, R. N.
'Reflections on the Protestant Ethic Analogy in Asia', *J.S.I.*, Vol. XIX No. 1, 1963, pp. 52–60. II

Berger, P. L.
'A Market Model for the Analysis of Ecumenicity', *Soc. Res.* 30/1, 1963. II

Beyhaut, G.
Raíces contemporaneas de América latina, Buenos Aires, Eudeba, 1964. IVb
—— *Süd und Mittelamerika II*, Frankfurt a.M., Fischer Weltgeschichte No. 23, 1965 (translated from French). IVb

Bieler, A.
La pensée économique et sociale de Calvin, Geneva, Georg, 1961. V

Birnbaum, N.
'Conflicting Interpretations of the Rise of Capitalism', *B.J.S.*, IV, 1953, pp. 125–41. I

Bloch-Hoell, N.
The Pentecostal Movement, London, Allen & Unwin, 1964 (1958, translated from Norwegian). V

Browning, W. *et al.*
The West Coast Republics of South America, London, World Dominion Press, 1930. IIIb

Calderon, L., Calle, A., and Dorselear, J.
Problemas de urbanización en América latina, Fribourg/Bogotá, F.E.R.E.S., 1963. IVb

Calley, M. J. C.
God's People. West Indian Pentecostal Sects in England, London, Oxford Univ. Press, 1965. II

Canclini, A.
Hasta lo último de la tierra. Allen Gardiner y las misiones en la Patagonia, Buenos Aires, 1951. IIIb

Centro de Estudios Cristianos.
Aspectos religiosos de la sociedad uruguaya, Montevideo, C.E.C., 1965. IIIb

C.E.P.A.L.
El desarrollo social de América latina en la postguerra, Buenos Aires, Solar/Hachette, 1963. IVb
—— *Problemas y perspectivas del desarrollo industrial latinoamericano*, Buenos Aires, Solar/Hachette, 1964. IVb
—— *Problemas y perspectives de la agricultura latinoamericana*, Buenos Aires, Solar/Hachette, 1965. IVb

Cerreceda, R.
Las instituciones políticas en América latina, Fribourg/Bogotá, F.E.R.E.S., 1961. IVb

Classification

Chaunu, P.
L'Amérique et les Amériques, Paris, Colin, 1964. IVb
—— 'Pour une sociologie du protestantisme latino-américain', *Cah. de Soc. écon.*, 12, 1965, pp. 5–18. IIIb

Corredor, B., and Torres, S.
Transformación en el mundo rural latinoamericano, Fribourg/Bogotá, F.E.R.E.S., 1961. IVb

Corredor, B.
La familia en América latina, Fribourg/Bogotá, F.E.R.E.S., 1962. IVb

Cruz Coke, R.
Geografia electoral de Chile, Santiago, ed. del Pacífico, 1952. IVa

Dahl, R.
'The Concept of Power', *Behavioral Science* 2, pp. 201–15. I

Damboriena, P.
'El protestantismo en Chile', *Mensaje* VI, 1957, pp. 145–54. IIIa
—— *El protestantismo en América latina*, Fribourg/Bogotá, F.E.R.E.S., 1962 (2 vol.). IIIb

D'Antonio, W., and Pike, F. (ed.).
Religion, Revolution and Reform, London, Burns & Oates, 1964. IIIb

Debuyst, F.
La población en América latina, Fribourg/Bogotá, F.E.R.E.S., 1961–62 (2 vol.). IVb
—— *Las clases sociales en América latina*, Fribourg/Bogotá, F.E.R.E.S., 1962. IVb

D.E.S.A.L.
América latina y el desarrollo social, Santiago, D.E.S.A.L., 1965 (2 vol.). IVb

Desroche, H.
Les Shakers américains, Paris, éd. de Minuit, 1955. II
—— *Socialismes et sociologie religieuse*, Paris, Cujas, 1965. II

Dimond, S. G.
The Psychology of the Methodist Revival, London, Oxford Univ. Press, 1926. V

Dirreccion de Estadistica y Censos.
XIII Censo de Población, seria B, Santiago, 1964–65 (25 vol.). IVa
Cifras comparativas de los censos de 1940 y 1952 y muestra del censo de 1960, Santiago, s.d. (1963?).
Población del país. Características básicas de la población (*Censo de 1960*), Santiago, 1964.
Población del país. Provincias, departamentos, comunas (*censo de 1960*), Santiago, 1964.
Población total por provincias (*1885–1960*), Santiago, 1964.
(and other D.E.C. publications).

Dominguez, O.
El campesino chileno y la acción católica rural, Fribourg/Bogotá, F.E.R.E.S., 1961. IVa

Classificat

—— *Sociologia rural*, Santiago, ed. del Pacífico, 1965. IVa

Dorselear, J., and Gregory, A.
La urbanización en América latina Fribourg/Bogotá, F.E.R.E.S., 1962 (2 vol.). IVb

Dumont, R.
Terres vivantes, Paris, Plon, 1961. IVa

Durkheim, E.
Les formes élémentaires de la vie religieuse (1912), Paris, P.U.F., 1960. II

—— *Le suicide* (1947), Paris, P.U.F., 1960. I

Dusen, H. van
'The Challenge of the Sects', *Christianity and Crisis*, XVIII, 13, 1958. IIIb

Duverger, N.
Méthodes des sciences sociales, Paris, P.U.F., 1964. I

Encina, F.
Nuestra inferioridad económica (1912), Santiago, ed. Universitaria, 1912. IVa

—— *Resumen de la historia de Chile*, Santiago, Zig-Zag, 1954(3 vol.). IVa

Engels, F.
Socialism: Utopian and Scientific, trans. E. Aveling (1892), London, Allen & Unwin, 1936. II

Eyzaguirre, J.
Ideario y ruta de la emancipación chilena, Santiago, ed. Universitaria, 1957. IVa

F.E.R.E.S.
Las Tareas de la Iglesia en América latina, Fribourg/Bogotá, F.E.R.E.S., 1964. IIIb

Festinger, K., and Katz, D. (ed.).
Research Methods in the Behavioral Sciences, New York, Holt, 1953. I

Fichter, J. H.
Sociology, Chicago, Univ. of Chicago Press, 1957. I

Gerth, H., and Mills, R. W.
Character and Social Structure, London, Routledge & Kegan Paul, 1954. I

Glock, C. Y., and Stark, R.
Religion and Society in Tension, Chicago, Rand McNally, 1965. II

Goslin, T.
Los evangélicos en la América latina, Buenos Aires, La Aurora, 1956. IIIb

Gozard, G.
Demain l'Amérique latine, Paris, P.U.F., 1964. IVb

Gurvitch, G. (dir.).
Traité de sociologie, Paris, P.U.F., t. I: 1958, t. II: 1960. I

—— *La vocation actuelle de la sociologie* (1950), Paris, P.U.F., 1963 (2 vol.).

Classification

—— *Les cadres sociaux de la connaissance*, Paris, P.U.F., 1966. I

Haddox, B.
Sociedad y religión en Colombia, Bogotá, Tercer Mundo, 1965. IIIb

Harper, M.
As at the Beginning: the Twentieth Century Pentecostal Revival, London, Hodder & Stoughton, 1965. V

Hayward, V. E. W. (ed.).
The Church as Christian Community: Three Studies of North Indian Churches, London, Lutterworth Press, 1966. V

Hollenweger, W.
Handbuch der Pfingstbewegung, Geneva, 1965 mimeo. (8 vol.). V

Hoover, W. C.
Historia del avivamiento pentecostal en Chile (1931), Valparaiso, Imp. Excelsior, 1948. IIIa

Hurtado, A.
Es Chile un paíd católico? Santiago, ed. del Pacífico, 1941. IIIa

Instituto de Economíca.
La migración interna en Chile, Santiago, Instituto de Economica, No. 19, Univ. of Chile, IVa
La población del Gran Santiago, 1952–1959, Santiago, No. 20, Univ. of Chile, 1959.

Iglesia Evangélica Pentecostal.
Fuego de Pentecostés, No. 1– . . . , 1933– . . . , Santiago. IIIa

Iglesia Metodista Pentecostal.
Chile Pentecostal, No. 1– . . . , 1911– . . . , Santiago. IIIa

Iglesia Pentecostal de Chile.
La Voz Pentecostal, No. 1– . . . , 1947– . . . , Curicó. IIIa
Manuel del Ministro, Curicó, 1950.

Jobet, J. C.
Ensayo crítico del desarrollo económico-social de Chile, Santiago, ed. Universitaria, 1955. IVa

Johnson, B.
'A Critical Appraisal of the Church–Sect Typology', *A.S.R.*, 22, 1957, pp. 82–92. II
—— 'On Church and Sect', *A.S.R.*, 28, 1963, pp. 539–49. II

Johnson, John James.
Political Change in Latin America, Stanford Univ. Press, 1958. IVb

Kelsey, M. T.
Tongue Speaking: An Experiment in Spiritual Experience, New York, 1960. V

Kluckhohn, C., and Kelly, William H.
'The Concept of Culture', in *Science of Man* . . . , Linton, Ralph, ed. I

Konetzke, R.
Süd u. Mittelamerika I, Frankfurt a.M., Fischer Weltgeschichte No. 22, 1965. IVb

Classification

Lalive d'Epinay, C.
'La expansión protestante en Chile', *Cr. y Soc.*, 9–10, 1965–66, pp. 19–43. IIIa

Lambert, J.
Amérique latine: structures sociales et institutions politiques, Paris, P.U.F., 1963. IVb

Landecker, W. S.
'Types of integration and their measurement', *A.J.S.*, LVI, 1951, pp. 332–40. I

Lannoy, J. L. de
Los niveles de vida en América latina, Fribourg/Bogotá, F.E.R.E.S., 1963. IVb

Le Bras, G.
Etudes de sociologie religieuse, Paris, P.U.F., 1955–56 (2 vol.). II
—— 'Problèmes de la sociologie des religions', in G. Gurvitch (dir.), *Traité de sociologie* II, Paris, P.U.F., 1960, pp. 79–102. II

Lee, Robert
The Social Sources of Church Unity, New York, Abingdon Press, 1960. II

Lee, Robert, and Marty, Martin E. (ed.).
Religion and Social Conflict, New York and London, Oxford Univ. Press, 1964. II

Léonard, E. G.
'Protestant français et protestant brésilien', *R.P.P.*, 8/1, Jan.–Mar. 1953, pp. 40–52. II
—— *L'illuminisme dans un protestantisme de constitution récente: Brésil*, Paris, P.U.F., 1953. IIIb
—— *O Protestantismo brasileiro* (1951–52). São Paulo, A.S.T.E., s.d. (1964?). IIIb

Lewis, O.
The Children of Sánchez. London, Secker & Warburg, 1962. IVb

Luthy, H.
'Calvinisme et capitalisme', *Cah. V. Pareto* 2, 1963, pp. 5–35. II

McLean, J. H.
Historia de la Iglesia Presbiteriana en Chile (1931), Santiago, Esc. nac. artes gráficas, 1954. IIIa

Magnet, A.
El padre Hurtado, Santiago, ed. del Pacífico, 1941. IIIa

Mattelart, A., and Garreton, M.
Integración nacional y marginalidad, Santiago, ed. del Pacífico, 1965. IVa

Marx, K.
Die Frühschriften (*1837–1848*), Stuttgart, Kröner Verlag, 1964. V

Medina, J.
Consideraciones sociológicas sobre el desarrollo económico, Buenos Aires, Solar/Hachette, 1964. IVb

Classification

Mehl, R.
Traité de sociologie du protestantisme, Paris and Neuchâtel, Delachaux & Niestlé, 1966. II

Mensaje
'Revolución en América latina', *Mensaje* No. 115, Dec. 1962. IVb
'Reformas revolucionarias en América latina', *Mensaje* No. 123, Oct. 1963.
'Integración de América latina', *Mensaje* No. 139, June 1965.

Mensching, G.
Sociologie religieuse, Paris, Payot, 1951 (1947, translated from German). II

Merton, R. K.
Social Theory and Social Structure (1949), Glencoe, Illinois Free Press, 1957. I

Miegge, M.
'L'oecuménisme est-il un phénomène culturel plus que théologique?' *Chr. social*, 72, Mar.–Apr. 1964. V

Miguez, J.
'Latin America', in Bates, M., and Pauck, W. (ed.), *The Prospects of Christianity throughout the World*, New York, Ch. Scribner's, 1964, pp. 165–82. IIIb

Missionary Research Library
Protestant Churches of Asia, the Middle East, Africa, Latin America and the Pacific Area. New York, M.R.L., 1959. IIIb

Moore, R. C.
Los evangélicos en marcha en América latina, Santiago, ed. bautistas, 1959. IIIb

Moraze, C.
Les bourgeois conquérants, Paris, A. Colin, 1957. V

Muñoz, H.
Sociología religiosa, Santiago, ed. Paulinas, 1956. II
—— 'Situación del protestantismo en Chile', *Mensaje* V, 1956, pp. 166–69. IIIa
—— 'Visión general del protestantismo en Latinoamérica', *Anales*, 11, 1960, pp. 62–73. IIIb

Nida, E. E.
'The Indigenous Churches in Latin America', *Practical Anthropology*, VIII, 3, May–June 1961. IIIb

Niebuhr, H. Richard
The Social Sources of Denominationalism, New York, Holt & Co., 1929. II
—— *Christ and Culture*, New York, Harper, 1951 (Torchlight, 1956). London, Faber, 1952. V

Niedergang, M.
Les 20 Amériques latines, Paris, Plon, 1962. IVb

Classification

Oyarzun, A.
Reminisciencias históricas de la obra evangélica en Chile, Valdivia, Imp. Alianza, 1921. IIIa

Perez, G., and Labelle, Y.
El problema sacerdotal en América latina, Fribourg/Bogotá, F.E.R.E.S., 1964. IIIb

Pin, E.
Elementos para una sociología del catolicismo latinamericano, Fribourg/Bogotá, F.E.R.E.S., 1963. II

Pinto Santa Cruz, A.
Chile, un caso de desarrollo frustrado, Santiago, ed. Universitairia, 1958. IVa

Plath, O.
Folklore religioso chileno, Santiago, PlaTur, 1966. IIIa

Poblete, R.
'Consideración sociológica de las sectas chilenas', *Anales*, 11, 1960, pp. 74–87. IIIa
—— *Crísis sacerdotal*, Santiago, ed. del Pacífico, 1965. IIIa

Pope, L.
Millhands and Preachers, New Haven, Yale Univ. Press, 1942. II

Rad, G. von.
Die Theologie des Alten Testamentes, München, Kaiser Verlag, t.1.1957, t.2.1960. V

Read, W. R.
New Patterns of Church Growth in Brazil, U.S.A., Eerdmans, 1965. IIIb

R. G. G.[3]
Die Religion in Geschichte u. Gegenwart (3rd ed.) Tübingen, Mohr, 1957–65 (7 vol.). V

Rosier, I.
Ovejas sin pastor, Buenos Aires, Carlo Lohlé, 1960. IIIb
—— 'Estudio del protestantismo en Chile', *Anales*, 11, 1960, pp. 88–120. IIIa

Rostow, W. W.
The Stages of Economic Growth, Cambridge Univ. Press, 1960. V

Rycroft, W. Stanley
Religion and Faith in Latin America, Philadelphia, Westminster Press, 1958. IIIb

St. Amand, E.
'Bon Dieu rit', *Rond Point* 11, 1960. IVb

Samuelsson, K.
Religion and Economic Action, London, Heinemann, 1961 (1959, translated from Swedish). II

Schweizer, E.
'Pneuma', *T.W.B.*, VI, 410. V

Classification

Scopes, Wilfred (ed.)
The Christian Ministry in Latin America and the Caribbean, Geneva/London/ New York, W.C.C., 1962. IIIb

Sebag, L.
Marxisme et structuralisme, Paris, Payot, 1964. I

Seguy, J.
Les sectes protestantes dans la France contemporaine, Paris, Beauchesne, 1956. II

—— 'Sectes chrétiennes et développement', *Archives* No. 13, Jan.–June 1962, pp. 5–15. II

—— 'Les oecuménismes du 17e s. et les relations internationales de l'époque', paper presented at *6e Congrès Mondial de Sociologie*, Evian, Sept. 1966. II

Sherill, J. L.
They Speak with Other Tongues, London, Hodder & Stoughton, 1965. V

Subercaseaux, B.
Chile o una loca geografia (1940), Buenos Aifes, Eudeba, 1964. IVa

Taylor, John V.
The Growth of the Church in Buganda, London, S.C.M. Press, 1956. V

Taylor, John V., and Lehmann, Dorothea A.
Christians of the Copperbelt, London, S.C.M. Press, 1961. V

Tiers-Monde.
'Bilan et perspective de l'intégration de l'Amérique latine', *Tiers-Monde* 6, 23, July–Sep. 1965. IVb

—— 'Industrialisation et intégration en Amérique latine', *Tiers-Monde* 7, 25, Jan.–Mar. 1966.

Torno, L. *et al.*
Historia de la Iglesia en América latina t. 1: La evangelización en A.l. t. III: La Iglesia en la crisis de la independencia, Fribourg/Bogotá, F.E.R.E.S., 1962. IIIb

Troeltsch, E.
The Social Teaching of the Christian Churches. New York, Harper & Bros., 1960, trans. Olive Wyon (first published 1931, Allen & Unwin, London, and Macmillan Co., New York). II

Umaña, M., and Guzman, O.
'Una Iglesia que nace', *Chile Pentecostal*, 12 Sept. 1959. IIIa

U.N.E.S.C.O.
'Sociologie des religions. Tendances actuelles de la recherche et bibliographie', *Current Sociology/Sociologie contemporaine*, 1956, Vol. 5/1, Paris. II

Vallier, I. (Project Director)
Anglican Opportunities in South America, New York, Bureau of Applied Social Research, Columbia Univ. 1963 (mimeo.). IIIb

Classification

Veloso, M.
'Visión general de los pentecostales chilenos', *Anales*, 11, 1960, pp. 121–37. IIIa

Vergara, I.
'Avance de los "Evangélicos" en Chile', *Mensaje*, III, 1955, pp. 257–62. IIIa
—— *El protestantismo en Chile*, Santiago, ed. del Pacífico, 1962. IIIa

Villeroy, M.
'Enquête sur les églises protestantes dans le Brésil en crise des années 1962–63', *Cah. de Soc. écon.* 12, May 1965, pp. 19–80. IIIb

Visser 't Hooft, W. A.
The Meaning of Ecumenical, London, S.C.M. Press, 1953. V

Wach, J.
Sociology of Religion (1941), Chicago, Univ. of Chicago Press, 1964. II
—— 'La sociologie de la religion', in Gurvitch, G., and Moore, W. (dir.), *Twentieth Century Sociology*, New York, Philosophical Library, 1945. II

Weber, M.
Gesammelte Aufsätze zur Religionssoziologie, Tübingen, Mohr, 1920 (3 vol.). II
—— *The Protestant Ethic and the Spirit of Capitalism*, trans. Talcott Parsons, London, Allen & Unwin, 1930. II
—— *Wirtschaft und Gesellschaft* (1922), Cologne, Kiepenheuer & Witsch, 1964 (2 vol.). I

Webster, D.
Patterns of Part-time Ministry in Some Churches in South America, London, World Dominion Press, 1964. IIIb

Wesley, J.
John Wesley's Journal, London, Curnock, 1905–16 (8 vol.). V

Willems, E.
'Protestantismus u. Klassenstruktur in Chile', *Kölner Z.S.S.* 12, 1960, pp. 632–71. IIIa
—— 'Protestantism and Culture Change in Brazil and Chile', in D'Antonio, W., and Pike, F., *Religion, Revolution and Reform*, London, Burns & Oates, 1964, pp. 91–108. IIIb
—— 'Religiöser Pluralismus und Klassenstruktur in Brasilien und Chile', *Int. Jahrbuch Rel. Soz.* I, 1965, pp. 189–211. IIIb

Wilson, B. R.
'Apparition et persistance des sectes dans un milieu social en évolution', *Archives*, No. 5, Jan.–June 1958, pp. 140–50. II
—— 'An Analysis of Sect Development', *A.S.R.* 24, 1959, pp. 3–15. II
—— *Sects and Society*, London, Heinemann, 1961. II
—— 'Typologie des sectes dans une perspective dynamique et comparative', *Archives*, No. 16, July–Dec. 1963, pp. 49–63. II

Classification

Wonderly, W., and Lara-Braud, J.
Los evangélicos somos asi?, México, Casa Unida de Publicaciones, 1964. IIIb

Yinger, J. M.
Religion, Society and the Individual, New York, Macmillan, 1957. II

Zamorano, M., and Munizaga, C.
Crimen y alcohol, Santiago, Univ. of Chile, 1963. IVa

Abbreviations of titles of periodicals

A.J.S.	*American Journal of Sociology* (U.S.A.)
Anales	*Anales de la Facultad de Teología* (Chile)
Archives	*Archives de Sociologie des Religions* (France)
A.S.R.	*American Sociological Review* (U.S.A.)
B.J.S.	*British Journal of Sociology* (England)
Cah. de Soc. écon.	*Cahiers de Sociologie économique* (France)
Cah. V. Pareto	*Cahiers Vilfredo Pareto* (Switzerland)
Chr. social	*Christianisme social* (France)
Cr. y Soc.	*Christianismo y Sociedad* (Uruguay)
Int. Jahrbuch Rel. Soz.	*Internationales Jahrbuch für Religionssoziologie* (Germany)
J.S.I.	*Journal of Social Issues* (U.S.A.)
Kölner Z.S.S.	*Kölner Zeitschrift für Soziologie u. Sozialpsychologie* (Germany)
Mensaje	*Mensaje* (Chile)
R.P.P.	*Revue de Psychologie des Peuples* (Switzerland)
Soc. Res.	*Social Research* (U.S.A.)

Other Abbreviations

C.E.P.A.L.	Comision Economica Para America Latine (United Nations)
D.E.S.A.L.	Centro Para el Desarrollo Economico y Social de America Latina (Roman Catholic)
F.E.R.E.S.	International Federation of Institutes for Social and Socio-Religious Research (Roman Catholic)

WORLD STUDIES OF CHURCHES IN MISSION
Published to date

The Growth of the Church in Buganda: An Attempt at Understanding, by John V. Taylor, 1958, SCM Press, London.

Christians of the Copperbelt: The Growth of the Church in Northern Rhodesia, by John V. Taylor and Dorothea A. Lehmann, 1961, SCM Press, London.

A Church Between Colonial Powers: A Study of the Church in Togo, by Hans W. Debrunner, 1965.

The Church as Christian Community: Three Studies of North Indian Churches, by J. P. Alter, H. Jai Singh, E. Y. Campbell, and Barbara M. Boal (ed. V. E. W. Hayward), 1966.

Urban Churches in Britain: A Question of Relevance, by Kofi A. Busia, 1966.

Stranger in the Land: A Study of the Church in Japan by Robert Lee, 1967.

Solomon Islands Christianity: A Study in Growth and Obstruction, by Alan R. Tippett, 1967.

Churches at the Grass-roots: A Study in Congo-Brazzaville, by Efraim Andersson, 1968.

Village Christians and Hindu Culture: Study of a rural church in Andhra Pradesh, by P. Y. Luke and John Carman, 1968.

All the above except the first two have been published by Lutterworth Press, London

INDEX